# VYGOTSKY
## *in 21st century*
# SOCIETY

PETER LANG
New York • Washington, D.C./Baltimore • Bern
Frankfurt • Berlin • Brussels • Vienna • Oxford

# VYGOTSKY
## *in 21st century*
# SOCIETY

*advances in cultural historical
theory and praxis with
non-dominant communities*

EDITED BY PEDRO R. PORTES & SPENCER SALAS

PETER LANG
New York • Washington, D.C./Baltimore • Bern
Frankfurt • Berlin • Brussels • Vienna • Oxford

Library of Congress Cataloging-in-Publication Data

Vygotsky in 21st century society: advances in cultural historical theory and praxis
with non-dominant communities / edited by Pedro R. Portes, Spencer Salas.
p. cm.
Includes bibliographical references.
1. Social psychology—Russia—History. 2. Minorities—Education.
3. Vygotskii, L. S. (Lev Semenovich), 1896–1934.
I. Portes, Pedro R. II. Salas, Spencer.
HM1027.R8V94   301.092—dc22   2011012283
ISBN 978-1-4331-1118-1 (hardcover)
ISBN 978-1-4331-1117-4 (paperback)


Bibliographic information published by **Die Deutsche Nationalbibliothek.**
**Die Deutsche Nationalbibliothek** lists this publication in the "Deutsche
Nationalbibliografie"; detailed bibliographic data is available
on the Internet at http://dnb.d-nb.de/.

**FSC**

**Mixed Sources**

Product group from well-managed
forests, controlled sources and
recycled wood or fiber

Cert no.  SCS-COC-002464
www.fsc.org
©1996 Forest Stewardship Council

The paper in this book meets the guidelines for permanence and durability
of the Committee on Production Guidelines for Book Longevity
of the Council of Library Resources.

© 2011 Peter Lang Publishing, Inc., New York
29 Broadway, 18th floor, New York, NY 10006
www.peterlang.com

Printed in the United States of America

# Contents

# Acknowledgments

Edited books, by their nature, reflect collective efforts and individual agencies. We recognize those here, particularly colleagues who helped keep the faith in this project alive. We owe much to the individuals who helped bring a cultural historical sense to our work and who cultivated much of the quintessence of cultural historical theory (CHT). Vygotsky's and Luria's legacies to various disciplines or fields are reflected in the breadth represented by the authors in this volume. Their efforts have been intense, and we are grateful to the contributors for sharing their insights. They wrestled with the demanding task set before them, helping to extend CHT to new generations while testing its very limits in everyday practical issues and problems in our societies. Some of the contributors are readily recognized senior scholars and some are newer voices, both aware of the timeliness of this volume and ready for the challenge of theorizing their praxes and illustrating the practical work at the borders and of inter-group learning and development. This collection is inspirited by their work and that of pioneers such as Luria, Mike Cole, Sylvia Scribner, Jim Wertsch, and so many others, some in this volume, serving as conduits to a new way of thinking and studying the mind. Our thanks also go to our responsive consulting board who reviewed chapter manuscripts with us: Patricia Baquedano López, Richard Duran, Inger Eriksson, and Peter Smagorinsky; and our students, Casey Nixon, Ashley Parker, and Jeremy Piña who unselfishly contributed to the needs of this project. Finally, we acknowledge the support of our colleagues at ISCAR and our AERA special interest group colleagues in cultural historical research who participated in the 2008–10 expositions of this project and of our colleagues from Cuba whose Vygotskyan roots and ideas until now had remained somewhat sidelined. In acknowledging the relevance of this discipline and what it can mean in the 21st century, we thank our readers in advance for their interest in learning more from an inclusive paradigm capable of integrating universal and dialectical principles openly. We also thank our contributing authors for their unique insights and sharing their grasp of the volume's primary themes.

We dedicate this volume especially to our spouses Tricia Michelle and Tesoro and our sons Andre' Sebastian Portes and Abel Salas for their support during this challenging project.

# Introduction

The idea behind *Vygotsky in 21st-Century Society: Advances in Cultural Historical Theory and Praxis with Non-Dominant Communities* was conceived during some of the early international socio-cultural conferences, particularly the ones after the 1990s in Madrid, Aarhus, Havana, and later Seville and San Diego. New communities of scholars began taking up issues regarding cultural differences at various levels—discussions motivated, in part, by migration and population shifts in developed nations as well as disparities regarding national minorities

Part of this renewed interest of course had to do with shifts in populations striving for a better life in the more developed nations as well as in already settled ethnic groups outside their traditional communities. The disparities in outcomes attracted attention to explanations that uncover how ethnic differences, like social class differences, were mostly *cultural* (i.e., connected to the development of certain cultural tools and the political economies that organized access to them through social and educational policies and practices). Nuances in what it meant to be in a dominant position (or not) quickly were reflected in how Vygotskyan-inspired writers drew implications from CHT around diversity as a new convention or code for what earlier in time had caused severe turmoil in terms of cultural deficit or difference views related to human development.

After the first re-discovery period (1956) when Vygotsky's legacy started to be known through Luria's agency (as *Language and Thought* and *Mind in Society*, 1978 were re-edited in various languages) and shared with great zeal, issues regarding what this culture-focused approach had to contribute in contexts where intercultural adaptations were taking place emerged rapidly. Primarily from the lens of those most proximal to the *oeuvre*, those seasoned scholars who first read these works and later interpreted the theory, interpreting the founders, and those most influential for the latter at that time, different understandings emerged and were established for the 21st century.

Later, as more evaluative, critical analyses of CHT surfaced in relation to activity theory, to its own socio-historical context and to other works by leading voices during these meetings, it became clear that diversity became a code in the new *Zeitgeist* for different types and levels of discussion and debate. For some in this field the appeal of Marxist social justice was more salient than for others interested in challenging or expanding psychology as an interdisciplinary science.

During this time, the fields of special education, educational, cognitive, and developmental psychology, language and literacy, cultural studies, linguistics, and others seemed to be transformed as each understood better the mechanisms that produced or sustained the so-called deficits and more than just higher-order thinking. Greater insights into the ways mediated experiences were linked to higher psychological functions became associated with disputed views of intelligence, teaching, and other socially organized practice. Soon it became evident that deficits, like differences, were difficult to pin down and locate from a CHT lens. They interacted and were situated along what appeared as a dominant vs. non-dominant dichotomy (DNDD) ultimately connected to objective and subjective aspects of identity. Concern with this DNDD, from a developmental lens, seemingly breathed new life in the work of those concerned most with the *practice* aspects of Vygotsky's legacy and the interpretation of it, particularly given the massive and growing levels of social inequality and the obvious failures in the social sciences to maximize social policies and praxes. Yes, this theory was founded on the study of cultural differences, but, at the same time, few outsiders were privy to its double meaning with respect to its defining characteristics in terms of:

1. Development as mediated by tools made by humans and cultivated historically through cultural transmission and
2. Communication-education practices, structures, and artifacts that in turn moderate material conditions.

In fact, it seems many associate Vygotsky directly with championing social justice today without regard to the historical development of his use of the term *culture*. Nevertheless, what this approach had or has to say depends greatly on the cultural history of the primary interpreters, their position, their settings, motives, and interests. Soon after CHT arrived, it is noticeable that the very narratives of academics influenced by Vygotsky varied considerably in content and their own position along the DNDD scale. The newer interpretations of Vygotsky worldwide and the reconstruction of CHT as a whole, as we will see in this volume, drew and still fuels debate.

This volume came about then as many of us met during various conferences and learned from a new generation of influential writings that are cited in these chapters. It was not difficult to notice that many Vygotskyan scholars were taking and extending CHT in different directions theoretically and in directions that reflected different interests and ends than others. The DNDD appeared to have something to "do with it." Some in this field were contending directly with the practical challenges involved in educating and serving other cultures in now post-Soviet era contexts. This dynamic was never clearer than in the triennial theme of ISCRAT in Aarhus "Dealing with Diversity." Indeed, this theme positioned some of us non-dominant co-participants in an interesting situation much related to this volume. We saw our peers attempting to press the CHT model to deal with or contend with growing national ethnic minorities or immigrants in ways that contrast with some chapters here. Our shared belief then was that CHT was ideally suited for this work relative to traditional, dominant disciplines; the question was exactly (or approximately) how so? Some invoked the question, "what would Lev Vygotsky say or do as CHT confronts the current sociogenesis of migrations and population/power shifts?" Others simply moved on and carved their niche.

While some non-dominant and dominant group members followed what appeared as the prevailing lead in extending Vygotsky during these meetings along theoretical lines as reflected in several leading books, others honed in directly to theorizing the practical side, buttressing and piloting transformative projects with CHT ideas. Moll's *Vygotsky and Education* (1990) edited book was the first major volume to concentrate on educational implications derived from this legacy, which in turn was later expanded by Kozulin et al.'s (2003) *Vygotsky's Educational Theory in Cultural Context.* Soon the emic and etic tensions could be detected within this growing CHT and AT community (a.k.a socio-cultural or socio-historical psychology). The issues addressed by this community directly impact how the approach is defined and consumed in the 21st century, and much seems to have to do with our own understandings of culture, identity, and development around the various levels in the waxing and waning of the *dominant or not* identity dialectic that everyone experiences at some level.

Finally, since many members in this CHT or AT community are multilingual or multicultural and have experiences, lived or otherwise, about being in non-dominant positions, the volume was designed to play with this finding and thus explore its value by actually doing it via this project. This volume aims to capture some of that *sense,* about how and where the field is moving, what is being discussed, by whom, and *why.* It has as its goal to renew a sense that, through both external and internal expeditions, cultural differences in development have much to teach us in our own backyards. Moreover, the reader will perhaps get a sense that a once promising discipline or field can thrive still and guide us interdisciplinarily in the future. With its sharp capacity for auto-reflection, CHT offers complex understandings of what might be termed as the stories within the story. For example, we can reflect on what it is exactly these chapters have in common or how the volume as a whole may change (or not) our conception of this discipline with its unique open-ended approach.

In noting how the initial CHT foundations emerged from the Uzbek expedition (Luria, 1976) and later from the subsequent research in Liberia (Cole & Scribner, 1974) when dominant group members/scholars studied the culturally different in situ, CHT now guides studies of non-dominant groups differently with immigrants or in their marginalized communities. Research designs, conceptualizations of the problem, and approaches to it often can differ by non-dominant scholars operating in different spaces and timeframes. Within this framework, we can consider the following typology as a heuristic:

| The Dominant working with and for dominant groups | The Non-dominant working with and for dominant groups |
| --- | --- |
| The Dominant working with and for non-dominant groups | The Non-dominant working with and for non-dominant groups |

However, the above does not consider instances that are increasingly common of individuals with much different cultural histories working together for either or both groups.

In short, we sought a different approach to organize an incomparable volume that would help join not merely those interested in CHT. More importantly, we hope, as the first chapter might suggest, that a better understanding of mind can help create better conditions for all children in the near future. We aimed to bring together prevailing concerns about how Vygotsky and CHT have been constructed and interpreted thus far, along with critiques regarding significant aspects of this legacy that remain uncovered. The best way we thought to do this was to create this space, one that would exemplify the challenges that still face CHT as a philosophy of science in advancing a holistic approach even if dialectic foundations cannot and are not meant to produce a unified discipline.

## Revisioning CHT in 13 Chapters

Rather than focusing on the past, the volume is aimed toward informing a once and future discipline (Cole, 1996) that is ever emerging as an open dialectical system. After a century of fragmented mini-theories that often fall into petty or false dichotomies established over the last century, we question those directions.

As we enter this second decade that very odd phenomenon of CHT's resilience and relevance concerns how our understanding of human consciousness "can improve" with a better grasp of the organizing principles of CHT and its focus on situatedness in time and space. Our purpose in organizing the present collection is to consider *decisive* CHT interpretations from a developmental perspective, from the problems it addresses and may have been neglected or misinterpreted. This book represents somewhat of an outlier perhaps in the genre of other books regarding Vygotsky and Luria. For our purposes here, it constitutes a challenge for what we construct as the more popular or prevailing positions held by those who first brought and interpreted for English speakers their research on Vygoskty and Luria's work. Of course some of our authors here did not have to rely solely on English translations, something which adds to the hybrid, diverse nature of what might be considered a sampler of writings that vary not only by foci but also by the cultural histories of each author.

The chapters are organized broadly around two sections. The first centers on historical and philosophical issues concerning theory that contribute to both practice and the advancement of a still-emerging theory. These particular chapters aim to fill voids that may be of interest to veterans as well as newcomers to CHT. The second section is more focused on field applications that stem from CHAT perspectives that illustrate how various scholars conceptualize praxis across contexts, developmental stages and against their own interpretations of the theory. It is important to note that there was never an a priori consensus regarding neither how CHT is to be construed nor a prescriptive organizational framework. There is no official story about how CHT works or should work in these chapters, nor is there a particular common view or focus. On the contrary, what the reader will find is that whatever the official story has been or what the prevailing view *may be* needs to be challenged and carefully reexamined. While the editors cannot speak for particular authors, one conclusion to be drawn at this point is that the observation or belief that CHT's time came, went, and is simply of historical value reflects an impoverished understanding of it.

Much of the education available to new students of sociocultural theory may be limited by current popular interpretations and elaborations of what can be regarded as an uneasy fuzzy alliance of cultural historical, activity, deconstruction, and critical, late modern, and other theories. For many of us, the transitions of this dialectical historical worldview and approach to psychology from Soviet/Russian psychology to the West are not linear or internally consistent. CHT cannot be located or restricted to a particular account in cognitive, psycholinguistic, child development special education, or other such areas. We see its modern relevance and semiotic nature as discussions moved from word meaning to other units of analysis or the relatively *new* interest in emotional IQ or the affective-motivation domain in educational research or other popular trends that seem to have their deeper roots in the CHT legacy. Readers may also question the extent to which cultural-historical theory as "located" in permeable professional associations such as the International Society for Cultural and Activity Research (http://www.iscar.org/) or the American Educational Research Association's cultural-historical research Special Interest Group (SIG) or the Laboratory of Comparative Human Cognition (http://lchc.ucsd.edu/) community or beyond may lay claim to extending CHT in the new century. A view that may emerge from the diverse chapters here is that CHT remains the core of that once and future discipline *is* still new to many and ever emerging as suggested by Cole (1996). Furthermore, it is holistic and integrates subjective and objective dimensions of consciousness as both forge a social and private reality simultaneously.

## Part One

The first section dealing with mainly theoretical challenges in CHT adds breadth and scope to this paradigm in incorporating the dialectics of materialistic and idealistic, qualitative, and positivist aspects without excluding any. The latter four aspects may be regarded more along a continuum than as dichotomous. The second section, on the other hand, reflects praxes totally within what may be regarded as an important, if not dominant collective of "U.S.-bred" scholars sharing in part a common history in extending CHT. In contrast to some chapters in the first section, the demonstration projects in the second part are theorized differently along the above dialectic domains of CHT in action. The unresolved issues regarding how the mind works and develops are also a central topic in this volume that extends from macro psychology (see Ratner) to mostly internal agency aspects connecting with subjectivity (Gonzalez-Rey) and to individual psychology that is well beyond what readers can find in textbooks such as Gredler and Shields's *Vygotsky's Legacy* (2008) or others.

Glick's essay, Chapter One, notes there are some novel reasons for highlighting contributions from some Latin American scholars in a volume such as this. The project was conceptualized in part by observations concerning the role of cultural history and ethnicity in how CHT appears to have some traction for scholars working with non-dominant groups and equity, and in how some of them employ and extend CHT in ways that in our view are not necessarily coincidental.

Over a decade ago at an annual meeting of the American Educational Research Association where a CHT research group was being founded, Kris Gutierrez, who was participating in a keynote session with Mike Cole, recognized how some of the Latino scholars in the back of the room were focusing this line of research in ways that appeared distinctive to CHT. While this volume remains diverse, it does bring together a blend of authors and topics that captures a sense or savor of difference relative to other books in this genre. The reader will decide about what to make of the intersections found there. Glick astutely examines CHT's origins in terms of a comparative historical-cultural research with Uzbeks in the last century, the relations between psychology and education in terms of cultural development around the Sputnik era, the positioning of Piaget and Vygotsky in the second half of 20th century in terms of learning and teaching, and all of these in relation to the issue of massive group-based disparities. At one point in his chapter, seasoned readers in this genre might remember the times when two mighty empires contested their future in terms of which had the best theory and educational praxes to prevail. Furthermore, Glick helps us to consider the centrality of this contest prior to and after controversies associated with Head Start as a compensatory avenue for non-dominant populations designed to "normalize" their next generations' success. Today one might see this theme played out in international contrasts of various societies' educational outcomes and how the "developed" ones treat their culturally-linguistically diverse non-dominant communities.

We chose to follow Glick's historical orientation chapter with Fernando Gonzalez-Rey's (Chapter Two) own synopsis of Soviet psychology after Vygotsky's last period. He ventures on another important dialectic aspect that we describe as an expedition into subjectivity and what difference a unit of analysis for CHT makes. This chapter captures the often-neglected third period of Vygotsky's legacy and opens wide a possibly new debate for readers. It validates much of what is to be found in the praxis-oriented second section chapters although from a different perspective outside the influence of the main Vygotskyans in North America.

However, this volume is far from privileging any one emphasis or interpretation. We purposely follow it with a contrasting view of how this legacy is being reconstructed and developed with Guillermo Arias's "The Process of Producing Knowledge: Vygotsky Revisited." In Chapter Three, Arias forcefully addresses several myths about Vygotsky's work; for example, the disputed idea that he was not truly a Marxist. He questions, as does the previous chapter, the issue of whether activity is the most or the only appropriate unit of analysis in CHT. The reader might ponder at this point the implications and the facile union implied by the acronym of CHAT as some aptly mix CHT with activity theory as Vygotsky's legacy. Arias's chapter also reflects some of his collaborators' contributions at the Universidad de la Habana Vygotsky Chair there.

In continuing the analyses of discord or consensus within CHT in this first section, we present an important example of the theory-praxis recursive loop by

Alex Kozulin, Chapter Four, whose work is already widely known and appreciated. His chapter shows a theory-based study with his extensions of CHT regarding cultural transition in relation to cognitive change outlined in three specific areas. His chapter lends continuity to Glick's opening chapter by revisiting the purposes associated with Vygotsky's earlier period along with Luria's expedition (1976) when they pursued building an approach partly based on historical changes that might occur in human cognition. He dispels the myth that they set out to study cross-cultural differences per se. As cultural changes emerge due to tools and migration across global societies, one value added by this report concerns the social situation described by Alex Kozulin in the case of Ethiopian immigrants in Israel that is not totally unlike that of other groups varying in literacy and being integrated in other parts of the world. With respect to how CHT may be extended in a developed context, Kozulin's contribution addresses other important levels at which CHT can operate, specifically those on which practices can be informed by theory in recursive fashion. He asks a critical question in CHT regarding cognitive and social adaptation differences that may differ qualitatively in contexts varying from traditional and oral practices to newer technologically mediated literacies. Finally, his work captures an important experimental tradition within CHT that is theorized differently to some extent by other projects and strategies as illustrated in the second part of the volume. How socio-cognitive interventions and counteractions (Portes & Salas, 2010) are conceptualized in this volume serves to illustrate the internal dialectic tensions within a paradigm that today may demand different mixed methods and perspectives to understand developmental and culturally mediated experience.

Kozulin's chapter opens with a shared question regarding the challenges facing groups, often immigrants who are developing amidst radical and in most cases politically charged cultural transitions. This theme is revisited in subsequent chapters that reflect much different (etic vs. emic) perspectives. More importantly, though, Kozulin's work with Ethiopian immigrants illustrates a comparative means with respect to understanding educational praxis under qualitatively different contexts (e.g., those in the Southwest of the United States where the Latin culture prevailed before 1848 and current economic conditions that reinforce cultural-linguistic continuity) and migration.

The first section ends with three also fundamentally diverse chapters by Ratner (Chapter Five), Portes (Chapter Six), and Dergan (Chapter Seven). These are theoretically inclined contributions concerning mental health extensions of the Vygotsky-Luria legacy. Each carries direct implications for practice in ways not available otherwise.

Carl Ratner's Macro Cultural Psychology challenges predominant beliefs that lean toward the internal, subjective processes in individuals and, like "Mind in

Society," considers macro culture as inseparable from human nature. He validates this side of CHT with the analysis of "Honor Killings" in Kurdish culture that captures the dialectics involved in human agency impacting society and society returning the favor through normative pressures. Ratner is well aware, as is Gonzalez Rey in his elaboration of subjectivity, that developmental processes in affective relational domains come into play in the tensions that peak during adolescence and later as macro culture is reconstructed by each generation within certain limits. Suicide in Romeo and Juliet situations and violence toward others in today's diverse contexts illustrate the complexity involved in understanding the minds of individuals, dyads, families, communities, and of larger collectives as each one exerts their will or agency for and against others. History is laden with collective minds perpetrating what is considered pathological more easily at the individual level, and this chapter stands as a solid frame of reference for examining other insights and aspects derived from a CHT lens.

His chapter, incidentally, comes amidst controversy involving a U.S. pastor threatening to burn the Q'uran around the anniversary of 9/11. Ratner's focus on pressing realities concerning cultural practices is complicated to frame around the old explanations of cultural deficit or difference hypotheses and take readers on a much different extension of CHT. Whether readers agree or disagree with a particular level of theorizing and pushing the limits of this paradigm, this chapter presents a convincing case for how society makes minds and still how individual agency can still prevail at times.

The sixth chapter, by Portes, explores further the connections involving Vygotsky and Luria in the areas of psychotherapy and counseling-oriented practice. He reviews the earlier interests by CHT founders with psychodynamic (Freudian) theory, which eventually left both disillusioned as a foundation for the study of mind. Portes notes that one figure thus far neglected in *Understanding Vygotsky* (van der Veer & Valsiner, 1993) may be Alfred Adler, a colleague of Freud's who understood much better the social forces that interacted with and were interwoven into the field he pioneered—individual psychology. This chapter also attempts to explain the peculiar situation regarding why the CHT paradigm has had relatively minor impact relative to other subdisciplines and within theories of counseling and psychotherapy. Examples of how both Vygotsky and Luria's legacy in this area remains fertile ground and of how Adler's compensation-related ideas that might have played a role in CHT's development are provided. Clearly this paradigm overall, and this connection in particular, is deemphasized as it appears in the authoritative Vygotsky's *Collected Works* (Rieber & Carton, 1993). Still, the chapter carries implications for education, counseling, and prevention but is of interest to clinically oriented practice.

Jose Dergan's chapter focusing on the Lurian influence in neuropsychology appears consistent in many ways with this rather neglected area of clinical theory and practice. In Chapter Seven, Dergan summarizes much in this field that will be useful for new scholars and those whose practice involves diverse client populations. He presents clinical data pertaining to assessment and treatment in illustrating the many ways the overarching theme of understanding cultural adaptation in which the hyphen found in *non-dominant* groups is critical for situating our narratives. Reflecting on this hyphen is essential also for the inseparable cultural-historical model and practices therein. Dergan employs current case studies of immigrants as a practicing bilingual neuropsychologist in the U.S. and provides the clinical field important implications for practice. Both chapters underline the important contributions of Luria.

## Part Two

As Part One illustrates, how Vygotsky and his legacy are understood depend in large part on which one of the proverbial blind men is holding on to what part of the elephant. However, in conceptualizing this collection, we were committed not only to potentially building theory through a juxtaposition of not completely harmonious viewpoints but also to illustrating how cultural historical thinking has been taken up in praxis. Part Two shifts, therefore, from discussions of Vygotsky and Luria's foundational work to their enactment by prominent contemporary researchers.

In Chapter Eight, "Only Life Educates: Immigrant Families, the Cultivation of Biliteracy, and the Mobility of Knowledge," Luis C. Moll opens a nuanced chapter that helps frame subsequent studies illustrating advances in praxes with non-dominant populations in the United States. He examines three distinct projects in Latino school/communities that cultivate U.S. Latino schoolchildren and families' dynamic and intergenerational "funds of knowledge" (González, Moll, & Amanti, 2005; Moll & González, 2004) to theorize the need for education that engages life beyond school walls. Thus, funds of knowledge, for Moll, are dynamic, intergenerational, and mobile and can be leveraged in students' participatory action research around social justice issues whereby formal schooling is recast as a means of empowering rather than curtailing their developmental trajectories. Moll's highly influential work surrounding "funds of knowledge" is evident in the chapters that follow, as are the generative effect of his earlier volume Vygotsky and Education (Moll, 1992) on subsequent scholarship for language and literacy education. He shows the funds to be mobile as well as the mediating structure of teacher study groups in cultivating biliteracies with delightful case studies and examples.

In Chapter Nine, "Computer-Mediated Learning and Young Latino/a Students' Developing Expertise," Carmen M. Martínez-Roldán and Peter Smagorinsky present a qualitative interpretation of the potential of the Amigos Clase Mágica—an after-school program *cum* collective zone of proximal development in which bilingualism, games, peers, and adults all mediated students' and interns' learning to argue for the re-conceptualization of classrooms as "permeable zones of proximal development in which children's learning is interwoven with culturally appropriate mediational tools and multifaceted proleptic possibilities."

In Chapter Ten, "An Integrated Approach to the Study of Transitions as Learning Activity: Two Cases from Spanish Immersion Classrooms," Patricia Baquedano-López, Ariana Mangual Figueroa, and Sera Jean Hernandez draw from two preschool Spanish immersion sites in northern California to illustrate the mediational nature of language in learning through an analysis of teacher and student practices during transition activity. Blending a language socialization paradigm with an ethnomethodological approach, the authors examine how classroom exchanges in between teaching and learning also socialize young children to the norms and expectations of their classroom communities. Fluid and complex, transition activities, the authors argue, are spaces for a range of actions—"From opportunities to test the parameters of permissible action to learning about the consequences of breaches to ongoing interaction."

In Chapter Eleven, Leticia Tomas Bustillos, Robert Rueda, and Estela Mara Bensimon theorize praxis on a collaborative-inquiry project among two-year college faculty. Describing the critical discussions centered on Latino achievement at the college, the authors argue the possibilities of re-mediating faculty's perception of remediation and Latinos in higher education. They extend us ways to reconceptualize discordination in higher education by design, as the next chapter would lead us to think and do.

In Chapter Twelve, "Praxis in Dis-coordination" Margaret Gallego and Olga A. Vásquez draw from fieldwork in two distinct Clase Mágica sites to argue for the practice of making the problems that arise from difference into opportunities for cultural awareness, resolution, and internalization. The idea of discoordination as opportunity in general that can be designed, particularly for multilingual children is pivotal for the future on non-dominant populations placed at risk. At this point, the reader can begin to connect with the mediation chains required from preschool to college or to the workforce that often engage learners within and beyond school settings, as Moll's initial epigraph intends and the next chapter elaborates thoughtfully at the family level.

Richard Durán, Chapter Thirteen, closes the volume with "Development of Latino Family-School Engagement Programs in U.S. Contexts: Enhancements to Cultural Historical Activity Theory Accounts." Illustrating how scholars and implementers can adapt a CHAT perspective to improve Latino parents' organizational capacity for school involvement, coupled with civic engagement in a systematic and multi-level integrated manner, Durán argues how "CHAT and Vygotskian [sic] approaches to human and organizational development are of relevance to researchers and program implementers serving Latino community members beyond the abstract contribution to knowledge." He concludes with a call for a better design in organizing, or as Gallego and Vásquez would argue, discoordinations that create zones for development for both sides of the NDDD hyphen.

Thus, now that we have concluded the first decade of a new century in psychology and education, this volume aims to help readers re-think some assumptions and problems that remain with respect to a more unified, cogent approach to the human mind. While for many, Vygotsky and cultural historical theory (CHT) remain mostly of historical interest as a paradigm that once was and that is no longer as relevant, we take the contrary position. In terms of both praxis and illustrating how this dialectical approach remains pertinent, the chapters here reflect a range that introduces novel twists across diverse foci and populations. The project evolves understanding that this legacy remains still largely misunderstood and limited in terms of its broader significance in forging a future, less fragmented discipline and just society in the future. It is our hope that readers will encounter a variety of reasons as well as ideas that suggest much of value has been ignored, missed, or misunderstood—and also how the CHT paradigm remains responsive to pressing issues and those that connect sociogenetic circumstances to the development of individuals and less dominant groups.

If, as Vygotsky wrote, "All the higher functions originate as actual relations between human individuals" (p. 57), then a mediating device such as cultural historical theory is not any less of a dynamic social practice—not separate from the social contexts in which it is taken up either directly or peripherally by individual participants and communities (see, e.g., Lave & Wenger, 1991). It is our hope that this volume will provide a useful precedent and a fresh context for increased interaction among scholars and their audiences, whose lived experiences too are recognized as an integral part of what cultural historical thinking and cultural historical psychology are and could yet be. In a century when the pace and nature of cultural change spin the mind as never before, we hope these chapters contribute to a dynamic integration of mind, development and evermore complex cultural portals of sense and meaning.

# Part
## ·1·

· 1 ·

# Dynamics in the "Sabor" of Vygotsky

*Joseph Glick*

*One of the most interesting and important contributions of
Vygotskian [sic] psychology is the proposal that human thinking
must be understood in its concrete social and historical
circumstances. (Moll & Greenberg, 1990, p. 319).*

A primary obligation of any approach that claims to be cultural and historical is
to find ways of integrating culture and history deeply into its praxis. Doing so
must have theoretical and analytic consequences. Too often these terms are used
in loose and ungrounded ways to merely legitimize a piece of writing as belonging to the proper theoretical school, bidding for a sympathetic and like-minded
audience.

Thus, this chapter will be less about "true" or "untrue" interpretations of
Vygotsky's theory. My focus, instead, is on the ways in which his theory was
received in different socio-historical contexts and with respect to different problems faced by the societies to which his theory was introduced (usually in translations, dated with little relation to the date of Vygotsky's writing).

The intent of this chapter is neither political (e.g., "was Vygotsky's theory truly Marxist?") nor hermeneutical (e.g., "Is the original text well translated or not? Are the meanings of the terms consistent in each language?"). My claim is that with the temporal distance that exists between the original Russian text (with the attendant political and social conditions that existed at the time of its writing) and the reading of that text within political and social conditions, and with respect to other texts that have been published in the interim, the "real, true original meaning" is a vain search. Rather we should look at the conditions of reception of the text (in varying social and political conditions) for an understanding of both the work and its implications for contemporary analysis, and theoretical meaning. This chapter seeks to locate Vygotsky's texts within the context of their reception.

For me, thinking about interpretations of Vygotsky leads to thinking about how history and culture are entwined not only in cultural-historical theory, but also in the historical dynamics that influence the way that theories are received in particular, concrete, historical situations. From that angle, I hope to find a way of constructively engaging in an international dialogue about varying emphases and interpretations of Vygotsky's work, and, in particular, looking for the meaning of Vygotsky's theoretical ideas as it may be extended to the unique problems faced within the "Latino" communities, either in Central and South America, but most importantly in North America where there has been an enormous wave of immigration and a problematic reaction to the "Latinization" of the United States.

This approach is particularly needed when dealing with "contemporary" interpretations of texts written long ago in historically different circumstances, which are, moreover, encountered by many in translation (which is itself historically situated) and with various forms of redaction. Vygotsky died in 1934, but his texts are often treated as contemporary, and they are treated as the basis for more contemporary approaches, e.g., Cultural-Historical Activity Theory (CHAT).

However, since Vygotsky wrote in the middle of a particular period in Russian and world history (i.e., both before and during the consolidation of power by Stalin), the status of his texts within Russia and, in particular, the circulation of his texts into translations into other languages have led to historical dislocations, where it is difficult to separate Vygotsky as he might or might not have intended himself to be understood and the uses made of his theory for contemporary purposes and different historical periods. As a trenchant example we might look at the reception of Vygotsky and of Piaget within the pantheon of important developmental theorists.

The first English translation of Vygotsky's "Thought and Language" appeared in 1962, translated by Eugenia Hanfmann and Gertrude Vakar, and introduced by Jerome Bruner. There are some interesting thoughts about issues of translation raised in the translator's preface that indicate the difficulties involved in penetrating the layers of history and culture that divide us from the author. I quote from the translator's preface:

> In the late thirties. One of the translators of the present edition, E. Hanfmann, in collaboration with J. Kasanin, repeated some of Vygotsky's studies of concept formation; she remembers vividly the struggle of winding her way through this text. When Vygotsky's collaborator and friend A. R. Luria approached her in 1957 with the request that she participate in the translation of *Thought and Language* she expressed her conviction that a literal translation would not do justice to Vygotsky's thought. It was agreed that excessive repetition and certain polemical discussions that would be of little interest to the contemporary reader should be eliminated, in favor of a more straightforward exposition. (Vygotsky, 1962; translator's preface, xi–xii)

The preface continues:

> The internal organization of the chapters has been preserved, except in Chapter 2, where extensive omissions resulted in the rearrangement of the text and in a greatly reduced number of subdivisions. (Translator's preface, xii)

Interestingly, and germane to my chapter, Chapter 2 of *Thought and Language* is titled "Piaget's Theory of Child's Language and Thought," which is based on Vygotsky's introduction to the Russian translation of Piaget's earliest books dealing with child thought—what we have come to know as "The language and thought of the child" (French language original 1923); (English translation 1926); (Russian translation, 1932) and "Judgment and reasoning of the child (French language original, 1924); (English translation, 1928); (Russian translation, 1932). As the translators note, these first books of Piaget are not fully representative of Piagetian theory as it later developed.

We shall return to the relations between Piaget and Vygotsky at a later point in this chapter. Suffice it to say that Vygotsky was commenting on an early Piaget whose focus was on observing schoolchildren's reasoning and thinking. Along with studying children's communications concerning logical relations, a great deal of focus was on the concept of the "egocentrism" of children's communication. Piaget's later focus, after he had his own children and was able to observe them closely, was on the constructive processes involved in the development of logical thought. This work was not available to Vygotsky at the time of his death, nor was it accessible to the rest of the non-French speaking world (see Flavell's historical and biographical note on what was quickly translated and assimilated, and what was not in Kessen & Kuhlman, 1962).

In thinking about the main theme of this volume, finding the "sabor Latino" in Vygotskyan theory, I have also had to confront the historical conditions in Latin America, and in the United States (including dates of translation, political and intellectual situation and the historical situation that prevailed at the time when the texts were received).

From this angle it seems that the use of "Latino" as if it yields a singular "Latino" of a single "type" is a complex and contestable concept, since the contemporary conditions that existed at the point when Vygotsky's texts were introduced varied widely throughout Latin America, at different publication dates, in different interpretive contexts, in differing political situations, ranging from dictatorships to revolutions, with accordingly different attitudes toward theorists and their national origins. The conditions varied from revolutionary praxis in such places as Cuba and Nicaragua to dictatorships (often right wing) in such places as Brazil. A cultural-historical analysis suggests that interpretations and uses of Vygotsky of his writings must have taken (if they were acknowledged at all) on very different forms within each context. They certainly influenced the order of appearance of translations. While translations of Piaget's early works seem to have been widespread, his later works were sometimes translated and assimilated to education and scientific discourse and sometimes not. Vygotsky, on the other hand was, in many instances untranslated, and when translated, for example, after the end of the dictatorship in Brazil, came out "backwards" with *Mind in Society* (published in English in 1978 and in Portuguese translation in 1984) appearing two years before *Thought and Language* (written in 1934 and published in English translation in 1962 and in Portuguese translation in 1987). This is the inverse of the order of publication dates in the United States. However, in Cuba, the Spanish translation of Vygotsky was published in 1964 by the Press La Habana: Edicion Revolutionaria.

Differences of contexts abound. In the United States there was a Cold War between the Soviet Union and the United States as superpowers, while in the Cuban case, there was a leftist revolution, with many of the academic Vygotskyans having been trained at Moscow State University.

Not only do political situations vary, but also the adoption of analytic traditions relates in some way to the evolving "problematic" of a society, i.e., the problems that it sees itself having to solve in order to be successful in its own terms or in terms that address contested versions of the social order. Thus, issues of culture and history necessarily find themselves embedded in societies and their histories. These vary across nations and across time periods. In this regard, one would include in the term *Latino* those who are living in the United States within "minority" or migrant communities (Moll, 1990).

This much having been introduced I would like to begin with a note of delicious irony. In a volume dedicated to the work and memory of Sylvia Scribner (one of the editors of *Mind in Society*), Jerome Bruner contributed a chapter titled "Reflecting on Russian Consciousness." He was writing of the great contradictions that exist within Russian consciousness and at that particular moment of his writing there was, in particular, a post-Soviet crisis as the Russian "White House" was being bombarded while its Parliament was reflecting on a new constitution. Bruner then goes on to say that one of the few people with whom he could talk about these issues was Sylvia Scribner. Reflectively, he goes on to say that

> I would have liked to consider the matter in more general terms—or even more particularly in terms of the American case. But, as for the general case, I simply do not have a deep enough grasp of the issues to know how to begin. And as for America and American psychology's place in our culture, I know all too well that the fish may be the last to discover water. (Bruner, 1995, pp. 67–68)

Paradoxically, I believe that analysis of the contexts for the adoption of Vygotsky's theories as they have developed in the United States does allow one to see American waters and, hopefully, to see how they have/or can apply to a Latino perspective that is neither distasteful nor poisonous (in other words, at this moment of writing in May 2010 they are not in the Gulf of Mexico).

The adoption has neither been smooth, nor linear, nor, in many cases in the spirit of the theory. The appropriations often do damage or create distortions— taking a part of a theory and making it seem to be the whole. In particular many changes in the conditions of the theory are related to the relation of the works of Piaget. Undoubtedly, this dynamic is a general issue that applies to the various Latin Americas as well.

While, undoubtedly there are "authentic" Vygotskyan texts that form the basis for a family resemblance among interpretations of his approach, interpretations are heavily influenced by three factors that I identify as (a) the function of the theory within an historical context (b) the textual "surround" (other writers, contemporary or historical) of the theory that I identify as its "inter-textuality" (the relation of any text to all of the other texts read before or contemporarily with that text) and, finally, (c) factors extrinsic to the field of theory and of texts, that have to do with historical events such as wars (hot and cold), civic movements, changes in political attitudes and actions, and (if they are different) natural and unnatural catastrophes.

In other words, the commonalities and different emphases in the interpretations of Vygotsky are not simply matters of appropriate or inappropriate readings of original texts. This issue is not hermeneutic; it is historical-material, political, and inter-textual. *how his text were interpretted here mor to do w/ what was going on at the time.*

# Vygotsky and Piaget Within the "Problematic" of the United States and the Cold War—Sputnik

Societies have faced very different sorts of problems at the time of Vygotsky's discovery and application as a theoretical resource and basis for social action, I can only speak with some degree of assuredness about the situation in the United States as I have experienced it.

One of the few advantages of age is one, if lucky, lives through a time of rapid change. In my case I will talk about developmental psychology in the United States, where there were major "paradigm shifts" in what has been taken to be the most interesting phenomena and most central social functions of theory.

When I began my studies as a graduate student, the "mainstream" in the United States was occupied by "learning theory" as a dominant theoretical paradigm. It saw changes in behavior as the result of either pairings of stimulus relationships within a stimulus-response paradigm or as operant responses preserved because they led to attainment of goals.

That theory began to become unglued in the late 1950s as structural aspects of learning, and constraints on what was or could be learned, came to be identified and appreciated. In 1959 Noam Chomsky (Chomsky, 1959) published a devastating review of B. F. Skinner's book on language. Chomsky showed that language had structure quite beyond anything that learning theory had been able to imagine. Experiments by others on the dynamics of transfer of learned responses began to show that transfer was related to structural properties rather than physical properties (e.g., that a response would transfer from a note to a musical fifth or octave rather than to a physically adjacent note). Learning theory began to give way to the beginning recognition that there were structural constraints on ability to learn.

Enter a new historical dimension into the picture—a dimension that was not from within developmental theory, but that deeply affected the way in which developmental theory was received and what was expected from it. In 1957, in the middle of a Cold War between Russia and the United States—a war partly political and partly technological—against all expectations by the United States about its technological superiority, Sputnik, the first object to reach orbit, was launched. The belief in the ultimate success of the "American Approach," culturally and technologically, was severely shaken by the Russians' starting and winning the space race by launching Sputnik. This defeat led to a huge investment in education, a search for new approaches—a new way to win or lose (in an era of ICBM-carried atomic weapons) the Cold War, a sense that something was amiss—that there was, in addition to a "Cold War" a "Space Race" and that "we" might be losing both.

In 1959 a conference was held in Dedham, MA, that focused on new ways of viewing the intellectual development of young children. The Dedham conference eventually led to a monograph edited by Kessen and Kuhlman that celebrated Piaget as a new foundation for educational practice. Though not explicitly stated, the conference was held in the intellectual atmosphere generated by the shock of Sputnik.

Another conflict was stirring in the background. The civil rights movement and the full recognition of the disparities in cultural and social capital were beginning to be realized.

In what was a typical response the educational system (now expanded to younger years) bore the burden, and cultural disenfranchisement was repackaged as "cultural deprivation," and the education system was given that task of being "compensatory," i.e., public means were expected to offer what families were unable or unwilling to provide on their own. This development led, in 1965, to the foundation of Project Head Start—and a plethora of "home-based" intervention programs designed to "rectify" or to compensate for what families lacked. At the same time, the educational system was pressed to provide "what was missing" in the technological competition between the United States and Russia.

To some extent, the interplay of these factors, the collapse of behaviorism, the dawning recognition of cultural and technological disparities, and the desire to regain "the leading edge" in science led to a search for a theory that could enhance education, in particular education related to the STEM disciplines (Science, Technology, Engineering, Mathematics), formed the interpretive framework for the acceptance, or not, of Vygotsky and Piaget within the United States.

I would like to begin my story of the place of Vygotsky in the United States in 1962, the publication date of two basic texts that had very different fates within the theoretical heartland.

The year 1962 witnessed the first English language translation of Vygotsky's *Thought and Language*. That very same year witnessed the publication of a monograph of the Society for Research in Child Development (SRCD—one of the mainstream developmental psychology organizations) edited by William Kessen and Clementina Kuhlman entitled *Thought in the Young Child: Report of a Conference on Intellective Development with Particular Attention to the Work of Jean Piaget*. This monograph not only had the imprimatur of the dominant professional organization in developmental psychology (SRCD), but it was also the product of a Social Science Research Council committee that was trying to define the leading edge of the psychology of the future formed in reaction to an emerging national need and forming ultimately a network of power brokers in the field (The Dedham conference). These people might have *read* Vygotsky, but they had *discovered* Piaget.

Though Piaget and Vygotsky were born in the same year (1896), Piaget's early works were widely available in many languages, and his later books continuously appeared (after the hiatus indicated by Flavell) in English. Vygotsky's major work only appeared in 1962.

However, by the time Vygotsky's work appeared in the United States, the stage was already set. Piaget's work, which, in his second phase, focused on problems of the construction of knowledge, was seen as immediately relevant to the needs of a technologically embattled society (the space race/the Cold War and, since it could be seen as adapted to preschool education from infancy onward, to current issues of civil rights).

Piaget had the advantage of being seen as immediately relevant to the development of social, scientific, and technological knowledge. The STEM disciplines seemed to have an immediate relation to the logical/operational foci of Piagetian theory. Moreover, since his theory began with infancy, there was immediate face relevance to the newly emerging educational needs spawned by the recognition of social disparities. It seemed in 1962 as if Piaget were treated as the new discovery and Vygotsky was carefully placed in the past or nowhere at all.

The Kessen and Kuhlman monograph which "legitimized" Piaget (after the fall of Learning Theory and the launching of Sputnik) was quickly followed by a book written by John Flavell (in 1963) attempting to synthesize the various writings of Piaget that had been available to be read in English, but which were now taken as canonical and as the "new wave" of post-behaviorist thinking. Piaget was systematically introduced in to mainstream developmental psychology and the Kessen and Kuhlman monograph was republished in book form in 1970 by the University of Chicago Press in the midst of a flurry of publications by and about Piaget. A massive compendium, *The Essential Piaget: An Interpretive Reference and Guide* was edited by Howard Gruber and J. Jacques Vonèche was published in 1977 complete with testimony by Piaget on the front cover "…In reading the explanatory notes, I came to understand better what I had wanted to do." Even so, this testamentary volume was, in some sense, the beginning of the end.

## The Re-discovery of Vygotsky in the United States

In 1978, after 16 or so years of Piaget-inspired research, two books appeared that began to crack into the hegemony of Piagetian discourse. The Scottish developmentalist, Margaret Donaldson, published *Children's Minds* with an opening line of a preface that reflects the time and a shift of framework. Donaldson writes, "In the course of this book I argue that the evidence now compels us to reject certain features of Jean Piaget's theory of intellectual development."

The second book that appeared was *Mind in Society* (Vygotsky, 1978) with Vygotsky named as author but edited and constructed by Michael Cole, Vera John-Steiner, Sylvia Scribner, and Elaine Souberman from a number of pieces of texts from various of Vygotsky's writings that A. R. Luria had put into Michael Cole's hands to get them "out" to an English-speaking audience. *Mind in Society* had an immediate impact on developmental psychology in the United States, though it was a long relay race from 1934 from Luria to Cole to Harvard University Press by 1978 (after translating, selecting, editing).

It became increasingly apparent that Piagetian theory was essentially "conservative" with Piaget's idea that structural developmental change must be in advance of learning, and in fact was a limiting factor on what could be learned. Thus it was ultimately found to be unsuited to a social scenario that was in "speed mode"—searching to catch up and succeed technologically and socially. Vygotsky was "re-discovered" with the publication of *Mind in Society* (1978).

One notion came to dominate the rediscovery of Vygotsky, the idea that developmental level was not structurally determined but could be influenced to a greater or lesser degree by learning experience. The re-discovered Vygotsky was almost exclusively received in terms of the notion of the Zone of Proximal Development (the ZPD). Looking backward, it was clear that the rediscovered Vygotsky, and, in particular the notion of the ZPD was a reaction to a decade and a half of Piagetian dominance that placed structural constraint as limiting possible speeding up of developmental progress (Glick, 1983).

What is interesting in all of this activity is that the ZPD was not the main focus of Vygotsky's work. There is no reference to it in the index of *Thought and Language,* and it is mentioned only in relation to the difference between spontaneous and scientific (schooled) contexts (Chapter 6 of *Thought and Language*). There it was used in two ways, the first showing that a child's unaided performance could be enhanced with help, and secondly, as identifying differences between children as to how much they could profit from such help (almost equivalent to the idea of IQ in the United States).

Where the ZPD was referenced by Vygotsky in *Thought and Language* in the "original" 1962 translation is in these words:

> Most of the psychological investigations concerned with school learning measured the level of mental development of the child by making him solve certain standardized problems. The problems he was able to solve by himself were supposed to indicate the level of mental development at the particular time. But in this way only the completed part of development can be measured, which is far from the whole story. Having found that the mental age of two children was, let us say, eight, we gave each of them harder problems than he could manage on his own and provided slight assistance: the first step in a solution, a leading question, or some other form of help. We discovered that one child could, in co-operation, solve problems designed for 12 year olds while the

other could not go beyond problems intended for 9 year olds. The discrepancy between a child's actual mental age and the level he reaches in solving problems with assistance indicates the zone of proximal development: in our example this zone is four for the first and one for the second. Can we truly say that their mental development is the same? Experience has shown that the child with larger zone of proximal development will do much better in school. (Vygotsky, 1962, p. 103)

Somewhat the same passage occurs in *Mind in Society* but with some critical following text that directly challenges Piagetian assumptions (even those of Piaget's more constructivist period).

To summarize, the most essential feature of our hypothesis is the notion that developmental processes do not coincide with learning processes. Rather, the developmental process lags behind the learning process; this sequence then results in zones of proximal development. Our analysis alters the traditional view that the moment a child assimilates the meaning of a word, or masters an operation such as addition or written language, her developmental processes are basically completed. In fact, they have only just begun at that moment. The major consequence of analyzing the educational process in this manner is to show that initial mastery of, for example, the four arithmetic operations provides the basis for the subsequent development of a variety of highly complex internal processes in children's thinking. (Vygotsky, *Mind in Society*, 1978, p. 90)

It is on this impact that I want to focus. I start by comparing the index of *Thought and Language* and the index of *Mind in Society*. In *Thought and Language*, there is no reference in the index to what U.S. developmental psychology, in 1978, took to be the hallmark of Vygotsky's theory—the Zone of Proximal Development. There were many references to the ZPD in the index to *Mind in Society*.

Moreover, the notion of ZPD as referenced in *Thought and Language* is essentially about the differential potentialities of children, those with larger or smaller zones of proximal development. In this sense, the notion is somewhat the equivalent of the measures of IQ in use at the time, with the addition of the idea that such differences reflect differences in "teachability." The expanded notion of the ZPD in *Mind and Society* goes much further, implying, but not detailing the idea that complex internal developmental processes that follow from this initial "boost." The major work of the ZPD in developmental terms then is in the internal processes that follow *within* the child and not *between* the child and the more capable other. What had happened during this time period? Why was Piaget immediately taken up by developmental psychologists in the United States, and why did Vygotsky have to be "rediscovered" in the late 1970s (with the publication of *Mind in Society* in 1978) and in delayed retranslations and a flurry of books that brought Vygotsky into central relevance. Why did the Vygotsky of 1962 have no reference to the ZPD while later works focused on that as his central conceptual contribution?

There is a story to tell—and it is a story that relates to the political structure of psychology that was developed within this historical period that is decisive for the interpretation of the meaning of Vygotsky's theory within the United States. My central theoretical claim is that somewhere in the process, Vygtosky became "Piagetianized"—framed as an "answer to" the limitations of Piaget's theory—rather than treated in depth as a theory in itself. In the process much has been lost. As such, treated as a reaction to Piaget, Vygotsky was treated within the context of learning instead of contexts that were amenable to his thinking, e.g., social mediation or cultural tools.

For example, the section quoted above from *Mind and Society* (1978) ends with most of the developmental processes empowered by the interaction with others submerged within the individual child.

> In fact, they have only just begun at that moment. The major consequence of analyzing the educational process in this manner is to show that initial mastery of, for example, the four arithmetic operations provides the basis for the subsequent development of a variety of highly complex internal processes in children's thinking. (p. 90)

My further claim is that by de-Piagetianizing Vygotsky, we can discover the way in which his work is directly relevant to the discovery of the many ways that an application of Vygotsky's work can contribute to an understanding of the issues facing a Latino community (or a Latin world) within contemporary conditions.

Being framed as an "answer to Piaget," Vygotsky's voice was changed, and he came to be thought of as a "stand in" for the learning theory that had been supplanted by Piagetian theory. The difference between the ZPD and that learning theory are, in fact, profound, but the depth of that difference was yet to be recognized. Indeed, the full thrust of Vygotskyan theory can be found in the differences between conceptualizing core developmental processes locked in "highly complex internal processes in children's thinking" or conceiving them in complex interactional, social, historical, and cultural processes.

# Mid-1980s: Wertsch, Bakhtin, and Sociocultural Theory

While many U.S. developmental psychologists participated in many Zone of Proximal Development studies in the post *Mind in Society* period, other voices and sources were coming into focus—some from other Russian theorists, for example, Mikhail Bakhtin. Under the stewardship of Michael Holquist and Caryl Emerson and others, a number Bakhtinian texts began to appear in English in the mid-1980s.

As a backdrop to Wertsch's contribution, the reader should be familiar with Vygotsky's own definition of his project.

This book is a study of one of the most complex problems of psychology, the interrelation of thought and language…. The structure of this book is perforce complex and multifaceted, yet all its parts are oriented toward a central task, the genetic analysis of the relation between thought and the spoken word…It might be useful to enumerate briefly the aspect of our work that we believe to be novel and consequently in need of further checking…(1) providing experimental evidence that meanings of words undergo evolution during childhood, and defining the basic steps in that evolution; (2) uncovering the singular way in which the child's "scientific" concepts develop, compared with his spontaneous concepts; (3) demonstrating the specific psychological nature and linguistic function of written speech in its relation to thinking and (4) clarifying, by way of experiments, the nature of inner speech and its relation to thought…we feel that in uncovering the problem of the relation of thought and language as a focal issue of human psychology we have contributed to some essential progress. Our findings point the way to a new theory of consciousness, which is barely touched on at the end of our book. (Vygotsky, 1962, Author's preface, Hanfmann and Vakar translation)

James Wertsch, a linguist by training, began to publish texts on Vygotsky—in 1985 *Vygotsky and the Social Formation of Mind* and in 1991 *Voices of the Mind: A Sociocultural Approach to Culturally Mediated Action* (1991a).

The core issue is put very tactfully by Wertsch (1991a) in his introductory remarks to chapter 3, titled "Beyond Vygotsky: Bakhtin's Contribution."

Vygotsky's analysis of higher mental functioning provides a foundation for a sociocultural approach to mediated action. In this connection, his investigation of the social origins of individual mental functioning and his claims about semiotic mediation are particularly important. Yet in certain essential respects he did not succeed in providing a genuinely sociocultural approach to mind. *In particular, he did little to spell out how specific historical, cultural and institutional settings are tied to various forms of mediated action.* (Wertsch, 1991a, p. 46, emphasis added)

Wertsch goes on to identify the problem in terms of Vygotsky's focus on "small group interaction, particularly the adult-child dyad." This small group focus does not allow for an understanding of how larger historical, cultural and institutional settings come to bear on human lives. Additionally, Vygotsky had defined the core issue as one of "word meaning"—a feature that could be thought of as equivalent to contemporary cognitive analysis.

By introducing Bakhtin, Wertsch shifted emphasis from "word" to "utterance." A word meaning is something that may develop within a person. It could easily be understood as having a cognitive but not social referent. However, an utterance is something that occurs between people (in groups small or large) and bears heavily on the relationships that exist and are articulated in language use.

In contrast to the STEM discipline focus of both Piaget and the partially social and partially internal notion of the ZPD, Wertsch introduced new topics to be addressed, in part introduced by the core ideas of Bakhtin. These topics had more to do with the dynamics of language and its use than they had to do with making better rockets. Some illustrative titles: "Problems of Dosteyevsky's Poetics"; "The Dialogic Imagination;" "

## Latin Issues and Bakhtin in Contemporary Context

Whether or not there is a "Latin American World" (as indicated earlier), it is clear that whatever world occupied Central and South America, it was not centrally the competition between superpowers in technological terms. While Cuba and Nicaragua were sucked into the Cold War imaginary, the problems facing the area were problems of development in multiple forms.

As Torres (1995) describes the situation, there were differences between the "developed cold warrior nations" and the majority of Latin America:

> Schooling in Latin America is segregated by class, with the poor attending public schooling and the middle and upper classes attending private education....With the exception of Mexico the important pre-school experience, which has proven decisive in shaping the cognitive structure of children is not widely available for the majority of children of the poor in the region. Illiteracy continues to be an educational nightmare for educational planners, and the gender gap to the disadvantage of women [is] widening....Shortcomings and omissions in adult education are not surprising considering the fact that literacy training and adult education services provided by the state in Latin America play mainly a symbolic and legitimizing role, although there has been expansion and diversification of services in some countries in the 1980's. (Torres, 1995).

Many of the articles in the Torres (1995) book deal with the tensions and difficulties encountered in addressing marked social differences between educators and those to be educated, and to the difficulties encountered when "nation" and "national standards" come face to face with indigenous groups.

The articles further identify additional "educational topics" that are of central importance to developing nations, adult literacy, and job training, and, of course, debt (which is incurred in attempting huge developmental strides in a short period of time). This dynamic led to the "lost 1980s" when the IMF began to call in loans, and investment in education was brought to a screeching halt. Clearly, larger social, historical, political and economic issues were at play.

As we are becoming increasingly aware, Latin America is not some distant place, it is both outside and inside our borders, with large numbers of immigrants, both documented and undocumented, living in North American cities.

This Vygotskyan/Bakhtinian voice could address fundamental issues of cultural membership, i.e., participation in language communities, the "life" of a culture as it is lived. It is a picture of a person engaged, discursively, interactively with a community. Perhaps this interaction is the deeper meaning of the concept of the Zone of Proximal Development. It is not a term that is a synonym for teaching—it is a term that refers to dialogical engagement with and within a culture. Meanings develop. They are not just acquired.

When we shift attention from teaching/learning to cultural mediation, a number of other factors in the developmental picture begin to emerge with some clarity. Fundamental questions can be raised that can apply to cultural formations that go beyond any that Vygotsky might have imagined in 1934. I will, in the rest of this chapter, focus on three basic ideas:

1.  A focus on "cultural mediational tools: as they are involved in activity of children, adults and, in general, culture members in a particular historical climate and
2.  The forms of activity invited and afforded by these mediational tools.
3.  The social, intellectual, and dialogical ecology that results.

In this way I hope to do what Vygotsky said (it is said) had to be done with Marx. Rather than the theory being "quoted" and its language applied, its fundamental concepts have to be reinvented in application to any concrete analysis.

## Sabor Latino, with or Without Vygotsky

As focus turns toward a dialogical approach and to larger societal units than the parent-child dyad, or the educational system per se, it is clear that Latin America and Latin Americans in the United States face formidable social problems. There are, within Latin America great disparities in wealth and with that cultural and social capital. It is also clear that there are many populations with differing social status and cultural formations (deriving from an essentially colonial past). They also came equipped with resources that are scarcely recognized within traditional developmental psychological approaches.

Several interesting lines of approach using sociohistorical theory (broadly conceived and somewhat based on Vygotsky and Bakhtin) are beginning to develop an approach that addresses these issues.

Moll and Greenberg (1990) have done ethnographic studies of Mexican communities living (ironically at this point in time) in Arizona. They have examined some of the dialogical and cultural resources that underpin the life of this community. They identify two critical points that sustain this community. One is a sense of solidarity and mutual trust—"Confianza." Additionally, they interestingly identify a variety of forms of Zones of Proximal Development—which have a more social and community basis—"zones of knowledge" and "zones of possibility"—which are based on a more fundamental notion that exists—seeing communities as containing "funds of knowledge" that form the basis for sharing and spreading of competencies within communities. In this work, it is clear that two fundamental extensions of Vygotsky's ideas are involved: a focus on social, trust and dialogical relations and the intellectual resources considered in a community as opposed to an individual intellectual basis. Moreover, the funds of knowledge are at the level of "how to" and hence very much tied to activities and possible activities.

In a detailed analysis of monolingual and bilingual schooling in this community, a further, and to my mind, essential element is added. The Bakhtinian notion of "dialogue" does not sufficiently distinguish the social positioning that exists within dialogical relationships. Communicative interactions, addressor-addressee relationships can take on several forms. They can be asymmetrical (master/student; knower/ignorant in need of teaching), or they can be truly dialogically engaged (considered as the mutual influence of equals on each other). Lessons can either be monologically imposed, or dialogically developed. Schools are caught between monologic "standards" and dialogic engagement with students. The two case studies presented focus on the importance of an essential factor in dialogical engagement-legitimization. Dialogical engagement ultimately rests on issues of mutuality and legitimization of the "other" as having a point of view worth considering. Similarly, Rogoff (1995) presented studies showing the multiple modes of cultural transmission, some involving, from my point of view, the issues both of transmission and of dialogical legitimacy.

In situations of uneven development and/or unequal status, the issue of having "a voice" that can be heard in dialogic encounters is critical. If dialogue involves exchanges of utterances, then the status of the person in the dialogue as a legitimate voice is critical to many of life's issues. For the Latino community in the United States, issues of language, skin color, opportunity will hinge on the degree to which the "other" is seen as a possible dialogical partner. Moll and Greenberg identify critical areas that I would call "legitimization moves"—for example, when the funds of knowledge possessed by parents of schoolchildren are brought into the school setting—and treated, indeed, as expertise.

Funds of knowledge are but one source of sustaining community and attaining legitimacy. Smolka, De Goes, and Pino (1995) address some of these same issues in terms of the relation of intersubjectivity and individual processes. Within a "legitimization" perspective, adopted here, intersubjectivity is not automatically achieved. The question is who is a "subject" with whom one can be intersubjective. From a dialogical perspective, this issue is critical. The authors, in their own terms, point out some of the critical points.

> We could say that in different approaches within the historical-cultural perspective, when intraindividual functioning is focused on, there is a concern with the risk of a 'dissolution of the subject' or of a 'dictatorship of the other' in the interindividual func-

tioning; on the other hand, when interindividual functioning is focused on, the question of the subject constitution is not directly addressed.

Wertsch's work can be identified as an important attempt to establish an articulated view of 'the two sides' of subject formation.... In these efforts, the semiotic and dialogic nature of human actions and development have been emphasized, in analyses predominantly inspired by Vygotsky and Bakhtin. (pp. 178–179).

Del Río and Álvarez (2007) developed an ecofunctional approach to the ZPD, which has important pointers toward the adaptation of Vygotsky's ideas to a cultural approach to Latin America. In this approach, they define the ZPD in several terms. I will focus here on a key passage that would allow for a consideration outside of the corset into which developmental psychology in the United States has put Vygotsky (Wertsch excepted).

Thus, the notion of the ZPD as scaffolding that would achieve full internalization of all mental functioning should be revised in order to construct a ZPD, and education itself from the ecology of mind. This involves accepting the existence of nonindividual mental subjects—communities, institutions, cultures—and the notion that an individual maintains, throughout his life, a large part of his individual functional systems distributed effectively in his personal Umwelt. (Del Río & Álvarez, p. 302)

This assessment, if taken seriously, would mean that it would be necessary to address concretely the social, political, religious community and activity structures of Latin America. It would mean that it would be necessary to legitimize aspects of persons' lives that are meaningful to them and that have an impact on them. From the perspective of a legitimizing analysis or even the seemingly irrational, it is mandatory to see the elements of dialogic encounter that could form a zone of development, proximally, socially, and politically. Religion and religious ideas, for example, would not be ruled out of a consideration of the ZPD.

Solís (2001, 2004) has dealt with these issues in directly political terms examining the difference in perceived agency and social action depending on whether Mexican immigrants (in New York) consider themselves to be "illegal" or "undocumented." Those assuming the position of "illegal" opt for silence and suffer exploitation, those assuming a position of "undocumented" are far more likely to be agentive and resistant to the many forms of exploitation that are possible (should one remain voiceless). We are currently entering a period within U.S. politics where these issues are becoming increasingly salient.

Issues of dialogicality are central to the emerging cultural scene now. Important contributions about "voice" are available, for example, see Cheyne and Tarulli (1999).

These issues are of profound importance. There is nothing less at stake than whether people, particularly Latinos, are considered sources of pollution and danger or are engaged as legitimate beings who can and should be dialogically engaged (consider the newly emerged issue concerning the 14th Amendment).

As "immigration reform" comes to be more topical in years to come, the issue of the dialogical positioning of the Latino communities in the United States is likely to arise in stark political terms.

The story told here is not the story of a theorist who died in 1934 and how he may be applied now. Rather we are involved in adapting that theory and the thinking of that theorist to issues that are both consequential and contemporary. Satisfactory use of that theory is based neither on ideological nor terminological grounds. It rests instead on the adaptation of a theory to contemporary conditions, with an array of understandings that have developed within the human sciences, and which relate to the application to contemporary problems. We are dealing with profound issues of human rights, cultural belonging, and the having of a cultural voice. A cultural and historical understanding is a key element to address these issues, whether that understanding comes in the form of applying a theory or expanding its scope and resources to deal with increasingly complex and inherently political issues.

# · 2 ·

# The Path to Subjectivity

## Advancing Alternative Understandings of Vygotsky and the Cultural Historical Legacy

*Fernando González Rey*

Vygotsky's brief intellectual trajectory in Soviet psychology was remarkably innovative—often contradictory. Indeed, over the past two decades, new interpretations of and counterpoints to Vygotsky's legacy have emerged that have led to reflections concerning his legacy and its consequences for psychology. (Yarochevsky, 1989, 1993; Leontiev., A.A, 1992, 2001; Zinchenko, 1997, 2009; Veresov, 1999; González Rey 1995, 2001, 2008, 2009). Even so, much of Western Vygotskyan-inspired scholarship still understands the approaches of Vygotsky and Leontiev as integrated in that numerous scholars lump both authors under the theoretical umbrella of Cultural Historical Activity Approach (CHAT) (Zinchenko, 1997; Lektorsky, 1999; González Rey, 1983, 1999, 2008, 2009; Veresov, 1999). Such an amalgamation needs to be questioned carefully and possibly even reconsidered. Specifically, in this chapter I focus on the topic of subjectivity.

After a brief historical presentation of the basis for the development of subjectivity as result of social and cultural experience in Russian thinking and in Soviet and Russian psychologies, I present alternative interpretations by Soviet and Russian[1] authors to argue that the dialectical orientations of the post-1917 October Revolution were not incompatible with the theoretical constructions of thinkers labeled as idealistics, such as Troistki, Chelpanov and Schpet—all of whom underscored the relevance of culture for the development of the human psyche. I discuss Vygotsky's orientation towards cognitive-emotional synthesis or "unities," the generative character of emotions, and the idea of psyche as a dynamic system. These features, I argue, all marked a new ontological definition of the human psyche based on cognitive-emotional processes grounded in culture. Despite their cultural genesis, such processes and formations were, for Vygotsky, singular in their organization and in their cultural and social influences. Thus, Vygotsky's conceptualization of the social situation of development in the final stages of his oeuvre was, in my opinion, closest to Rubinstein's views. However, with the advent of Activity Theory, such unity was essentially considered, in its movement from activity to consciousness, as a reflection of reality rather than the production of realities by the child's consciousness (Zinchenko, 2002). I underscore that for Vygotsky external influences were made relevant to individuals as "perezhivanie," which appear as a result of the actual personal psychical organization. Perezhivanie thus represented the individual psychical production rather than the mere and exclusive effect of external influences.[2] That is to say, external facts are involved in a self-regulatory process of personality at the moment of one's living a concrete experience or series of experiences. Emotion is an expression of the personality's self-regulatory movement facing new experiences. Through the concepts of "perezhivanie" and social situation of development, Vygotsky introduced a theoretical representation of human development underscoring the self-regulatory movement of personality in the face of lived experiences from which appear "perezhivanies" leading to ruptures and, consequently, the beginnings of new development. After an examination of the evolution of these concepts and positions as the basis for the consideration of subjectivity from a new cultural-historical approach, I theorize ways of developing the topic of subjectivity from the concepts of subjective sense and subjective configurations. I argue for understanding human psychological processes as rooted in social, historical, and cultural genesis and development.

## Materialistic and Idealistic Thinking
## in Soviet Psychology

With the emergence of the Soviet state, the conflict between idealism and materialism became ideological in nature. All idealistic thoughts or concepts were synonymous with the conservative and reactionary, and, by consequence, the old political order. Adherents to idealistic positions were potential or real enemies of the Revolution and the subsequent target of repression in academic and scientific institutions. Idealistic philosophers who played an important role in the consideration of culture as a source of subjectivity in Russian thought were effectively banished from the official versions of Soviet psychology history. To that end, Troitski (1882) who had argued that concepts themselves "configured the social cultural form of human thinking, appearing as a powerful organ of social relations" (p. 62) was officially abandoned. Troitski had been the principal professor of Philosophy at the University of Moscow and president of the Moscow Society of Psychologists when psychology was considered part of philosophy in Russia. The prestigious Soviet psychologist Budilova, devoted to the study of history of psychology, noted Troitski's seminal contributions describing his doctoral thesis as: "The first Russian historical psychological work" (1983, p. 19).

The struggle between idealism and materialism mirrored the tensions between arguments for framing the origins of human thinking as cultural or physiological. For example, A. N. Leontiev and the Kharkov's group criticized Vygotsky's verbal reductionism in the comprehension of psychological functions. Even earlier, Soviet psychology was characterized by the confrontation between a mechanical interpretation of Marxism with an objective and concrete understanding of the genesis of the psyche versus the idea of the human psyche as a specific phenomenon grounded in the cultural character of human existence. Materialistic interpretations prevailed and informed the subsequent definition of an objective psychology

Two psychologists long stigmatized in Soviet psychology nevertheless, defended consciousness as a qualitatively singular phenomenon, distinct from the physiological processes: Chelpanov and his disciple Schpet. The relevance of Chelpanov and the first references to Schpet were raised in the early eighties (Budilova, 1983; Radzijovsky, 1982). Culture, consciousness, and subjectivity were re-introduced as important topics for Russian psychology in the beginning of the 21st century, even when the topic of subjectivity was explicitly brought into light at the 1980s (Abuljanova, 1980; Chudnovsky, 1988). The reluctance in considering subjectivity also affected the acceptance of cultural differences among the different ethnic groups that integrated the former Soviet Union. As Zinchenko (2007, 2009) argued, the influence of Schpet on Vygotsky seemed to be relevant in his interests for the development of a cultural psychology.

With the Fifth Congress of the Society of Soviet Psychologists (1977), a fault line emerged between the prevalence of a more official and restricted domain of an objective or "Marxist" psychology and the emergence of new approaches still "Marxist" but not restricted to an objective version of psychology—illustrated, for example, in the principles of Leontiev's version of object based activity.

## Subjectivity During the Soviet Period and Implications for Psychology

Although the topic of subjectivity was largely suppressed during the Soviet era, Vygotsky and Rubinstein nevertheless left clear, though distinct, notions about the active and generative character of individuals in regard to social influences. Rubinstein (1957) outlived Vygotsky by several decades and explicitly addressed subjectivity in *Social Being and Consciousness* where he argued that a particular quality of human psyche was its irreducibility in relation to external processes that participate in its genesis. That irreducible quality or qualities were a starting point for a truly dialectical comprehension of the relation between culture and the human psyche. In other words, although the human psyche had a cultural genesis, the human psyche was not reproduced in its nature by those external processes involved in its genesis. That said, Soviet psychologists, including Rubinstein and Vygotsky, consistently referred to subjective matters through other theoretical concepts such as gnoseological processes, consciousness, personality, psychological formations, and so on.

It is quite impossible to amalgamate Vygotsky's thought into a coherent and unique narrative. Even so, Western psychologists have done exactly that—constraining Vygtosky's theoretical position mainly to the period between 1928 and 1931. As such, Cultural Historical Theory is limited to Vygotskyan notions of sign, semiotic mediation, internalization, and higher psychological functions. Indeed, Vygotsky's focus during the 1928–1931 period, or cultural historical period, largely revolved around these notions. However, his earlier notion of a psychological system capable of integrating emotions and cognitive processes, ideas that reappeared in his last works, are today largely misunderstood if not ignored in Western literature on Vygotsky.

As previously stated, Vygotsky's orientation towards cognitive-emotional synthesis or "unities," the generative character of emotions, and the idea of psyche as a dynamic system together marked an ontological definition of human psyche based on cognitive-emotional processes grounded in culture. When Vygotsky introduced the concept of social situation of development at the end of his work, he extended Rubinstein's attempt at unifying consciousness and activity. However, in Activity Theory, such unity was essentially considered in its movement from activity to consciousness, as a reflection of reality and not as the production of realities by the child's consciousness (Zinchenko, 2002). For Vygotsky, "The emotional experience [perezhivanie] arising from any situation or from any aspect of environment, determines what kind of influence this situation or this environment will have on the child" (1994, p. 338). Through concepts such as "perezhivanie" and the social situation of development, Vygotsky avoided the concept of reflection, which between 1928 and 1931 was embodied in his use of "vrachivaniya"—translated as internalization.

Vygotsky's use of the terms *personality* and *consciousness* in his earlier and later writings resembled Rubinstein's definition in that psychical systems were not to be reduced simply to activity. Renewed interest in the topic of consciousness in Russian psychology has since revived discussions of the ontological specificity of human psychical phenomena. V. P. Zinchenko (2009), a contemporary advocate of this new approach to consciousness, explained:

> The task of any science that lays claim to studying consciousness is to fill it with concrete ontological substance and meaning. After all, consciousness is not only born in existence and not only reflects and therefore embodies it—to be sure, in a reflected or distorted light—but also creates it. (p. 46)

Zinchenko's oriented consciousness as an active and generative subjective system not controlled by external influences or contingencies. The continued search for an ontological definition of subjectivity was therefore important since subjectivity could only be recognized through its heuristic value in identifying new problems, in particular those related to motivation of the systemic functioning of human psyche.

Emphases on behavior, relations, and the social and discursive origins of human consciousness resist the subject's ability to create and produce his or her own alternatives through lived social experiences. The subject is not an exclusively external production. Rather, what counts is the configuration of organized experiences interwoven within the subject's system of subjective configurations— capable of generating new networks of subjective senses and possibilities for the subject's actions. In short, the re-prioritization of the subject challenged the extended idea that subjectivity and the subject are mere epiphenomena of discursive, semiotic, and linguistic practices.

Over time, Soviet psychology split into two different camps. The first camp oriented to an objective definition of psychology which chronologically focused on three different concepts, "Reflexological," whereby the psyche was explained on the basis of physiological processes; "Behavioral," whereby behavior was the objective focus for the explanation of consciousness and associated the concept of internalization; and object based activity that focused on the object and on the external in detriment of the concepts of subject and, consequently, subjectivity. The second camp represented a minority opinion with respect to the latter position and became salient in the study of personality and motivation in ways that separate both concepts from the immediate determinism of external facts, dominant in Soviet psychology due to the principle of reflection. They attempted to overcome the determinism that resulted from the hegemony of the concept of object based activity.

Rubinstein, L. I. Bozhovich, V. I. Miasichev, and some of Rubinstein's followers such as Abuljanova, Antsiferova, and Aseiev dealt explicitly with issues of personality. With Leontiev's activity theory, motivation and personality were understood through the lens of activity. Only in the 1970s did the issue of personality become an object of empirical inquiry within the frame of Activity Theory as evidenced in Leontiev's book *Activity, Consciousness and Personality.*

If motivation and personality gradually became of consequence in Soviet psychology, this was due to the gradual realization of the limitations of Activity Theory in its treatment of subjective processes and phenomena. Eventually, L. I. Bozhovich (1978) one of the members of Kharkov's group, and Vygotsky's disciple, broke with Leontiev and the Jharkov group. She explained,

> In the beginning we shared the same position related to needs and motives sustained by Leontiev. However, based on our first research we came to a different practical definition of motive because it was impossible to use "motive" while always taking into account certain objective things....In trying to analyze which needs "crystallized" in one or another "motive," what is behind the child's inclination toward one object or another, we found a complex knot of needs, desires and intentions where it was difficult to understand which was the object of an activity and which the motive. (pp. 19–20)

In contrast to Leontiev who had framed motive as the object of activity, Bozhovich drew from Vygotsky to examine the complex psychical organization of motives. Likewise, Davydov critically analyzed A. N. Leontiev's conceptualization of internal activity as identical to external activity whereby the object was framed as a motive. Or, as Davydov (1980) explained in a joint paper with his disciple Radzikhovskii,

> They (Kharkov group) took another decision (in relation to Vygotsky concerning the internalization of external activity). They conducted the "psychologization" of the methodological activity approach through the essentially new idea of individual activity as a trace of external activity. This idea was the basis of A. N. Leontiev and collaborators' cycle of works from 1930 to 1970. (p. 76)

Bozhovich's orientation to the study of personality via development represented a break from more traditional clinical approaches of understanding personality. Bozhovich's contribution was the specification of personality as an essential topic for general psychology—much as it had been for Vygotsky.

Chudnovsky (2009) in his recent biography of Bozhovich notes:

In 1939, she defended her candidate of sciences dissertation.[3] A significant conclusion reached in her dissertation research was that schoolchildren's assimilation of knowledge is significantly conditioned by their personality[-related] relationships to the material. This conclusion would go on to become a core focus of her scholarship. (p. 4)

Bozhovich consequently developed a line in Soviet psychology—resurrecting Vygotskyan concepts suppressed by Leontiev's dominant interpretation. The creative subjective approach to learning, in contraposition to the objective-based object approach centered on assimilation, became a central topic to Soviet and Russian psychology some years later (Yakimanskaya, 1989; Bruschlinsky, 1996; Davydov, 1999, 2002).

In my opinion, motivation and personality are central for the development of the topic of subjectivity from a theoretical account of the creative subject. I define subjectivity as those processes of subjective sense[4] in their multiple and constant configurations in different human activeness. Subjectivity is always involved in subject action, as a subjective configuration that organizes itself based on ongoing action. Motivation is more than a simple psychical function. Rather, as a central core of subjectivity, motives must be analyzed as particular moments of the subject's subjective configurations in his or her multiple and simultaneous expressions. From this perspective and within a cultural-historical approach, motivation is central to the ontological distinction of the subject and subjectivity.

Traditionally, motive has been taken as a given content driving human action and almost always has been considered as embodied in a concrete content, e.g., the motive to study, the motive to play a sport. Via the motive, the concept crystallizes as a concrete entity. A subjective configuration frames motive as a network of different subjective senses, emanating from a continuum of an individual's lived experiences converging at the moment of the subject's action. The "motive" to learn or to achieve is configured in the child as the result of multiple subjective senses. We could imagine, for example, a specific case where different subjective productions of the child, such as the shame the child experienced about his or her social status, or the fear of his or her father who physically abuses his or her mother are combined in a complex subjective network that will mediate emotionally and symbolically the child's perception about the way the teacher establishes or doesn't establish relations with him or her. These intricate affections and symbolical expressions are organized as a subjective configuration that characterize those chains of subjective senses and, consequently, shape the child's behaviors in a classroom or school. Thus, isolated content cannot be defined as motive. Motive is always a configuration of subjective senses permanently produced on the course of human activity.

Also important in developing an understanding of subjectivity within a cultural historical framework is the notion of communication—first introduced as a specific psychical concept in Soviet psychology in the 1970s as a means of counteracting explanations that limited all psychological concepts in terms of object based activity (Lomov, 1978, 1984; Abuljanova, 1973, 1980). Communication as presented by Lomov (1984) integrated both the subject of the process of communication and its subjective character. Thus, following Lomov, "Communication appears as an autonomous and specific form of subject's activeness. Its result is not the transformation of the object (material or ideal), but the relations with other persons" (p. 248). Lomov's questions were later advanced by Davydov (2002) and Smirnov (1993)—both adherents of Activity Theory. Rejecting communication as an activity, Smirnov (1993) argued:

> According to the main conceptual apparatus of the theory of activity, those processes that appear between two persons looking into each other's are not evident without making any external or internal act. There are bases to state that these processes of communication have completely different bases than those on which rest the concept of activity. (p. 99)

Reductive attempts to reduce psychological process exclusively to activity impoverished Soviet psychology to the extent that all psychological processes and phenomena were conceptualized as objective operations crystallized in the organization of activity. The polemical character of Soviet psychology in the late 1970s and the 1980s was indicative of a rupture with the previous Soviet agenda for defining psychology—a break that gave way to revised interpretations of the history of Soviet and Russian psychologies and the rehabilitation of figures previously stigmatized such as Schpet, Chelpanov, Bakhtin, and others (Budilova, 1983; Radzijovsky, 1985; Yarochevsky, 1993; Abuljanova & Bruschlinsky, 1989; Zinchenko, 2007, 2009; A. A. Leontiev, 1992, 2001).

## Subjectivity Revisited

New alliances such as the one between Davydov and Bruschlinsky emerged— theoretical partnerships that produced multiple positions and alternatives. For the purpose of this chapter, I focus on those relevant to the development of the topics of subjectivity and subject from a cultural-historical standpoint. In 1988, subjectivity appeared explicitly in V. E. Chudnovsky's "Problem of Subjectivity in the Light of Current Tasks of the Psychology of Education" in *Voprocy Psykjology*. Arguing that subjectivity could not be reduced to the assimilation of external influences, Chudnovsky (1988) underscored the active character of subjectivity through which individuals' produce their distinct "realities":

> The fact that the genesis of subjectivity results from communication and joint activity is true. But it is not all the truth. As it was stated before, subjectivity has its active side, it not only is engendered by the facts, it influences them and it is this dialectic that is the key to understanding subjectivity. (p. 17)

Or, as I have argued, the "generative capacity of psyche" (González Rey, 2009) is crucial for understanding the subjective nature of culture—two moments of the same recursive system. Within this system, cultural events gain continuously subjective expressions in persons and institutions, and subjective processes become cultural accounts that are perceived as objective for persons, as a subjective effect that could be named as the naturalization of a given fact. Moscovici (2000) emphasized this subjective character of socially produced phenomena in his explanation about the objectification of social representations. Subjectivity, in this cultural-historical definition, cannot be considered only as an individual phenomenon because it involves the subjective sense productions and configurations that characterize the different social spaces within which human experience takes place. Each family has its own social subjectivity that is not the sum of the individual psychologies of its members. Differently from the systemic paradigm in psychotherapy, the concept of social subjectivity permits understandings of how subjective senses result from other social spaces and social discourses that assemble into the familiar subjective configuration. Each social space is configured on a subjective configuration that is revealed by its belonging to a more complex social subjectivity.

The entrance of the topics of subject and subjectivity in Soviet psychology (see, e.g., Rubinstein, 1957; Abuljanova, 1973, 1980; Lomov, 1978, 1984; Chudnovsky, 1988, 2007; Bruschlinsky, 1996, 2002) and the growing force of such topics in those years also influenced two psychologists who were part of the Activity Theory group: Davydov and Zinchenko. Davydov first revisited and remodeled the topic of activity on a completely new basis. Zinchenko focused on the topic of consciousness in its more subjective definition—as Vygotsky had in the final moments of his unfinished oeuvre (Vygotsky, 1987, 1994).

Like Chudnovsky, Zinchenko (2002) defended the generative character of the human psyche centered on consciousness:

> Once it appeared, consciousness emancipates from activity and it begins to create new forms of activities, to create the world and not only to reflect it, subordinating to it…. Empirical justified an asymmetrical relation between consciousness and activity, not its unity. A slave work not always leads to a slave consciousness. Precisely the contradiction between consciousness and activity acts as driving force of human development. (p. 79)

Central to his definition of consciousness was its emancipation from activity and its capacity to create new realities and the basis of a psychology oriented to human creation rather than assimilation. Similarly, Davydov maintained that activity was an interdisciplinary concept and not a purely psychological one—ideas that Lomov (1978, 1984) had suggested more than a decade earlier. Attempting to rework activity as a psychological concept, Davydov introduced desire[5] as part of activity structure. In so doing, Davydov advanced the subjective aspects or "subjectivization" of activity.

Davydov (2002) explicitly referred to two important ruptures with the Activity Theory of his day. The first was associated with the Russian philosopher Bibler and the second with Bruschlinsky's definition of the subject of activity. Davydov identified three weak points in the more classical definition of activity in Leontiev's works. First, Davydov argued that activity could not exist as a psychological concept without the integration of desire as a central element of its structure. Along those same lines, Davydov introduced the concept of the subject of activity—with a nod to Bruschlinsky's contribution. Finally, Davydov argued the idea of collective and interpersonal activity. Davydov's extended arguments drew from Lomov, Zinchenko, and Bruschlinsky—who besides Zinchenko had never before been recognized by adherents of activity theory.

Integrating the idea of the subject of activity and desire as central for the psychological relevance of activity, Davydov (2002) overcame Leontiev's objective definition of the structure of activity centered on individual acts and operations with objects. While his death prevented him from developing further his revision of activity theory, Davydov nevertheless began the work of revising the representation of activity given by Leontiev. Unlike A. N. Leontiev who only took into account individual activity, Davydov extended the concept to social relations and contexts.

Many of the ideas discussed in this section have been overlooked by Russian and Western psychologies. As this chapter is an attempt to defend the possibility of understanding the topic of subjectivity on a new basis, it is important for the reader to know not only Vygotsky's contributions but also to know different positions and discussions within Russian and Soviet psychologies. This approach allows us to demystify the so-called "troika" as a monolithical position organized as result of the integration between Vygotsky, Luria, and Leontiev.

## Vygotsky's Legacy in Soviet and Russian Psychologies After the 1980s: Different Approaches to the Topic of Sense

The critical interpretations of the Vygotskyan legacy that emerged in the 1990s (A. A. Leontiev, 1992, 2001; Zinchenko, 1997; Yarochevsky, 1989, 1993; Van der

Veer & Valsiner, 1994; Veresov, 1999) have impacted a relatively small population of researchers—with dominant interpretations of Vygotsky still remaining resistant to extensions of that legacy or to innovations by others. With the exception of Yarochevsky (2007), few have pursued the relevance Vygotsky assigned in his early writings to the generative character of emotions and the subjective processes. I (González Rey, 2009) consider the psychology of art and Vygotsky's first works on defectology as his initial foray into questions closely related to subjectivity within an evolving cultural-historical framework.

Attention to "sense" and the social situation of development has been largely excluded from current Vygotskyan-inspired thinking. That said, the topic of sense did gain some currency inside Soviet and Russian psychologies at the end of the 1970s. In particular, these two issues appealed to some of the younger generation of Activity Theory (Asmolov, Bratus, Stolin, D. Leontiev)—energized by A. N. Leontiev's redefinition of sense in "Activity Consciousness and Personality," which, as the title suggests, attributed more importance to personality than had been the case previously. However, the ways Leontiev's followers have historically treated sense suggest a number of contradictions. Alternatively, as A. A. Leontiev (1992) explained:

> There are many theoretical ideas in these works, however, that were not picked up by the Kharkov group or were only partially accepted (he referred to Vygotsky's ideas after 1930). These were hardly noticed by Vygotsky's historiographers and were deliberately ignored by his critics. The most important of these ideas was that of "sense", or "sense field. (p. 41)

By contrast, D. Leontiev (1994) argued:

> This concept (the author referred to sense) first appeared in L. S. Vygotsky's late writings (e.g., Vygotsky, 1934/1987). He used this concept in his analysis of the complex psychological relationships between thinking, inner and outer speech, and intended to reveal the "sense structure of consciousness, considering sense to be "a relation to the outer word" (Vygotsky, 1982, p. 165). However, it was merely a declaration on the part of Vygotsky, who failed to go beyond the sphere of consciousness in his interpretation and use of the concept of sense. ( p. 9)

D. Leontiev, a critic of Vygotsky's use of the concept of sense, attributed to A. N. Leontiev, his grandfather, the merit of having approached the psychological character of sense. If the concept of sense was really so central to A. N. Leontiev as D. Leontiev's interpretation argued, it could have avoided the critiques of determinism, individualism, objectivism, and universalism addressed to Activity Theory from important Russian psychologists from different fields since the 1970s (Abuljanova, 1973, 1980; Lomov, 1978, 1984; Bozhovich, 1978; Bruschlinsky, 1977; Pushkin, 1977; Nepomnichaya, 1977; Zinchenko, 1997).

D. Leontiev's position is unsustainable because of the precarious presence of sense in the main works of more orthodox Activity Theory. A. A. Leontiev (1992) argued:

> Only many years later did A. N. Leontiev (in relation to the Vygotsky's use of the term) speak publicly of "personal sense" (most clearly in his 1974 work, "The Psychological Problem of the Consciousness of Learning"). There appears to be a gap between Leontiev's "personal sense" and Vygotsky's "sense field", but it is in fact not the case. (p. 41)

I identify two distinct interpretations of sense. The first reduced the category to a concrete based object activity. The second, as emphasized by A. A. Leontiev and with which I generally concur (González Rey, 2009), considered sense as a new psychical unity critical to a new systemic comprehension of the human mind. D. Leontiev's genealogy of the issue of sense in Soviet psychology took A. N. Leontiev's definition of personal sense as a starting point—a descriptive concept aligned with based object activity whereby in the relationship between the goal and motive of activity, motive was framed as the object of activity. Alternatively, as D. Leontiev (1994) explained: "Sense in our understanding is always sense of something or of someone—sense of certain influences, facts, phenomena, objective reality for the concrete subject who lives in that reality" (p. 278; taken from D. Leontiev, 2007, p. 83).

D. Leontiev (2007) explained, "Personal sense from the beginning in… Leontiev's representation meant the link between consciousness and activity" (p. 90). Thus, personal sense in Leontiev's work is understood within activity— as a reflection of phenomena from an objective reality. For Vygotsky, sense had a completely different meaning (González Rey, 2009, 2010). D. Leontiev (2007) further argued:

> It could be possible to take [perezhivanie] as an initial psychological fact and therefore to recognize that it determines in some extent the way in which a given situation or, a given object of reality influences the subject. We answer no….. [ Perezhivanie] effectively takes part of each subject's act within human activity, but [perezhivanie] is not the activity, neither its cause. Rather than the cause of activity, it is the consequence of it. (p. 81)

Unlike Vygotsky, D. Leontiev subordinated the subject to the moment of any concrete activity. Thus, for example, for D. Leontiev, the emotional reaction from one young boy to his result in mathematics will result in the way he involves himself in the activity oriented to learning mathematics, being the "perezhivanie" that emotional reaction to the performance in the activity of learning. D. Leontiev (2007) subordinated the subject to the moment of any concrete activity, as is clear in the following statement:

It is possible, in a first approach to sense, to define it as the relationship between subject and object or phenomenon of reality, which is defined by the place of the object
(phenomenon) in the life of the subject. In this process the object become a representation of the world embodied in the structures of personality that regulates behavior
in relation to that object. (p. 114)

For D. Leontiev, sense was an external given entity at the moment of individual
performance in a concrete activity. The object was embodied in personality as a
representation of the world, as a reflection of a given object. Sense was reduced
in that definition, to the internalization of the object, which in terms of image
or representation becomes an element of personality. Nothing new is produced
from the current subject's psychological organization at the moment of living a
given experience with the object. The objectivistic and mechanical ground of
this representation is evident.

By the mid-1970s, A. N. Leontiev's concept of the "formations of sense" and
his re-orientation of Activity Theory to issues of personality had gained new currency. Nevertheless, Leontiev's orthodoxy concerning reflection, a principle that
historically ruled Activity Theory, resulted in consciousness and personality being
explained again in terms of activity and reflection. Asmolov (1984) explained:

Therefore, a cardinal difference of dynamic systems of sense from those systems that
exist in the consciousness surface formations, like subjective [pereshivanie] (desires,
wishes, etc) is given by the fact that change of the personal senses and formations of
sense always are mediated by activity changes, which takes place as the subject's objective relationship with the world. (p. 65)

For Asmolov, personal sense and formations of sense were the results of changes
in concrete activities. Thus, these attempts to revise Activity Theory appear to
have been thwarted by a ubiquitous objective psychology.

Authors such as D. Leontiev and Asmolov did not see a new alternative in
Vygotsky's definition of sense. They attempted to constrain it to the limits of the
logic centers of the object that prevailed throughout A. N. Leontiev's trajectory.
Zaporochets and A. A. Leontiev's historic attempts to integrate A. N. Leontiev's
legacy with the last period of Vygotsky's work took a radically different path from
that of D. Leontiev in his attempt to emphasize Leontiev's and Vygotsky's differences concerning sense.

## Advancing Vygotsky's Legacy Toward a New Conception of Subjectivity Within a Cultural Historical Approach

In the last thirty years, concerns about the reification of relational and social
practices have brought the issue of subjectivity front and center (Guattari 1992;
Elliott, 1992; González Rey 2002, 2005, 2007; Blackman, 2008). Vygotsky's brief

elaboration concerning sense was remarkable as were the contributions of Bakhtin, Voloshinov and Schpet on this topic. Vygotsky (1987) interpreted sense as a process of consciousness, as an "entirety of all psychological facts that emerge in our consciousness as a consequence of the word." Two of Vygotsky's points are notable. First: psychological facts are not intentionally created; they emerge. Second, his definition of psychological facts did not exclude emotion.

Vygotsky's cognitive-emotional concept of sense is one that needs to be re-defined in ways that recognize more fully the unity between symbolic processes and emotion—a continuous movement between the subject's actions, relations, and psychological states. Subjective senses qualify the subjective character of human activities—not through their content, structure, or object, but as a subject's subjective production grounded in subjective configurations as the psychological space of any human activity.[6]

Not guided by some sort of rationality, subjective sense is a motivational concept involving emotions—a truly subjective production of women and men grounded in subjective configurations and new experiences, which always involve unexpected emotions and symbolic productions. The confluence of a multiplicity of subjective senses and emotional states that together create relevance, subjective configurations have, nevertheless, a relatively stable character.

Subjective senses and subjective configurations characterize the uniqueness of human actions, relationships, or psychological states. Thus, every human function is a subjective function. As Zaporochets (1986) argued:

> We have reason to believe that, in contrast to the intellectual control that regulates behavior in relation to the objective meaning of the conditions of the problem to be solved; emotional control guarantees a correction of the action adequate to the subject's sense of what is being done with respect to the satisfaction of present need. Only this coordinated functioning of two systems, only, as Vygotsky expressed it, the 'unity of affect and intellect' can guarantee a full realization of any form of activity. (p. 283)

Once a psychological function involves emotions, those emotions are inseparable from the whole subject's subjective system. Any psychological function expresses itself as a subjective configuration, as a subjective production that embodies the emotional symbolical dynamic of the function *in media res*. As Zaporochets pointed out, the full realization of any activity only could be guaranteed on the basis of that "unity of affect and intellect" produced by a subject's sense. Even when Zaporochets did not go further on the psychological nature of motive, his position was congruent with my understanding of motive because the multiple subjective senses obtain a new qualitative expression through subjective configurations within which they join together as the basis of any subject's performance. More specifically, children can involve themselves in their play's performance more than the cognitive element. Their tactics and actions embody emotions and symbolic processes, expectancies, images, anticipations that are not cognitive at all but truly subjective productions. They are the result of the subjective configurations of those processes that appear as the real motive of those performances.

Subjective sense and subjective configuration as defined here are inseparable from the subject and social subjectivity (González Rey, 1991, 2002, 2007, 2008, 2009). With subject as the person who actively produces new subjective alternatives within a given social situation, entering in contradiction to standardized rituals, procedures, and values dominant in that specific situation, the subject is always singular and grounded in his or her own subjective configurations. The person as subject is always subversive in relation to the dominant current social status, which appears to the persons who live in those spaces as naturalized and objective. The alternatives to those naturalized patterns are always subjective alternatives that contain a new social status as a subjectively produced option.

In other words, the subject is capable of developing subjective alternatives to dominant norms in any type of human activity. Simultaneously, the subject's creativity emerges in not being subordinated to the given or expected, but rather by questioning, reframing, and generating alternatives.

The emergence of subject is an important signal of personal development in any social practice. Even so, the subject is in flux—changing as a result of his or her subjective production as a crucial moment of social practice. The teacher does not change his or her way of working through the passive accumulation of knowledge. Instead, those ideas associated with his or her emergence as a teacher develop in the process of teaching, not as cognitive operations, but as operations of subjective sense in which cognitive operations are a moment of the functioning subjective configuration. The emergence of the differentiating subjects among those who participate in a communicative event is one important expression of the dialogical character of that event. Dialogue is made of the shared spaces and tensions that arise between participants in dialogue.

The subject's decisions and options represent possible sources in the genesis of new subjective senses. In this subject's processes, subjective senses appear behind the conscious intention, having unpredictable effects on the ongoing course of action. During a mathematics exercise in a classroom, one child carries out multiple emotions and symbolic expressions that integrate into a subjective configuration of his or her different cognitive operations in front of that mathematics exercise. This complex configuration and the subjective senses that are interwoven in this process are rather a subjective production than a real event. Generally, these complex subjective dynamics are completely overlooked in our practices as a result of our ignorance about subjectivity due to our illusion of control and objectivity. Those psychological states are not only emotional; they are symbolic-emotional processes configured as a recursive chain within which those processes interrelated to each other become a subjective configuration. The expression of that configuration will always involve in the options and decisions taken by persons in their ongoing daily life.

This definition of subjectivity involves the idea of the subject as an active person immersed in his or her performances, whose initiatives and ideas are inseparable from the ongoing process of subjectivization that characterizes any human performance. Without subjective involvement, human acts become merely repetitive processes. Even when most of the postmodern authors have chosen language, signs and discourse as the site on which the subject is organized, the categories of subjective sense and subjective configuration claim the central *place* of emotion with symbolic processes that are inseparable as the ground on which subject and subjectivity should be understood.

# Conclusion

In this chapter, I have attempted to begin a discussion about subjectivity within a cultural-historical approach. I have highlighted processes and phenomena that are involved in any human action, practice and organization, overcoming the common trend to define subjectivity as an individual or intra-psychical phenomenon—a tendency that has led to conceptualize subjectivity as a remnant of modernity. It was the emergence of culture as a key topic for philosophy and social sciences in general, one of the elements that permits us to address the topic of subjectivity as a new quality of human processes through which it is possible to discriminate psyche as grounded in culture. This distinction facilitates overcoming several dichotomies some of which I want to emphasize.

Social processes and their effects always appear in subjective terms, not as reflection but as a true subject's subjective production grounded on singular subjective configurations interwoven with social subjectivity at the moment of living current social experiences. Individuals are active and creative producers within social scenarios; they are not simply effects. Subjectivity is not a reflection. It is a production that cannot be deduced from the external circumstances within which human actions take place.

In Russia, philosophy and linguistics were important roots for the development of the topic of subjectivity in psychology. However, the irruption of Soviet power gradually imposed an objectivistic and deterministic version of Marxism, banishing the topic of subjectivity from the agenda of psychology. It was in this context that Vygotsky, Luria, and Leontiev found their place in the University of Moscow as part of Kornilov's group, a key figure in the development of a Marxist psychology.

In retrospect, after the period of reflexology and behaviorism in Soviet psychology, the hegemonic paradigm that ruled Soviet psychology was Activity Theory, whose center was the concept of object-based activity. Under the domain of Activity Theory, Vygotsky's works re-appeared as fragmented and incomplete. In what was an obscure and contradictory relationship between Vygotsky and Leontiev, the Vygotsky of the time period between 1928 and 1931 was officially taken as the mature Vygotsky, keeping in the dark the relevance of the first and last works of this author. Rubinstein, in contrast to the pioneers of Soviet psychology, studied philosophy in Germany and did not participate in that beginning of Soviet psychology. In spite of his differences with Vygotsky, both of them maintained a particular sensitivity in relation to dialectics. Both of them also emphasized the idea of human psyche as a system and the need of new concepts to be able to integrate cognitive and affective processes. In this regard, Rubinstein gave special attention to the topic of consciousness and personality. On the other hand, Vygotsky, even working on personality in his first works—like Rubinstein—centered in his last works on concepts like sense, "perezhivanie" and the social situation of development.

Besides sharing a critical route in the development of subjectivity within a cultural-historical psychology, in this chapter I presented three main characteristics of the human psyche: its cultural historical origin, grounded in cultural and social human practice; its generative character, that is to say, its capacity to create processes that are not objectively justified but which should be recognized as an essential part of human reality; and the inseparable unity between symbolic and emotional processes, a unity configured on complex subjective systems at individual and social levels.

Subjectivity, from this perspective, is inseparable from the subject's action. Each expression by the subject (person), in any field, is subjectively configured. This configuration emerges in the course of the ongoing subject's experiences. Despite the fact that there are more stable subjective configurations, which may be organized in the human personality, the fact is that none of those configurations determines human behavior. They appear through multiple and different subjective senses in the continuum of human experience within which new subjective configurations continuously emerge.

## ENDNOTES

1   I define the category "Soviet" as all the literature produced during the Soviet Era from 1917 to 1990.

2   Perezhivanie acquired meaning in Vygotsky's work that in my opinion is different than that given to this concept in most English translations in which perezhivanie is translated as

"emotional experience" (Van der Veer & Valsiner, 1994). "Perezhivanie" emerged in Vygotsky's work as a new unity for the analysis of development, which carries out the integration of cognitive and affective into a new qualitative system that characterizes human development. As Yarochevsky (1993) explained: "In 'perezhivanie,' the logic of ideas and logic of sentiments lawfully come together, leading to the change of 'formations' influenced by maturation. 'Perezhivanie' should be understood as a self-regulated psychological system of personality" (p. 268).

3    The word -*related* was added by the editors to this quote for clarity.

4    Unlike sense, subjective sense is configured as a network of emotional and symbolic processes that emerge from the collateral effects of living an ongoing human experience. These subjective senses flow as an interwoven movement of emotional and symbolic processes where the emergence of one of them evokes the other without becoming its cause.

5    The Russian word used by Davydov in his original was "nuzhda." It was translated to the English (1999) as desire. Even so, I understood the employed original term as a "state of need."

6    The difference between my concept of subjective configuration and that provided by Gestalt theory is that subjective configurations result from the integration into a new qualitative psychical organization of multiple subjective senses grounded on social cultural personal experience, including an inseparable emotional symbolical unity, which was not explicit in Gestalt psychology, an approach that is much more representational.

· 3 ·

# The Process of Producing Knowledge

## Vygotsky Revisited

*Guillermo Arias*

*To question everything, not to believe blindly in anything,
to demand the bases and sources from all theses is the first
rule in science methodology. (Vygotsky, 1997, p. 301,
as cited in Arias, 2005, p. 131)*

The purpose of this chapter is to challenge some of the current views shared in what is CHAT today. The challenge stems from the idea that life and its circumstances change over time and across contexts, and therefore knowledge and its acquisition change constantly. More specifically, the chapter addresses still incomplete analyses of Vygotsky's work, given that it has been fragmented and misconstrued or ignored as Luria, Leontiev, and others have argued (Leontiev, 1966, 1981; Luria, 1979a). Misguided interpretations appear to have already misled new generations of neo-Vygotskyans or critics. In effect, an attempt to integrate some of the loose or lost threads I, and some of my colleagues of the

"Vygotsky Chair" in Cuba, consider it significant to define this endeavor, one that may hopefully contribute to various disciplines influenced today by CHAT.

This chapter is organized into developmental stages that unfold into the main historical periods over which CHAT has evolved. First, I consider CHAT'sessential historical legacy stemming from Vygotsky's explanations that are supported by dialectical and historical materialist philosophical ideas based on German classical philosophy. Second I will introduce some of the critiques of Vygotsky`s hypotheses and explanations. In addition, I will also show the peculiar way in which CHAT's followers conducted these critiques (Bozhovich, 1976; Puziréi & Guippenréiter, 1989; Leontiev, 1981).

Third, I examine some problems still being considered in present-day studies and interpretations of the way *mediation* has been considered (Van der Veer & Valsiner, 1996; Wertsch, 1998, 2007; Daniels, 2002; Kozulin, 1990a, 1998; Arias, 2005; Fariñas, 2005). Essential aspects of Vygotsky`s work have been seen as incomplete and simplified in a fashion that diminishes their value and significance. Finally, I summarize some ideas that remain open to debate.

This analysis illustrates how from his immediate followers' times up to the present, Vygotsky's work has been criticized without being taken into account as a whole and using inaccurate terms. Many critiques have been then answered with arguments that allegedly belong to the author but actually are merely a rephrasing of Vygotsky's own ideas. For example, since their emergence in the 1920s and 1930s, the main ideas reflecting cultural-historical activity theory (CHAT) have been the object of criticism (Shuare, 1990; Leontiev, Luria, & Teplov, 1987). Nevertheless, Vygotsky's initial works left a legacy that needs to be clearly defined and critically analyzed, taking into account subsequent ideas that have not contributed to a critical systematization. This interpretation has led some present-day scholars to refer to these concepts as "CHAT's myths" (Kozulin, 1990 quoted in Daniels, 2002; Blanck, 2001).

These differences seem to be the cause of the estrangement between Vygotsky and his collaborators. All these dissentions, which so far have been kept hidden and undisclosed, now re-emerge with only few possibilities of enlightenment due to the fact that all those ideas were initially brought forth over 20 years ago.

# The University of Habana Vygotsky Chair: Vygotsky's Legacy in Cuba

Even in Vygotsky's lifetime, critical analyses carried out on his work were mediated by or related to different contexts, real-life conditions, and historical processes (Febles, 2001; Arias, 2005a; Postone, 2006; Acanda, 2007). These, in turn, have been expressed in different ways by different authors. Such analyses inevitably reproduce the complex processes that still characterize psychology as a science within CHAT's communities of practice concerning the formation, existence, and development of subjectivity or the psychological realm (Fariñas & Arias, 2002). Thus, even today, it is difficult for the cultural historical approach to explain the formation, development, and existence of subjectivity in psychology. Current theories tend to emphasize one component or another, one mechanism of construction or another and to note the importance of one element or another.

This method of analysis presents a very complex problem since it requires the explanation of concepts that are constantly moving and changing (subjectivity and the psychological), concepts that do not depend on one content or another separately and that are constantly modified by the subject's real-life experiences in varied contexts as well as by constant internal processes. The present challenge is to explain what components and specific contents are mediating the process and, at the same time, to define mediation, i.e., to lay out its movements and changes, as well as its connections and inter-determinations (Vygotsky, 1991, 1995). This process becomes more complex due to the fact that one of the many mediating conditions is the historical aspect, that is, the movement and change that take place over time. Thus, it is not possible for us to agree with those who attribute subjectivity essentially either to the socio-cultural domain, to institutions, or to social organization. Moreover, I do not share the belief that its evolution is a result of an internal process of subjectivity itself, one that reaches independence or autonomy in which, for instance, the unconscious, behavior, cognitive processes, language, meanings, and senses are determining factors.

The *troika* and their followers within the frame of Soviet psychology recognized this problem in psychology as a science (Luria, 1979a; Leontiev, 1991). However, since Vygotsky's death, in this specific psychological model, there has been a certain disintegration of the elements of mediation. More specifically, I refer to different authors who began to emphasize certain components of the process of formation of subjectivity. This development led to a loss of consistency, flexibility, and complexity that entails the assumption of the existence and the consequence of mediation or mediated activity, thus producing fragmentation and an operational effect.

The above description exemplifies the fact that Soviet psychology was not as homogeneous or monolithic as is frequently assumed given the basic principles of dialectical and historical materialism. Even within the frame of this philosophical conception, there have been, still are, and will continue to exist different ways of interpretation. This dynamic constitutes the eternal problem of the psychological or subjectivity not yet convincingly explained by psychology. It just spins around a possible explanation without ever being articulated in a conclusive way.

Vygotsky is one of the scientists who comes closest to an explanation, given his historical and dialectical point of view on the methodology of science and his exceptionally dialectical and complex understanding of nature and of the way subjectivity is formed. However, his scientific program became shattered first by his premature death and later by the fragmentation and misinterpretations by others.

These are the essential reasons that an integral critical analysis of CHAT as a whole needs further research as well as closer scrutiny of the different approaches and interpretations that claim to be based on Vygotsky's work or that of Luria, Leontiev, or other representatives of this way of thinking and advancing psychology (Arias, 1999a, 2002a, 2002b, 2002c, 2004). I have been carrying on my systematization work since the 1990s, starting from the study of the original sources, theoretical and empirical research on the subject, and my professional practice. These have been presented in *La persona en lo histórico cultural* (The person in the historical cultural approach) (Arias, 2005b), a book published in Brazil. In sum, this systematization is not only a result of my work but of the collective endeavor of the members of L. S. Vygotsky's Chair, over which I have presided since its creation in 1997 (López Hurtado & Siverio, 1986; Corral Ruso, 1999; Fariñas, 1999; Febles, 2001; González Serra, 2003; Labarrere Sarduy, 1996b; Pedrol & Casanova, 2005).

## Critiques of Vygotsky by His Contemporaries

Among the critiques made of Vygotsky based on erroneous assumptions are the following:

1. His non-Marxist orientation
2. His pedagogical orientation
3. His not having conducted critiques of western psychology
4. His having produced hypotheses and explanations without sufficient empirical data
5. His erroneous classification into natural or elemental physical functions and higher physical functions
6. His having attributed an exaggerated significance to *mediation*
7. His highly schematic and even naïve (Shuarte, 1990; Kozulin, 1990; Leontiev, Luria, & Teplov, 1987) systemic structure of conscience.

The critiques are addressed and analyzed relative to two essential contents in this approach, those that simultaneously concern the social and cultural nature of human psychology with the concepts of *mediation* and *vivencia*. The critiques have undermined Vygotsky's philosophy as a whole.

## Bozhovich and Vygotsky: Their Meeting Points and Differences

First, let us examine the critique of Vygotsky by Lidia I. Bozhovich. It was recorded from an attendant's transcript of a lecture that was possibly published without Vygotsky's revision. Vygotsky died shortly after its appearance.

> However, we believe that in this regard Vygotsky took a step backward, for in some way he moved back from his former limits. He considered that the nature of (perezhivanie) (vivencia) is ultimately determined by the way in which children understand the circumstances influencing them; that is to say, by the level of development of their generalizations. [1] (Bozhovich, 1976, p. 100)

The meaning of "ultimately" is, here, extremely important because, as it can be noted in the lecture Bozhovich is talking about, it is never used there. It refers to the dialectical idea of process. It means that before this cause or reason there has been a process allowing this last cause or reason to produce the result. It does not mean at all that comes in the sentence after this phrase is the only and fundamental reason, but just the last cause in a process that has a complex genesis and mediation. From the beginning, Bozhovich herself is accumulating arguments for my refutation of her critique.

Later, when supporting this critique, and after having an interpretation has nothing to do with what was stated in the transcript, she states:

> In a way it was as if Vigotsky [sic] had closed his reasoning circle. He started by denying the intellectual and atomistic interpretation of a child's psyche. He saw vivencia as an indivisible whole, as the unit that allows us to understand the nature of the influence of the environment on the course of psychical development, and then talks of this vivencia as depending on the level of the child's intellectual possibilities. (Bozhovich, 1976, p. 101)

Finally in the same paragraph she introduces an idea that has no correspondence whatsoever to what Vygotsky said about *vivencia*, neither in that transcript nor anywhere else in his complete works. She states:

> If the concept of *vivencia* created by him, (the concept of the child's affective relations with the environment) got us closer to the interpretation of the true causes of the child's development, his further search for the link determining this development , a search that ends in the concept of generalization, brings us back to intellectualist positions. (Bozhovich, 1976, p. 101)

Here Bozhovich introduces the idea that Vygotsky did not conceptualize in any of his writings. It seems as if Vygotsky were made to speak nonsense or make mistakes for other writers to correct. Ideas are attributed to Vygotsky that he never articulated. We will see this when I quote Vygotsky's concept of *vivencia*. Then Bozhovich ends categorically:

> L. S. Vigotsky's [*sic*] thesis about vivencia being ultimately determined by the level of development of generalization, that is, by interpretation, is also mistaken.[2] (Bozhovich, 1976, p. 101)

> Consequently, although L. S. Vigotsky [*sic*] proposed the general theory that the child's vivencia and the course of his/her psychical development is determined by his/her level of understanding the environment, to explain the case described by him he practically analyzed the real situation of each child, which in fact determined the child's vivencias, his/her behaviour and the specific features of his/her development (Bozhovich, 1976, p. 111)

And thus, she contradicts the interpretation she made ten pages before.

> On the contrary, the elder child, that was already ten years of age when his mother was sick, was put in an adult's position, being made responsible for all the family, so that during his mother's fits of illness and in keeping with his possibilities he would be in charge of his younger brothers and sisters, organizing their family life. His fate— Vygotsky states—to have such a special role in the family was what conditioned the kind of development that became characteristic of him.[3] (Bozhovich, 1976, p. 111)

Thus, according to Bozhovich, Vygotsky insisted only in this example, a child at ten years of age, and in spite of his developmental retardation, possibly as a result of the very social situation he was enduring, had a greater understanding of such a situation than his siblings. Consequently, he reacted and behaved differently, which does not contradict the negative effects of that situation on his development (Valsiner & Van der Veer, 1994).

Vygotsky assumes that *vivencia* encompasses all that is psychical. In this case he is insisting, aside from the relationship and unity between the affective and the cognitive, on the fact that because the child is ten years old, the cognitive (constrained by maturation) or the affective is not on a different level than in his siblings. However, Vygotsky maintained the importance of the role of the cognitive in this case. Indeed, he never neglected this relation, and thus he never exaggerated the cognitive or the intellectual, or the aspect of generalization. In this case, he just wanted to show the relationship with the younger siblings who had more unpleasant *vivencias* and a greater rejection, hate, fear, and ambivalence in their attitudes and behaviors.

In fact, based on Bozhovich's analysis and on the one I am making now, I cannot believe we can conclude that Vygotsky adopted the general explanation of *vivencia* based on the degree of generalization. Above all, after having read his work on the seven years crisis, and the other crises, the theory of emotions, his concept of mediation in the higher psychical functions, and after reading all his references to what *vivencia* meant for him as a functional unit of everything psychical, particularly of personality and his analogy with the cell's function in the system of biological functional units, all this appears as another myth (see Vygotsky, 1987, 1993c, 1995, 1996, 2004).

For all these reasons, I cannot agree with this critique of Vygotsky that presents him as mechanist, reductionist, intellectualist, and above all as nondialectical. As a last resort, I would say that in his analysis of this case or cases, his insistence only on the cognitive or intellectual, because of the young age of the child in question, was unfortunate. He should also have addressed the possible changes in the system of needs and motives, affective aspects that may have affected development.[4] Vygotsky referred to this aspect in the case analysis in his lecture (Valsiner & Van der Veer, 1994). In other words, my critique can only say that the case analysis was incomplete, but I would not dare say that this example changed Vygotsky's theory or explanation.

Nevertheless, I cannot underestimate the fact that the fundamental law of the dynamics of development or the social situation of development is Vygotsky's first attempt to introduce us to this very complex problem, (Vygotsky, 1996). This aspect is very well dealt with by Bozhovich, but it is unfortunately lacking in the work of current scholars and of those interpreting the cultural-historical model. They insist only on the referents of the theory of activity and essentially on the contents expressed in the book about the development of the higher psychical functions, which does not prepare them to consider it. Regarding the question of age and the social situation of development or the dynamics of development, Vygotsky states: "At the beginning of each age period the relationship established between the child and the surrounding environment, particularly of the social environment, is particular, specific, unique and unrepeatable for that age" (Vygotsky, 1996, p. 264).

This analysis is evidence that Vygotsky has definitely gone beyond Baldwin's developmentalism, Piaget's mentalism or constructivism, and Janet's more social behaviorism. Therefore, it is so important to *rescue* his legacy.

Second, and closely associated with the above is the concept of *vivencia* that is developed in the documents of the crises and more elaborated on in the material of the crisis of the seven years, but to my mind it is still deserves more empirical and theoretical elaboration. Vygotsky states:

> Vivencia has a bio-social orientation, it is something in between, which means the personality and the environment; it reveals the meaning of a given moment of the environment for the personality. Vivencia determines the way in which this or that element of the environment influences the child's development...what is essential is not the

situation itself in absolute terms but the way in which the child lives that situation. (Vygotsky, 1996, p. 383)

However, it is not in the work on the crises where Vygotsky defines what a unit of analysis means to him but in his book *Thought and Language*. He defines vivencia as the unit of conscience and personality. I will quote here his explanation of this very important problem. Vygotsky points out:

> Unit means the result of the analysis, that in contrast with the elements, has all the fundamental characteristic properties of the whole and that constitutes a living and indivisible part of the total. The key for the explanation of the defining properties of water cannot be found in the chemical formula of water, but in the study of its molecules and of their movement. That is why the living cell, with all the fundamental properties of life that define a living organism, is the true unit of biological analysis. (Vygotsky, 1993c, pp. 19–20)

Vygotsky explains *vivencia* as follows:

> Vivencia is the true dynamic unit of conscience, the full unit constituting the basis of conscience. (Vygotsky, 1996, p. 383)

> This reason imposes on the researchers a profound internal analysis of the child's vivencias...that is not reduced to the study of the external conditions of his/her life (Vygotsky, 1996, pp. 383–384).

Can anyone think that he abandons the essential idea that he was formulating during 1933 when he wrote about the crises[5]?

With such ideas presented from a conceptual and theoretical perspective, there is no reason to believe that he abandons the initial concept to take the concept of generalization or the intellect, to a particular aspect, which stresses the case of the third child, as pointed out by Bozhovich.

For this reason, I assume the meaning of the term *vivencia* as the basic functional unit of the psychological, or the mind or subjectivity, in correspondence with the system of functional units and the basic function of living organisms; specifically in the psychological meaning as the complex functional unit between language and thought.

For me, the best solution is to call it the basic functional unit, because it is a unit, a complex element that allows us to explain the dynamics of the psychological functioning of its process of constitution, formation, and development in other contents or psychological systems, as Vygotsky calls them (Arias, 2002c). It is not only a question of semiotic or verbal analysis but an analysis of what is supposedly functioning undoubtedly through language, but also goes beyond speech and language. That is why I prefer to speak of a basic functional unit of the psychical, of conscience, and of personality.

## Leontiev and Vygotsky, Continuity and Divergence

Let us now analyze the critiques of how Vygotsky considers the role of activity and communication in the development of human psychology from Leontiev's point of view. In this sense, Puziréi and Guippenréiter can describe this more accurately than Leontiev himself by highlighting the continuity in these two authors and the role that they play in forming a new view of psychology.

> How does Leontiev solve the problem of the driving force in the development of conscience? In response to the question of how to represent the determination of the development of concepts in the child, Vygotski [sic] advanced a fundamental thesis; communication takes place after the development of meanings, of concepts. "Generalization, that is, the structure of meaning—Vygotski [sic] states in one of his last reports about the problem of conscience, written in 1933– depends on the form of communication" but Leontiev does not agree in principle with this statement. The opposition observed here seems to have been stated during Vygotski's [sic] lifetime. In any case, in a series of articles and statements from 1934–1935, Leontiev repeats a thesis that contradicts very clearly Vygotski's [sic] statement about communication as the final explanation of the problem of meaning and conscience: "After the word (and after communication)—Leontiev insists—activity happens." (Puziréi & Guippenréiter, 1989, pp. 22–23)

It is Vygotsky's dialectical and complex tendency to see the components in a dynamic unity or in a mediation, where activity and communication are an inseparable unit as forms of expression of the interpersonal or the system of social relations and *vivencia* processes, the formation of meanings and senses, all acting in a dynamic and complex unit, as the bases for the formation of personality.

This assessment attests to the mediated nature of the psychical (mind) that is not just any form of mediation but a dialectical and historical one. The pattern person-object-person is just this unit between activity and communication. Vygotsky never equaled or reduced communication to activity or vice versa as Leontiev did.[6]

These differences exist due to Vygotsky's more consistent use of dialectics. To be precise, he assumes they have different conditions as to their nature, but they are intimately linked and mutually mediated in function in the dynamic and historical process of interpersonal relations, the production of means of work or of life and throughout the process of human formation and the development of personality formation. This entire pattern gets reversed when Leontiev (1981a) considers activity as the unit of analysis. This is a mistake because he is not taking into account the levels of complexity in the dialectical process that goes from the interpersonal to activity and communication, mediated in turn by the *vivencia*. For Vygotsky, the *vivencia* constitutes the functional unit or the unit of basic analysis of personality and conscience, although this is not explicitly stated and can only be inferred from his analyses at different periods. This issue must be debated at length.

Marx's idea that the essence of human beings is social relations and not activity or work only is very important. Indeed, social relations encompass work and other relationships (Marx & Engels, 1986).

If Leontiev's work represents a continuation of Vygotsky's, there is no place for substitution of one explanation by another. Leontiev just went deeper into the moment that occurs after the constitution and operation of the driving forces generating human psychological development: activity, its organization and structure. However, I agree with Lomov and González that it is not right to absorb or dilute communication within activity because they are different in nature, structure, and organization (Lomov, 1989; González, 2002, 2010). They must be seen in their unity and diversity but most of all in their dynamics or movement, irrespective of which of the two has a central role.

I have reread *Thought and Language* in order to reaffirm these ideas, and I have confirmed my initial judgment that Leontiev's disagreement is unjustified. Vygotsky identifies the process of meaning formation in close connection with objective reality. The interpersonal and the *vivencia* take place in activity and communication, that is constituted as the process of relations between the subjects and their contexts, the objects, the others, and the self. Vygotsky states:

> The new method is free from these flaws, because the functional conditions for concept formation are just the axis of research. The concept is formed in relation with a given task or need generated in the mind in association with a given understanding or communication, related to the accomplishment of a task or instruction that cannot be accomplished without the concept formation. (Vygotsky, 1993c, p. 121)

In his analysis, Vygotsky explains the superiority of this method. Furthermore, the way in which he assumes the dynamic unit of communication and activity or mediated action becomes clear: the interpersonal, the *vivencia*, activity, and communication through action or mediated activity are central to human interaction. Later, he keeps insisting:

> As we have stated before, the objective does not explain the process. The first and fundamental problem related to the process of concept formation, and of the activity oriented towards an objective in general, is the problem of the means by which any psychical operation takes place, the problem of the way in which any goal-oriented activity occurs (Vygotsky, 1993c, p. 125).

According to my interpretation of what Leontiev states later in his theory of activity, there is an analogy in this statement by Vygotsky and what the former's theory says in relation to the motive, the object, the goal, and the action. This assessment makes Leontiev's critique incomprehensible.

If what my colleague and friend, Leontiev's disciple María Febles, told me is true, about an underlying fear of reducing to idealism these explanations taken of Leontiev's summary or notes about human psychology (Febles, 2001), I can assert, without being afraid of idealism, that aside from mediated action they also suggest that: "A generalized reality always takes place in meaning" (Vygotsky, 1991, p. 128).

In addition, it is mediated by *vivencia* and constructed by its persistence and strength; it is accomplished because through *vivencia* humans find sense in the events in which they are involved, and they generalize them (no matter how irrationally at times), depending on the subjects, their histories, and the contents constituted up to that moment. This dynamic reflects the role of *vivencia*, in the event, in activity, in communication, through discourse, through inner speech, through interiorization,[7] in conscience, and in the process of personality formation.

Finally, Vygotsky makes it clear that there is no possible idealist derivation:

> At the beginning was the event (not the event was at the beginning) and at the end the word emerged, and that is the most important thing (L. S. Vygotski [sic]). What is the meaning of what we have said? As to me, to be aware of this is enough. I mean, I am satisfied with the problem having being stated. (Vygotsky, 1991, p. 130)

For me, and I think that perhaps for others, too, it means that the event (whether generalized, conceptualized, in meaning and word in a semiotic sense, in a generalization according to the kind of communication) is present in one way or another and that the word was not the beginning but the event, the action, the interrelation with the object and the subject in its unity. This concept presents the dialectical and historical materialist principle. For all these reasons, the critical analysis of Vygotsky's ideas based on Puziréi and Guippenréiter's statements is incomprehensible. They provide grounds for the differences between Vygotsky and Leontiev. These are Leontiev's further insistence that give *activity* the role of the unit of analysis, including communication in place of the primary or initial condition of the interpersonal, and the role of *vivencia* in the other psychological systems that become more and more complex, including activity and communication to the point of those defining personality.

There are many other reasons that be discussed in future publications. However, I would like to examine the following observation:

> But even this, understanding another person's thought is incomplete if you do not grasp the motive, the reason for the expression of thought. In the same fashion, the psychological analysis of any expression is only complete when we find the deepest internal and more hidden level of verbal thought, its motivation. (Vygotsky, 1993c, p. 343)

This quote shows how several essential assumptions of Vygotsky's general conception and explanations are denied when he is accused of having abandoned the concept of *vivencia* and when the role he assigns to *vivencia* as a basic functional unit of the physical, of personality and of conscience is questioned.

Vygotsky's concept of *viviencia* as the way in which a subject lives an experience is replaced by Bozhovich's phenomenological and traditional conception of *viviencia* as the affective relations with the context or environment in which they evolve. This conception ignores Vygotsky´s assertions concerning the complex relations entailed by the cognitive-affective, the social-biological and cultural, and the context personality. To these concepts I add the conscious and the unconscious, the individual and the collective, which are also contained in *vivencia* (Arias, 2005b). These are merely two examples, but a similar analysis may be conducted about most aspects often depicted as deficiencies in Vygotsky's work.

This analysis is expressed one way or another in CHAT's present situation. That is why I mention the need for at least three critical systematizations on the work of Vygotsky and his collaborators; to begin, the productions following his death up to the 1980s; second, research in western psychology from 1962 to the present; third, a critical systematization focused on what has been produced by other psychological models and their contributions to CHAT (Arias, 2002a).

## Some Problems Still Being Debated in Contemporary Studies and Interpretations

We are still in the process of submitting to discussion controversial aspects such as communication-activity derived from the consideration of the category of activity by Leontiev and his followers. Later Lomov and his followers present arguments that consider communication to be a quasi-universal category. This interpretation is another explanatory principle that explains almost nothing (Vygotsky, 1991; Arias, 2005a).

A similar exchange occurs in the debate between the experimental quantitative and the qualitative dichotomy, which is also present in science in general and in Vygotsky's thought in particular, as an indissoluble unit and a process of inter-determination. This issue is worthy of prolonged discussion, and we should continue going deeper in its analysis to avoid dichotomies, reductionism, and *a priori* conclusions.

Next, it is also essential to analyze the problems of interpretations of the concept of internalization in Vygotsky and the historical cultural in general (Santamaría, 2005), the mechanistic vision attributed to it, and the solution with the concept of appropriation, which was already used by Marx. The last-named gives origin to the concept of interiorization in Vygotsky as a way to explain psychologically how appropriation takes place (Arias, 2005a). A discussion of this issue would be very important indeed.

A similar process occurs with the overemphasis of the role of language and semiotics in that the role of meaning is highlighted; in fact, it has generated another psychology—cultural psychology—but it disregards history (Mescheryakov & Zinchenko, 2000), the understanding of history is an indispensable skill for the cultural-historical model (Vygotsky, 1978).

All these issues and others derive from an incomplete or formalized concept of mediation and depart from Vygotsky's work and his references to Marx and Hegel. As Vygotsky states:

> Hegel rightly attributed a more general meaning to the concept of mediation and considered it the most characteristic property of reason. Reason, Hegel says, is shrewd as well as powerful. Its shrewdness consists in general in the fact that mediating activity, by allowing objects to interact according to their nature and be consumed in this process, does not directly participate in it but carries out, nevertheless, its own objective. Marx quotes these words when referring to work tools and says: "Man uses the mechanical, physical and chemical properties of the things he employs as tools to act upon other things according to his objective." (Marx & Engels, vol. 23, Russian edition quoted by Vygotsky, 1995, pp. 92–93)

> The use of signs should, to our understanding, be also included in mediated activity […]. According to Vygotsky the use of signs and tool does not exhaust reasoning activity (Vygotsky, 1995, pp. 92–93).

Considering these ideas as stated by Vygotsky, it is important to note that they cannot be considered equivalent in their significance and importance or by the function they perform, which does not exhaust all the dimensions of mediating activity.

Also relevant is the real life of human beings, according to Politzer, its drama, ideas which Vygotsky also expresses at different points in his work. According to Politzer's (1965) expression, "what works is not the muscle but man," it is valid to make the same statement about memory: what memorizes is not memory but man. Meaning is established when functions have established a new relation among them through personality (Vygotsky, 1996, p. 244).

Based on the preceding reasoning, Vygotsky's concept of mediation has been insufficiently studied by present-day scholars (Wertsch, 1998, 2007; Daniels, 2002). Mediation includes instruments, signs, and language with all of them having a central role. However, these are not the only mediators to be considered or the ones that explain everything. I share Kozulin's analyses on activity theory and Leontiev's intentions in the search for other essential mediators (Kozulin, 1990a, quoting Daniels, 2002). However I do not agree with him on the point that these are the result of political problems in the former Soviet Union. However, I consider essential references to inadequate interpretations of Marxism, which date back to the times of Marx and Engels and still exist. Indeed, they constitute the cause of the political problems mentioned by Kozulin while, at the same time, they are related to the material conditions of life, the conditions of production, and to human relations that existed in the former Soviet Union and still exist in our present world (Marx & Engels, 1986; Rodríguez Ibáñez & García Báez, 1996; Postone, 2006; Acanda, 2007).

We also consider that present-day scholars' interpretation of CHAT is mediated by the belief that the socialism, real or traditional, that developed in the former Soviet Union, was Marxism (Rodríguez & García, 1996). This conception is also mediated, in our times, by similar life conditions. An example of the previous observation is the fact that in the former Soviet Union as well as in present-day Russia, the concept and application of what mediation is from the point of view of dialectical and historical materialism have been incompletely interpreted.

That is the reason for my insistence on going back to Vygotsky, but I want to be able to go on, not to repeat him as such, as some colleagues' critiques have suggested. Vygotsky writes of activity and communication in their inter-determination, of the qualitative and the quantitative or experimental, of activity or mediated action, as well as of the interpersonal, the objects, the signs and symbols, activity and communication, the others, the groups, and even the subject itself as mediated (Vygotsky, 1993c; Arias, 2005a).

Possibly, communication and activity could be included among the different forms of expression of the interpersonal that becomes the source of the intrapsychological and the psychological, once constituted, turns to the social and the cultural mediating them (objectification or crystallization), again according to Vygotsky (Vygotsky, 1987b, 1999; Arias, 2005a; Fariñas, 2005).

Methodologically speaking the whole can be broken down into its parts; the parts can even be explained one by one, but we cannot lose sight of the whole, and above all, of its present and historical dynamics, and of what happens with the links established, that is, the movement of the process of object constitution (Fariñas, 2005). These ideas, reflections, and interpretations are mediated by a particular relationship, which is that very early in life I was connected to the cultural-historic approach to solve problems of the educational and clinical practice together with many other colleagues in my country. Unquestionably, this practice has been for me and for others an essential mediator for the individual process of knowledge production, that is what we are devoted to, and I insist on the fact that it cannot be reduced to the statements of instrumental and sign mediation (Venguer, 1976; Novoselova, 1981; Arias & Llorens, 1982; Roloff et al., 1987; López Hurtado, 1996; Labarrere, 1996b ; Siverio Gómez, 1988, 1995; Arias, 1979, 1986a, 1986b, 1999a, 1999b, 2001, 2005a; Rivero, 2001; Echemendía

Tocabens, 2006; Roche, 2000; Betancourt, 2002; Fariñas, 2005; Rico Montero, 1996; Figueredo, 1999; Torres Dávila, 2006; García Tejeda, 2007).

## By Way of Conclusion

Vygotsky's essential legacy consists in having emphasized the need for an integral dialectical and complex analysis of subjectivity and establishing and stressing the dynamics and movement of this process conceptualized in the definition of mediation. It does not consist in the mere placement of a third situation in the middle of two pre-existing ones, influencing or affecting these two or the three as a whole. There are multiple conditions that are often imperceptible but which in some way affect the process depending on the relations they establish as the approach to complexity subsequently tries to demonstrate.

Moreover, in this conception about the mediated nature of subjectivity, the legacy of Marx and Engels is present when they consider that productive activity and communication historically only occur intertwined with real and material life conditions and the interpersonal (social relations). According to them, they all constitute the source and origin of the formation and development of subjectivity which conforms to the inner subject according to its own laws, to take into account the subject's own active role.

In the explanation of the historical and cultural nature of human subjectivity, Vygotsky introduces for the first time the term *vivencia* as the basic functional unit in the process of formation and development of subjectivity, conscience, and personality as a whole. It is not the affective relation with the context, or the experiences only, but it is the most elemental complex unit in the process of subjectifying all elements coming from external sources, as well as the socio-cultural and historical context. It is the way a subject lives an experience or what derives from that material or interpersonal context. Regrettably, *vivencia* as the basic complex unit of psychology is no longer being used and studied systematically. It has been replaced by other complex units, which is not the basic complex unit such as activity, communication, meanings, and the senses, which essentially become elucidating principles. What has been previously stated are the consequences of separating hypotheses and theses from their theoretical and methodological bases. This dynamic determines the need to demand the basic foundation of every thesis. Post-Vygotskyan interpretations are in need of this process since from their very beginning, they were the object of partial, functionalist, and pragmatic interpretations. Thus, it is difficult to understand these in their real essence and origin. This problem has an effect on mediation and *vivencia*, which has repercussions on subsequent analyses and explanations of other aspects, also relevant to CHAT. These are all good reasons to continue the study and debate on the bases and sources of our explanations about human subjectivity.

I finish this chapter as Vygotsky once did[8]: "(...) I am now content with the problem having been stated." (Vygotsky, 1991, p. 130)

## ENDNOTES

1   We must take into account that there is not a word in the English language for the translation of the word *vivencia*. It does exist in Spanish, Portuguese, Russian, and German, and it must be roughly translated as experience or *emotional experience* a term very well created by Van der Veer and Valsiner in the book and paper by Vygotsky mentioned above (Van der Veer & Valsiner, 1994).

    Call it experience or the form in which an experience is lived, or living a social situation, or the process of producing or working, but we must always insist on that it is a way of living emotionally and cognitively, individually and collectively, biologically and psychologically for what is already constituted; a situation, an experience that allows the subject to give meaning and sense to what it is living because it is the *vivencia* of something inside the subject that it lives and will continue living. These observations can be seen as a follow-up of Politzer's study of human drama.

2   She uses this phrase correctly again. However, by using it she is denying all the analysis made from a dialectical perspective or one of mediation. This is to my mind what makes Bozhovich's conclusions regarding vivencia by Vygotsky erroneous.

3   This feature reflects an important piece of information that had not come up so far in Bozhovich's analysis. Also note, the mother's disease was alcoholism.

4   He insists on these aspects in other analyses. It makes me think that the person who prepared the transcript did not consider it.

5   This lecture must have been delivered in 1933 or 1934.

6   More modern interpretations state that activity refers to the subject-object relationship and communication subject-subject. However, Vygotsky's way, formulated long before these more recent analyses, is better because he presents a complex unit: person-object-person.

7   That is why those studying, analyzing, and interpreting the process of internalization in Vygotsky do not give it the meaning and sense that this process has for me.

8   I also want to thank the editors for allowing me to express these ideas.

## · 4 ·

# Cognitive Aspects
# of the Transition From
# a Traditional to a Modern
# Technological Society

*Alex Kozulin*

Looking at human history one immediately perceives transitions and translations. No culture is a product of its own autonomous development. Each time a
certain ethnic group establishes contact with another one, the transition process
is set in motion—it was true of the Germanic culture when it came in contact
with Roman civilization, and it is equally true today when African villagers
migrate to Paris or London. Cultures also evolve through translations—a set of
stories and rules initially transmitted orally and later in writing in Hebrew and
Aramaic eventually became a codex of biblical texts in Greek and Latin and
then appeared in all European vernaculars. Each translation brought with it new
meanings and served as a basis for inter-cultural dialogue and discussion. All

these transitions and translations are thoroughly studied by historians and linguists who focus on cultural artifacts—words, pictures, buildings, and tools. But what about cognition? Do people of the 21st century think exactly the same way as people thought in the first century with just a change in the content? Is there a qualitative difference between the cognition of people who still live in traditional oral societies and those in technologically advanced countries? Finally, what are the challenges facing people making radical cultural transitions today?

In this chapter I will discuss the issue of cultural transition by taking the perspective of Vygotskyan cultural-historical and sociocultural theory and using immigrants from rural Ethiopia in Israel as a case study. The chapter starts with a brief introduction to the Vygotsky and Luria (see Luria, 1976) concept of cognitive change and points out those aspects of this concept that require further elaboration and critique. An overview of the processes and circumstances of Ethiopian immigration follows and the challenges facing immigrants in modern technological society are outlined. Following this overview, three sections are dedicated to exploring the immigrants' cognitive transition in three different contexts: First, the acquisition of initial literacy and cultural orientation during the first year in the country; second, challenges facing minority young adults in vocational training; third, problems associated with admission to such prestigious academic tracks as engineering.

## The Cultural-Historical Approach to Cultural Transition

Two main approaches to a study of human cognitive processes in general and to the problem of cross-cultural differences in cognition in particular can be discerned. The first, psychometric approach is based on the belief in the basic uniformity of human cognition, with cross-cultural differences explained as quantitative in nature. In other words, all human beings irrespective of their culture and experience are assumed to have the same cognitive functions. These functions can be evaluated with the help of psychometric tests. Both individual and ethnic differences are attributed mostly to the genetic component of intellectual abilities that is resistant to significant change (see Herrnstein & Murray, 1994).

The second, culture-centered approach originated in the work of Vygotsky and Luria (1993) and was later developed by their followers in different countries (Cole & Scribner, 1974; Tulviste, 1991; Kozulin, Gindis, Ageyev & Miller, 2003). This approach identifies culture as a main source of both the development of cognition and the inter-group differences. According to Vygotsky and his followers, only the most basic, "natural" cognitive processes are universal, while all higher mental functions, including those required for problem solving, are formed in the course of sociocultural activities. The development of specific cognitive functions on an individual as well as on a group level is associated with gradual internalization of symbolic psychological tools available in a given culture. Internalized symbolic tools and activities become inner psychological tools. Confronted with the same task, people who have different sets of psychological tools will approach the task differently.

Initially Vygotsky and Luria (see Luria, 1976) were interested not so much in cross-cultural differences as such, as in finding a model for a study of historical changes that presumably occurred in human cognition. The logic of their "quasi-historical" study was as follows. Since it is impossible to conduct an empirical study of human cognition in different historical periods, the best approximation would be a traditional society with economy, lifestyle and learning patterns more or less corresponding to the previous historical periods that underwent a rapid sociocultural change. Vygotsky and Luria thought that they had found such a natural historical "experiment" in Soviet Central Asia of the early 1930s. The unique sociocultural situation of this region was determined by a very rapid invasion of Soviet power into a traditional and mostly non-literate agricultural society. As a result of this invasion, people belonging to the same economic and sociocultural group and sometimes even to the same extended family found themselves in very different sociocultural contexts. Some of them, especially those in the remote villages, retained all aspects of a traditional non-literate culture and way of life. Others became involved in new agricultural or industrial enterprises set up by the Soviets, but still without access to systematic formal education. Finally, some not only changed their occupation and work environment but also attended adult literacy courses and even teachers' colleges.

The main conclusion reached by Vygotsky and Luria was that informants who remained out of contact with the new occupational and educational opportunities tended to solve problems by using functional reasoning reflecting their everyday life practical experience and rejected the possibility of looking at classification, generalization, or drawing conclusions from another, e.g., more abstractive point of view. Exposure to modern technology and involvement in jobs based on division of labor tend to increase the informants' readiness to solve problems both in functional and in verbal-logical ways. It was observed, however, that informants who did not experience formal education easily reverted to purely functional reasoning. At the same time informants who received some form of formal education demonstrated a clear preference for the verbal-logical form of problem solving.

Taking into account that the Vygotsky-Luria study has been a subject of considerable discussion and controversy (see Cole 1990; van der Veer and Valsiner 1993, chapter 10), it seems important to clarify certain theoretical points. First of all, the Vygotsky-Luria position was often perceived as Euro-centric because the authors obviously considered cognitive skills associated with formal schooling as superior to those based on everyday experiences in pre-technological society. This "superiority," however, should not be considered as absolute. Vygotsky and Luria made no claim about the relative adaptation value of various cognitive functions for survival in the informants' traditional environment. In other words, functional reasoning based on everyday experience might be highly adaptive in a stable pre-technological society. What Vygotsky and Luria observed, however, was the situation of a forced transition from traditional agricultural life to a life in technological society based on literacy and formal schooling. This point seems to be important in a more general sense, because the vector of migration or change is usually from traditional to technological society, not in the opposite direction. As demonstrated by Serpell (1993), formal schooling may indeed be of little relevance for success in a traditional African village as long as its life continues to be centered on subsistence agriculture and supported by the respective traditional social order. A different question, however, is which cognitive functions become adaptive when the villagers migrate to the urban areas or to more technologically developed countries? Thus, Vygotsky and Luria should be credited with posing a question about the cognitive value of different sociocultural activities, including formal education, in the situation of transition from a traditional to a technological society. In the late 20th and early 21st century, a time that was characterized by a considerable influx of immigrants from the so-called "Third World" to Europe and North America, this question becomes of considerable practical interest.

Posing the question, however, does not mean providing a comprehensive answer. With the wisdom of hindsight, one can distinguish a number of lacunae in the Vygotsky-Luria approach. One of the more significant of them is the lack of elaboration of different aspects of sociocultural change such as the acquisition of literacy, formal classroom learning, exposure to modern technology, and participation in labor activities based on the formal division of labor. In the Vygotsky-Luria model, all these aspects were lumped together, thus obscuring possible differential impact of each one of them on the development of certain cognitive functions. A certain degree of elaboration of these parameters was provided by Scribner and Cole (1981), who demonstrated that literacy and schooling may have a differential cognitive impact. By conducting their research in an African society where literacy in three different languages was associated with different acquisition and application contexts (school, home, and religious institution), Scribner and Cole showed that literacy does not have an overall impact on problem solving but affects specific cognitive functions corresponding to each one of the contexts. Formal education has a predominant impact on problem solving in the tasks that resemble those used in school.

In a more recent study Greenfield, Maynard, and Childs (2003) investigated how the overall change in the sociocultural practices affected the problem-solving patterns of Mayan children in a rural Mexican community. They compared the data collected in the 1970s when the predominant form of economy in this community was subsistence and agriculture with data of the early 1990s when wage economy and commerce had become predominant. The tasks given to children were based on visual patterns derived from traditional textiles produced in practically every Mayan family. The authors were able to identify the transition from subsistence and agriculture to wage economy and commerce as the main factor leading children from more concrete to more abstractive representations. At the same time, in more complex tasks that required the continuation of the model pattern schooling proved to have the strongest relationship with the choice of a more abstractive and less imitative strategy, with the involvement in the "new" economy coming second.

Somewhat similar results were reported by Gauvain and Munroe (2009), who documented changes in cognitive performance associated with modernization and schooling in four different cultures. The authors concluded that modernization and schooling can be seen as two relatively independent factors imparting children's cognitive performance.

Another problematic point in the Vygotsky-Luria model was their apparent belief that adult literacy courses are sufficient for shifting the informants' problem solving from functional-contextual to verbal-logical. This belief might be related to Vygotsky's conviction that properly organized classroom learning not only uses the already mature cognitive functions, but also helps to develop the emergent ones. As demonstrated by Vygotsky's followers in Russia (Davydov, 1988), such a situation, however, is more an exception than the rule. In the majority of classrooms, educators presuppose that all the students' prerequisite cognitive functions are in place and when they are not these children are labeled as "learning disabled" and placed in special education groups. Education continues to be mostly content-oriented. Vygotsky's model of development generating teaching is still waiting for its systematic implementation (for an example of a cognitively-oriented math curriculum see Kinard & Kozulin, 2008).

As I will demonstrate later in this chapter, the mere immersion of immigrant children and adults into formal education does not seem to be sufficient for promoting the full range of cognitive functions expected in modern technological society. These functions should be deliberately developed through specially designed educational activities. This actually follows from Vygotsky's theory of psychological tools that associates the emergence of the new higher mental functions with acquisition and internalization of symbolic tools characteristic of the given subculture (Vygotsky, 1979; Kozulin, 1998). One, therefore, cannot expect an immigrant learner to fully benefit from the study of the new language when it is not accompanied by an acquisition and internalization of a much broader system of symbolic tools and learning strategies.

The following sections are based on a number of studies conducted with new immigrants from Ethiopia in Israel and are aimed at documenting challenges experienced by immigrants at different phases of their transition from traditional to modern technological culture. The choice of this specific immigrant group carries in itself a number of advantages as well as limitations. The advantages are associated with the fact that the Ethiopian group is rather typical of the rural African community with traditional agriculture and crafts and limited access to school-based literacy. Thus, the transition to modern technological society was dramatic and had all the signs of the radical change discussed by Vygotsky and Luria. An additional advantage is that integration of Ethiopian immigrants into Israeli society, including housing, education, and employment was not individual and spontaneous, but planned and closely monitored by the relevant governmental agencies. As a result the processes observed are typical for an entire group rather than individual or idiosyncratic. The limitations appear to be the other side of the above advantages because many immigrant groups (e.g., in the United States) have a cultural background very different from that of Ethiopians, and the process of their integration into a new society is largely individual. As a result the reported findings about Ethiopians cannot be automatically generalized to other groups.

## From Ethiopian Village to Technological Society

Since the mid-1980s, Israel has received and integrated more than 100,000 immigrants from Ethiopia. The majority came from rural areas where they were engaged in traditional agricultural work and crafts with a limited access to school-based literacy (Avinor, 1995). Many of the new immigrants received no formal education in Ethiopia and were completely unfamiliar with the learning tasks typical in the Israeli educational system. Those who attended schools in towns or larger villages were exposed to teaching methods based on frontal teaching, continuous repetition, memorization, and drill. Solving a problem usually meant recalling the correct solution of the same problem previously demonstrated by the teacher (see Kozulin, 1998, chapter 5).

Though Israel has a rich experience of integrating immigrants from different countries, the Hebrew language courses are based on the assumption that immigrants are fully literate in their native language. For the majority of new immigrants from Ethiopia this assumption was not valid (see Lifshitz, Noam, & Habib, 1998). The Israeli system of teaching Hebrew to new immigrants also presupposes personal initiative, competitiveness, and independence. Ethiopian tradition, on the contrary, seems to encourage cooperative rather than individual activity, total compliance with existent patterns and discouragement of younger students' initiative in the presence of older people (Berhanu, 2001). Adult Hebrew classes tend to be large and very heterogeneous including some younger literate adults as well as older people some of whom have never seen paper and pencils in their lives. Many new immigrants complained about the ineffectiveness of the Hebrew study (see Berhanu, 2001). A number of studies confirmed that observation. For example Lifshitz, Noam, and Habib (1998) reported that 50% of the adult immigrant parents could not conduct a simple conversation in Hebrew after a few years in Israel, and 70% could not read a simple letter. Levin and Shohamy (2008) showed that even ten years after immigration, Ethiopian students still lagged considerably behind both non-immigrant Israelis and immigrants from Russia in their Hebrew reading comprehension. It seems significant that only 41% of the adults interviewed in our survey of 139 immigrant families mentioned Hebrew classes as a part of their educational experience (Kozulin, 2005a). In other words, even if they attended these courses, the study failed to become a turning point in their cultural transition process.

In terms of employment, the integration efforts had a limited success. According to Habib et al. (2001), the unemployment rate among Ethiopian immigrants reached 40% for males and 75% for females, while for non-immigrant Israelis it was about 7%. Moreover, the absolute majority of Ethiopian immigrants were employed in poorly paid menial jobs with limited social mobility.

The following sections discuss the cognitive aspects of transition from traditional Ethiopian to modern technological culture with focus on three different facets of the transition process. The first is the transition to the new educational and vocational environment by the new immigrants during the first year after arrival. The second is the challenge of young minority adults being admitted to more prestigious vocational training programs. The third is ways of helping minority students to be accepted to a competitive college of engineering.

# The First Year in the Country: Cognitive Aspects of Educational and Vocational Integration

The study described here aimed at exploring the cognitive aspects of the cultural transition process in adult new immigrants attending intensive Hebrew literacy courses during their first year in the country (Kozulin, 2005b). Responding to less than successful acquisition of Hebrew by the new immigrant adults, the agency responsible for immigrant integration created a pilot project aimed at giving an opportunity for more intensive study of Hebrew and other relevant subjects during their first year in the country. The candidates for the program were single adults in the age range from 17 to 26 with high motivation for intensive study and subsequent vocational training or academic studies. The program was residential—students were provided with dormitory style housing and stipends to cover their basic expenses. Students differed significantly in their previous educational experiences, literacy in Amharic or another language, and their familiarity with modern technological society. The period of study was about nine months and included intensive Hebrew studies comprising communicative language, reading and writing, a basic study of Jewish tradition, mathematics and computers. During the first year of the project, the curriculum was limited to the above subjects and included no general learning skills program. The results were somewhat disappointing because many graduates failed the exams required for the entry into more challenging vocational training courses or pre-academic programs in colleges and universities. In terms of the Vygotsky-Luria model, a mere immersion in the literacy curriculum failed to prepare immigrants for integration into technological society.

It was thus decided to add for the next cohort the cognitive enrichment activities aimed at the development of general learning strategies and problem-solving skills. The activities were based on the "Instrumental Enrichment" (IE) program (Feuerstein, Rand, Hoffman, & Miller, 1980). The IE materials include 14 sets of paper-and-pencil tasks covering such areas as analytic perception, orientation in space and time, comparisons, classification, and so on. IE lessons are conducted by specially trained IE teachers who mediate the material to students using the criteria of mediated learning experience elaborated by Feuerstein et al. (1980). The IE program promotes acquisition of general learning strategies serving as the core prerequisite for any formal learning. Such emphasis is particularly important for those students whose native culture does not foster formal learning mechanisms. Another aspect of the IE program particularly important for culturally different students is its saturation with various graphic-symbolic devices (schemas, tables, graphs, plans, and maps). These graphic-symbolic devices provide the basis for psychological tools that students in the advanced technological countries usually acquire in the course of their "natural" learning experiences, and which are often missing in immigrant students (Kozulin, 1998). As a research project the study aimed at responding to the following questions: First, will the addition of the IE activities be effective in changing the students' cognitive performance as measured by non-verbal problem solving tasks? Second, does the IE have a moderating effect on the predictive power of the students' previous educational experience? Third, how does the change in cognitive performance contribute to the success of the new immigrants' vocational and academic advancement.

The first question was answered by comparing the students' non-verbal cognitive performance as measured by the Raven Progressive Matrices test at the beginning and the end of their participation in the program. The second research question was answered by examining the correlation between the students' education received in Ethiopia with their cognitive performance at the beginning and the end of the program. The diminishing correlation would indicate the moderating effect of the IE program. The third question was answered by comparing the students' cognitive achievements during the program with their success at joining academic or vocational training programs after graduation. If students with greater cognitive achievements were accepted into more prestigious academic or training programs this would indicate the impact of the cognitive enrichment activities on vocational and academic advancement.

The results of assessments conducted at the beginning of the program showed that immigrant adults experienced serious difficulties with Raven Matrices and positional memory tasks (Kozulin, 2008). The matrix tasks include no verbal elements and do not require any culture-specific knowledge except recognition of simple geometric shapes. The positional memory test is even simpler: the participants are shown a poster with a grid of 25 empty squares organized in a 5 by 5 pattern of columns and rows. The evaluator then points to a specific square in each column and says "here, here, here, here, and here." In this way five positions are indicated, each one in a different column and row. After a ten second delay, participants are asked to mark the same five positions in the first 5 x 5 grid printed on their answer sheet. After the participants finish marking the positions, the procedure is repeated. Three consecutive errorless identifications of all five positions are considered to be the criterion of correct performance. If a considerable number of students in the group fail to reach the criterion level, the presentation of the same patterns continues up to 12 trials. Though at first glance the task appears to be culture-neutral, the results of the new immigrants turned out to be significantly lower than those of educated European subjects. The analysis of mistakes indicated that for many immigrant participants, the grid of columns and rows apparently failed to serve as a reliable framework for identifying the "address" of each indicated position.

In the matrix tasks, the choice of the correct answer depends on systematic comparison of designs belonging to the same row and column as well as generalization of the rules of each row. One could say that the use of tables and grids is deeply ingrained in European culture, both in formal education but also in everyday life with its ubiquitous presence of the rectangular organization of space, designs, and printed materials. Two points are important for our discussion. First, non-verbal tasks like matrices and positional memory are often included into psychometric tests used for job selection or admission to higher education.

Second, a typical language study rarely includes tasks of this nature into its curriculum. As a result, if not specially trained in using various symbolic devices new immigrants will remain disadvantaged when confronted with vocational or scholastic tests.

Activities based on the IE tasks seemed to be effective in improving the immigrant students' performance with matrix and positional memory tests. It is important to emphasize that students were not coached on how to solve such tests. IE tasks do not include matrices or positional memory exercises. At the same time they are rich in various symbolic devices including tables, diagrams, and charts.

Initially stronger students were tested with Raven Standard Progressive Matrices (RSPM), while initially weaker students were tested with simpler Raven Colored Matrices. The application of the IE program with stronger students produced a statistically significant change (t $_{22}$=5.76, p<0.01) and demonstrated a very robust effect size of 1.1. (Effect size is estimated by dividing the gain score by the mean standard deviation of the average pre- and post-test scores. Effect size 0.5 is considered medium, and 0.8 is seen as large, see Cohen, 1988.) At the end of the program initially stronger students on average reached the normative Israeli level of problem-solving performance in the RSPM test. Only two students in the entire group scored below one standard deviation from the norm. The IE program effect size with initially weaker students was less impressive (0.76), but the pre- to post-difference was statistically significant ($t_{16}$=3.09, p<0.01). The initially weaker students were also post-tested with RSPM and four (25% of the group) reached the results within one standard deviation of the Israeli norm. It can thus be concluded that IE was effective in improving the non-verbal problem solving skills of immigrant students, particularly those who started the program with somewhat higher results.

The second question posed in this study was the influence of previous schooling on the students' cognitive progress and the possible moderating effect of the IE program. The results indicate that the correlation between the level of the students' previous schooling and their cognitive performance was significantly stronger at the beginning of the program ( r = 0.76) than at the end (r = 0.52). This assessment signifies that students who had less schooling in Ethiopia benefited more from the IE program and at the end of the program received results closer to those of students who had more years of schooling. Some students who had had as little as two or four years of schooling scored on the post-test on par with students who had studied for ten years. At the same time students who never attended school showed poor results both at the beginning and at the end of intervention. A certain minimal level of schooling seems to be important for a student to be ready to benefit from the cognitive intervention program given in a relatively heterogeneous classroom. On the other hand, beyond this minimal requirement the years of schooling do not offer a strong predictor for the students' progress in problem solving. The IE intervention is effective in moderating the effect of schooling and advancing the students with limited previous school experience.

The third question posed in this study was whether the change in cognitive performance contributed to the vocational and academic advancement of immigrant students. This question was answered by comparing the students' cognitive achievements at the end of the program with their success at joining academic or vocational training programs after graduation. In order to compare the graduates' cognitive achievement with their academic or vocational advancement, all students were divided into a subgroup of "High scorers" (above median performance) and "low scorers" (below median performance) using Raven Matrices scores. Some students who were placed in the pre-academic college program later dropped out of it. Though a number of social and economic factors contributed to their decision, one cannot help noticing that many more of the "Low" group students dropped out. Table 1 shows the placement of "High" and "Low" group students. The Chi Square test indicates that there was a greater than chance probability for the members of the "high" group being accepted to the university or college pre-academic program and staying in this program.

TABLE 1. Number of students admitted to university or college preparatory programs or vocational training courses and number of students who dropped out of the college program.

| | University | College | Dropped out | Vocational training |
|---|---|---|---|---|
| High group (N=18) | 6 | 10 | 2 | 0 |
| Low group (N=18) | 0 | 7 | 6 | 5 |

The study confirmed that challenges facing new immigrants from traditional agricultural societies are not limited to learning a new language and orienting themselves in everyday life of the new country. Cognitive functions expected for educational and vocational advancement are culturally specific, and there is no reason to believe that they will be spontaneously developed by immigrants. A study of the new language and some curricular subjects such as math and computers may not be sufficient for the acquisition of the new symbolic tools and their internalization. Specially designed cognitive enrichment programs, such as IE, seem to be effective in filling this gap.

## Dynamic Assessment as a Tool of Vocational Advancement of Minority Students

Admission to both academic learning and vocational training is typically based on the results of the candidates' static psychometric exams. These exams are based on the assumption that current psychometric performance can serve as a reliable predictor of future learning achievement. As has been discussed at greater length elsewhere (Feuerstein & Kozulin, 1995; Feuerstein et al., 2002), these assumptions are not as obvious as they may seem. First, there is a sufficient amount of research indicating that human intelligence is not a stable entity but a dynamic process amenable to change even in adults. Psychometric tests may then more or less accurately assess the more stable components of the intellectual activity, but they miss the dynamic ones. Static administration of psychometric tests limit the possibility of evaluating the individual's learning capacity, as distinct from performance capacity. The time-limiting administration of tests shifts the focus of assessment from that of intellectual functions to that of speed of processing. Finally, there is a considerable argument regarding the accuracy of psychometric tests in predicting the level of professional achievement (Sternberg, 2000).

Contrary to the psychometric paradigm, the dynamic assessment (DA) paradigm perceives intellectual processes as dynamic, flexible, and amenable to substantial modification not only in children but also in adults. The two paradigms differ in the goal of assessment. While the psychometric approach searches for stable characteristics of intellectual functioning, DA searches for signs of modifiability and change. Psychometric tests focus on the individual's current performance, while DA assessment responds to the question regarding the individual's ability to learn and change his or her performance in the future. The differences in the goals of assessment also influence the instruments and procedures of assessment. The DA approach selects tasks amenable to learning and includes the learning phase in the assessment procedure. The learning phase is based on active interaction between the assessor and individuals being assessed. The latter are provided with positive feedback that enhances their feeling of competence.

The DA system developed by Feuerstein, Rand, and Hoffman (1979) has been applied with various populations of socially disadvantaged and culturally different children and adolescents. The results of DA have consistently demonstrated that static psychometric tests significantly underestimate the learning potential of these populations of students.

The first large-scale application of this method with new immigrants from Ethiopia was undertaken in 1985 and 1986 (see Kaniel et al., 1991). Three hundred new immigrant adolescents were examined using the group format of the DA battery. The initial level of the students' performance on such non-verbal and presumably culturally neutral tests as RSPM was much lower than that of the Israeli norm. On average fifteen-year-old new immigrant students performed on the level of ten-year-old native Israelis. If only this static measure of the new immigrant students' intelligence had been taken into account, many of them would have had to have been placed in special education frameworks. The results after DA procedure that included a learning phase based on a small number of model items from the RSPM test were, however, dramatically different. The performance of students who received DA procedure was compared to a control group consisting of their peers who received the same tasks but without mediation. The first important finding of this study was that mere familiarity with the test material does not help much in solving the tasks. The control group students who solved the RSPM test twice improved their performance only by 3%. The second finding was that exposure to the learning phase materials without mediation also has little effect on the students' performance. While the control group students, who worked without mediation, were able to solve only 21% of the learning tasks, the experimental group that received mediation was able to solve 65% of the same tasks. Finally, the results of the post-test indicated that the majority of new immigrant students became much closer in their performance to the Israeli age norm.

The study described below (see Kozulin, 2006) was prompted by dissatisfaction with the fact that young minority adults of Ethiopian origin are underrepresented in the more challenging setting of the vocational training courses. As mentioned above, the results of psychometric tests play an important role in decision regarding selection for specific training courses. Since a relatively small percentage of Ethiopian candidates received the required scores, they were routinely directed to low level training courses. As a result, their professional advancement was stymied and their self-perception as learners was undermined.

There were three main research questions: First, does the DA procedure allow for a different ranking of subjects vis-à-vis their problem-solving abilities from a similar static psychometric test? Second, is the subjects' learning potential a better predictor of their performance at the end of a short-term cognitive intervention program than their static performance score? Third, will minority subjects selected by DA for more challenging training courses successfully graduate from them?

Ninety-four young adults (20 males and 74 females) participated in the study. All of them were of Ethiopian origin but were either born in Israel or immigrated to Israel with their families during early childhood. All participants had successfully finished 12 years of schooling in Israel and were about to start studying in professional training courses. Participation in the DA assessment and the subsequent cognitive training program were voluntary, indicating that the present sample had a relatively high achievement motivation.

The subjects first underwent a standard placement examination (conducted by an independent testing company) that included a battery of standard psychometric tests, interviews, and evaluation of their school matriculation transcripts. At the end of the placement examination, each subject received his or her placement score. Then the DA assessment was conducted for two days with groups of 15 or 16 subjects. The group DA battery included a variety of DA tests (see Feuerstein et al., 2002), but in the present research, only the data from Raven Standard Progressive Matrices (RSPM) used as static pre- and post-tests, and two DA tests, Figural analogies ("Var-1") and Set variations (Var-2) similar to the RSPM series C, D, and E tasks, are discussed. DA tests "Var- 1" and "Var-2" have a number of sample tasks that serve as models for the problem-solving strategies actively mediated to subjects by the evaluator. After the period of mediation, the subjects are given test items similar but not identical to sample tasks.

After DA assessment the subjects were assigned to six groups that received cognitive enrichment based on the Feuerstein et al. (1980) *Instrumental Enrichment* (IE) program for two weeks (65 hours). It is important to emphasize that IE material does not have any items or activities similar to RSPM or "Variations." After the end of cognitive training, the subjects were post-tested statically using RSPM.

The first question posed in the study was whether the DA assessment allows for a different ranking of subjects' problem-solving abilities from a similar static test.

This question is answered by comparing the results of the static Figural Analogies Test (from the standard placement examination) with the results of the DA figural analogies test (Var-1). The correlation between static and DA test results was not trivial ($r = 0.46$), but could not be considered particularly strong, taking into account a considerable similarity of the items in the two tests. The question is thus whether the lack of a stronger correlation stems from the difference in the testing procedures, or from a random "drift" of the test results. If a random drift is responsible, then it should be present in equal measure in high and low performing students. The analysis of the difference between z-scores of static and dynamic tests demonstrates, however, that there is a definite tendency for the static test to underestimate those students who performed better in the dynamic test.

All subjects were ranked according to their "Var-1" scores and subdivided into three subgroups: high scorers, medium scorers, and low scorers. The comparison between average dynamic and static scores in each one of these subgroups revealed the following: Members of the "high" group on average were significantly higher in their dynamic than in their static scores; members of the "medium" group were somewhat higher in their dynamic scores, but the difference was not significant, and members of the "low" group were on average significantly lower in their dynamic than static scores. This result clearly indicates that static psychometric testing systematically underestimated students with stronger learning potential, and overestimated students with good static performance but relatively weak learning potential.

The second question posed in this study was whether the subjects' learning potential is indeed a better predictor of their performance at the end of the cognitive intervention program. The students' learning potential was operationalized as their score in the DA "Var-2" test. Their initial level of cognitive performance was established by the RSPM static pre-test. Cognitive advancement was evaluated with the help of the static RSPM post-test at the end of 65 hours of cognitive intervention program. Because subjects with higher RSPM pre-test static scores tend on average to have higher learning potential, it was decided to test the above hypothesis by using matched groups of subjects with identical pre-test RSPM scores but contrasting learning potential. If learning potential had impact over and above subjects' pre-test performance level, then the high learning potential subjects should achieve better results on the post-program test than the matched lower learning potential subjects. The results confirmed this hypothesis—the post-program score of the subjects who demonstrated higher learning potential was significantly higher than that of subjects with lower learning potential though their pre-program static performance level was the same.

The third question posed was whether the subjects whose standard placement scores were much lower than required for placement into more challenging professional training courses would nevertheless be able to successfully graduate from these courses. The duration of training ranged from two weeks for less challenging courses to 24 weeks for more challenging ones. At the end of this period data were collected regarding the success of subjects in finishing the courses, as well as the number of drop-out and transfer cases. Similar data were obtained regarding cultural majority subjects from the same courses who were placed there on the basis of standard placement procedure.

Seventy-seven out of 94 minority subjects, i.e., 81.9%, successfully finished their training courses. The graduation rate for cultural majority students in the same courses is about 85% to 90%. These results should be evaluated against the difference in standard placement scores in these two groups. Because we are interested primarily in more challenging courses that were traditionally completely "off limits" for minority subjects due to their low placement scores, we will focus here on a subgroup of high learning potential minority students (N=31) who were offered an opportunity to study in these particularly challenging courses. The mean standard placement scores of the minority students who were admitted and successfully graduated from these courses were significantly lower (48.2; SD=2.4) than the admission scores of the cultural majority students (52.42; SD=0.56). The difference was statistically significant and the effect size of $d=2.85$ very large. This indicates that the DA procedure was effective in successfully selecting minority candidates with high learning potential whose standard placement scores were on average 2.85 standard deviations below the ordinary admission level. The graduation rate in this minority subgroup was 83.9% as compared to about 90% among the cultural majority students. It can thus be concluded that DA assessment procedure was able to "close the gap" the size of 2.85 standard deviations and reach the high accuracy in placing minority students into the training courses corresponding to their learning potential.

The results of the study indicate that even after many years in the country, young minority adults experience certain disadvantages when confronted with standard psychometric exams. There are several possible reasons for this state of affairs. One of them is that psychometric exams are given via computer while many minority students do not have sufficient experience with such a problem-solving interface. The second possible reason is that all psychometric tests are time-limited, while the culture of time in Ethiopian families seems to remain very different from that of the "Western" notion. Finally, the socioeconomic status of Ethiopian families on average is rather low, and children usually attend schools situated in the poverty areas. The amount of enrichment activities they have beyond the standard school curriculum is thus limited.

At the same time, the study demonstrated that the minority adults' potential for change is much stronger than their static psychometric performance. Psychometric and DA assessment procedures aimed at the same cognitive area resulted in different intra-group ranking of the same subjects. Static psychometric tests systematically assigned lower ranks to subjects with high learning potential and higher ranks for subjects with relatively low learning potential. The study also answered positively to the question regarding the propensity of individuals with higher learning potential to benefit more from cognitive intervention. The comparison of the two subgroups of subjects who had identical static pre-test scores but contrasting learning potential scores, confirmed that indeed high learning potential subjects made more significant cognitive gains during the short-term cognitive intervention program. It has also been confirmed that DA assessment can indeed be a tool of professional advancement of minority students by offering an alternative procedure for their successful placement into more challenging vocational training courses. The use of DA proved to have a considerable advantage over the psychometrically based placement exams and allowed a large number of cultural minority students to gain access to vocational training that would otherwise be completely beyond their reach.

## Minority Students in a College of Engineering

The ultimate step toward transition to modern technological society is associated with the access to higher education. A considerable number of minority students who succeed in passing the high-school matriculation exams take them at the "minimal" level that is not sufficient for admission to Israeli universities and colleges. In 2003 only 19% of immigrant students passed matriculation exams sufficient for university admission, while for the non-Ethiopian students this percentage reached 53% (*Brookdale Memo*, 2004).

Minority students find it particularly difficult to gain admission to more prestigious and eventually economically rewarding study tracks such as engineering, medicine, and law. In 2002 only 40 Ethiopian minority students studied in these tracks (Wurztburger, 2003). There seem to be several factors contributing to the low admission numbers. One of them is the relatively low scores that minority students receive in time-limited psychometric tests (similar to the SAT). This factor has already been discussed in the previous section in connection to admission to vocational programs. The second factor is the relative underachievement of minority students in such high school curriculum subjects—mathematics, science, and English-as-a-second language.

One of the mechanisms called upon to remedy this situation is the pre-academic program (*mechina*) that gives a second chance to students who failed to obtain matriculation exam results sufficient for their direct admission to higher education. The students study at the pre-academic programs for ten months taking those subjects in which their matriculation results were insufficient. Thus, candidates for admission to schools of engineering or technology colleges usually need to improve their results in mathematics, physics, and English-as-a-second language. Though the pre-academic programs proved to be beneficial for some students, the success rate of minority students of Ethiopian origin remained unacceptably low. One of the possible reasons for a relatively low success rate is that pre-academic programs focus exclusively on curricular subjects and pay little attention to the development of students' more general learning and problem-solving skills often considered to be the necessary prerequisite of successful curricular learning (Costa, 1999). The utility of adding a cognitive enrichment element to the pre-academic English-as-a second language curriculum has already been documented (Garb & Kozulin, 2004). Here, however, I would like to describe a new project aimed at linking cognitive enrichment with a study of physics and mathematics (Gouzman & Kozulin, 2011).

Unlike the projects described in the previous sections where the main goal was to enhance general cognitive and learning functions required for education and advancement in a technological society, the current study focuses on cognitive functions specific for a given curricular area. Theoretically, this approach extends Vygotsky's claim that human higher mental functions are shaped by culturally specific activities. It would thus be incorrect to imagine the higher forms of reasoning as a combination of specific (e.g., physical) curricular content plus general cognitive function. Rather than being "generic" the higher mental functions themselves become shaped by content-specific activities, so that one can distinguish physical, biological, historical, and linguistic types of reasoning. Thus, the introduction of cognitive enrichment activities on the level of higher education requires what we call "a round trip from cognitive functions to curriculum and back."

One of the first steps in this direction was made by Mehl (1991), who applied the principles of cognitive enrichment via IE with first year physics students in South Africa. After giving students two mechanical tasks, Mehl performed the cognitive analysis of the students' mistakes. The following cognitive functions and operations turned out to be responsible for the majority of mistakes: poor visualization of the given physical situation, insufficient use of such graphic tools as sketches, difficulty with identification of implicit data, poor formulation of the problem and planning its solution, impulsivity in dealing with the data, difficulty in relating to two sources of information simultaneously. Mehl then created a series of physics tasks that allowed the instructor to mediate to the students the underlying cognitive principles leading to the efficient solution of the tasks. In the mid- and end-of-year exams, the experimental group that used these tasks significantly outperformed the control group of students who received a regular physics curriculum.

A pioneering effort of "bridging" the cognitive principles to the math curriculum in the university pre-academic program for minority students from Ethiopia was undertaken by August-Rothman and Zinn (1986). Students who received cognitive intervention via IE linked to the math curriculum during the first year of the preparatory program scored better at the end-of-year math exams than the control group who received no cognitive enrichment, though the effect size was rather small (.35). Students also continued improving their results during the second year of study. Seven out of 15 minority students were accepted to the university after two years of such preparatory program, in contrast to the previous period when only one out of 15 students was accepted.

The study summarized here (see Gouzman & Kozulin, 2010) was conducted under realistic conditions of the pre-academic program in one of the prestigious colleges of engineering in Jerusalem. For a number of years the college accepted young adults of Ethiopian origin to the pre-academic program with the aim of enhancing their knowledge in the field of physics, mathematics, and English-as-a-foreign-language and preparing them for passing exams on a level sufficient for subsequent admission to the college. The success rate, however, was less than 50%. Thus, it was decided to add the cognitive component to the physics and mathematics curriculum during the second semester of the pre-academic program. Eleven minority students participated in the program. Before the start of the program, all of them received a DA assessment (Feuerstein, Rand, & Hoffman, 1979) the results of which were used to advise them about their strong and weak points in learning and problem solving. The enrichment program was conducted for four hours per week for the duration of the semester. The program was based on a selection of IE tasks that allowed identifying and developing cognitive functions central for problem solving in physics and mathematics. Immediately after such an exercise a physics or mathematics problem was presented, and students were asked to analyze it in terms of cognitive prerequisites. Students were also taught to conduct an opposite procedure—first analyze the curricular task cognitively and then demonstrate the same cognitive operations in their "pure" form in an IE task.

The-end-of-year exam results in mathematics and physics demonstrated that students in the experimental (IE) group received much higher scores than students in the comparison group who received no IE session. Experimental group students also took more difficult, advanced level exams. For example, all students in the experimental group took the advanced level physics exams, while in the comparison group only one student took the advanced level while the rest chose the basic level exam. In mathematics, five students in the experimental group took the advanced level and two took the intermediate level exams, while in the comparison group only two students took advanced-level and the rest intermediate-level exams. The choice of more challenging exams reflected, in our opinion, the enhanced self-confidence of the experimental group students. Their confidence was not misplaced because the experimental group on average achieved significantly better results both in mathematics and in physics, with the effect size in mathematics being very large ($d = 2.06$), and in physics medium to large ($d = 0.76$). All of them passed matriculation exams at the level sufficient for admission to the technological college.

The above study confirmed that even on the university level mere access to curricular studies is often not sufficient to prepare minority students for the challenges of higher-level math and science exams. It is important to realize that in this respect minority students are not exceptional but belong to a relatively wide range of students from low-SES families whose advancement in higher education is often blocked by the lack of more efficient learning and problem-solving strategies. The integration of cognitive and curricular tasks appears to be the best approach leading to academic acceptance and success.

# Conclusion

Transition from traditional to advanced technological society appears to be associated to a considerable extent with acquisition and internalization of the new sets of symbolic tools and sociocultural activities. In this respect the Vygotsky-Luria model still retains its original theoretical value. Moreover, with modern technology becoming more and more information based and less object based, the importance of symbolic tools and interfaces becomes even stronger. To what extent is a simple immersion in the everyday life of a technological society sufficient for supplying immigrants with the new psychological tools? Studies presented in this chapter indicate that a mere immersion or even access to a formal study of the new language do not seem to be sufficient for fulfilling this function. A systematic mediation of new symbolic tools and learning strategies appear to be a more efficient method for providing new immigrants with the required set of psychological tools.

One of the major stumbling blocks on the immigrants' path to achievement in the new society is static psychometric exams. These exams ignore the test-takers' learning potential and ability to change. In Vygotsky's terms, only the current development is taken into account, but the zone of proximal development is ignored. This is true for all test-takers, but for immigrant and minority students the gap seems to be wider and more persistent. The application of the dynamic, rather than the static assessment, model promises to bypass this stumbling block and provide a more reliable estimate of the minorities' potential than the currently used static tests.

Responding to the questions posed at the beginning of this chapter one may hazard the following tentative answers. Human cognition is changing historically and it is different culturally. There is little reason to make a sharp distinction between the content of thinking and its form. A new content requires re-shaping cognitive mechanisms and in this way new forms of thinking are generated. Transition from traditional oral culture to technologically advanced societies includes acquisition and internalization of a wide range of new psychological tools. The situation of a multicultural classroom may thus be operationalized as a dialogue between different systems of psychological tools. A study of cultural transition teaches us many things about our cognitive processes over and above the practical question of immigrant integration.

# Macro Cultural Psychology, the Psychology of Oppression, and Cultural-Psychological Enrichment

*Carl Ratner*

Approaches to cultural psychology rest upon their definition of culture. By definition of culture I mean both its content—that is, the components of cultural factors and which factors are most important for structuring social and psychological activity—and also its form or how the factors are organized, whether as a sum or sequence of discrete variables or a structured, integral whole, as a set of equals or with certain ones being more central, as static givens or dialectically dynamic. Macro cultural psychology construes culture as composed primarily of macro factors—social institutions, artifacts, and cultural concepts.

The main principle of macro cultural psychology is that psychological phenomena such as perception, self, emotions, cognition, and mental illness are based on macro cultural factors, developed in macro cultural factors, publicly objectified in macro cultural factors, and socialized by macro cultural factors;

they embody macro cultural factors and function to sustain macro cultural factors. Macro cultural factors comprise the operating mechanism of the psyche. We think, perceive, and feel through macro cultural factors. Macro cultural factors are the explanatory constructs, descriptors, and predictors of emotions, perception, cognition, memory, motivation, self, sexuality, mental illness, and developmental processes (Ratner, 2011a, 2011b).

Contrary to predominant thinking about psychology, psychology does not emanate from natural or personal processes internal to the individual. Culture determines *that* we think, perceive, remember, and emote (in human terms), as well as *how* we think, remember, emote, and perceive, and also *what* we think, remember, emote, and perceive. Macro culture is the basis of abstract (essential) aspects of psychology and concrete aspects. Macro culture is our human nature.

Durkheim (1914/2005) put it well when he said:

> Society cannot constitute itself unless it penetrates individual consciousnesses and fashions them in its image and likeness....We cannot live without representing to ourselves the world around us and the objects of every sort that fill it. But by this alone, that we represent them to ourselves, they enter into us and thus become part of ourselves.... Consequently, there is in us something other than ourselves to call up our activity.... Ideas and sentiments developed by the community...move our will.... ( pp. 35, 38, 42)

This is what I mean when I say that culture is the operating mechanism of the psyche.[1]

Vygotsky (1998) similarly emphasized the point:

> The structures of higher mental functions represent a cast of collective social relations between people. These [mental] structures are nothing other than a transfer into the personality of an inward relation of a social order that constitutes the basis of the social structure of the human personality. (pp. 169–170)

He (Vygotsky, 1986) also elaborated this point through such statements as the following:

> Verbal thought is not an innate, natural form of behavior, but is determined by historical-cultural process and has specific properties and laws that cannot be found in the natural forms of thought and speech. Once we acknowledge the historical character of verbal thought, we must consider it subject to all the premises of historical materialism, which are valid for any historical phenomenon in human society. It is only to be expected that on this level the development of behavior will be governed essentially by the general laws of the historical development of human society. (pp. 94–95)

Durkheim emphasized a central point of macro cultural psychology, that society is not an extension of the individual nor a sum of individuals. "Society has its own nature and consequently altogether different demands than those that are involved in our nature as an individual" (1914/2005, p. 44). Psychological phenomena are part of the macro cultural system and dynamics. Psychological phenomena construct cultural factors and are constructed by them.

# Honor Killings

An example of these points is honor killings among devoutly religious people: For choosing a lover outside of her Kurdish community and living with him, Fadime was brutally shot and killed by her father at point-blank range in front of her mother and younger sister in 2002 in Sweden at the age of 25. Her father shot her in the face as he shouted "you filthy whore." The father felt no regret; he felt the killing assuaged the shame that Fadime had brought upon him and his family (Wikan, 2008).[2]

Honor killings exemplify a complex of emotions, perceptions, reasoning, self-concept, and sexuality organized in cultural norms. These norms are represented by sexual honor. Sexual honor embodies and sustains a social system of proper male-female interactions and proper interactions between daughters and parents. Violating sexual norms violates the entire normative system of gender and familial relations, which sexual honor represents. This is why it is so serious and why it must be corrected. Sexual honor is made serious by attributing it to an entire family, not to an individual. The siblings of a disgraced woman are disgraced and become unfit for marriage. This social construction of sexual honor gives family members a vested interest in preventing her disobedience against the entire social system.

Honor and shame are social constructs with socially specific and variable content. Wikan (p. 64) observes that honor takes on other forms/qualities in other societies. Some societies define honor as the value of a person in his own eyes. The Kurdish notion of honor practiced by Fadime's father was more collectivistic.

The emotional fury and murderous behavior directed at the miscreant daughter is organized by the social construct of honor; it incarnates the social construct, and it sustains and reinforces the social construct of honor. The emotional fury contains the code within itself as its operating mechanism. The code is what generates the fury at particular activities of the daughter in particular circumstances (when non-family members discover the tabooed behavior). The code is also what mandates particular behavioral responses to assuage the fury.

The fury bears the quality of the code. It is *disgraced fury*, not some other kind of fury. Fadime's father's fury was not related to jealousy or abuse, nor was it blind passion. It was a calculated response based upon knowledge that outsiders were aware of the daughter's disgraceful sexual behavior and the inability of the parents to control it.

Disgraced fury is nuanced differently from the fury a mother feels at her child who runs into the street without looking for approaching cars that might injure him. The latter fury is tinged with concern for the child's well-being, not family honor. The eliciting event, the quality of the emotion, and resolving behavior form a system in both cases.

Macro cultural psychology does not regard fury as a neutral, natural, fixed, universal, independent process that becomes associated with—conditioned to— various events/stimuli in various conditions. Rather, we regard fury as specifically formed by macro cultural factors such as honor codes, in order to achieve specific cultural states. The same is true for love, memory, perception, and reasoning. Psychology is not generic, it is culturally specific.

The cultural code was inside the psychology, modulating and organizing it; but psychology was also inside the code. The cultural norm of honor and dishonor regarding sexual behavior of daughters rested upon particular perceptions, emotions, sexuality, self-concept, self-control of impulses, and reasoning. These psychological phenomena were the subjective element of the code.[3]

Wikan observes a principle of macro cultural psychology, namely, that the cultural concept of honor, which formed the basis of the family's psychology, is political. It incarnates, expresses, and promulgates a system of social practices that are political. Family honor rests upon submissive behavior by women that supports male dominance over a monogamous family. Honor is also ideological in that it purports to enshrine noble behavior, but it really enshrines submissive, oppressive, ignoble, dishonorable behavior by women that violates their humanity and dignity. Honor is additionally political in that it is defined by the ruling elite. "Those in power have waded into the European debate in an attempt to take charge of 'honor'" (Wikan, 2008, p. 68).

Since psychology is the subjective side (element) of macro cultural factors, it contained the politics of the honor code. The father's psychology (his emotional fury and shame) and behavior triggered a political act that sustained the subordinate position of women within the monogamous family. Women's psychology that conformed to the honor code was similarly political in that it reinforced their subordination.

Because psychology emanates from, embodies, and facilitates participation in macro cultural factors, we may say that *psychology is a cultural state of being, a cultural state of mind, a cultural identity and membership.* As Vygotsky and Durkheim emphasized in their statements cited earlier, psychology is not pure consciousness or subjectivity; psychology contains and expresses a social order.

Fadime's father's fury and shame at his daughter's "disgraceful" behavior placed him in a highly visible social position vis-à-vis his community; it testified to his membership in the community; finally, it promulgated a wide range of social relations regarding daughters' social position vis-à-vis parents and young men.

Macro cultural psychology argues that Fadime's father's psychology was constructed at the macro cultural level, objectified in macro cultural factors, organized by them, socialized by them and also maintains them. Indeed, this honor killing exemplifies the cultural nature of all psychological phenomena.[4]

Macro cultural psychology argues that psychological phenomena are public, definite, objective, cultural tools/means whose form and content are culturally organized to be suitable for achieving cultural purposes (see Lewis, 1989; Ratner 2011b, for example).

As a result, subjectivity, psychology, and agency bind the individual to the culture and also bind the culture together through shared individual behavior. Fadime's father's psychology is a telling example. This cultural function of psychology refutes the popular notion that psychology is essentially a personal construct. Psychology is a macro cultural factor that does cultural work.

The psychological phenomena we have discussed are only explicable in macro cultural terms. Reducing them to natural biological mechanisms, or individual personality processes, or personal-subjective choices and meanings cannot account for the cultural specificity of this psychology, its widespread prevalence throughout the culture, and its obvious dependence upon cultural codes and concepts.

Macro cultural psychology does not simply describe cultural differences in psychological expressions; it identifies the cultural operating mechanisms (mediational means) that generate (and explain) those expressions. This reveals culture in psychology rather than psychology in culture.

Macro cultural psychology emphasizes the complexity of culture that is composed of different macro cultural factors with their own contents, processes, histories, vested interests, and position vis-à-vis other factors. Factory work is qualitatively different from family life. There are contradictions and interactions among these cultural factors. Each contributes differently to psychology. At the same time, there is an overarching unity to culture that holds it together and prevents it from becoming decimated by conflicting pressures. This unity stems from the predominant power of the political economy over other cultural factors. The political economy of capitalism dominates other institutions such as government, family, entertainment, sports, medicine, scientific research, news media, and religion. I propose that the social structure takes the form of a cone with political economy at the stem (Ratner, 2011b, chap. 3; Williams, 1973; Pred, 1984; *New York Times*, Aug. 1, 2010, "The Academic-Industrial Complex").

Because psychology is formed in macro cultural factors, it is designed and controlled by whoever is in charge of those factors. Psychology is only as democratic as the culture in which it is formed.

Every society for the past 10,000 years has been structured in a pyramidal hierarchy in which the upper class has dominated the subaltern classes. The structure is only maintained by exploitation and oppression—people would never voluntarily and rationally consent to it.

> Inequality is produced by specific institutional mechanisms that are all variations on exploitation and…discrimination…. The contemporary political economy of the United States is riddled with categorical mechanisms that produce unequal distributions of material, symbolic, and emotional resources along the lines of race, class, and gender…. Under capitalism, categorical mechanisms of inequality are often built into the social organization of the market itself—they are embedded within its laws, regulations, conventions, understandings, and institutions, both formal and informal. (Massey, 2007, pp. xv–xvi, 36)

For example, in the last quarter of 2009 and throughout 2010, American businesses shed employees at a massive rate and have extracted more productivity from the remaining employees (through lower wages) so that profit margins will reach 9% at the end of 2010, an all time record! (*New York Times*, July 26, 2010). From the fourth quarter of 2007 to the fourth quarter of 2009, real aggregate output in the United States, as measured by the gross domestic product, fell by about 2.5%. However, employers cut their payrolls by 6%. They threw out far more workers and hours than they lost output. At the end of the fourth quarter in 2008, corporate profits began to dramatically increase, growing by $572 billion by the first quarter of 2010. Over that same time period, wage and salary payments fell by $122 billion. That kind of disconnect had never been seen before in all the decades since World War II. Worker productivity has increased dramatically, but the workers themselves have seen no gains from their increased production. It has all gone to corporate profits. This dynamic is unprecedented in the postwar years. Executives are delighted with this ill-gotten bonanza. Charles D. McLane Jr. is the chief financial officer of Alcoa, which recently experienced a turnaround in profits and a 22% increase in revenue. He assured investors that his company was in no hurry to bring back 37,000 workers who were let go since 2008. "We're not only holding head-count levels, but are also driving restructuring this quarter that will result in further reductions" (*New York Times*, July 31, 2010, editorial).

According to the Internal Revenue Service, in 2005 the top 1% of income earners received more than twice as much income as everyone in the bottom 50% combined.

The primary function of the state is to enforce the dominance of the upper class over the subaltern classes. Most of the security apparatus designed by the state over the past quarter-century

[i]s a political response, not to rising criminal insecurity, but to the diffuse social insecurity wrought by the fragmentation of wage labor and the shakeup of ethnic hierarchy. The punitive slant of recent shifts in both welfare and justice policies points to a broader reconstruction of the state coupling restrictive "workfare" and expansive "prisonfare" under a philosophy of moral behaviorism. The paternalist penalization of poverty aims to contain the urban disorders spawned by economic deregulation and to discipline the precarious fractions of the postindustrial working class. Diligent and belligerent programs of "law and order" entailing the enlargement and exaltation of the police, the courts, and the penitentiary have also spread across the First world because they enable political elites to reassert the authority of the state and shore up the deficit of legitimacy officials suffer...(Wacquant, 2010, p. 198)

The U.S. class structure has become more pyramidal and oppressive over recent decades (Massey, 2007, p. xvi). From 1975 to 1996, the poverty rate for American children has increased 33%, making it many times higher than that of other wealthy countries. Upward mobility in the U.S. has declined in every decade since the 1970s.

The class and state domination extends to the subjective psychological elements of this social structure. For example, the Index of Social Health of the United States provides a composite measure of social health or well-being. Based on a scale of 100, it declined from 69.6 in 1973 to 53.2 in 2005, a drop of 23.6% (Wisman & Capehart, 2010, p. 951). The psychological effects of oppression must therefore be a central topic for comprehending concrete cultural psychology.

# The Psychology of Oppression

Conditions of oppression and the psychology of oppression are mutually dependent and reinforcing, just as social conditions and psychology always are. Oppressive conditions limit people's creativity, understanding, and control over their social life. Conversely, oppressed psychology maintains people in a subservient social position and therefore reinforces the oppressive conditions.

Psychology is active subjectivity that embodies macro cultural factors. Subjectivity in an oppressive society actively embodies oppression, and it activates oppressed behavior. Activating oppressed behavior is an oppressive act. Consequently, oppressed psychology is oppressive psychology.

Oppression works from within the psyche, as well as from outside. The mind is an agent of oppression just as much as external cultural factors are. People oppress themselves through their own oppressed subjectivities. This "learned helplessness" is the concrete manifestation of Durkheim's remark that "society cannot constitute itself unless it penetrates individual consciousnesses and fashions them in its image and likeness."

Psychology does cultural work just as institutions, artifacts, and cultural concepts do. "Durable embodied cognitive schemes, acquired by children in class environments, are a principal cause of observed class variation in educational performance" (Nash, 2003, p. 174). In this way, psychology is a macro cultural factor.

---

FIGURE 1. The Cultual Psychology of Oppression

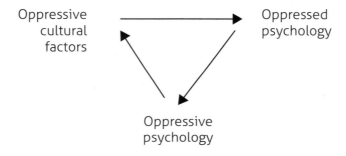

The psychology of oppression is a serious psychological issue that limits people's self-understanding, social understanding, critical faculty, and imagination of substantive alternatives to the status quo. An illustrative example is the manner in which segregation persists in the spontaneous, personal behavior of individuals, long after official segregation has been prohibited. Since discrimination deprives both groups of valuable human relationships with the other group, it is a psychology of oppression that illuminates key aspects of this phenomenon.

## Racial Psychology

Thomas (2005) empirically researched this issue of how high school students promulgate racial segregation in a South Carolina high school. Thomas began with a perspective congruent with macro cultural psychology. She sought to investigate ways in which "race endures through the everyday practices of subjects.... Race is enacted through the symbolic, psychic, and social activities of subjects" (pp. 1233, 1234). She characterized the process in this manner: "This performative process occurs in a social field of power that conditions a subject's practice and agency" (pp. 1233, 1234). Additionally, she stated "Performativity is impelled by the demands of powerful social normativity" (p. 1240). This observation echoes my statement that oppressed psychology is oppressive psychology.

Thomas corrects the conventional theory of performance that construes it as a free act of self-expression (cf. Pred, 1984; Ratner, 2011b, chapter 6 for additional critiques). She echoes Bourdieu's notion of a *habitus* that is a set of creative tendencies which reproduce politically charged macro cultural factors. Agency is cultural agency.

Thomas discovered an important point about the subjects' cultural agency: it was unaware of its cultural basis, characteristics, and function. The subjects misinterpreted their own subjectivity and behavior. They built their subjectivity and behavior as free constructions that expressed their own personal desires. They acted in these ways because "they wanted to," "that is how they felt comfortable." The students did not realize that their desires were culturally conditioned habitus.

The students stated that their school was a happy family where anybody could sit next to anyone they chose during lunch in the cafeteria. In fact, however, seating arrangements—spatiality—were thoroughly segregated. The students perceived this scenario but attributed it to free choice and comfort levels, not to any sociostructural factors such as macro cultural practices and values beyond the lunchroom.

When Thomas directly asked a white girl about the obvious racial segregation of seating arrangements during lunch, she hazily replied, "Blacks usually hang out together, and like whites hang out together, but we...you know." "I don't know, maybe I, maybe that's how they're more comfortable. But it's not like, oh, 'we don't like you' or you know?" (pp. 1237–1238).

Thomas criticizes these self-interpretations as inadequate for failing to comprehend the social structuring of their behavior: "Their words of harmony in the lunchroom, of the ways its segregated space 'doesn't matter' cannot be taken for granted" (p. 1241).

Commenting on one white girl's account, Thomas says, "She establishes her practices of race as nonracist, and even as non-racial, although her spatial practices at lunch produce the space of separation.... She construes herself as a subject who is able to travel across racial boundaries as she chooses" (p. 1238).

A black girl, Bryana, manifested the same lack of understanding as her white classmate: "I really do not understand why black people sit by all the black kids in the cafeteria because that's just something we do" (p. 1239). This is a telling statement about the psychology of oppression; for it reveals that people do not understand the reasons for their own oppressed and oppressive behavior.

Thomas explains this phenomenon:

The students accept and reinforce the social boundaries and produce the differentiations of racial and gendered categories, though they may be confounded by the invisible power that guides their lunchroom spatial practices—and despite the fact that they articulate sense of choice in the matter.... These reincarnations [of racial and gendered categories] remain often unnoticed, unanalyzed, and unapproachable to the subjects themselves. (p. 1241)

Thomas "explores racial boundaries and shows how girls *enforce* racial difference at school despite their idealization of school as a racially mobile space" (p. 1241).

Thomas observes that the subjects "seek to explain the [segregated] spatial practice in their own time and place as their practice. However, as their everyday practice of sitting down in [the] same race groups reproduces the space and continues racial segregation, the girls embody and repeat the norm of segregated seating" (p. 1239).[5]

Given the functional importance of spatial segregation for broader social stratification, This spatiality cannot be imagined as simply a result of girls' agency, nor, despite the girls' language, as a result of their choice and action (for example, as something they 'do'). Girls...come to accept, repeat, and embody racialization by invoking normative racial identities and recreating racial symbolism. (Thomas, 2005, p. 1241, p. 1246)

The agency that students display is cultural agency, not individual agency.

Students enacted racial segregation in areas where they were not directed to do so by immediate external cultural factors. This fact makes it the psychology of oppression. It has become the students' own agency which they then implement as agents of oppression against each other and against themselves. Alexander and Tredoux found the same dynamic in their study of segregation in informal, interpersonal spaces:

Informal spaces are possibly more amenable to segregation simply because individuals are able to choose who they wish to interact with, without concern for official monitoring or sanctions....However, racial divisions in space may emerge even in more formal or structured settings such as a classroom or lecture theatre, provided that individuals are able to exercise a certain degree of choice in their use and occupation of a given space. Haber conducted a study of lecture theatres at a university in the United States and observed that, when given enough seating choice (more than one seat available for every student), dominant (White Anglo-Saxon) and marginal (Blacks and other ethnic minorities) students placed themselves more often on the spatial center and periphery of the classroom, respectively. Their particular locations were not only structured by the differential social status and broader power relations between the two groups, but simultaneously reflected students' understandings of their "proper place" within the classroom setting. Thus, broader social relations and localized spatial configurations may be mutually reinforcing. (2010, p. 370)

Alexander and Tredoux (2010, p. 381) found that seating patterns in South African tutorial classrooms were significantly segregated, even in the absence of pressure to do so by the educational system, per se. In fact, 71% of Black students would have to change seats within classrooms to achieve an integrated seating pattern. "Overall, these findings suggest that the probability of interracial contact occurring in psychology tutorial classrooms is very low."

The same situation exists in elite American universities. Espenshade and Radford demonstrate the myriad threads of class and racial distinctions which permeate admission to elite universities, and campus life within them. They found:

> The odds that black students socialize very often with white students are just 14% of the odds that white students socialize this frequently with other whites.... On average, nonwhite students are 31% as likely to interact socially with white students as whites are to mix and mingle among themselves.... Non black students are just 16% as likely as black students to interact with the blacks.

> Black students have "621% greater odds and white students have 481% higher odds of having social relations with coethnics than with non-coethnics" (Espenshade & Radford (2009, pp. 214, 215). Thus, being together in university does not necessarily generate a coming together to overcome segregation. Taking a course about one's own ethnic group is negatively related to interacting with members of other ethnic groups (ibid., p. 194).

Finally, racial segregation is organized by social class. The higher a student's social class background, the less likely he or she is to have substantial social relations with a student from a different racial or ethnic background. Lower class students are generally just 1 percentage points more likely to interact with a same-race student than with an other-race student, 27 percentage points for working class students, 37 for middle class students, and 43 for upper middle class and 44 percentage points for upper class students. (p. 190)

These findings demonstrate that racism is embedded in children's consciousness and is manifested when their consciousness is given free reign in unregulated, protected, interpersonal interactions. The children themselves promulgate racial segregation in their choices of companions. They did not resist segregation by developing alternative personal meanings. They did not even realize the segregationist character of their subjectivity/agency. Giving individuals reign to express their desires, paradoxically gives reign to predominant *cultural* motives which comprise their *habitus*. Mere co-presence (contact) of groups in a space does not facilitate intercourse because the unrestricted physical space is overlain by social distinctions that divide the space (Erasmus, 2010; Dixon, Tredoux, & Clack, 2005, pp. 404–405.

Alexander and Tredoux (2010, p. 384) said it well:

> The fact that classrooms were significantly segregated in our study at the very first tutorial [with first year students], when students were relatively unfamiliar with both the space and its occupants, provides support for the argument that, even where pre-

established norms do not exist, groups will seek to reestablish and reproduce the prevailing social order through the racialization of space…. Even in desegregated contexts, opportunities for contact may be thwarted by informal practices that reproduce group boundaries.

Thomas and Alexander and Tredoux recognize that, while public universities prohibit discrimination on their premises, unnoticed social relations foster it. Racial segregation throughout society is a macro model that affects students' racial thinking and behavior. The United States today is as racially segregated in housing and neighborhoods as it was before civil rights legislation was passed.

The 1990 census shows that 30% of African Americans lived in neighborhoods which were 90% or more black, while the remaining percentage of African Americans still lived in predominantly black areas. In fact, 62% of African Americans lived in areas that were at least 60% black. While 86% of suburban whites, on the other hand, lived in communities that were less than 1% black.

Housing segregation produces educational segregation in neighborhood schools. In 1997, nationwide, nearly 70% of African American students and 75% of Latino students attended predominantly minority schools. More than one-third of the students in each group were in schools where 90% or more of their classmates are minorities. Meanwhile, the average white student was enrolled in a school where more than eight in 10 of his or her classmates also were white.

Within schools, teachers treat ethnic groups differently despite formal prohibitions against this demeanor (Panofsky, 2003). Teachers of first-grade pupils respond differently to *equivalent* reading errors depending upon whether pupils are white and middle class or black and working class. Children were treated in ways that perpetuated stereotypical psychological (cognitive, emotional, motivational) and interpersonal activities associated with the different classes. In this case, teachers focused on the social aspects of students' responses rather than the technical aspects of their reading competence (which were equivalent). Teachers' response to students' technical reading competence were colored by their social features. Teachers used reading not simply to teach neutral, technical aspects of reading, but as a means to socialize class-appropriate psychological competencies. Psychology becomes a mechanism of social control (Panofsky, 2003, p. 423).

These conditions—along with racial differences in poverty and employment—give children a sense of social differences that carry over into their interpersonal interactions.

In addition, enduring social divisions promote psychological and behavioral differences in the groups (Portes & Vadeboncoeur, 2003), which make interactions difficult in free spaces. Interpersonal relations are not outside culture, but they are deeply embedded within it.

Dixon, Tredoux, Clack, (2005, p. 409) explain:

If the micro-ecology of segregation constitutes a sui generis level of reality, this does not mean that this reality is autonomous from processes operating at other spatial scales. Clearly, the patterning of face-to-face interaction within a given setting is invariably structured by wider political, economic and historical factors.

Massey (2007, p. 7) concurs:

Social relations and day-to-day behaviors at the microsocial level become oriented toward ranked categories, so that decisions about who[m] to befriend, who[m] to help, who[m] to share with, who[m] to live near, who[m] to court, and who[m] to marry are made in ways that assume the existence and importance of asymmetric social categories.

The apparent banality of everyday spatial practices should not disguise their political resonance…. Notwithstanding the official demise of petty apartheid, social relations continue to conform to a supposedly defunct logic of (racial) hierarchy, division and withdrawal (Dixon, Tredoux, & Clack, 2005, pp. 407, 408).

Elucidating "how the endless dialectic between practice and social structure expresses itself locally…clarifies how individual practices of boundary regulation are both enabled by broader systems of segregation and the means whereby such systems are reproduced or transformed" (Dixon, Tredoux, & Clack, 2005, p. 403).

This research indicates that even when individuals are granted a space within culture that is freed from direct pressure to behave in a certain way (e.g., in schools and beaches that do not mandate segregation from other groups), individuals continue to behave in ways that they have learned from broader, distal conditions. The psychology of oppression is so ingrained in consciousness that it cannot readily be repudiated even when given somewhat of a chance.

Contrary to popular thinking, broad, encompassing, difficult to discern (and pin down) macro cultural factors are more influential on psychology than immediate, proximal circumscribed conditions. Direct efforts to alter immediate, proximal situations are less effective than changes to broad macro cultural factors—which are, unfortunately, more difficult to alter. The easier the changes, the less effective they are (Ratner, 1991, p. 287).

## Personal Meanings

Macro cultural psychology acknowledges that within shared cultural meanings necessary for social coherence and for individual participation in culture, individuals also develop personal modulations, or senses, of psychology. Individual students will practice segregation more or less intensely depending upon their backgrounds. Individual Muslims will practice the honor code more or less strictly, as well. These personal modulations are generally slight variations in the cultural norms (Ratner, 2002, p. 93). They do not subvert norms. That is clearly the lesson of the students' interpersonal interactions in school cafeterias. Cultural coherence—and the advantages it offers to people—requires that personal idiosyncracies function within the parameters of macro cultural requirements. Personal idiosyncracies cannot be allowed to subvert this dynamic.

Consequently, the way to transform culture is through developing a new social organization that provides a cultural coherence to individuals.

## Reformulating Psychological Constructs in Accordance with the Psychology of Oppression

The psychology of oppression indicates that social processes that organize psychology may stultify psychology. This dynamic requires that we reconsider concepts such as "zone of proximal development," agency, and activity, as agents of oppression. Psychological constructs must reflect real, concrete, cultural content of psychological phenomena.

It is wrong to accuse macro cultural psychology of overlooking agency in emphasizing macro cultural factors. I have emphasized the active subjectivity of people in conducting honor killings, segregation, and so on. Macro cultural psychology criticizes oppressed and oppressing agency; it does not deny agency. The criticism is meant to enhance genuine agency.

## The Cultural Psychology of Liberation

The psychology of oppression problematizes social reform and psychological improvement, for the psychology of oppression limits people's intellectual and psychological resources that are available to make changes (Lukes, 2005). Consequently, current subjectivity and psychology are not reliable guides to understanding and improving oneself or society at large.

Oppressed people may endorse fascism; lynch Negroes; blame immigrants for social problems; endorse religious mysticism (see Ratner, 2009a for discussion). A troubling example of indigenous people being complicit in their psychology of oppression is a tribal Saudi Arabian woman who recently had her husband arrested because he lifted her veil to see her face. They had been married 35 years, had 6 children, and he had *never* seen his wife's face. She had so internalized the depersonalization of women in her tribal society that she prosecuted her husband for trying to circumvent it. She actively opposed her husband's effort to establish a more personal, sensual relationship.

In his revolutionary work, Mao Zedung worried about the culturally-based backward thinking among the Chinese peasantry with whom he worked for decades. He said: "given the various kinds of deep-rooted feudal relationships in the countryside, it will not be an easy task to raise the class-consciousness of the peasants to the extent that they all realize that, in the end, it will be essential to eliminate the feudal remnants" (cited in Knight, 2007, p. 98).

Wikan (2008, p. 68) emphasizes the relation between oppression and conservative thinking/action: "because the Kurds have been an oppressed and stateless people, the consequence has been that, at home and in exile, they cling to old traditions which include clan mentality and violence against women" (see also Frank, 2005).

When oppressed people take power from their oppressors, as has happened in many African countries, the new social order is often as bad as the old one. Thus, "Fanon hammers away at the inadequacy of national consciousness for it is at the very moment that the victory of colonialism seems to be won that a more serious problem appears—an exploitation that wears a black face" (Gibson, 2005, p. 91; Gibson, 2011).

Because subjectivity has become oppressed, it does not necessarily comprehend itself or society. Subjectivity utilizes cultural concepts to understand itself, and when these mediational means are mystified, they distort people's self-understanding. The students in the segregation studies did not comprehend the significance and origins of their own behavior, nor do most people thoroughly comprehend their own society because they utilize mystified cultural concepts to understand it.

Recent interviews with high school girls in Los Angeles after a racial conflict reveal the sadly limited understanding and suggestions that these participants had (Thomas, 2008, pp. 2869, 2875). A question was put to all of the girls: What do you think the school should do to prevent future violence?

Nane: "They should just tell us every day, like, encouraging words or something. Have more events where we could all, like, get into."

Grisselle: "There shouldn't be fights against race because we're all people, we all have feelings, we all [share] stuff. It's just stupid."

Interviewer: "So why does it happen then? What do you think?"

Grisselle: "I guess the people who are in the fight are not understanding."

Anne: "They just think it's cool, oh, 'we're like fighting,' you know, 'in a riot.'"

Alexis: "So it's just sad how closed minded they are."

Chibi-Kim: "We're all the same [...]. I think it's very stupid."

Zelda: "Why can't they like, set their animosities aside and just like, harmonize."

Chibi-Kim: "Peace."

Thomas (2008) identifies the limited understanding of self and society these statements express: "The girls deny and disavow their own racism and racialization by proclaiming multicultural ideals and highlighting the good and essential sameness of humanity. By articulating so clearly their commitments to multiculturalism, they likewise perform the liberal move of eschewing difference, and even violence, and focusing on individual rights and justice. "A confined focus on the self, I argue, is done at the expense of asking difficult questions of what processes racialized identifications and racist practice entail for the subject, such as how racist practice and resentment might be as heartfelt as peace to subjects." (pp. 2876–2877).

These examples of oppressed/oppressive psychology generate little confidence that social and psychological improvement can spring from ordinary subjectivity. Social and psychological improvement requires an external, objective, scientific perspective that overcomes the limitations of mystified beliefs. (As an American bumper sticker advises: "Don't believe what you think.")

Macro cultural psychology engages in this kind of analysis. It elucidates the political economics of oppression and liberation—i.e., whose interests were instrumental in founding and maintaining cultural and psychological factors; how these interests may form an oppressive social system that runs counter to the real interests and fulfillment of the populace; what the structural mechanisms are that promote exploitation, class society, the psychology of oppression; and what viable alternative social organization of cultural and psychological factors would eliminate these evils. Because the political economy is the dominant, core macro cultural factor that radiates throughout the others to one extent or another, significant social change requires changing the political economic core of society (Ratner, 2009b; Ratner, 2011b , chap. 7).[6]

Macro cultural psychology (consistent with historical materialism, as Vygotsky said)—which maintains that consciousness follows historical developments in macro cultural factors—is not simply an intellectual (scientific) doctrine about consciousness; it is also a political doctrine about the need for political transformation. For the scientific fact that psychology is stunted by deleterious social conditions is also a political fact that people are oppressed by their social system. In addition, the scientific implication that psychological improvement demands humanizing social conditions is also a political implication that the status quo must be politically restructured.

Vygotsky made this argument himself. He says that capitalism impedes psychological fulfillment: "the source of the degradation of the personality [lies] in the capitalist form of manufacturing." Vygotsky links psychological fulfillment to social change. He says the contradictions of capitalist political economy are "being resolved by the socialist revolution....Alongside this process, a change in the human personality and an alteration of man himself must inevitably take place (Vygotsky, 1994, pp. 180, 181).

Vygotsky is proposing an external, objective, social solution to psychological problems. He is not reporting on people's subjective opinion about what should be done.

Macro cultural psychology uses social critique to work on the political level to change macro cultural factors, and also on the personal level to help people understand and circumvent their culture's deleterious psychological and social effects. On the personal level (in schools, in therapy), we would remediate existing forms of agency/consciousness with substantially different *cultural* values and practices drawn from an objective macro cultural psychological analysis. For example, we would suggest to the students who practice segregation that their behavior is far more than personal preference for in-group members. Their behavior stems from and recapitulates racial practices in macro cultural factors. They need to understand these factors and their effects on their psychology and then systematically repudiate these effects and the formative macro cultural factors. They can accomplish this goal on a personal/psychological level, and also on the political level. In this case, we are helping to alter the subjects' consciousness through a social critique. We do not accept their cultural psychology as is. We believe that the students will not significantly change their segregationist psychology/behavior unless they understand its cultural origins and devote attention to critiquing and circumventing them.

When Marx spoke of a working-class perspective as the guide for social change, he was not referring to contemporary outlooks by workers. He was referring to an objective theoretical perspective that had workers' interests at its core. It was a perspective that comprehended the political economic basis of the exploitation of workers and the need for a new socialist political economy that would realize their material and psychological interests. The working class does not have this deep understanding simply by virtue of being oppressed. The working-class perspective is not the perspective of the working class as currently constituted.

# Other Psychological Approaches to Enriching Psychology

Other psychological approaches seek to enrich society and psychology without substantively transforming macro cultural factors and people's cultural consciousness. Three approaches are prominent.

## Agency theory

It is common to extol agency as an intrinsically liberatory aspect of human subjectivity/psychology. A recent example is Skandrani et al.'s (2010) enthusiasm about how "Oppressed populations defended their traditions as a means of resisting French or British colonial power." Algerian women "used the veil as a means to express their agency and subjectivity" (p. 303). "In this interethnic game, Maghrebine migrants eventually appropriated the 'Maghrebine' trait, interiorized it, revalorized it and claimed it as a positive emblem of their identity" (p. 304).

The authors also extol the Indian practice of sati, in which a widow immolates herself on her husband's funeral pyre: "[I]n India, the practice of sati became a symbol of the nationalist and anti-colonial movement, a symbol of resistance against the British colonial power" (p. 304).

The fact that victims of colonialism assert a custom is valorized as active, intentional self-expression, empowerment and resistance to society—even when the custom leads to their death. Simply engaging in action is valorized abstractly without any consideration of its cultural content or even the lethal effects on the practitioner. I identify this point of view as "agency theory."

Veils and head scarves are used in Islam to ensconce women from social participation and personal expression under the myth that veils and scarves hide women from Satan. Before we exalt the wearing veils and scarves by Muslim girls as innovative, transformative agency, we must be sure that they repudiate their oppressive cultural signification and behavioral effects. We would have to be sure that the girls instead use them for personal enhancement during social participation rather than a restriction on their behavior.

However, it is not clear that they acted in this fashion. According to the description, the women identified with indigenous cultural practices and subjectively invested them with the significance of resistance. However, this dynamic may simply be a subjective inversion of significance rather than extirpating the oppressive aspects of the indigenous practices. Indian women, for example, continued to die from the oppressive aspects of their indigenous practice of sati, which makes their subjective inversion of sati from colonialist oppression to resisting colonialism purely illusory.

Stubbornly reclaiming oppression as one's own liberation is a psychology of oppression. This set of behaviors can be seen in all sorts of prideful, self-destructive behaviors. The Saudi woman who defended her depersonalization against her husband's efforts to pierce it is a case in point. Obese women proclaim that "fat is beautiful." Indians living near the Ganges River believe the river is blessed by God, and they throw dead animals and people into it, thus polluting it and sickening people who drink and bathe in it. They resist efforts of "outside experts" who implore them to stop this self-destructive indigenous behavior. Many deaf people identify with their disability and refuse to overcome it by inserting cochlear implants that could significantly expand their fulfillment, e.g., by hearing Mozart's music. Reclaiming and holding debilitating practices as one's own is ethnocentric thinking which refuses to accept the debilitating reality of one's behavior.

It is akin to American consumerism which is financially and psychologically oppressive, but which is adopted by consumers as their own way of feeling happy, attractive, confident, self-expressive, self-fulfilled, and even natural.

Given this mystification, an external, objective analysis of culture and psychology is necessary to disclose the fact that subjective feelings of satisfaction are culturally organized, conformist, and disempowering.

This point is evident in another example from Skandrani et al. (2010). They glorify the ways that Muslim girls in France reconcile sexual mores of Islam with those of France. These girls maintain the letter of the law of virginity while simultaneously engaging in sexual acts other than vaginal intercourse (p. 308). "Rather than passive victims of a rigid norm of virginity, these young women show themselves to be creative agents, capable of appropriating and reinterpreting cultural proscriptions to their own ends" (p. 312). "All of the interviewees used creative and original strategies to defend their position regarding the norm of virginity" (p. 307).

This interpretation overlooks the cultural constraints on the girls' behavior and makes it appear to be a free, personal choice. A macro cultural psychological analysis reveals that the girls' sexuality was buffeted by two contradictory cultures. Their agency simply played off one against the other, undoubtedly at great psychological cost. (It is not easy to satisfy two different masters.) The girls applied French sexual norms to find loopholes in Islamic law. While this approach requires some dexterity, it hardly qualifies as a creative, original strategy, or social reform.[7]

In fact, their sexual compromise leaves them subservient to an irrational, autocratic, oppressive religious sexual prohibition against intercourse. This hypocritical practice should be renounced entirely and not be used as an anchor that must be appeased through compromise. Their compromise neither liberates them (psychologically or sexually) nor transforms their oppressive culture. The girls' agency is limited to working within the systems.

"Agency theory" decontextualizes agency from its cultural origins, characteristics, and function. This scientific distortion is based on fallacious individualistic politics that seeks to free the individual from social pressures rather than transform the pressures.

However, pretending that oppressed people are liberated compounds their oppression because it overlooks behavior, psychology, and macro cultural factors that truncate agency, and which must be changed in order to achieve true creativity, liberation, and social change.

Psychological enrichment requires keen societal awareness of the political origins and consequences of customs. It also requires political activity that challenges the macro cultural constituents of psychology and replaces them with humanized macro cultural factors, as Vygotsky insisted.

From this interpretation, it follows that personal growth and social change both require dispelling the myth that agency is an individual phenomenon that produces social and personal change on the micro, mundane, and individual levels. Dispelling individual agency does not negate agency, per se; it dispels truncated, alienated agency that is confined to operating within the status quo and is oblivious to real social and psychological transformation necessary for genuine agency. In other words, dispelling personal, subjective agency actually enhances agency by acknowledging and improving its cultural constituents. As Adorno (2006, p. 203) put it, "we must abandon the illusion that freedom is a reality so as to salvage the possibility that freedom might one day become a reality after all."[8]

Macro cultural psychology speaks to the level of analysis that is necessary to enrich psychology and society. Individuals and small groups certainly initiate this enrichment. However, in order to effectively enrich psychology and society, the pioneers of social change need to be cognizant of macro cultural factors and challenge their concrete social organization.

Indigenous people can utilize this perspective as a general guide for analyzing their particular conditions; they may also refine the general theory and methodology. However, indigenous ideas and practices are too limited (despite their good intentions) to displace the general theory and methodology of macro cultural psychology.

## Labeling Theory

One form of the foregoing liberation psychology is known as labeling theory. It argues that oppression consists of a dominant power labeling subaltern culture and psychology as deficient. If the labels were removed, then subaltern people would be recognized as capable.

While it is true that the dominant class does stigmatize subaltern groups, it also rules by materially and psychologically oppressing lower classes. Oppression is real, and it is not merely symbolic and linguistic.

Oppression does not end by removing pejorative labels and recognizing the true capability of oppressed people. Labeling theory minimizes oppression by converting it into a linguistic phenomenon or an attitude.

Labeling theory romanticizes oppressed people by insisting that they are capable despite their oppression. The solution is to accept them as they are. But, since people are truly oppressed, their cultures and psychology are oppressed and oppressing. Oppressed culture and psychology are obstacles to liberation which must be overcome, not idealized.

## Diversity

Labeling theory is an element in the philosophy of diversity. Diversity insists that ethnic groups be respected because their distinctive customs broaden the aggregate experiences of a society. The quantitative breadth of experience is deemed to be beneficial, and this understanding requires respecting different customs. Stigmatizing a group denies the value of its distinctive customs and reduces the breadth of social customs.

Diversity is an abstraction. It privileges the number of customs over their content. Multiculturalists do not critically examine the politics behind cultural customs. For instance, they do not examine the autocratic leadership structure of the Catholic Church, which is not elected by church members. They do not examine the system of slavery that was practiced in Tibetan Buddhist temples under the rule of the Dali Lama, nor do multiculturalists critique devout religiosity that subjects people to autocratic, oppressive, mythical, irrational, mystifying religious dogma. Multiculturalists treat cultural practices as quaint, unique customs divorced from their institutional, structural base and from their political content. Oppressive, irrational, mystifying customs are encouraged and accommodated, as in the case of Muslim girls wearing hoods and scarves, and fundamentalist Christian girls wearing skirts and not pants, and the belief that Jesus is watching your behavior, and the belief that your current status in life reincarnates your behavior in a previous life. Religious prohibitions against sex education, sexual activity, birth control, and abortion are also happily accepted as interesting, diverse perspectives that can teach us about the world (the only exception being physical mutilation).

Identifying a practice as cultural, spiritual, or religious commands respect for it and exempts it from evaluation: "How dare you question a person's deeply held spiritual belief that gives meaning to her world?" Critical evaluation is denounced as intolerant.[9] Skandrani et al. (p. 304) make this claim. In this way, "culturalism" and multiculturalism may obscure oppression and implicitly condone it. What begins as abstract acceptance of behavior in general winds up accepting concrete cultural forms that are often oppressive.

If existing forms of agency are acceptable, then there is no need for social reform. Society must already be positive in allowing ethnic agency to flourish. Applauding extant subjectivity is conservative politics because it (implicitly) applauds the status quo that generates it. The focus is on enabling marginalized people to express their voice (which presumes they already have one), not on transforming conditions to give people a voice in controlling their society.

Diversity theory also militates against social critique and transformation in the way it treats the psychology of out-group people. Diversity theory suggests that out-group individuals become more tolerant or accepting of in-group behavior. Prejudice and intolerance are chastised. However, no change in social structure or political economy is proposed to stimulate and support this kind of psychological change. Multiculturalists only press for increased opportunities for social contact in the belief that mere contact will foster tolerance and cooperation. Providing opportunities for contact in classrooms, workplaces, and beaches, e.g., through civil rights legislation, does not touch the political-economic principles that structure social relations. There is no suggestion of new, cooperative ownership of property, cooperative management of institutions and distribution of wealth that would overcome these principles and facilitate concrete cooperation among groups, increase the opportunities of minorities, and foster tolerance among dominant cultural groups. When concrete cultural contexts and forms of behavior/psychology are reorganized along specifically cooperative lines, social cooperation is successfully achieved, as Sherif et al. 1954/1988 experimentally demonstrated.

Diversity expands the ethnic composition of the social hierarchy, but it does not alter the structure and principles of the hierarchy. Diversity allows marginalized people to join upper echelons of society, but it does not alter the pyramidal structure in which a few wealthy, powerful individuals dominate the populace. Diversity diversifies the participants in the system without changing the system. Thomas (2008) terms this "banal multiculturalism."

Multiculturalism rests on the false belief that individuals change systems through their individual qualities; no direct change in the principles that govern the system is indicated. Even so, we know after decades of civil rights legislation that changing the gender and ethnicity of social participants does not change the system. The presence of Obama, Condoleezza Rice, Margaret Thatcher, Hillary Clinton, Alberto Gonzalez, Imelda Marcos, and Clarence Thomas in positions of governmental leadership has left the pyramidal, exploitive social structure of capitalism intact.

Michaels (2006) explains another reason why multiculturalism cannot generate substantive social equality among ethnic groups or social classes: it focuses on cultural issues such as prejudicial attitudes and ignores political economic change: "If we can stop thinking of the poor as people who have too little money and start thinking of them instead as people who have too little respect, then it's our attitude toward the poor, not their poverty, that becomes the problem to be solved. [Then,] we think of inequalities as a consequence of our prejudices rather than as a consequence of our social system, and [we] thus turn the project of creating a more egalitarian society into the project of getting people to stop being racist, sexist, homophobes" (p. 19). "You're a victim not because you're poor but because people aren't nice to you because you're poor" (p. 106). This leads to attacking people's attitudes toward oppressed people rather than attacking the conditions that cause the oppression.

For instance, while cultural diversity is increasing at elite universities, of the 146 "selective" universities, 3% of students come from the lowest socioeconomic quarter of American society while 74% come from the highest. You are 25 times more likely to run into a rich student than a poor student" (ibid. pp. 95–96). Thus, diversity is window dressing on the homogeneity of social class (Melamed, 2006).

This dynamic is illustrated in the cultural treatment of domestic violence. It emphasizes the gender dimension—males abusing females—while obscuring the class dimension. Domestic violence is said to be a male-female problem that exists in all classes. While domestic violence does technically exist in all classes, it is greatly overrepresented in the lower class, by a factor of seven times. "We take a problem that significantly involves people's economic status and pretend instead that it's a problem about the relations between the sexes" (Michaels, 2006, pp. 117–119). This understanding exempts political economic class from criticism. Moreover, since class is a more powerful cause of domestic violence (and all social psychological problems) than gender (and ethnicity), obscuring class leaves domestic violence (and all social psychological problems) irresolvable.

The discipline of sociology recapitulates this ignoring and obfuscating of class and capitalism: "Although stratification is arguably the subject area of greatest interest to sociologists, the American Sociological Association does not have a section on the sociology of stratification. What the association does have are sections on the sociology of sex and gender, Asians and Asian Americans, Latinos and Latinas, and racial and ethnic minorities, and one section devoted specifically to the interaction of race, gender, and class" (Massey, 2007, p. 37).

Michaels shows how culture does not simply displace social class, but also how it converts it into a cultural category which prevents recognizing it as a political phenomenon (Michaels, 2006, p. 172). "When the problem is inequality, the solution is identity" (p. 161). "The debate about inequality becomes a debate instead about prejudice and respect" (p. 173). In fact, about half of poor people are white, so poverty is not a matter of discrimination but rather of cruel economic forces (p. 172).

Diversity impedes solving the problem of inequality, segregation, and prejudice; criticizing the obstacle facilitates solving the problem.

# Conclusion

Because psychology is formed by macro cultural factors that are the cornerstones of society, it follows that psychological and social enrichment requires a transformation of macro cultural factors. This understanding reflects the unique political thrust of macro cultural psychology. Social psychological transformation entails a social critique that takes full account of its concrete nature and the viable possibilities of change. Social critique cannot emanate from acultural abstract psychological principles such as agency, tolerance, communication, self-expression, nor can immanent social critique emanate from abstract social principles such as "justice," "peace," "tolerance" and "human rights" (McIntyre, 2008). Extra-cultural abstractions are uninformed by concrete macro cultural factors and cannot generate concrete, viable alternatives that avoid concrete impediments to them.

As I explain in Ratner (2011a), the battle for the concrete is the foremost intellectual and political struggle of our time.

## NOTES

1　Durkheim (1914/2005, pp. 37, 41) also said that social existence and social consciousness are contradictory to innate, natural, individual processes. "We cannot give ourselves over to moral ends without unsettling the instincts and inclinations that are the most deeply rooted in our body." "Our activity displays two altogether opposite characteristics depending upon whether it is under the sway of sensory or rational motives." Vygotsky made the same important distinction between natural, lower behavioral mechanisms and higher, social, conscious mechanisms. However, where Vygotsky resolved the contradiction by subordinating natural to social mechanisms, Durkheim felt the contradiction is unresolvable and constantly buffets and torments human beings.

2　Honor killings are generally supported by the entire family including mother and sisters. Honor killings can also be committed on males who seduce women.

3　Portraying cultural factors and psychology as independent and dependent variables, respectively, misrepresents the relationship. It presumes that culture pre-exists psychology and generates it as a by-product. It presumes that psychology is outside of cultural factors and is "influenced" by them in a secondary manner.

4　Thus, there is nothing unfathomable or "inhuman" about honor killings, or the psychology of evil in general. Its commonality testifies to its normalcy. Assuming that the psychology of evil is peculiar and violates human nature, it is erroneous to assume that human nature has a natural beneficient content that requires some abnormal countervailing influence.

Recent research by Wendy Lower reveals that German women actively perpetrated the Holocaust; they were not insulated by any natural feminine nurturing tendencies. Women constituted about 5,000 of the extermination camp guards. Furthermore, "in many cases where genocide was taking place, German women were very close by. Several witnesses have described festive banquets near mass shooting sites in the Ukrainian forests, with German women providing refreshments for the shooting squads whose work often went on for days." In the occupied territories, "Women ran the storehouses of belongings taken from Jews" (*New York Times*, July 18, 2010).

5 Massey (2007, pp. 19, 195) explains the importance of spatial segregation for social stratification: "Spatial segregation renders stratification easy, convenient, and efficient because by investing or disinvesting in a place, one can invest or disinvest in a whole set of people." "Throughout history, therefore, whenever the powerful have sought to stigmatize and subordinate a particular social group, they have endeavored to confine its members to specific neighborhoods...." "As the U.S. polarized economically during the last third of the 20th century, it also polarized spatially [poor people concentrated in neighborhoods with other poor people, while rich people lived in physical concentration with other rich people]. As poverty became more concentrated spatially, of course, so did everything associated with it: crime, violence, disorder, substance abuse, welfare dependency, poor health, and lagging educational achievement....The end result was the emergence of a new geography of inequality—a categorical segmentation of America's social geography that gave rise to a new set of self-reinforcing political, education, social, economic, and cultural mechanisms that hardened the lines of class stratification and deepened inequality in the United States."

6 Macro cultural psychology recoils from punishing deficient individuals. Punishment implies that individuals, not society, are responsible for misdeeds, when, in fact, oppressed people are not the authors of their own behavior. Personal responsibility is an inappropriate term in oppressive societies. It falsely attributes power to people who do not have it. Punishment is political in sustaining a benevolent or neutral view of society. Punishment thus embodies and promotes a theory of behavior and society.

7 Skandrani et al. briefly acknowledge this phenomenon: "Their religiosity is a more individual experience than that of their parents, which was strongly buttressed by a community of believers. Moreover, this association of religious practice with the private realm represents an adaptation to secular principles and calls for individuation fostered by the French society" (p. 307). It is the norms of French society that have generated the girls' subversion of Islamic codes; their resistance was not an original, inventive act that liberated them from social pressures. However, the authors do not integrate this observation into their theory of agency.

8 Conservative defenders of the status quo are the most avid advocates of individualism because it supports the social pyramid. If individualism truly enabled people to alter their class position and join the ruling class in controlling resources and social life, the ruling class would never support individualism. Conservative politicians and businessmen know that as people are thrown onto their "own" resources, the influence of social class organizes their behavior. The best way to ensure class hierarchy is to call for individual resourcefulness, responsibility, and choice—and to oppose public support systems that could more equally distribute resources in ways that would truly overcome the class hierarchy.

Individualism is thus the most mystifying ideology that has ever been invented. No other ideology has so completely disguised social determinism as freedom.

9 Many cultural psychologists reject macro cultural psychology's objective, concrete macro cultural analysis. They feel it imposes external, expert analysis on oppressed people and it prevents people from collectively figuring out their own solutions. However, this objection is as faulty as denouncing medical science because it was not invented by "the people."

It is more humane to provide people with useful scientific information that can enrich their lives than it is to encourage them to "dialogue together" to find their own solutions that may not be adequate. It is more humane for a few scientists to teach people how to treat their water than it is for a multitude of people to come up with some popular, unscientific solution. Similarly, it is more humane for macro cultural psychologists to use a scientific analysis to teach people how to reorganize specific macro cultural factors in ways that will provide for viable, democratic social organization than it is for people to spontaneously dialogue and fail to reach this conclusion (as was the case with students in research presented earlier). Individualistic, liberal cultural psychologists privilege the interpersonal process of discovery over scientific, structural results. However, viable structural end-points provide the extensive and enduring framework that people need for improving their lives.

*[handwritten annotation, top margin:]* cultural tools = internet, SES, books, race, skin color etc.

# · 6 ·

# Vygotsky's Significance in Advancing Counseling and Psychotherapy

*Pedro R. Portes*

> As a general rule, one could say that the further a syndrome stands…from the primary cause, from the handicap itself, the easier it will be to eliminate it by psychotherapeutic and curative-educational means, all other things being equal (Vygotsky, 1993b, pp. 269–270).

*[handwritten annotation:]* CHT = → How culture shapes your mind ↳ speaks about the "tools" you have-gained from your "culture"

This chapter acquaints readers interested in how cultural-historical theory is connected to counseling and mental health applied areas of psychology and how it can advance the practices as well as theory. Cultural-historical theory (CHT) has received minimal attention in mainstream mental health disciplines in psychology relative to other fields such as developmental and educational psychology. However, because counseling and psychotherapy are essentially educational activities, some of the work concerning the application of essential concepts in the model has already been initiated (Katz & Hadas, 1995; Kozulin, 1990b;

*[handwritten annotation, bottom margin:]* Dialectical Theory? · inspired by Vygotsky

Miltenburg & Singer, 1999; Portes, 1993; Ryle, 1991; Wilson & Weinstein, 1990). Counseling and psychotherapy are specific types of educational activities that have emerged in many parts of the world mostly through institutionalized, formal, cultural practices. Counseling and therapy essentially represent re-mediational practices that, as a rule, aim to socialize the client anew, particularly when other socialization practices have failed or when stressful events overwhelm the individual. Re-mediation can and does take place ordinarily at both individual and group levels (Katz & Hadas, 1995). The client may learn new ways to remediate or alter external conditions as well. At the individual level, self-help books and practices, as well as sessions with experts, form part of what is essentially mediated learning (Karpov & Haywood, 1998) involving advanced helpers, others, activities, and tools. However, efforts to extend CHT holistically in this area have been limited in terms of scope, populations, and foci (e.g., Green, Kern, Blaff, & Mintz, 2000; Redlich, Hadas-Lidor, Weiss, & Amirav, 2010).

## Cultural-Historical Theory and Mental Health

(Developmental)

From a historical standpoint, mental health counseling or psychotherapy was not a direct concern for Vygotsky, Luria, and CHT as a whole (Vygotsky, 1978). This is quite understandable for a number of reasons. Counseling, as a cultural practice, had not been well established in the West except for psychodynamic theories during the early part of the century. Luria's pioneering work in medicine with head injury and psychotic patients, and Vygotsky's analysis of thought in schizophrenic adolescents focused mainly on the relation between the regulatory functions of language, inner speech, and cerebral organization of verbal structures and comprehension. This work was significant, yet far removed from the secondary intervention focus associated with more formal, institutionalized practices in counseling or clinical psychology as they have evolved in developed Western nations. In the first half of the last century, the counseling profession, as it exists today, was only beginning to emerge from practices based on psychodynamic models and behaviorism. As noted elsewhere in this volume, CHT originated in a Soviet context that took a much different course under different political and economic conditions (cf. Gonzalez-Rey, 2011).

In the early 1920s Luria, and to a lesser extent, Vygotsky, had a strong interest initially in psychodynamic theory (Valsiner & Van der Veer, 1993; Wertsch, 1990), but both became disillusioned with its adequacy as a general model for the emerging discipline of psychology. This was not because of its inadequacy in dealing with mental health problems specifically, but rather because it did not present a unified model for the scientific study of the mind that would meld both positivist and interpretative-subjective dimensions of human consciousness. It was concern for the latter that later led them to establish the cultural-historical school in response to a deeper crisis in psychology as a discipline (Cahan & White, 1992). This crisis has prevailed in Western psychology, long after psychodynamic and behavioral theories moved away from the core of the discipline of psychology in the U.S. and other parts of the world. Even today, this crisis has not been resolved and the CHT's quest for a unified discipline remains fragmented in three major directions; first, those who follow what may be termed the External/Society→Mind orientation once critiqued by Fodor (1972) such as the materialistic aspects of activity theory or macropsychological lens (Kozulin, 1998; Ratner, 2011a/2011b); second, those who interpret Vygotsky as leaning mostly in the other (idealistic) direction mainly in terms of subjectivity with interpretative, qualitative methods mostly reflected in the literature, including some chapters in this volume; and third, various others focused primarily on cognitive, critical theory or deconstruction aspects that generally lack a deeper understanding of the CHT quest for synthesizing mainstream objective and interpretative models within cultural psychology (Cole, 1996; Portes, 1996).

## Different CHT Foci and Goals

The cultural-historical theory model requires not only attention to the means though which the client can be helped to change or develop, as in the case of acquiring new problem-solving skills, new affective-cognitive perspectives and actions. CHT encompasses questions that concern ontogenesis, microgenesis, sociogenesis; and phylogenesis (see Kozulin, 1990a; Wertsch, 1990), that are most relevant to the counseling and clinical fields. It also requires attention to the affective relations between the client and others, including the therapist, in the larger cultural context that often defines mental health and learning problems. CHT attends to the roles of the therapist and of particular institutions from various perspectives in an open-ended manner as opposed to a reductive one to serve a particular purpose. The *means* through which an individual acts and adapts are central issues for counseling that this model examines in terms of past and present patterns of mediation both in and outside of the brain. Vygotsky's and Luria's model attempted to integrate affective and cognitive learning experiences as they are mediated culturally and, in turn, influence development in semiotic fashion.

CHT is not the same as activity theory (AT), nor is AT the heir of CHT. The paradigm remains open as a cultural psychology (Cole, 1996), one that is different and broader than what might be regarded as the dominant scientific psychology that remains fragmented within the APA, or other associations still framing the discipline, mental health problems, and units of analyses in the individual's mind. While the semiotic connections among the major intersecting lines of developmental analysis (Portes & Vadeboncoeur, 2003) are regarded as essential in CHT for understanding the mind or psyche, many new Vygotskyan-inspired models appear to lean exclusively on either the objective or interpretative side. Some of the more interpretative, sociocultural work based on this broad paradigm ignores that CHT pioneers employed scientific experimental methods. CHT thus cannot be defined or restricted solely by activity-based, metacognitive, participatory, research models or by Marxist or deconstruction/postmodern-oriented interpretations. For CHT, any advancement in the application of the model at the individual level (as with a purposive application orientation in counseling/psychotherapy) would have to simultaneously consider the very practices and roles of other minds or tools available in the larger societal context. This is an unfamiliar practice in counseling since psychopathology has ordinarily been situated in "the head" of the client, as has been the case with other traits and (dis)abilities.[1]

In cultural-historical theory, the unit of analysis cannot be reduced simply to heredity, behavior, thought, or the environment. Rather, it is the person acting, feeling, and thinking with cultural tools, who, in interacting with his or her environment and heredity, can develop beyond them without being totally constrained by them. This non-dominant psychology also has implications for both dominant and non-dominant parts of society, i.e., from multiple perspectives based on lived experiences over time. The reduction or extent to which the study of the human mind shall be confined is arbitrary, of course, and is at this moment being forged in particular contexts by different communities. In this model, what a person chooses to do with a given set of socially and biologically influenced conditions matters and defines agency. Even so, CHT does not only consider the development and constitution of mind as it reflects the interaction of subjective and objective conditions related to individual adjustment but also of mediation in a reciprocal sense. Whether in the classroom or the counseling office, teaching and learning involve two or more planes (teacher/counselor and student/client) and their histories in terms of that holistic unit of analysis that houses affective-cognitive and purposive/motivation interrelated lived experiences. In contrast to CHT, counseling and psychotherapy today view these as different domains co-existing and brought together in the psyche *somehow*. For CHT the domains cannot be compartmentalized, studied, treated, or evaluated separately from each other as we see with affective or eating disorders diagnoses.

Efforts to understand the social construction of psychopathology or various disorders from a psycho-social standpoint (e.g., Erikson, 1968; Goffman, 1961) have been noted since CHT entered in the field. However, these models have served mainly for organizing critical observations of cultural practices without directly becoming part of counseling within a unified framework. This is not to say that CHT offers a particular way to accomplish this goal, given how it is situated at present as a loose federation of developers and followers of particular persuasions. In sum, what many of us have referred to loosely as a CHAT approach that combines CHY with AT into one is, after a close examination, not internally consistent *theory* but rather a convenient identity for some in this community.

The acronym CHAT originated in the United States as some of us founded the cultural-historical research Special Interest Group (SIG) at the American Educational Research Association meetings as a counterpart to European-based colleagues' ISCAR/ISCRAT meetings and organizations where AT may have appeared as the best CHT extension for a time to some in these groups. One might understand why CHT, shrouded for years and complex in its simultaneous interpretative and objective approach, failed to be considered in modern counseling and clinical fields already influenced by psychodynamic, Gestalt/cognitive, behavioristic and existential paradigms. Cultural-historical theory thus cannot be reduced simply, as some have, to deconstructing other models and practices. In effect, CHT *is* a special tool with which to understand the development of human consciousness.

## Mediation of Development Through Language and Other Tools

To the extent that psychological adjustment is influenced by cognitive-affective experiences and development, one sees that the mind the client brings to therapy has been constructed largely through the lived co-experiences situated in the micro and macro culture through words, evaluations, and other cultural signs and means. The emergence of language as a way of mediating experience is one of the most critical areas for further study in counseling. The way language is employed in a given setting and how it mediates development is relevant to understanding "psychopathology" or disorders developmentally in terms of how different psychological functions emerge or fail to develop. This point is relevant to some of the techniques currently found in the field such as neuro-linguistic programming, brief solution, reality or rational-emotive, behavior or chemotherapies. CHT would seem critical for counselors who strive to understand how communication experiences and processes shape the mind's higher psychological functions. This dynamic is particularly important as it applies to the counseling process where much of the re-socialization efforts are generally attempted via verbal communication and modeling. The "talking cure" directly impacts regulation of thought, behavior, internalization, and socio-emotional learning and motivation.

Why then is it so difficult to obtain meaningful change in the client? Why is the "talking cure" so evanescent? From a CHT view, it is not just insight by the client that leads to change. When permanent change occurs, several important concepts might require attention; the zone of proximal development, the first law of cultural development, development of complex functional systems, and the double stimulation method. Unfortunately, a full discussion of these and related dimensions of this model remains outside the scope of this chapter.

## CHT Premises

A semiotic relationship exists between mind and culture that is generally overlooked by models that presume culture to be either a constant in the individual or an external factor that like gender or ethnicity must be controlled. The lack of continuity in the types and use of meanings and mental tools found in the counseling context is characteristic of some clients' adjustment problems. Clearly, a mismatch between a client's set of meanings and that of others is related to subsequent motivational, affective, and behavioral difficulties.

Cultural-historical theory addresses developmentally (historically) many of the ways through which environmental processes influence cognition, learning, and behavior. It distinguishes the natural from the cultural line of development as well as the learning of natural "spontaneous" and scientific concepts (Vygotsky, 1978). The development of executive processes, voluntary attention, and cognitive skills appears largely structured by external, inter-psychological relations, communication, and routines in culture. The person's maturing cognitive structure and culture regulate reasoning, and affective growth interacts with social-interactive processes. The implications here are most helpful in understanding how culture forms the higher functions of mind. The model attends to both between group and within group analysis of differences in values, attitudes, mental health, and intellectual ability and thus, is by design culturally and developmentally sensitive. It addresses social formation of institutional and professional definitions and identities that may be arbitrary and situated in particular contexts.

Cultural processes and communication patterns influence the transition from simple to complex functions through speech and other symbolic means and semiotic devices. They influence the type as well as the timing of such psychological processes. The term *cultural* in this model is often misunderstood and refers to (psychological) tools or other means that mediate development and behavior. One implication from the model is that maladjustment often leads to the development of "different" meanings and adaptation schemas that, in turn, are likely to affect the person's potential for change or development. These differences sometimes occur in areas related to social norms and mores that can vary greatly in diverse societies.

## Understanding CHT in Psychotherapy in a Historical Context

Although earlier during the development of this approach efforts were made to integrate it with psychoanalytic theory, by the late 1920s both Luria and Vygotsky had abandoned the monism inherent in psychoanalysis as a theoretical system in favor of a more comprehensive approach that would consider socio-cultural factors more directly. While various threads have evolved in other fields since that time (mainly in education and developmental psychology), implications for a cultural-historical approach have been rather scarce in counseling and psychotherapy for reasons examined further in this chapter.

Vygotsky's search for a unified theory was influenced by Adler, Kretschmer, Jaspers, and Freud (see Valsiner & Van der Veer, 1992). Luria had been an enthusiastic follower of Freud until several critiques (see Van der Veer & Valsiner, 1993; Wertsch, 1990) led him to also reject the psychodynamic model altogether. Both founders of cultural-historical theory were not directly concerned about causes and cures for psychopathology generally in a post-revolutionary social context where psychotherapy clashed with Marxism-Leninism. Their search or focus was for developing a unified theory of mind, which would provide a broad foundation for various subdisciplines such as education, social development, or special education, and in this chapter, perhaps for counseling and clinical psychology. In retrospect, psychology's subdisciplines evolved without a unified framework, a reality that explains today's fragmented landscape. For example, counseling in the United States has always had a focus on career development while clinical psychology operates in the shadow of the biologically grounded psychiatric community that is focused on psychopathology and follows a medical model. School psychology is heavily influenced by the latter, and test and measurements based on a brass and experimental approach to a *scientific* a.k.a. objective psychology. Unlike the physical sciences, however, psychology has a different *subject* of study and requires a different approach that demands the inclusion of subjectivity. Vygotsky's student L. Bozovich remains relevant if for no other reason than clarifying how activity theory falls short and how the troika myth may be but another social construction (see Arias, chapter 3 in this volume; Gonzalez-Rey, chapter 2 in this volume). As with the psychodynamic approach where Freud and Adler were the cofounders and a student, Jung, the student of that threesome in psychodynamic theory, in CHT we have Luria and Vygotsky as founders, with Leontiev as a key student, that in this volume, we come to find out was a peer of Elkonin, Bozovich, Galperin, and others in that generation of Soviet psychology.

Cultural-historical theory offers a paradigm that is multi-level and complex, and thus might be regarded as a *metaparadigm* relative to other forces in the field, such as cognitive-behavioral, psychodynamic, existential, humanistic or other models. Development is constantly being extended by human agency reciprocally within the contexts of sociogenesis and perhaps with phylogenesis as we evolve a head taller or more sedentary in the new century. Notwithstanding, this legacy is reconsidered here in the broader context of writings found in earlier decades (see Cole, 1996; Kozulin et al., 2003; Moll, 1990; Van der Veer & Valsiner, 1994, Wertsch, 2008, and others.

CHT's potential is already evident in both interpretative areas as well as in cognitive/educational sciences and related disciplines, such as special education (Kozulin, 1990a; Feuerstein & Feuerstein, 1991; Feuerstein, Falik, & Feuerstein, 1998), and developmental (Valsiner, 1987), and educational (Portes, 1996) psychology. Only recently, have there been several writings that attempt to link Vygotsky's work to mental health that vary considerably in interpretation and application. Some stem from the psychoanalytic thread (Green et al., 2000; Kozulin, chapter 4 in this volume; Leiman, 1992; Ryle, 1991) and others (Dreier, 1997; Miltenburg & Singer, 1999).

## Insights from Abandoning the Psychoanalytic Framework

In the early 1920s, both Luria and Vygotsky still believed that psychodynamic theory provided a valid framework for psychology. In the case of Luria, the influence of Freud was more intense (see Luria, 1925/1978) initially, although later its rejection was much greater than that found in Vygotsky's writings (Valsiner & Van der Veer, 1992). Both appeared to endorse psychoanalysis initially as a great advance as reflected in their introduction to Freud's publication, *Beyond the Pleasure Principle*. By 1926, psychoanalysis was no longer regarded in the Soviet Union as sufficiently materialistic, and as some critics noted, it suffered actually from the problematic idealism associated with Trotsky that was viewed as inconsistent with efforts to forge a truly Marxist psychology (see Newman & Holzman, 1993). Freud's model for a discipline of psychology was repudiated after critiques from Bakhtin, Jurinets, and Vygotsky himself, although Vygotsky respected the originality and heuristic value of Freud's work in advancing the cause for a more scientific psychology (Van der Veer & Valsiner, 1993).

Why Vygotsky disagreed with Luria and others' early, enthusiastic effort to integrate Marxism and psychoanalysis appears due to Adler's influence. From Vygotsky's perspective, Freud probably would not have agreed that his system was monistic, not that he followed historical materialism as some contended at that time. Vygotsky felt such efforts to marry the two models were filled with distortions and that psychoanalytic theory was much closer to a conglomeration of insights, beliefs, and facts than a complete model (Van der Veer & Valsiner, 1993). Vygotsky's analysis and critique of psychoanalysis must be understood, thus, in context of his search for a general, unified psychological science that went beyond the positivist and idealistic limitations and which would remain *empirical, scientific* and anchored in *praxis*. In spite of appreciating the analysis of various areas and principles (e.g., pleasure, death) he felt that a number of premises, such as pansexualism and the blanket explanation of form and content according to primordial drives to the exclusion of social factors compromised the model. He felt Freud's focus on the biological or phylogenic line tended to exclude attention to the socio-genetic line of development. Nevertheless, he did not condemn psychoanalysis entirely and focused positively on some of its contributions to psychology as it strove to become a more complete science. He considered Freud's work on the unconscious reaches of the mind highly creative.

Many of the fundamental problems and issues in psychology today were anticipated by Vygotsky's search for a causal, objective psychology that would evolve from social practices, applications, and their scientific study (Cahan & White, 1992). Interestingly enough, among the areas that lend themselves most directly to practices guided by theory are (special) education and psychotherapy. Since practice is the most exacting test of theory, Vygotsky argued that the traditional theory-down-to-practice order should be changed recursively where practice routinely informs the development of theory. As Van der Veer and Valsiner (1994) note, for Vygotsky:

> The growth of branches of applied psychology, such as psychotherapy, paedology (including intelligence testing), and educational counseling, forced researchers to be explicit in their assumptions and to re-examine their theoretical concepts. It was against this background of rapid social reforms and the need for scientists to contribute to these reforms, that Vygotsky agreed with those who consider practice to be the Supreme Court, the ultimate judge of truth. (p. 150)

# Alfred Adler

An underestimated important influence in Vygotsky's thinking is found in Adler's theory (see Ansbacher & Ansbacher, 1964) that focused on individual action and social *motives*. His views on the purposiveness of behavior and his ideas about compensation appear to have influenced Vygotsky's work in defectology and in general. Adler believed that behavior is goal directed and understanding. Thus, the future course of behavior allows for a prospective or historical approach in the study of mind. In a way, one might even link the metaphor of the zone of proximal development to developmental/historical analysis, which is now becoming integrated in the mainstream of psychology. This functional, goal-directed point of view allowed for a more sophisticated understanding of how individuals negotiate the complexities found in a future full of options, contradictions, and possibilities. Adler's own thinking about human behavior appears to have been influenced by both philosophy and fiction (art) as was the case for Vygotsky. Among his favorite authors were Goethe, Shakespeare, Marx, Dostoevsky, Arthur Conan Doyle, and Edgar Allan Poe. They contributed in varied ways to the investigation of basic principles underlying behavior that included both unconscious and social motives. Whereas Adler focused on encouragement to influence the individual's development, Vygotsky stressed later the idea of mediation in relation to that of compensation and what the editors of this volume refer to as counteraction (Portes & Salas, 2010).

Adler believed that all psychological phenomena can be related to the preparation for some future goal which is generally social in nature, that of reaching a superior or advantageous position in life relative to others. The feeling of inferiority, on the other hand, represents a basic principle for motivation, which is of particular importance for children who wish to become adults, or children and adults with physical or psychological challenges. Vygotsky and Adler agreed most in theory and advocating an open system where problems or treatments in one area might reconfigure the structure of the psyche and allow for compensation in functioning in another area (Vygotsky, 1993a). Vygotsky stressed the vital need for developing new means and approaches for those with "defects" or mental problems in order to adapt socially. His attention to the role of the social context often imposed on institutionalized persons anticipated changes in the field by more than half a century. Ironically, cultural historical differences such as those concerning schooled versus less schooled groups (Uzbeks in the 1920s) could be understood along similar lines to the social treatment given to those served by special education or by most high-poverty schools today.

## Psychotherapy as Special Education

For Vygotsky, the treatment or the analysis of a handicap (i.e., as in special education), or of psychotic and neurotic disorders, should be based on the analysis of mental functions and principles of human psychological development. Compensatory "psychotechnics" could help the organism compensate for a defect by building a superstructure, which would permit sufficient compensation to deal with social demands. Whether particular tools are internalized by the individual or remain external is a relative issue (Zinchenko, 2001) although the main implication here is clear. That is, with the aid of lived experiences (*perezhivanie*) as tools provided externally, individuals' success and that of treatment are maximized and defined by the extent self-help or agency (as in the case of a recovered alcoholic) is mastered. Here the main concern for Vygotsky and Luria seems centered on the cultural consequences of the problem.

Vygotsky suggests that often the main consequences concerning a biologically based problem or defect are not just the resulting limited functioning and action potentials but *how* social relations are changed in ways that exacerbate or ameliorate the problem. Some institutionalized practices, such as assimilation-oriented, anti-bilingual education attitudes/practices in the United States can serve to further debilitate the potential of groups while in other contexts, additive bilingualism and encouragement of additive multilingual cultural identity development are forms of developing greater social capital for a society. One of Vygotsky's main contributions lies in this early insight that remains underdeveloped, which can be coupled with a developmental approach to the treatment of any exceptionality. He envisioned more than just an individual effort to compensate for structural problems such as those found in a natural experiment as in the case of the blind or deaf, which can lead to compensation involving the replacement of one function with extensions of another.

In the case of multilingual children of immigrants in the United States and other contexts, dominant society constructs an educational defect for those in the process of acquiring proficiency in the dominant (second) language. Many of these children, in turn, can develop secondary order "disorders" such as aggression, helplessness, unusual conduct, affective or cognition-related differences in that process. Vygotsky saw a great opportunity to aid the development of a protective, adaptive (socio-biological) superstructure around most individual problems by altering certain social relations around the person. Such an approach would allow progress in the development of cultural tools and mediated action that would lead to significant improvement. For example, the treatment afforded to autistic children can be improved in relative fashion by incorporating work-related activities and spaces (i.e., off-hours restaurant help) into the daily routine, (i.e., they can help set tables before customers arrive). In effect, his interaction with Adler's ideas appeared to have led him to the insight that just as blindness is not only the lack of vision, any psychophysiological problem causes a "deep restructuring of all the forces of the organism and the personality" (1982, pp. 86–89) and by extension of social relations outside. The thinking here is systemic, ecological, and dialectical in the understanding of psychopathology and most other bio-social conditions. This is illustrated in his "Defects and Compensation" chapter (Vygotsky, 1993) when he cites Adler noting:

> Adler's individual psychology bears a revolutionary character...
>
> Adler introduces "the basic psychological law of dialectical transformation: as a result of a subjective feeling...(a) defect will be transformed into a psychological drive to compensate and overcompensate" (Adler, 1927, p. 57)

The above thinking, coupled with the Uzbekistan scientific venture investigating the impact of cultural tools or education/literacy on unschooled or less schooled individuals illustrates why this approach is the only framework that incorporates crucial levels of analysis (Cole, 1990) With non-dominant groups today, one may extrapolate these principles to the relatively similar case of immigrant unschooled migrants in the developed societies today (see Kozulin, chapter 4 of this volume; Portes & Smagorinsky, 2010), who suffer not organic but socially framed defects or exceptionalities.

Part of the problem with the deaf, blind, and others who are challenged, lies precisely in the difficulty of developing a second (signal) functional system of communication and/or operations. Second, how the development of such an alternate system affects higher levels of cultural adaptation and development is the most important aspect of the problem. The second signal system for the deaf is sign language and for the blind Braille, and in each case, cultural development can proceed relatively well with respect to higher-level functions. In the case of most immigrant children, mastering the dominant group's tools *early enough* is pivotal in reaching normative standards and the pathways these open and that are synchronized in time and space. Without them, development and cultural adaptation are constrained. In a sense, this is a *two-factor* model that could be applied not only to learning disabilities but also to a variety of numerous socio-psychological problems. For example, Ritalin (or such) may be the Braille of the ADHD child or bilingual education for an immigrant child placed at risk; Lithium may be considered akin to allowing the manic-depressive to function in society, and so on. However, chemical or other socio-cognitive treatments or counteractions such as Instrumental Enrichment (Kozulin, chapter 4 in this volume) may not necessarily form a reliable superstructure in the person's life in every case. Moreover, from a broader perspective, from individual counseling to socially organized intervention programs where specific psychological skills can be co-constructed and improved, this basic explanation for how re-mediation works can be applied remains well beyond what the majority of people understand by this term. Improvement is, in sum, achieved through the acquisition of new emotionally and socially mediated experiences, which can be designed in a variety of ways.

The above examples show how cultural tools can be appropriated by the individual or at the group level and can be converted into means for goal-oriented actions. As Van der Veer and Valsiner (1994) note, such views "to a great extent only reiterated Vygotsky's earlier point of view that defects had to be overcome by the word" (p. 74) or more broadly, by counteractions. This dynamic provides probably the most elegant rationale for the "talking cure." On the other hand, some critiques found in the literature concern loose ends and contradictions because he saw development spurred not by smooth, socially shaped transitions but propelled often by conflict between the natural and cultural aspects of development. The implications that a social compensation or a *counteraction* approach addressing group-based inequalities (Portes & Salas, 2010) entails in human development have yet to receive full attention in contemporary clinical work or social policy, particularly in the context of new (social) practices such as chemotherapy, zero-tolerance, or managed care. For Vygotsky, it was not the treatment of *clinical* cases no psychopathological conditions as defined in the West that were of concern in forming the core for a new science of mind. His was a general framework that included human development, learning, psycholinguistics within a cultural psychology that others would have to systematize in the future. From this 1924 to 1931 golden period in Vygotsky's legacy, he anticipated current views framing defect more in terms of "risks" or of vulnerability, resilience, and skills development that are quite in line with the future orientation of prevention (primary to tertiary) connecting social practices to group and individual change. He praised Adler's historical thinking in relation to goal-directed aspects of personality and development in general and wrote:

> The entire psychological life of an individual consists of a succession of combative objectives, directed at the resolution of a single task: to secure a definite position with respect to the immanent logic of human society, or to the demands of the social environment (Vygotsky, 1993, p. 55).

If we understand this situated defect terminology more in terms of cultural differences and their social consequences, we can follow Vygotsky's own goals during that socio-historical period and his admiration of Adler's work from his non-dominant situation. Furthermore, he concludes that the main area of application for Adler is pedagogy, which

> occupies the same place as medicine does for the biological sciences, engineering for physics, and chemistry and politics for the social sciences: namely, the highest category of truth, since man proves the truth of his thoughts only by application (Vygotsky, 1993, p. 55).

In the final period for his life, Vygotsky addressed some clinical problems from the newly created cultural-historical theory, including Pick's disease (a type of dementia), Parkinson's, and schizophrenia in relation to other types of psychopathology. He dealt with schizophrenia in adolescent thought disorders (Valsiner & Van der Veer, 1992; also in the Cuban translation of Volume V of his collected works), particularly with attention to the role of mediation. For example, early on he was interested in the works of Kretschmer (1936) who noted that schizophrenics responded quite differently to life-threatening situations (bombing during the war). Schizophrenics were not among the masses of hysterics who filled area hospitals during WWI. During that period, a contemporary of Vygotsky named Levenshtein derived an experimental method to determine whether some schizophrenics are susceptible to psychotherapy or not (see next section). This work led Vygotsky to postulate that psychotherapy or remediation of psychosocial relations might counteract some part of the actual negative effects a biological defect or problem has on socio-psychological functioning. His writings suggest that disturbance in such functioning could be mainly caused by biological, hereditary predispositions or by disturbances in social conditions such as war, unemployment, or alienation. In such cases, he was optimistic about prognoses in general since he saw the potential benefit of providing re-mediation to faltering functions at the psychogenic level and also through more enlightened social treatments. However, this area has remained disconnected from that of developing proximal zones in psychotherapy. A fuller understanding of the zone of proximal development as a metaphor is lacking in the field today in spite of numerous writings in other areas regarding praxis.

Vygotsky agreed that as in some cases of schizophrenia, *defects* arise that last a long time and are not susceptible to psychotherapy. However, he thought that if one knew more about the "internal dynamic" or the interplay of sociobiological forces, one could intervene strategically in some cases. Vygotsky noted from the work of Jung and Bleuler (Bleier) that atop the schizophrenic's organic symptoms there exists a complex (simple elementary functions), or what he regarded as a reactive psychic superstructure. Vygotsky noticed in Levenshtein's work the implications of a psychological test or experiment in which some schizophrenics' manifest hysteric symptoms or behavior under stress. The results of this test suggested that in cases where schizophrenics' "superstructure" resembles or is similar to that of hysteria (neuroses in general) cases, there appeared to be a greater opportunity for psychotherapy to have a positive effect. This puzzle presented by Kretschmer's observations during the First World War (see Vygotsky, 1989, *Obras Completas*, vol. 5, p. 263) led Vygotsky and his student Surajeva to examine more closely why a proportion of that population is so disposed. While they believed that sometimes the biologically based endogenic schizophrenia is susceptible to psychosocial remediation, there is little clinical data with respect to treatment effectiveness. At that time, empirically based treatment or theory applications were not a main concern since such cases, and others, served as essential clues in the development of an empirically consistent "theory" which was still in the making. It remains so today as can be noted with victims of explosive devices. The main concern here was with the explanation as to why this response to psychotherapy (however defined) was the way it was. It seems to be based on a more general logic or synthesis regarding the structuring and deconstructing processes that shape the mind. For example, in electro-shock and other perhaps less primitive treatments, a similar question arises as to why they might work for some and not for others.

It should be noted that this example for theory building is related also to studies of concept formation involving the simple, "thinking in complexes" and pre-operations (see Piaget, 1964) found in young children, *primitives* and psychotic persons relative to more advanced others functioning with abstract, formal operations (Luria, 1929/1979; Vygotsky, 1962). With adolescent schizophrenics, a delay in that phase of development in line with Erik Erikson's concept of "sturm und drang" was noted (Vygotsky, 1993b), suggesting they differ in *not* manifesting the typical effects of formal operational thinking in adolescence. The analyses of these cases illustrate the detective work behind an emerging theory, much of which remains untested today. At present, there is little evidence to suggest the above thread concerning within group differences in the schizophrenic population has been studied systematically in the fields of psychiatry and clinical and counseling psychology. What is important to note, however, is that even during the initial period of forging a cultural-historical approach, questions relevant to counseling and psychotherapy were being considered. This work and Luria's in particular, remain important to current fields focusing on rehabilitation of persons suffering from physical and psychological trauma.

## Implications and Conclusions for Counseling: The Zone of Proximal Development

While the ZPD construct or metaphor has been discussed primarily in the context of learning and education (Moll, 1990), this chapter explored the usefulness of some of Vygotsky's ideas in a number of cultural practices, particularly that of counseling. Vygotsky noted an aspect of human development that is generally overlooked and that is of equal, if not greater, importance than individual (test) performance or behavior. The zone of proximal development (ZPD) is a metaphor defined by mental "functions that have not yet matured but are in the process of maturation, functions that will mature tomorrow but are currently in an embryonic state..."(Vygotsky, 1986, p. 86). For example, two persons may score similarly on an assessment protocol and might appear comparable in terms of maturity, social background, overall adjustment, or age. Even so, they could differ considerably in terms of learning readiness, motivation, or their response to various areas related to treatment.

Vygotsky argued that learning activates developmental processes that become functional, initially, through social interaction with more advanced agents. For him re-mediation was necessary in both endogenic disorders such as mental retardation as well as in more psychogenic cases such as neuroses, although he did not focus on the latter. This view suggests that therapy and education can be most helpful when focused on learning potential and second, by how learning is mediated and transformed in context. Counseling, just like education, needs to focus on the "buds or flowers" in a developmental process as much if not more than on the "fruits" of children's development (test performance). This goal can be accomplished by learning activities that are sensitively arranged ahead of a person's or group's actual level of adaptation. This theory helps account for "how culture acts" and could be organized differently with regard to developmental disparities related to equity and ethics in education and health.

Finally, the method of Double Stimulation found in the cultural-historical model, deserves some attention in counseling and psychotherapy. As Portes, Smith, Zady, and Del Castillo (1997) note, social interaction, particularly educational (teaching and learning) involve the presentation of stimuli, means, or signs that may be employed by an individual in advancing her own development. In the process of education or counseling, the acquisition or internalization of skills, beliefs, attitudes on the part of the client is often the intermediate objective that leads to achieving the future goal of praxis. The advice, insights, suggestions or, skills offered by the helper directly or incidentally represent a menu of neutral stimuli *any one of which* might be appropriated and employed by clients to change their future or present condition. Therapy, like education, offers a *production zone* for new meanings, feelings, motivations, and skills to be developed. It may be organized in various ways, yet the principles regarding the creation and maintenance of zones of proximal development, the transitions from external to internal regulation (Zinchenko, 2001), and such appear important in extending the development of professionals in mental health, as in other related areas. This approach offers a dynamic grasp of development, which challenges the traditional separation of mind from society in ways that require attention to both objective and subjective stances.

## Conclusions

The seminal ideas spun by Vygotsky and his co-workers led to an interdisciplinary renaissance in psychology and related fields that is currently known as the cultural-historical model. This model has remained powerful because it addresses fundamental questions that still confront us today.

In retrospect, it is not surprising that Vygotsky's seminal work on the formation of mind would be eventually recognized in counseling and psychotherapy. The fact that CHT has not been fundamental to those areas speaks to the extant of the dichotomies noted in this volume and to unresolved integrations within cultural psychology (Cole, 1996).

His and Luria's work in defectology and the social and biological aspects of development and mediated action are all directly pertinent to the fields involving education, counseling, and psychotherapy. While the context in which the practice of psychotherapy was being institutionalized in Vygotsky's era is quite different from that of today, various communities of practice define and are subject to psychopathology, treating it according to various standards and *best* practices. It should be noted then that although useful insights may be derived in a historical analysis of CHT, one should not expect to find a neat or finished theory with a defined set of techniques.

At this point, a deeper understanding of cultural-historical theory in the profession seems unlikely soon because as a meta-theory, it challenges (deconstructs) traditional worldviews and requires considerable synthesis, which is unlikely to be integrated into professional training or practices defined by a dominant view. In sum, how cultural-historical theory is to be integrated within counseling as a culturally situated social practice has yet to be clearly defined.

Based on how theoretical knowledge about how humans learn and develop, each major psychological theory has been infused into practices and techniques that range from how to define and assess health problems to specific methods to effect change in the client(s). This process may occur in the present case as it once did with psychoanalysis and behaviorism if it becomes integrated with a generally fragmented mainstream psychology. Present-day psychology still remains in a crisis which dates to the turn of the last century and which ultimately extends into all applied professions.

The extent to which this approach will fit the mood of the present century remains in question and is relative to the beliefs and main intellectual systems of a new information age. In Mannheim's (1952) terms, such are conditioned by existing socio-economic structures and by human activities or experiences in enacting roles within that structure. Perhaps CHT does not insist on uncovering a particular objective truth and to the manner in which *disorders* and gaps are to be defined socially, yet it may be less vulnerable to critiques leveled at behaviorist, intellectual orientations. cultural-historical activity theory addresses how the content and perhaps the structure of human thought changes within an intellectual system that predates Weber's (1964) insight regarding the interplay between socioeconomic conditions and intellectual systems. Both appear to recognize what Marx and other sociologists of knowledge missed. The central idea here is that sociocultural conditions do not produce intellectual orientations directly, but they do produce differential receptivities to such intellectual systems. At present, the cognitive-behavioral and the medical model paradigms still reign in the field, and they appear to have well established economic conditions in the eyes of some depending on power and ethics. The crux of the question here thus lies in determining how and to what extent cultural-context factors may change and bring about a change in future practices. The interdisciplinary, dialectical nature of cultural-historical theory is a double-edged sword in making a prediction with respect to future goals and directions. As this century progresses, evidence exists that a slow change is occurring toward a cultural-developmental intellectual system, as evidenced perhaps by the rejection of a computational model of mind (Bruner, 1990), the introduction of terms such as situated cognition, communities of practice and the very notion of a cultural, interdisciplinary psychology. It may appear less ironic than that because application-focused areas within psychology (clinical and counseling) have not experienced a major paradigm shift since the cognitive–behavioral models were blended. To conclude then, for both areas a broader understanding about the semiotic relationships among *adjustment* problems, their cultural contexts, and particularly the cultural history of individuals and groups (Portes, 1996, 2005) needs deeper consideration in the 21st century.

## ENDNOTE

1    Although sub-disciplines such as developmental psychopathology and others would seem to be an ideal in addressing these concerns, few have been able to "step out" of their professional setting and their paradigm to consider and elaborate upon these issues.

# A Cultural-Historical Approach to NeuroPsychological Treatment

## Understanding Latino and Other Non-Dominant Groups

*Jose Dergan*

> *It seems surprising that the science of psychology has avoided the idea that many mental processes are social and historical in origin, or that important manifestations of human consciousness have been directly shaped by the basic practices of human activity and the actual forms of culture. (A. R. Luria, 1976, p. 3)*

Almost everyone would agree that the translation of Luria's extensive work, originally published in Russian and mostly restricted in the West, became a key cornerstone for the subsequent development of neuropsychology. Based on his intersystemic functional model, new principles of cognitive rehabilitation with the brain-injured population were developed and enriched by Luria and his coworkers over approximately fifty years. As a result of the cognitive revolution that took place during the 1970s, clinical psychologists began to change their outlook, particularly in the area of analysis and interpretation of quantitative results obtained from psychometric data (Golden & Moses, 1984). Rather than conforming to the medical model, they took a different route, shifting towards the discovery of underlying internal processes and attempting to develop a qualitatively different approach to the treatment of various behavioral disorders (Fuster, 2002; Gauggel, 1997). Subsequently, Luria's systemic view of cognitive processes and his qualitative approach to the analysis of cognitive impairment were accepted enthusiastically by many American neuroscientists (Goldberg & Bougakov, 2009).

The Lurian influence on American neuropsychology is twofold. On the one hand, during the 1980s, Golden (1984) and his associates ventured to take Luria's examination techniques, previously translated and adapted by Christensen (1975), to establish statistical parameters among a variety of brain-injured patients (Golden and Moses, 1984; Cristensen, 1975). In fact, by overlooking Luria's early criticism of psychometrics, Golden grouped his basic assessment techniques in a psychometric battery (Golden & Moses, 1984). The Luria Nebraska Neuropsychological battery (LNNB) evolved as the counterpart to The Halstead-Reitan Battery. According to Golden (1984) and his followers, the LNNB has not only provided sufficient statistical power, but contrary to the Halstead Reitan, it may also provide the clinician with valuable data to enhance a qualitative interpretation of functional units.

According to Golden, this approach may help analyze and interpret cognitive deficits preserving Luria's major premises (Golden & Moses, 1984). Nevertheless, this assumption is still very far from the scientific truth. Golden has been widely criticized by those who believe that data quantification distorts Luria's conceptualizations considerably (Christensen, 1975).

Concomitantly to Golden's contribution to neuropsychological assessment, Sohlberg and his associates implemented a set of cognitive systems to help brain-injury patients restore their cognitive deficits (Sohlberg & Mateer, 1989). By utilizing the major postulates and contributions made by the Lurian school, Sohlberg and Mateer were able to implement operational concepts such as plasticity, systemic reintegration of impaired functions, and the creation of cognitive programs to restore functional units at a maximum potential (Sohlberg & Mateer, 1989).

Despite Luria's major contributions in cultural-historical theory, its main relevance remains overlooked, particularly, when it comes to the analysis and interpretation of clinical data in patients from multicultural contexts. A main problem is fitting theories and methods with populations with different cultural histories (Portes, 1990, 1996). However, rather than analyzing the relationship between culture and the development of dysfunctional behavior, most behavioral and cognitive models view psychopathology (e.g., anxiety) as a universal construct. Although some psychological problems appear to have a strong biological component, their development, manifestation, assessment, and treatment are context bound.

One of the major contributions made by A. R. Luria and his disciples dealt precisely with the social formation of all higher-order psychological functions and dysfunctions (Luria, 1980). Following this line of thought, cultural-historical psychotherapy and neurorehabilitation assess psychological dysfunctions without taking them apart from the patient's social historical context. Understanding the relationship between social mediators (e.g., language, social symbols, cultural customs, and so on) and psychopathology is of paramount importance for case conceptualization and treatment planning.

## The Problem

In the West the origins of psychotherapy and rehabilitation had a different historical root. At the end of the nineteenth century, as electronic equipment replaced steam-based machinery, there was an increase in the overproduction of means and a subsequent profitable investment for certain social groups. At that time, psychotherapy was just seen as an unscientific, speculative approach to the treatment of deep-seated intra-psychic problems. Its major source of influence was the classic Freudian analytic view which emphasized the liberation of sexual energy as its major therapeutic goal (Parker, 1999).

As industrial societies became more sophisticated and the division of labor strengthened the need to refine psychometric tools to differentiate different social groups based on their abilities, traits, and potentialities emerged (Portes, 1996). To help adjust injured and emotionally unstable patients to the demands of the social system, there was a need to seek a more efficacious way of treating mental illnesses in a manner that was more time and cost effective to the private health industry.

After World War II, the acceptance of behaviorism as the leading school of thought in most western countries played a striking role in increasing the use of the operational methods of assessment, behavioral change, and therapeutic outcomes (Eysenck, 1973). A reductionist stimuli-response (S-R) model influenced a variety of areas such as program evaluation, psychiatric medication management, therapy evaluation, assessment scales, treatment planning, and therapy efficacy (Eysenck, 1973).

During the 1970s, cognitivism was introduced to most behavioral psychologists in the clinical field. Far from helping patients become liberated from social alienation and repression, the main therapeutic goal was to decrease emotional disturbance through the use of empirically proven behavioral and cognitive techniques (Eysenck, 1973; Parker, 1999).

Since social events and scientific discoveries are mostly causally related, they are connected to the historical context from which they originated. For example, during the seventies, community mental health services were created and funded by the U.S. Federal Government. At first, the initiative was seen as an attempt to de-institutionalize psychiatric facilities and also to make treatment more accessible to the low income and low-middle income classes (e.g., African Americans, Latinos, and other minorities among them).

As a clinician practicing both psychotherapy and neuropsychological rehabilitation in various clinical settings, I had the opportunity to observe the constant implementation of this reductionist approach to clinical rehabilitation of patients from the non-dominant culture. It was often observed that patients from different cultural minorities (e.g., Latino, African American, Asian, and so on) were evaluated and treated with similar psychometric and therapeutic tools when compared to patients from the mainstream culture (e.g., Anglo-Saxon). The social factors were only described as part of the demographic characteristics but never analyzed deeply in understanding various individual-context dynamics.

Another example where the most common medical problems associated with work-related accidents can be noted concern spinal cord and brain injuries in the field of rehabilitation (Ashley, 2004). Often and shortly after patients are discharged from acute hospital care, they are referred by the worker compensation insurance company to a rehabilitation setting in order to be involved in a time/cost effective, goal-oriented treatment (pain management or head injury rehabilitation). The major treatment goal is to help patients decrease pain, increase memory and attention, increase ambulation, physical strength, appropriate speech, decrease depression associated with disability, and so forth. However, most Latino patients are discharged from various programs (e.g., pain management, head injury, and so on) without having even achieved basic therapeutic goals. Upon discharge, they continue to show severe neurological and orthopedic symptoms, which make their return to work very difficult. During my consulting work with various rehabilitation centers, I frequently find that patients either do not adjust to the program regulation (e.g., missed sessions, passive attitude, lack of motivation, refusal to be assessed), or they do not fully understand the guidelines. The majority of Latinos and African Americans are labeled as "pain magnifiers" or "malingerers," who are solely seeking financial compensation by taking advantages of the system (Dergan, 1997). The Anglo-Saxon patients who do not make progress are also discharged back to work. They are generally labeled differently (e.g., uncooperative, negative, or attention seekers). There is also abundant evidence that during the intake, no significant effort is made to understand the cultural-historical context of participating patients. There was no documentation as to how chronic pain interacted with previously learned cultural symbols, word meanings, and general attitudes toward physical impairment commonly manifested by specific non-dominant groups.

The above examples demonstrate that, by failing to understand physical pain in humans as a complex functional unit derived from a historical social formation, therapists deal with clinical problems by having as their main goal the attenuation of symptoms without analyzing the specific mediators pertaining to cultural and individual parameters. Their psychological reports do not generally describe how cultural artifacts from a specific non-dominant group mediated the therapeutic process (e.g., cultural perception of pain; the role played by family members in the rehabilitation process, the concept of becoming disabled and unable to provide).

In brief, the major pitfall in the rehabilitation process with patients who are treated for head trauma after a work-related accident lies in the ethnocentric tendency to treat them with techniques designed for the dominant population. As a result, most African American, Asian, and Latino patients do not benefit as well nor understand the therapeutic process, resulting in a much slower progress and therapeutic resistance (Dergan, 1997).

By overlooking cultural-historical factors, clinicians have the tendency to minimize the role played by the acquisition of values and social perceptions pertaining to a specific ethnic group. This wrongful approach appears to be the major limitation when rehabilitating patients in various clinical settings in the United States and elsewhere based on experiences with my peers. Therefore, the analysis of cultural-historical complexities is crucial to understand individual pathology and rehabilitation. In the next sections, I will analyze the contributions made by Luria and his school in order to understand the multifunctional treatment of neuropsychological and psychological dysfunctions within a cultural-historical framework (Luria, 1973; Jantzen, 2004).

## A Cultural Historical Perspective

## Historical Foundations

As Hegel (1969) and Marx (1952) proposed, the historical analysis of social formations is of paramount importance to discover the driving forces formed in each stage of social development. As these social forces are driven permanently by internal and external opposing elements, they inevitably form critical contradictions that, in turn, lead to qualitative changes in the social system. Thus, through sophisticated social activity, speech and thought became the most complex culturally mediated processes accounting for the origin and development of the individual psychological structure (Wallon, 1937; Marx, 1952; Hegel, 1969; Luria, 1973; Vygotsky, 1978).

> I believe that this premise is essential and a stepping stone to understand subsequent development in psychology. As with most of the humanistic sciences of the post romantic period, psychology emerged as an academic, sophisticated field of knowledge linked to philosophy. Later on, as the development of the industrial society progressed and the need to understand the complexities of human behavior was created, the mental processes began to be understood more objectively, and psychology became an independent field. (Gauggel, 1997)

Historically, there was an attempt to explain human behavior within a more complex perspective linking basic processes to higher psychological functions (Wundt, 1921; Cole, 1996). In fact, Wundt proposed the creation of two psychologies: one experimentally oriented to explain scientifically basic psychological functions (e.g., sensations and perceptions mostly related to the immediate experience) and the second brand, which he called *Völkerpsychologie*. He stated that *Völkerpsychologie* could not be studied experimentally because it would transcend the principles of individual consciousness. Its major goal was to study higher psychological functions in a descriptive way, taking into account elements of cultural variations, linguistics, religious values, and so forth. He strongly believed that the two psychologies were supplemental to each other and that, through a synthesis of their respective insights, a holistic analysis could be achieved (Wundt, 1921; Cole, 1996).

Dewey (1938/1963) revived most of the Wundtian principles pertaining to the second psychology, particularly when studying cultural differences among ethnic groups. In both Germany and France the second psychology also influenced the emergence of the Gestalt theory and Durkheim's social theory. Unfortunately, in most texts of general psychology, Wundt's contribution is primarily linked to his early experiments in which he studied introspection.

Following the contribution made by German scholars, new initiatives emerged to explain human behavior within the cause and effect paradigm. Freud's major contribution was seen as the first attempt to understand, holistically, the structure of the human mind. However, apart from its controversial reductionist view (e.g., pansexualism, the emphasis on instinctual forces); one of the major limitations of Freudian psychoanalysis was the lack of understanding of complex social factors and, the differences among cultures in the origin of complex psychopathology (Wallon, 1984). His views were later criticized and opposed by a number of scholars such as Adler and Jung (Oberst & Stewart, 2003).

This set of historical changes in the study of complex psychological processes emerged precisely when Europe was going through a critical period of political uprisings. It was indeed, this political transformation that led to drastic changes in the philosophy of science during the first decades of the Soviet Revolution.

Debates among Soviet intellectuals were frequently carried out at different levels (Blunden, 2009). The main issue seemed to be the need to understand man as a social entity determined by his material needs but without depriving him from the right of freedom and social justice.

In psychology, a wave of new young scientists, influenced by European schools of thought, proposed the creation of a Marxist psychology. There was a constant search to find a theory that could conceptualize man, following the new parameters of the revolution. At that time, Bechterev's concept of reflex was linked to Pavlov's discovery of the conditioned reflex paradigm helping crystallize the Leninist theory of reflex as a subjective, sensorial category of the external world. As a result, Soviet scholars viewed psychological science as being akin to behaviorism ( Wallon, 1937; Cole, 1978; Blunden, 2009).

Despite the official's attempt to explain social consciousness as a reflected, subjective activity and to use the principles of conditioning to explain the material basic unity of the psyche, many young psychologists, including Lev Vygotsky, used these principles, not as a major foundation, but as a stepping stone for the upcoming creation of a sophisticated psychological theory (Vygotsky, 1978).

Even though Vygotsky found conditioning a useful scientific explanation, his conception of the human mind goes far beyond this point. He and his coworkers proposed that the relationship between the newborns and their external world is not as simple as conveying different factors in a linear fashion. On the contrary, by going through different stages, the psychological activity is hierarchically developed and formed by the dialectical interaction between social activity, culturally mediated artifacts, and the development of higher cerebral structures. The end result is the acquisition of human consciousness as a subjective reflex of external reality. At first, by using primitive tools to modify and establish communication, children become unique subjective reflections of their social world. Later on, by separating themselves from the syncretism created by attachments with affectionate figures, they become very independent, active parts of their own social transformation. Lastly, by becoming socially conscious and capable of internalizing their plans and intentions, modifying them internally, and changing the contingencies of their social system, they become free to create their own destiny through social activity (Vygotsky, 1978; Voyat, 1984; Wallon, 1984). This premise is based on the principles of dialectical materialism and has strongly influenced the ulterior development of the cultural-historical psychology (Ratner, 1991; Cole, 1996).

Luria's major goal lay in the analysis and explanation of more sophisticated internal psychological processes such as memory and the structure of conscious processes in pathological states. At first, he tried to explain the dialectical interaction between psychological structures using psychoanalysis as a major reference (Luria, 1979; Cole, 1996; Jantzen, 2004). Later on, as a result of major political contradictions affecting Soviet science, he focused on the analysis and interpretation of cognitive deficiencies as a result of cerebral insult, subsequently formulating his main contribution in the neuropsychology of higher psychological processes (Luria, 1973).

Vygotsky proposed a qualitatively different methodology based on the concept of units of analysis. Rather than targeting isolated elements of the psychological structure, he proposed that the major objective of a scientific psychological theory was the objective analysis on the relationship between thought and speech (Vygotsky, 1978). These ideas were manifested in his historical manuscript published in 1929 known as "The Crisis of Psychology" (Blunden, 2009). In that classical work, he concluded that solving this problem would lead to the scientific explanation of human consciousness as a material category. Later, Leontiev (1978) focused on the development of a social activity theory to explain how the mental processes permanently change as the result of social formation and how this permanent dialectical interaction forms the essence of social consciousness, human motivation, and the use of problem-solving activity to attain specific goals (Leontiev, 1978; Luria, 1979).

Ever since that time, the *troika* developed various methods to prove the validity of the artifact-mediated activity as the central key to the formation of higher psychological processes (Vygotsky, 1978; Blunden, 2009; Ratner, 1991). This new era in the scientific development of psychology was soon darkened by the Soviet censorship. In 1929, Leontiev was forced to leave Krupskaya Academy as a result of his "refusal" to accept a psychological theory solely based on the reflexology as the unique, scientific explanation of psychological processes (Luria, 1979; Blunden, 2009).

In 1931, Luria and Vygotsky's famous expedition in Uzbekistan investigated how formal education affected the cognitive development of peasants living in remote areas. Following unique historical contextual situations, they carried out a sophisticated cultural-historical experiment on the relationship between artifact-mediated activity and differences in cognitive development (Cole, 1978).

Most likely as a way of circumventing a direct confrontation with the government, Luria, who had already obtained a degree in psychology, decided to go back to medicine. Ironically, the patriotic war that took place in the Soviet Union following the Nazi occupation served as an opportunity for him to work closely with soldiers who came back from the front with different kinds of cerebral traumatic injuries (Luria,1979).

Since Luria viewed psychological processes as complex units of socially mediated activity originated in historically determined social relationships, he devoted most of his scientific work discovering the organization of such complex functional units and their underlying complex physiological mechanisms. By analyzing different clusters of psychological disturbances, he identified complex physiological mechanisms, which took part holistically in the development of higher psychological processes.

As a result, he developed the foundations for his three-level intersystem neuropsychological model. His major contributions in the field of neuropsychology (e.g., aphasia, memory disturbance, and rehabilitation) derived from his systematic analysis and interpretation of a variety of cognitive impairment (Luria, 1979).

By viewing the organization of functional zones in the cerebral cortex, not as a passive entity, but rather as a direct context-specific cultural-historical neuronal circuit, Luria's contribution opened the path to the creation of a sophisticated psychological theory of man ( Luria, 1973).

## The Lurian Contribution to Modern Neuropsychology and Clinical Psychology

During the latter part of the nineteenth century, irreconcilable and opposite views such as Cartesian dualism, mechanical materialism, and subjective idealism underlined the basic foundations of psychology. However, the scientific development of disciplines such as medicine, physiology, and biology created the need to understand the mechanisms underlying both simple and complex behaviors within the scope of traditional science (Wallon, 1937). During this time, neurology and other disciplines became interested in the localization of specific anatomical centers in the human brain to explain psychological processes (Wallon, 1937). Inspired by Gall's attempt to create phrenology of psychological faculties, the concept of cortical "maps" gained momentum but was rapidly forgotten. There were other attempts to identify specific cortical areas responsible for both simple and complex cognitive and motor behaviors. The discoveries made by Broca and Wernicke on specific centers underlying sophisticated mechanisms of both motor and sensorial speech were considered of paramount importance for the discovery of complex mental functions as a direct result of the work of specific cortical areas (Luria, 1973).

However, years later, due to the failure to localize anatomical centers of complex psychological activities, other views flourished opposing the attempts to connect specific areas in the cortex and complex psychological functions. One of the greatest opponents to this localization "quest" was the British neurologist Jackson who proposed that complex mental processes should be approached by analyzing the way they are hierarchically constructed rather than by analyzing isolated cortical areas (1874/1932). Misunderstanding Jackson's critiques regarding the localization, many scientists opted for rethinking Cartesian dualism and agreed with the old hypothesis that spiritual systems transcend the physiological structure of the human mind (Luria, 1973).

Taking Jackson's views into consideration, Luria stated that a function is not the result of a single, isolated cortical area, as proposed by the localizationists. On the contrary, following Anojin's model of functional systems, he proposed that functional cortical units involve different components, and according to the complexity of a specific internal activity, they participate in a hierarchically organized fashion, on the elaboration of complex psychological programs. These programs are used by man to assimilate, modify, anticipate, and create new external systems through social activity (Anojin, 1963; Luria, 1973; Leontiev, 1978; Jantzen, 2004). Influenced by Vygotsky's concept of the *analysis into units*, he proposed that in order to attain this higher organizational task; the cerebral activity is functionally and permanently interconnected to its inseparable component: social history. The cultural artifacts, learned through the history of civilization and then assimilated through ontogenesis, are pivotal in order to understand the interconnectivity of different cortical zones in both simple and complex psychological activity (Vygotsky, 1978; Luria, 1973; Ratner, 2002).

The significance of Luria's work transcended his contribution in the field of clinical assessment and neurorehabilitation. Luria understood neuropsychology as the branch of science which would serve as the framework for the subsequent development of a sophisticated psychological theory of man (Luria, 1980). By following this principle for many decades, first as a psychologist in a defectology institute, and then as a medical doctor working with war veterans, he discovered, through years of arduous scientific work, the basic mechanisms underlying complex psychological activity (Luria, 1979).

During most of his life, Luria emphasized on the creation of a psychological system capable of explaining mental processes without reducing the human mind to its parts. By taking advantage of the socio-historical conditions of his time, he developed, through neuropsychology as a discipline, the keys for the understanding of the complexities of psychological activity. A thorough detailed analysis of Luria's work is beyond the scope of this chapter. Therefore, I will only outline his major contributions.

Since the very beginning, Luria proposed that the human brain is composed of three blocks or functional zones, differentiated by their hierarchical organization, their neuroanatomical structures, and their specific functions. Since the brain works as a complex holistic system, all of these functional units are necessary when sophisticated psychological activity is performed (Luria, 1980).

The first system is known as the unit for regulation of general physiological activity. Its neuroanatomical structure is composed of the reticular ascending system (RAS). Its major function is displayed by its role played in the awakening states and also in maintaining attenuated cortical tone while context-specific cerebral activity takes place (Luria, 1973).

Luria's major assertion has been vastly demonstrated by scientific evidence. For example, clinical observations conducted with patients exhibiting a lowered cortical tone due to pathological states showed an interesting clinical picture. Despite their intact specific gnostic abilities, they could not maintain appropriate levels of activation while a specific cognitive task was performed. This dysfunction usually breaks the *law of strength* as proposed by Pavlov (1957) and creates a dysfunctional lower cortical state that interferes with appropriate levels of cognitive-emotional processing (Luria, 1973; Dergan, 1987; Fuster, 2002; Prigatano, 2009).

The second unit is known to play a crucial role in the sensorial analysis, interpretation, and storing of incoming external stimuli. Its neuroanatomical structure lies in the posterior area of the cerebral cortex which involves the occipital (visual processing), the parietal (general sensorial), and the temporal (auditory) cortex (Luria, 1973).

Contrary to the gradual process of activation and deactivation carried out by the first functional unit, the second functional zone is modality-specific and operates in a hierarchical fashion. Input from the outside world is analyzed by a primary layer of neurons (layer IV), then synthesized by associative neurons (layers III and II) and lastly, the information from various functional systems is overlapped by the tertiary associative zone (associative layers located on the boundaries of the occipital, parietal, and temporal zones) (Luria, 1973).

The two major features of this second functional zone are in the principle of modal organization and interhemispheric specialization. At this level of organization, the human brain is highly distinguished from inferior mammals by means of social historical mediated activity (mostly of semantic origin) (Luria, 1973).

The third functional zone is considered the major achievement of social evolution. It is the unit for programming, regulating, and verifying mental programs as they dynamically participate in social activity (Luria, 1973). Its neuroanatomical structure lies in the frontal portion of the cortex (anterior to the posteromedial sylvan fissure). The major role of this third system is to react actively to external stimuli, by modifying internal programs intentionally directing words, images, sensations, and emotions to goal-oriented activity. The major primary projection outlet for this unit is the voluntary motor activity which interconnects, through an efferent input, to different lower components of the motor system (Luria, 1973).

As a result of social history, the anterior zone of the human cortex evolved as a qualitatively unique system. Its sophisticated development was dialectically determined by the interconnectivity between the manufacturing of social artifacts and the development of sophisticated biological and physiological systems.

Therefore, by comparing different sophisticated clusters of information, verifying their relevance, monitoring its intensity, and creating qualitatively new mental and emotional strategies, the third unit is considered the realm of human consciousness (Vygotsky, 1978; Luria, 1973; Jantzen, 2004).

## A Clinical Analysis and Interpretation of Psychological Disorders

The following case presentations illustrate the need for a reformulation based on Luria's perspective that will end this chapter.

## Case 1

Manuel R. is a 72-year-old Mexican male who is a resident of Miami-Dade and illegally immigrated to the State of Florida 20 years ago, where he has survived as a tomato picker ever since. He lives on a small farm in the outskirts of Homestead, Miami-Dade with his family. In October of 2009, due to severe memory loss, slurred speech, and spatial disorientation, he was admitted to Central Hospital (neurological unit). Results from the MRI of the brain without contrast indicated enlargement of ventricles consistent with his age but did not indicate any pathological state. The psychiatric evaluation was positive for dementia, Alzheimer's type. As a result, Seraquel 100mg, Lexapro 10mg, and Aricept 10mg were prescribed by the staff psychiatrist. Neuropsychological testing was also indicative of dementia with primary dysfunctions on verbal memory, attention, concentration, and poor levels of basic alertness. According to the recommendation made by the staff, the patient was in a critical stage (dementia) with only limited potential for recovery. They suggested that Manuel should be referred to a closed, supervised environment and that his family should be prepared for an unavoidable gradual deterioration of higher psychological functions. They were informed that at the stage he was in, Manuel would never recover. Far from understanding this concept, relatives became very upset. They refused to accept these assertions and insisted that they were going to take Manuel back home. The staff suggested that cognitive retraining, physical, and speech therapies should be provided at least three times per week in an inpatient setting. Despite this recommendation, Manuel was taken home by his relatives. Subsequently, treatment was rendered on ambulatory basis.

Review of the clinical chart indicated that Manuel was provided with cognitive rehabilitation. It consisted of six sessions of verbal memorization with familiar cues and also double-cognitive training using retrieval. For evaluative purposes, both the Rey Verbal-auditory test and the de Prose memory test from the Memory

Assessment Scale (MAS) were used. These exams were administered twice, prior and post treatment, and Manuel's scores prior to the treatment fell within 3% percentile (severe impairment) on both the Rey Verbal scale and the Prose memory exam. At the end of the sixth session, the neuropsychologist from Central Hospital indicated that the patient did not meet the criteria for further cognitive training. This decision was made based on the patient's poor progress upon the retrieval of these two scales. According to the written report, at the time of his discharge from the retraining program, Manuel's scores maintained the same level of impairment (3% percentile). His condition remained the same.

A few weeks later, a family member contacted me at the mental health unit at the University hospital for a second opinion on Manuel's condition. After reviewing extensive documentation, it was concluded that Manuel was very unfamiliar with techniques provided by the rehabilitation team at Baptist. During my first session with Manuel, I conducted a syndromic analysis in order to determine what culturally based artifacts should be added to the new rehabilitation plan. It was decided that due to his lack of cultural knowledge on the verbal cues presented during both procedures, Manuel was not responding adequately to the treatment. It was also concluded that regardless of his memory deficit, he possessed an adequate level of general alertness and his executive functions were still intact. It was also noticed that most of the words and expressions used during the rehabilitation lacked cultural meaning to Manuel. Subsequently, the list of words was changed arbitrarily by using a vocabulary well known within the Mexican culture. The story from the MAS (Memory Assessment Scale) was also arbitrarily changed to include culturally sensitive artifacts for the Mexican culture.

Intriguingly, after six sessions of this cultural mediated procedure, Manuel was able to answer almost 90% of the questions adequately. Furthermore, he was able to generalize memory retraining to real-life situations and reported a considerable improvement. At an emotional level, according to the Geriatric Depression Scale (GDS), he felt motivated and did not report symptoms of depression any longer. A neuropsychological evaluation (post training) was conducted using the same procedures that were used on the previous evaluation conducted at Central Hospital of Miami. Results indicated that Manuel had improved by almost 50% in both verbal memory and general emotional functioning.

Three months later, during a follow-up session, it was found that Manuel was living independently and did not need any extra help from any relative. He was highly motivated to continue on his own with memory exercising. Self-motivation was validated by his social competence and mastering of compensatory memory programs.

This case study clearly shows how the clinician's lack of knowledge of the cultural artifacts involved in the patient's pathology may affect negatively any effort to work with specific ethnic groups effectively. As shown in this case study, the importance of identifying and selecting culturally mediated artifacts for cognitive recovery emphasizes the learning of new compensatory cognitive-emotional units to help patients assimilate and reprocess their needs and motives through social activity. Since Manuel preserved his ability to generate planning, to initiate, and internalize (the third functional unit), he was able to learn compensatory strategies through self-motivation. As Luria stated:

> This active process of restoration of a function naturally demands great will power from the patient, and diligent, steadfast work. It is quite obvious, therefore, that the preservation of a steadfast and intensive motivation, stabilizing the patient's inclination to work on the compensation of his defect, is an essential condition of the successful restoration of a disturbed function. (1943, p. 232)

After all, it is not about making a psychometric exam or a therapeutic tool more sensitive to cultural variations. It is rather about determining how artifacts from a given cultural minority, assisted by clinical methods, can be used for recovery. Thus, the goal of cultural-historical clinical interventions goes far beyond statistically designed instruments and techniques.

## Case 2

Juan T. is a 27-year-old Nicaraguan male, referred to me by the civil judge in charge of his workmen's compensation case. Juan was involved in a job-related accident in which, as a result of electrocution, he fell approximately 10 feet to the pavement, injuring his lower back, neck, and both lower extremities. As part of his WC (workmen's compensation) treatment plan, he was referred to see a clinical psychologist for severe depression and anxiety.

After having treated Juan for 12 weeks, the psychologist concluded that Juan had regained control of his life and that he did not have any major emotional problems. As a result, although WC continued providing him with medical assistance, they cut his benefits pertaining to mental health. Juan T. disagreed with his psychologist and stated that he fell coerced by him to go back to work. He stated that far from being emotionally ready, he was feeling worse, had problems with his family, and felt constantly anxious, hopeless, and inept.

Clinical documents sent by the treating psychologist were reviewed. In fact, results from the MMPI-2 were indicative of a "faking bad" response pattern. It also showed that Juan had responded with a randomized "true or false" pattern. On the McGill pain questionnaire (MPQ), the psychologist interpreted that Juan was a pain magnifier trying to obtain secondary gains through his complaints. The psychologist also referred to the inconsistencies in his statements and concluded that there could be a strong possibility of malingering.

During our first session, Juan T. was freely allowed to ventilate his anger towards the system, the legal case, the insensitivity of those who were in charge of his case, and so forth. He revealed that he was raised in a small village near the city of Leon, Nicaragua. His parents were peasants working in the country-side. He also stated that, because of financial limitations, his education was limited to elementary school. When asked about his cultural concept of pain and medical illnesses, he indicated that he strongly believed that when people get sick, they must be helped by all family members (close and extended), who take turns not to leave the sick one alone. In fact, he had to go back to his country five years earlier to help his youngest brother recover from a car accident. He also stated that, because of this situation, he lost his job in Miami. During the session, he also vocalized how he and his family felt abandoned by the system and how lawyers and paralegals think that he is abusing the system.

After having researched cultural attitude toward physical illness in the countryside of Nicaragua, I came to the conclusion that Juan T.'s attitude towards psychological assessment and treatment can be seen as "crying for help." He felt abandoned by his employer and felt hopeless, suffering from severe lower back pain and physical limitations. On the other hand, he thought that his employer, lawyers, and doctors would not believe him. This situation led him to exaggerate a bit his responses towards his illness to obtain the attention he was culturally supposed to have when a member from his ethnic group was seriously ill. Subsequently, by establishing an interpersonal alliance, psychological therapy was set to validate his complaints. He did not feel any longer coerced and threatened. His wife and three children were also brought to therapy. Following the Lurian model, psychotherapy was geared towards increasing self-regulation through both emotional and cognitive processes. Thus, he regained *self-internalization* as a primary source of self-reinforcement and positive self-appraisal.

Contrary to what the WC lawyer would have expected, in only a few sessions of culturally mediated psychotherapy, Juan T. regained emotional control of his life, continued making medical progress, and finally regained useful employment. The judge was convinced by the new clinical evidence that the testing originally administered did not reflect objectively the cause of Juan T.'s emotional disturbance. He also legitimized the cultural-historical interpretation of Juan's clinical complaints. In a six-month follow-up session, it was found that although still complaining of moderate pain, Juan is working full time, and carrying out his job duties.

## Recommendations and Conclusions

In analyzing the above clinical cases by succumbing their views to the guidelines stipulated by the dominant culture, most clinicians rely solely on the interpretation of psychometric results and the standard use of therapeutic strategies. As a result, interventions are very limited at best. These lack the proper understanding of complex functional systems (e.g., the relationship between clinical signs and social attitudes, language, family values, specific ethnic cognitive development, and so forth) underlying overt pathological signs. Unfortunately, this situation prevails among the majority of clinicians dealing with patients from various ethnic minorities frequently leading to a simplistic and erroneous interpretation of their psychological dysfunctions. In sum, even though the works of Luria and Vygotsky in particular have impacted some areas of psychology in the United States during the last two decades, few attempts have been documented to analyze psychopathology within the scope of the cultural-historical-activity theory (Portes, 1999). Following the model developed by A.R. Luria and a cultural-historical based psychotherapy and neurorehabilitation model can be proposed without decomposing the social nature of a patient's own subjectivity (e.g., the dynamics of his social activity, the social formation of his consciousness, his physiological activity, and so on.

First, to begin to solve the social situation facing clients from non-dominant and immigrant minorities, a critical analysis must be conducted to refurbish the basic foundations of applied branches of psychology. This approach will help deconstruct a reductionist view of the mind, opening the key for the construction of a broader cultural-historical activity approach. This model shall approach psychological activity as a sophisticated entity regulated by the permanent dialectical interaction between an individual's internal mental system and one's socially mediated experiences. Patients will no longer be seen as just "being appropriate for specific techniques," but rather as unique entities, mediated by social artifacts from both, their own ethnic group and the mainstream culture (Ratner, 2002).

The origin of dysfunctional behavior arises when the demands of the external group cannot be adequately assimilated and reprocessed by the individual's internal mental structure. By creating a constant interactive negative loop, different levels of pathophysiological states may intercalate with an altered conscious activity, forming a biphasic dysfunctional category (cognitive-emotional). The constant dialectics of this pathological entity will result in an alienated cognitive-emotional state, preventing the individual from objectively analyzing, reprocessing, and searching for new strategies to solve the problem (Dergan, 2007a).

When helping patients from the non-dominant culture, the major goal of cultural-historical therapy should be focused on helping them increase appropriate assimilation and reprocessing of culturally mediated artifacts from the mainstream culture, without abdicating the ones from their own ethnic group. On the contrary, by no means does this process imply that the objective of these therapeutic interventions is for social re-adaptation. This would result in social alienation with the mainstream culture (Dergan, 2007b).

Thus, the therapeutic process must enhance the learning of qualitatively new cognitive-emotional strategies in order to assure adequate coping with context-specific problems (e.g., depression, pain management, anxiety, head injury, and so on). Since it is of paramount importance to go from the concrete analysis toward a more complex identification of different levels of impairment, Luria's assessment methods are crucial to understanding the genesis of the various psychopathologies caused by physical trauma (e.g., head injury), marital conflicts, drug abuse, eating disorders, and personality disorders. In regard to this concept, he wrote:

> The symptom of a disturbance of praxis (apraxia) is an assign of a local brain lesion; however, by itself this symptom tells nothing about any specific localization of the focus causing its appearance. Voluntary movement constitutes a complex functional system incorporating a number of conditions or factors dependent upon the concerted working of a whole group of cortical zones and sub cortical structures, each of which makes its own contribution to the performance of the movement and supplies its own factor to its structure. (1973, pp. 37–38)

By following this line of thought, it may be concluded that symptoms, when only superficially analyzed (e.g., overt behavioral system, statistically based hypothesis), are only reflecting the surface of a pathological entity usually misleading the subsequent process of clinical treatment. Therefore, when analyzing specific cognitive and emotional disturbance with various multiethnic population, a syndromic analysis will lead us to the question as to how the specific pathology reflects his own socio-bio-psychological entity (Jantzen, 2004).

By identifying and analyzing objectively how different functional systems interact to form a complex pathological activity, a clinician will be in a position of making appropriate interpretations as to how specifically context-related functional systems are disturbed and how they can be restored by clinical intervention. For example, when evaluating an adult who suffers from attention deficit disorder, we must first analyze how symptoms such as wandering off, forgetfulness, and low academic achievement are all interconnected and affect their social activity, self-appraisal, emotionalism, and self-motivation.

Unfortunately, the political prevalence of social dominant groups controlled by powerful institutions exerts coercion on both the educational and mental health services (Parker, 1999). As a result, the provision of clinical services conforms to the norms imposed by the social establishment. By adjusting statistical norms and parameters from the mainstream culture, and turning them into socially sensitive instruments, clinicians usually feel that they provide an efficient therapeutic service. Nevertheless, by limiting their intervention just to the effects of specific techniques and neglecting the impact that social mediators have on psychopathology, they fail to provide patients from non-dominant cultures with adequate tools to attain valuable therapeutic changes.

In brief, although Luria's major premises were mostly derived from his work with cerebrally impaired patients, the essence of his contribution goes beyond the scope of neuropsychology. Luria's major legacy to the present and the future of cultural-historical psychotherapy and neurorehabilitation can be regarded as twofold:

First, by understanding that social history and its complexities are the dynamic force underlying psychological processes, Luria proposed a cultural-historical analysis of higher psychological functions as a way to establish the foundation for a true scientific rehabilitation of complex cognitive-emotional disturbances within different populations. This concept originally developed by Vygotsky is the key for understanding how specific disturbed psychological processes are the result of a multiple overlapping between faulty social activity, poor problem-solving strategies, dysfunctional physiological activity systems, and social rejection from dominant groups.

Second, by conceptualizing psychological processes from a three-level-based functional model, Luria presented a very sophisticated view of higher psychological functions. This model is valid to explain the overlapping between different pathological functional systems. For example, in the second case presented it was clearly seen how the external acceptance of the patient's socially mediated attitude towards his illness (second functional unit) played a crucial role during his reprocessing (through self-internalization and self-motivation: the third functional unit). In fact, by actively learning to solve medical issues, through different therapeutic techniques (e.g., pain management, relaxation, cognitive restructuring, interpersonal dynamics, especially those first and second functional units), he regained both emotional and cognitive endurance. No longer did he feel exploited and coerced by the dominant system, but rather he felt motivated to direct his social activity to fulfill his own needs.

Due to global financial conditions, the turning of the 21st century has witnessed drastic political changes worldwide. As a result, there has been an increased influx of immigrants to the United States (mostly from Latin American countries). As the number of immigrants increases, there is more potential for social and emotional dysfunction, physical injury, and a subsequent need for rehabilitation services and counseling (Portes, Nixon & Sandhu, 2008). By understanding the cultural-historical nature of human psychopathology and its role in rehabilitation, the ideas discussed in this chapter have proposed an alternative to current treatment guidelines for Latinos and other ethnic minorities in the United States.

# Part
## ·2·

## · 8 ·

# Only Life Educates

## Immigrant Families, the Cultivation of Biliteracy, and the Mobility of Knowledge

### Luis C. Moll

> *Our only concern is that there exist within the very nature*
> *of the educational process, within its psychological essence,*
> *the demand that there be as intimate a contact, and as close*
> *an interaction, with life itself as might be wished for. Ultimately,*
> *only life educates…(Vygotsky, 1997b, p. 345)*

In this chapter, I discuss how my colleagues and I have appropriated ideas in our educational research related to the concept of the cultural mediation of thinking, which I take as paradigmatic of the Vygotskyan approach. My goal here, then, is not to provide any sort of summary account of Vygotsky's contributions, which has already been done ably by others (e.g., van der Veer, 2007), or of the varying interpretations of his work (e.g., Arias, this volume; González Rey, this volume). The goal instead is to show how Vygotsky's concept of mediation, coordinated with contemporary anthropological concepts, particularly those that challenge essentialist notions of culture through an understanding of culture as practices or lived experiences, has helped determine our approach to literacy and schooling, especially for Latino children in U.S. schools. At the very least, I want to provide a sense of how we are, as Glick (this volume) suggests in his chapter, integrating this seminal concept of mediation deeply into our praxes, giving it a particular take or "sabor."[1]

As Kozulin (1995) has pointed out, Vygotsky's notion of mediation includes three large classes of mediators: signs and symbols, interpersonal relations, and individual activities (p. 119). Vygotsky (1978, 1987b) concentrated primarily on what he called "psychological tools," the semiotic potential of systems of signs and symbols (most significantly language) in mediating thinking (see also, Wertsch, 2007). Pontecorvo (1993) summarizes well the Vygotskyan idea of mediation: "Mediation tools include the semiotic systems pertaining to different languages and to various scientific fields; these are procedures, *thought methodologies*, and cultural objects that have to be appropriated, practices of discourse and reasoning that have to be developed, and play or study practices that have to be exercised" (p. 191, emphasis added).

I will concentrate on relating these ideas to three areas of research mentioned in the subtitle to this chapter. In particular, I will emphasize the centrality of the processes of appropriation and recontextualization of cultural resources, either by teachers or by students, in the formation of such "thought methodologies" for educational action. I start by summarizing some elements of research that we initiated about 20 years ago involving mostly immigrant (and second-generation) households, which we refer to as "funds of knowledge" research (González, Moll, & Amanti, 2005). The central idea here is that families, regardless of social class or economic standing, can be characterized by the practices they have developed and knowledge they have acquired in the living of their lives. Furthermore, this knowledge base can be treated pedagogically as cultural resources for teaching and learning in schools. This attempt to relate, document, and utilize funds of knowledge helps define the families as possessing valuable resources for their children's education. A key here is for teachers to become "cultural protagonists," a term I borrow from Labarrere Sarduy (1996a), in establishing contact with social practices and funds of knowledge as part and parcel of their pedagogy.

Similarly, for several years I have been interested in the development of biliteracy in children. Here I am using the term biliteracy to refer to competence with print literacy in two languages, a limited and perhaps inadequate definition given the proliferation of new technologies, variability and hybridity of ways with literacy today (García, Bartlett, & Kliefgen, 2007). I am also not nearly as interested in biliteracy in terms of its linguistic factors or "variables," as I am in understanding biliteracy as a cultural practice or way of life (e.g., Reyes, in press). I propose that literate bilingualism has important consequences for children by allowing them, the pedagogy willing, as I shall explain, to gain access to a broad array of cultural resources for thinking. It is the expansiveness afforded by biliteracy that impresses me, its boundary crossing, its transculturation, one could say; how it blurs boundaries between languages and social worlds, and how it facilitates the mobility of knowledge for social or academic purposes.

This is what Mignolo (2000), inspired by Anzaldúa (1987), calls languaging or bilanguaging, thinking and writing between languages. His interest, as he writes, is in "moving away from the idea that language is a fact (e.g., a system of syntactic, semantic, and phonetic rules), and moving toward the idea that speech and writing are strategies for orienting and manipulating social domains of interaction" (p. 226). Important for present purposes is that Mignolo (2000) emphasizes understanding "languaging" as both cultural practice and power struggle. That is, as a way of both being in the world, as one lives through both languages, and as a way of questioning power and domination by revealing the ideologies of uniformity in "monolanguaging." As he puts it, this is a way of questioning if not fracturing the hegemonic, and a way of decolonizing and relocating knowledge. Biliteracy, then, especially in the U.S. context, with the hegemony of English, always involves issues of "power differentials and tensions about linguistic rights" (García et al., 2007). Hence the interest in bilanguaging as autobiography, as a way of life, as a form of intellectual decolonization, one could say, and as a way of translating our thinking for others to benefit, not simply as decontextualized skills that can be assessed and marked by so-called measures.

I will then turn to the idea of the mobility of knowledge. I take this term from Montgomery (2002), who examines through multiple examples the crucial role of translation, and hence of biliteracy in various forms, in the history of scientific knowledge and in the building of Western science (see also, Chabrán, 2007; Varey & Chabrán, 1995). "Knowledge," Montgomery writes, "whatever its contents, has always been a mobile form of culture" (p. 2). The movement of knowledge, however one defines it, he adds, as facts and hypothesis, or as products of specific forms of labor, has occurred through trade and commerce, war and conquest and, of course, through all forms of immigration, to become a basic "feature of daily life along national and linguistic borders, both within and between cultures" (p. 2).

I will feature a project where students participating in an action research project develop new forms of mediation for the creation of knowledge about social issues that matter to them, and for mobilizing this new knowledge for political ends. As such, central to this work is not only the development of new meditational means, in the form of students' writings and uses of media, but also the re-contextualization of their emergent knowledge as part of their action research. Moreover, as important, through that inquiry and transformation, the students transform themselves.

## Immigrant Families

Contemporary forces of globalization have spurred the mobility of scientists and highly skilled professionals, and that of laborers in the form of massive international migration, all of them, in one way or another, involved in the mobilization of knowledge. Here I am most interested in what some would call ordinary, but no less important, knowledge. For example, it is common in the immigration literature to depict working-class immigrant families as having little or no human capital. This concept is usually operationally defined by a combination of level of occupation and years of schooling, criteria by which these families do not fare well. There are, to be sure, dire consequences to a lack of human capital, including economic stagnation, and a corresponding lack of school success for their children. A depressed socioeconomic standing, as is well known, has major implications for the schooling of children, both in terms of their preparation to begin school (Lee & Burkam, 2002), and of inequalities regarding the quality of their experiences in school (Oakes, Joseph, & Muir, 2004).

I argue that these depictions of immigrant families as bereft of human capital are misleading, at least in terms of conceptualizing a pedagogy that may help their children in school. Our studies have documented that immigrant households are generally characterized by a broad variety of experiences, skills, values, and practices that life, including going to school, has given them, which we refer to as "funds of knowledge" (González, Moll, & Amanti, 2005; Moll & González, 2004; Ríos-Aguilar, 2007). Furthermore, as a feature of daily life, there is mobility to these funds of knowledge that makes them particularly valuable. One is that this knowledge travels well, it is not checked in at the border, the immigrants bring it, and it may be activated to become part of either the formal or informal sector of the economy. For example, funds of knowledge about construction are often viable and expandable within the U.S. urban economy, but all that can change rapidly, as the current economic problems have shown.

A second way these funds of knowledge become mobile is inter-generationally, depending on the particular circumstances for living. We had some families in our studies that purchased small plots of land that they turned into gardens, where they could teach their children how to cultivate plants and vegetables and help them appreciate the value of such labor. These were deliberate attempts to transfer funds of knowledge and values to a new generation. We also had families who discovered that valuable knowledge generated by their labor history, for example, knowledge about horses from working at a ranch, or about the medicinal uses of plants, became irrelevant in the urban context, and thus often difficult to transfer to a new generation.

Yet another mode of mobility was through relations of exchange with other households as part of their social networks. For example, a person with knowledge about roofing might offer another to help fix his or her roof in exchange for mechanical knowledge necessary to help fix a car. Notice that the currency in this transaction is of funds of knowledge, hence the metaphor. What we referred to as "thick" or multiple social networks generally facilitate the exchange of such funds of knowledge among households. In contrast to these households, "thin" social networks usually characterize classrooms, where teachers and students rarely reach beyond the classroom walls as part of their routines for living and learning in schools.

Building on these observations, we made the case in our work for making funds of knowledge pedagogically worthy by transporting them into classroom contexts. As we have detailed elsewhere (González et al., 2005), central to this work have been teacher-researchers entering households as learners with an ethnographic eye toward documenting funds of knowledge. These household visits provided teachers with an important "cultural framing" of families and students, with implications for the teaching of literacy or mathematics as meaningful practices. Also central in this work, however, has been the formation of teacher study groups. We refer to this group formation, following Vygotsky (1978) as a "mediating structure": a setting where we could mutually shape our research practices and our understanding of the data collected in households in ways that help define working-class families as possessing valuable cultural resources for instruction, challenging perceptions that they would be lacking in such assets, while helping teachers develop both theory and methods on which to base their pedagogy. In brief, the emphasis has been on treating diversity, as manifested in the lives of people, as a pedagogical resource. The goal has been to provide not only an understanding of diversity, but a diversity of understandings to make sense of the heterogeneity of living.

## Cultivating Biliteracy

A related area of research has been on *cultivating* in students new funds of knowledge, in this case, *bilingual literate practices.* The power of such biliteracy, I propose, resides in its *boundary crossing*, in one's ability (and disposition) to read in one language, either word or world, and discuss (or write) what is read in the other. This form of code switching or interliteracy is what helps students garner and combine valuable funds of knowledge from their multiple environments for personal or academic use; that is, biliteracy serves to expand, one could say, the students' cultural and intellectual geographies in a transnational world.

Dyson (2001) makes a related point about "the centrality of the cultural symbols and practices through which children construct their own varied childhoods" (p. 11). She elaborates as follows:

These cultural resources reveal children's powers of adaptation and improvisation—their symbolic and discourse flexibility—and it is children's exploitation of these cross-cultural childhood strengths (Stephens, 1995; Sutton-Smith, 1997) and their ways of stretching, reconfiguring, and re-articulating their resources, that are key to literacy learning in contemporary times (p. 11).

Consider this third-grade example of biliteracy, where two girls collaborated to write a bilingual story (from Moll, Saez, & Dworin, 2001, p. 444). Lupita and her close friend, Racheal, have written a story about a new girl in the neighborhood, and the ethnic resentment she encounters, but they also provide an ending featuring a harmonious (and humorous) resolution. For clarity, I have included a typed version of the hand-written original but one that retains the girls' punctuation and spelling:

### The new Girl in the Neighborhood
By Lupita and Racheal

One day a new girl moved in my neighborhood. She was poor. I did not like her. She also was a Mexican girl. I went to her house and asked her name. "Mi nombre es Raquel," she replied. "I know a little bit of Spanish," I told her. "I know a little of 'ingles,'" Raquel told me. "Mi nombre es Michelle I don't like you." I yelled and then I yelled "Your not supposed to by holy today your supposed to be holy Sunday." She started to cry, then ran inside.

The next day my teacher said, "we have a new girl", "her name is Raquel." I screamed "What's the matter the teacher asked. "nothing I though I saw a spider"

After school I went to Raquel's house and asked "What were you doing in MY classroom"? "Para aprender a escribir y leer en ingles." She answered. "If YOU SHOW UP TOMorrow at my school Ill hurt you. And then she said. "No te entiendo." I got so mad that I screamed and ran away. The next day I went to her house and we talked and I found out that we had lots in common. And we were friend for ever.

The End

Notice the themes in this imaginative text, which include bilingual exchanges, humor, irrational dislikes, literacy learning, hostility to others who are different, and similarities leading to friendship. With the teacher's help, any one of these themes could have been elaborated more fully in writing or through discussions in class or study groups. As we wrote then, "The text represents an example of bringing life into the writing, and of using writing, and its conventions, to examine issues of life. But it also represents the extent to which languages can interconnect and interact with each other as part of the children's writing" (p. 444). What we failed to mention at the time was how affect-laden the text is; how emotions permeate (and mediate) the storytelling and how both languages are used, indeed, cleverly manipulated, to capture and display those essential elements of the story and their experiences. Here I am reminded of González Rey's (this volume) proposal for understanding the important generative character of emotions in the development of thinking.

The above is just one of many examples we could have presented from classrooms in which writing is fostered daily for many purposes and in which the use of both languages is encouraged and supported in a variety of ways for the expression of thinking and the elaboration of meaning. The broad range of communicative resources that such practices afford help constitute what Kenner and Kress (2003) have called the "multisemiotic resources of biliterate children." Central among these resources is the ability to cross social, linguistic, and cultural borders as part of their intellectual work with literacy. This is what Dyson (2001) refers to as the "recontextualization process" by which cultural resources are transported and adapted by children across social boundaries as part of their strategies for learning.

How feasible is it to foster biliteracy en masse? Quite feasible. For many bilingual schools, producing biliterate children early in their schooling is a routine achievement. In the school we studied, which featured a dual-language immersion model, children became literate in Spanish and English with relative ease, regardless of ethnic background, social class, or home language. However, the faculty and administrators established the vitality of Spanish by monitoring the proportion or distribution of use of the language in the school (Moll & Cammarota, 2010). That is, in the ideological context of the U.S. southwest, the staff's policy decision and goal was to make Spanish an *unmarked* language in the context of the school, what Luke (2008) calls establishing the school's *lingua franca*. English needed no such protection; it predominated among the children.

What may be some of the long-term consequences of early biliteracy in children? As Ortner (2006) has pointed out, "the playing out of the effects of culturally organized practices is essentially processual and often very slow: the construction of social subjects, often from childhood; the practices of life of young people and adults; the articulation of those practices with larger events in the world, often moving to a very different rhythm" (p. 9). As she adds, although one can form hypotheses about the long-term implications of such practices, especially in terms of social reproduction or transformation, their effects are often not visible until some time later.

However, we get a good sense of some of the long-term implications of cultivating biliteracy from the decade-long longitudinal work of the sociologist Alejandro Portes and colleagues on second-generation adaptation into U.S. society (Portes & Rumbaut, 2001; Portes et al., 2008).[2] Rather than the assimilationist model that so many policy makers embrace, with its complete disregard for preserving languages other than English, by far the most successful mode of adaptation was what they refer to as *selective acculturation*. Here children learn English and U.S. ways, while retaining important elements of the home culture, most notably fluency in the language. In this scenario, fluent bilingualism is key to preserving intergenerational communications, and with it parents' ability to provide discipline and direction for their children, monitor their academic progress, provide vigilance regarding their social relationships, and facilitate appreciation and respect for the parental culture, funds of knowledge and values. As their data show, selective acculturation and fluent bilingualism are significantly associated with several positive outcomes in late adolescence, including higher school grades, self-esteem, and educational aspirations, and lesser intergenerational conflict with families (Portes et al., 2008). These findings illustrate how bilingualism, especially if made fluent and literate through years of additive schooling, becomes not only a transformative resource for the students, but also a critical aspect of the cultural capital and knowledge necessary for social and academic advancement.

## Mobilizing Knowledge

I want to conclude by summarizing the work of some colleagues in developing a new "activity system," participatory action research, that has as a goal mobilizing students to address social issues of importance to them and their families by generating new knowledge through their studies and research (from Moll & Cammarota, 2010; see also, Cammarota, 2007, 2008). This work is known as the Social Justice Education Project (SJEP). The project began in 2003, in a course with 17 high school students. Currently, the program offers more than 150 students five courses at three different high schools. The majority of the students are from the predominantly Latino communities of the city. Most are children from poor or working-class families, and most have not experienced continued success in school.

The goal of the SJEP is to help the students achieve academically while helping them conduct critical research on issues that matter to them (Cammarota, 2008). Thus, students to satisfy their social science requirements for their senior year and read college-level material in critical race theory, critical pedagogy, and participatory action research (Cammarota, 2007). The goal is ensure that students meet state standards while developing the critical awareness vital for questioning and improving their social and educational experiences.

In brief, SJEP promotes critical reading and engagement, and students learn how to apply ethnographic methods to the study of their schools and communities. Students conduct observations, carried out weekly for several months, of social settings and document their findings via field notes, poetry, photos, and videos, which become their tools for thinking. The process of observing and recording eventually leads to the creation of new funds of knowledge, as students gain insights, often for the first time, into the details of social problems, such as racism and other forms of discrimination. These insights help motivate the students to prepare themselves to become advocates for social justice.

For example, the students' first video, "Questions for Answers," documents how the south-end portion of their high school is structurally inferior to the northern end, which tends house projects mostly attended by white students (from Moll & Cammarota, 2010). However, most students at the school (63%) are working-class Latinos, while Whites are in the minority (19%); the Native American (12%) and African American students (6%) comprise the rest of the student population.

The video shows the southern section, the space that most students of color inhabit, with broken bathrooms and water fountains, pipes protruding from walls, and library shelves with missing books. The video also offers a contrast to the northern section of campus, where floors and walls are immaculate, there is a fully stocked law library for a special study program, and computers abound. The video and its analysis were presented to teachers, students, and administrators as evidence of the discrepancy of resource allocation, even within the same high school.

Of note is that each semester, SJEP students hold "*Encuentros*" (encounters; public meetings) with their families to explain their work and the new knowledge that emerged from their research. In essence, students develop not only solid academic identities but also new subjectivities: they start seeing themselves as public intellectuals acting on behalf of fellow students, family members, and themselves. This work, then, features a similar intergenerational relational dynamic around matters of schooling and life that Portes et al. (2008) deemed crucial for student success.

## Discussion

I have presented three separate summaries of projects that cohere around efforts to improve schooling. Central to each is the need to engage life by going beyond the walls of the school, as Vygotsky proposed in the epigraph. Each project featured, in different ways, multiple modes of mediation for the appropriation of cultural resources and the recontextualization of knowledge and practices. Our strategy in the funds of knowledge work was to help teachers conduct visits to students' homes to facilitate establishing relations of trust with the families, to whatever extent possible, and to be able to start documenting social practices and the knowledge that the family has derived from their experiences. The goal here was not only to inform teachers about the knowledge available in these homes, but for teachers to take action by developing their own inquiries into these households to collect firsthand data about their funds of knowledge. To accomplish these goals, we established a teacher study group that would serve as a mediating structure to do the work. We would meet as a group prior to the home visits and subsequent to them to discuss what we had learned. Similarly, the planning of a pedagogy that would strategically incorporate the families' knowledge would also take place in the study group, where we would help each other think about teaching. In addition, it is in the study group where teachers would learn the theory and methods by which to carry out the visits, and where we would learn to talk about families in terms of the resources they possess, as documented through our studies, rather than on any assumed deficits. This mediation helped establish a more forthright representation of families, any vulnerabilities notwithstanding, characterized by an abundance of funds of knowledge.

In a second project, we claim that the development of biliteracy is a way of providing children with powerful and expansive meditational tools for thinking. The claim is straightforward: biliteracy helps students garner resources from not just one but two sociocultural and literate worlds. As illustrated in the example above, it helps young children use both languages to represent and convey an imagined scenario in writing, in this case, a playful take on cross-cultural and bilingual life's issues. One caveat for classroom teachers: the advantages of biliteracy do not necessarily accrue automatically; the teacher must provide an additive pedagogy, one that respects and fosters the dual development of language as assets for learning and development. In the context of the United States, this is a pedagogy against the grain, both in fostering bilingualism, especially in Spanish, a marked language, and given that tightly scripted curricula are the norm in teaching, in providing children with the openness to innovate and develop their sense of agency as learners. As shown earlier, and as Dyson (2001) underscores in her research, the students' "sense of agency, of possibility, comes from recontextualizing, that is, from rearranging, re-articulating, and stretching their ways with words" (p. 14).

The third project is an attempt to engage students, all of them adolescents, in social practices that seek to question and challenge the status quo; this a critical form of civic engagement to improve conditions in their schools and communities (Cammarota, 2007, 2008; Cannella, 2009). Central to the work is the students' development of a more elaborate symbolic repertoire in conducting research and in representing the findings of their work for multiple audiences, notably not only school authorities or peers but also their own families. What my summary intends to capture is the transformational potential of these mediating practices; that in doing action research, the students are also forming new subjectivities as "sociohistorical analysts and actors," to use Cannella's phrase (2009), with important consequences for their view of and investment in formal schooling as empowering rather than curtailing their developmental trajectories.

I close by extending the opening quote from Vygotsky (1997b),[3] which captures the essence of this chapter:

> Ultimately, only life educates, and the deeper that life, the real world, burrows into the school, the more dynamic and the more robust will be the educational process. That the school has been locked away and walled in as if by a tall fence from life itself has been its greatest failing. Education is just as meaningless outside the real world as is a fire without oxygen, or as is breathing in a vacuum. The teacher's educational work, therefore, must be inevitably connected with his [or her] creative, social, and life work. (p. 345)

## ENDNOTES

1    Portions of this paper appeared in Moll and Cammarota (2010).

2    Their sample, based mostly in Miami and San Diego, two prominent receiving communities for immigrants, consisted initially (1992) of 5,200 students, who were then in ninth grade. They collected data subsequently in 1995–96, when the students were high-school seniors, and then in 2002, when they were about 24 years old, or young adults.

3    I initially found this quote, in abbreviated form, in Terrell (2009).

## · 9 ·

# Computer-Mediated Learning and Young Latino/a Students' Developing Expertise

*Carmen M. Martínez-Roldán & Peter Smagorinsky*

It was Thursday, and a group of 16 second-grade Latino/a students had just finished playing online games in the Amigos Clase Mágica [Friends' Magic Classroom], a new after-school computer-mediated program at their elementary school. Diana, one of the undergraduate students from the university providing assistance to the children, wrote in her field notes about Oscar, the boy she had been mentoring for two months, and added an observer's comment (OC) with her reflection:

> He learned how to measure the distance and speed…so that he could stop at the right time and not have the bicycle turn over and lose a life. He also learned which keys to use to make the bicycle go forward; I figured it would be the left arrow key but it was the down arrow key so I learned something from him even though we both were new to the game. (OC: I was surprised that he was able to pick up on this kind of stuff faster than me but I think it has to do with the newer generations and that their world is surrounded by technology more than my generation.) (Field notes, April 22, 2010)

In the excerpt above, 20-year-old Diana, an intern (teacher candidate) in the Bilingual Professional Development Service (PDS) Program at the University of Texas-Austin, reflected with surprise about how fast Oscar, an eight-year-old student, was learning (all names are pseudonyms). Diana was one of the 31 university students who participated in the after-school program created by the first author[1] for bilingual students to support their reading and their digital literacy learning. The program simultaneously provided the interns with face-to-face interactions with bilingual learners and opportunities to conduct informal assessments. The after-school program was inspired by La Clase Mágica (LCM) developed to equip bilingual youths between the ages of 3 and 16 with the academic, cultural, and social skills that they need to meet and exceed state educational standards (Vásquez, 2003).

On this day, Oscar was playing the online game Neopets and surprised Diana by discovering the right key to engage with a part of the game. Diana found herself learning something from this youngster in an educational context in which she had been considered the more expert. She acknowledged that there might be a gap between these second-grade Latino/a children and her generation, one characterized by the distinction between *digital natives* who grow up exposed to new technologies and *digital immigrants* who have not (Prensky, 2001).

The opening excerpt was typical of the dynamics involved in the interns and students' collaborative computer use during the last two weeks of the program. Like Oscar, other students in the program were developing expertise in some computer games, surprising the interns, who found themselves learning from the students. The line between expert and learner got blurred for many of the children and the interns participating in the program, raising questions about the nature of the mediation in the zone of proximal development for both children and interns. Using Vygotsky's (1978, 1987c) concept of mediation, and drawing on New Literacy Studies (The New London Group, 1996) and related scholarship on multimodality (e.g., John-Steiner, 1987, 1995; Smagorinsky, 1995a, 2001), we address the ways in which the learning of digital literacies was mediated in this after-school program for Latino/a students.

# Cultural-Historical Factors in Teaching and Learning Mediation in the Zone of Proximal Development

Vygotsky's (1978) cultural-historical theory of learning and development provides a useful framework for examining children's learning as they interact with different people and different tools and artifacts, such as computer games in joint activity with adults and peers. Two themes relevant to this study are Vygotsky's argument that individuals' higher mental processes have their origins in social processes and cultural practices and that mental processes can be understood only if observers understand the cultural-historical nature of the tools and signs that mediate them (Wertsch, 1985). Vygotsky (1978) described interactions between children and adults or more capable peers as central to children's learning and development. His concept of mediation in the zone of proximal development highlights such a role: "what a child can do with assistance today she will be able to do by herself tomorrow" (p. 87).

Teachers and adults undoubtedly have a crucial role as mediators of children's learning, yet differential levels of digital expertise across generations complicate conventional notions of who is teaching whom what. Although there is an agreement on the crucial role teachers and adults play, the nature of the assistance and mediation has been the subject of debate, and researchers are still trying to understand how much assistance and under which circumstances this assistance supports students' learning (Smagorinsky, 1995b). The research we report in this chapter lends credence to sociocultural constructivist conceptions of teaching and learning relationships that allow for considerable agency on the part of learners-as-teachers. Dyson's (1990) rejection of the "scaffolding" metaphor in favor of a "weaving" metaphor illustrates this more interactive, mutually instructive conception of the ZPD, one that we found at work in the Amigos Clase Mágica.

Rejecting reductionist interpretations of the concept of mediation in the ZPD, Moll and Whitmore (1993) underscore that the ZPD involves "the child engaged in collaborative activity within a specific social (discourse) environment" (p. 20). The ZPD is thus not what Wilhelm, Baker, and Dube (2001) describe as a "cognitive region, which lies just beyond what the child can do alone. Anything that the child can learn with the assistance and support of a teacher, peers, and the instructional environment is said to lie within the ZPD" (p. 16). It is, rather, an interrelated set of social contexts that are deeply rooted in cultural and historical traditions, practices, and artifacts (Moll, 1990). ZPDs thus lack the sort of containment asserted by Wilhelm et al. and involve more of the "weaving" implied by the etymology of the term "context" (Cole, 1996) and recognized by Dyson (1990). Moll and Whitmore (1993) propose that the key to understanding learning in classroom contexts is to attend to the social transactions that make up classroom life: "Within this analysis the focus of study is on the sociocultural system within which children learn, with the understanding that this system is mutually and actively created by teachers and students. What we propose is a 'collective' zone of proximal development" (p. 20).

The notion of a collective zone of proximal development is related to the concept of distributed cognition (Salomon, 1993), since knowledge is shared among participants in sociocultural activity and manifested in the artifacts of human production (Rogoff, 2003), each with unique affordances and constraints available both through the material form of the artifacts themselves and the social practices that guide action in particular settings (Wertsch, 1991a). Individuals, for instance, would find it materially difficult to eat a thin soup with a fork and be socially discouraged from combing their hair with a fork at a formal dinner, possible though it might be.

Moreover, an apt definition of the ZPD applied to classroom practices for Moll and Whitmore (1993) must include the active child *appropriating* and *developing* new meditational means for learning. Shifting the emphasis from the adult/more-competent-peer and child dyad to what an individual can accomplish through participation in joint sociocultural activity opens up possibilities to understand the kinds of learning and dynamics that occur in computer-mediated environments in which the participants play games and use digital resources. Although gaps between those assigned different formal roles such as teacher and student might remain superficially in place, these gaps can mask other ways in which task-and-setting appropriate knowledge can be distributed more equitably across relationships.

This sociocultural perspective enables researchers to study people's use and transformation of cultural tools and technologies and their involvement and participation in the social, discursive, and cultural practices of their families and communities. Such practices are not fixed but rather change in relation to the protean dynamics of interpersonal and intrapersonal action and the teleological goals toward which action is directed in relation to task, setting, and participant factors (Rogoff, 2003; Smagorinsky, 2001; Wertsch, 2000). Two contexts that have experienced much change in the last decades involve literacy and play, which have prompted the "digital turn" in literacy research. Next we review briefly some studies about learning in computer-mediated environments.

## Learning in After-School Programs via Computer Games

Play, schooling, and work have been identified within the cultural-historical perspective as three leading activities mediating people's development. "In play," Vygotsky (1966/1933) maintains, "a child is always above his average age, above his daily behavior; in play it is as though he were a head taller than himself" (p. 25). It is important to note that the notion of "play" cannot be equated with "having fun" from the perspective we are taking via Vygotsky. Rather, play involves experimentation, playing with ideas, testing boundaries, trying out possibilities, and engaging in other forms of open-ended activity that might involve failure rather than fun. Because, however, the stakes of the experimental activity tend to be low—there is no external punishment for failure—an unsuccessful playful effort can benefit the learner's knowledge by helping to inform the next attempt and the development of a conception of the activity.

Recognizing the role of play activity in children's development, Griffin and Cole (1984) examined elementary children's learning in the computer-mediated after-school program of the Fifth Dimension. They developed the Fifth Dimension as a device to organize the students' activities with computers without imposing a school-like control structure of the sort that establishes a top-down teaching-and-learning relationship as opposed to the more reciprocal notion of the ZPD we endorse in this chapter. The program combined play and education to support children who were facing academic challenges at school. The children played different games, solved problems, and communicated online with the Wizard, a magical electronic entity whose role was played by a Fifth Dimension adult acting as part of the fantasy world of the program.

Playing different computer games in the Fifth Dimension created ZPDs for the children in which they could collaboratively organize themselves and perform beyond themselves given that they chose to fully enter into the activities. Their participation in this computer-mediated environment supported children's development of creative analyses and problem solving. Unfortunately, the team working on the Fifth Dimension had tried to entice bilingual students to join the program with no positive results. This concern prompted some initial adaptations that finally led to the innovation of La Clase Mágica (Vásquez, 2003).

La Clase Mágica expanded the Fifth Dimension to include early childhood, adolescent, and adult participants with a special interest in the children's families. Undergraduate students, called Amigos and Amigas, work with the children to help them move through a series of prearranged computer and online communication activities: "the students and the system of artifacts (e.g., maze, task, and constitution) prompt children to imagine themselves in a journey through a bilingual-bicultural fantasy word ruled by the magical electronic pal known as *El Maga*" (Vásquez, 2003, p. 8), the counterpart of the Wizard in the Fifth Dimension. Within the complex activity system of LCM, the cultural relevance of the program became one of the most salient meditational means of student learning. Students' language and culture were integrated in all aspects of the program including the meditational artifact of the maze that included the games the children could navigate (Vásquez, 1993).

## Digital Literacies

New Literacy Studies conceive of "reading" as an act undertaken with texts comprised of any configuration of signs into which a meaning potential may be built (Kress & van Leeuwen, 2006; Street, 2003; cf. Smagorinsky, 2001). Youths become parts of discourse communities that employ specialized languages as they develop interest and expertise in certain topics out of school (Gee, 2007b; Shaffer, 2006). Moreover, Gee (2007a) has proposed that a variety of learning principles are built into good video games, especially in "epistemic" video games in which students learn the "ways of knowing" of a community of practice or profession (Shaffer, 2006).

Electronic gaming is but one area of scholarly inquiry that has developed since the mid-1990s in the wake of widespread access to the World Wide Web and its successors. Digital spaces afford youths the opportunity to remix the worlds that they inherit into new configurations that suit their needs in shaping their identities in the malleable worlds that they find online (Knobel & Lankshear, 2008). These spaces, including those available at the Amigos Clase Mágica, stand in stark contrast to the learning environments of school, which are remarkably durable in perpetuating an authoritarian culture that both teachers and students find difficult to change (Smagorinsky, 2010).

## Context of the After-School Program

The after-school program was inspired by La Clase Mágica (Vásquez, 2003), including the procedure by which an undergraduate supports a student's interaction with computer games based on instructions provided on a Task Card to play a game at the beginning, intermediate or expert level. The games are included in a maze that the students need to follow, and there is a fantasy entity (El Maga, comparable to the Fifth Dimension's Wizard) who communicates with the children through email. The undergraduates working with the child write field notes describing the students' learning and their own. The Amigos Clase Mágica adapted most of these components, and a lesson plan was added to provide the interns with some direction.

Twice a week for two months, 31 interns taking a bilingual reading class with the first author met with second graders for an hour after the school day. Half of the interns worked with the children on Wednesdays and the other half on Thursdays. The sessions formally opened with the reading of a children's book. The interns read to or with the children a Latino/a literature text in English or Spanish. The selection of the literature responded to the nature of the game the students were going to play. For example, the day when the students used the website *Maya and Miguel* (http://www.scholastic.com/mayaandmiguel/), the interns chose books such as *El sancocho del sábado* (Saturday sancocho) (L. Torres, 1995) and *The empanadas that Abuela made/ Las empanadas que hacía la abuela* (Gonzales Bertrand, 2003) to make connections with the game *Cocina con abuela* (Cooking with Grandma) within the website.

The interns could also select books based on students' interests. For instance, during the first week Antonia learned that César had some favorite wrestlers and watched wrestling shows in Spanish and English. For the next meeting, she brought to the session the book *Lucha libre: The man in the silver mask: A bilingual cuento* (Garza, 2005) instead of the one she had previously chosen. After 15 minutes of reading, the students used the computers to play a game.

The games were listed in a maze or *laberinto*. Each pair of undergraduates working with the same child presented a different game or website to the undergraduate class (Figure 1 shows the maze created with the undergraduates) and prepared a weekly lesson plan and a task card with instructions to the children to engage with the games.

The weekly plan included the Texas Essential Knowledge and Skills (TEKS; see http://www.tea.state.tx.us/index2.aspx?id=6148) components that could be supported through the game; a description of the game explaining how it could be considered an epistemic game; information regarding whether the game encouraged problem solving, creativity, biliteracy, or identity development; and an anticipation of what sorts of identities the game seemed to support. The plan also included the titles of the two children's books used in the Reading compo-

FIGURE 1. The Laberinto or Maze

nent that week and criteria for selecting the texts. The interns were told that the most important factor was to be responsive to the children's needs.

The sessions ended with the children writing to El Maga and reading its emails and a short debriefing as a class in which the children shared which games they visited within the sites and which ones they liked most, enabling the children to learn of other possibilities from their peers.

## Findings

This section is organized around three major themes. We begin by offering some additional background for the interactions, using examples of the conversations between Antonia and her student César to illustrate how the students were being introduced into the program (i.e., into playing online games and using email). These interactions also involved the fluid use of Spanish and English mediating their interactions and digital learning, and the roles the Interns played in mediating this learning. Second, we pay attention to the kinds of digital literacy learning the students demonstrated while using websites aimed at supporting their production of multimodal texts and digital media. Third, we discuss and analyze examples in which the locus of authority began to shift, and the students began to learn from each other. The data illustrate the interactive nature of the ZPD afforded by the Amigos Clase Mágica in the manner outlined by Moll (1990) and the ways in which bilingual children whose linguistic potential is underestimated in their schools demonstrate expertise when provided settings for learning that encourage their agency.

## Creating a Bilingual Community Around Books and Computer Games

During the first three days of the program (Week One and Two), the two major goals were to introduce the students into the program and to learn about their digital literacies and experiences with computers. The coordinator (a graduate student) and the first author began to build a sense of group and community as members of La Clase Mágica program through a series of activities that we thought could help us introduce the fantasy and playful aspect of the program and a sense of identity as bilingual Latino/a students. We used a culturally relevant fictional story to introduce the fantasy entity of El Maga, whose identity and gender were unknown and to whom they would be sending emails. The first author read aloud the story *Prietita and the ghost woman/Prietita y la Llorona* (Anzaldúa, 1996). The children eagerly contributed comments in response to the story and shared experiences about La Llorona, and from there we introduced the fictional entity of El Maga. After the reading, collectively we developed some rules that would help everyone enjoy the program, and everyone, children as well as interns, signed them. The last part of that first day was used to set up an email account for each child so that they could send and receive messages from El Maga.

To introduce the students into the online games while informally assessing their digital learning, we chose a game, identified a website that was simple to navigate, used Spanish and English, and made reference to the bilingual Latino children Maya and Miguel. The game is actually based on a PBS TV program for children with the same name. The Maya and Miguel game was a success for most students. A couple of them who had experience with more complex games found it a little boring, and yet they engaged with it. In addition to the emails the children sent to El Maga, these games helped the interns to get to know the children as persons and digital literacy users and helped the kids get to know the two interns or Amigos/as who would work with them.

The interactions presented next between Antonia, the intern, and César were typical of what transpired between children and their mentors during the first three days. We present the language used in conversations as they used it, codeswitching between English and Spanish. We use italics to represent the Spanish part of the sentences followed by English translation in brackets, while we will use roman print to represent English as used by the participants. The children's codeswitching reveals the manner in which their use of their bilingual capabilities contributed to their learning opportunities in this out-of-school learning environment, in contrast to what is often available to immigrant children in school (Gutiérrez, 1999).

| | |
|---|---|
| Intern: | *Ahora vamos a hacer un email: ¿Sabes lo que es un email?* [Now we are going to create an email. Do you know what an email is?] |
| César: | Uhum. |
| Intern: | *¿Tú tienes un email ya?* [Do you already have an email?] |
| César: | *No.* |
| Intern: | We are going to create you one. *Tú le vas a escribir al Maga.* [You are going to write to El Maga]. (Antonia helps the student answer questions to create an email account). |
| Intern: | Is it male or female? Male *significa* [means] *hombre* [man] *y* [and] female *significa* [means] *mujer* [woman]. |
| César: | Boy |
| Intern: | *Casi siempre te preguntan eso….*[They almost always ask you this question]…(César chooses the pseudonym Rey Misterio or Mystery King). |

Intern: *Dice:* [*It says:*] this is not available; *es que alguien ya lo tiene...* [someone already has it]...(They make changes to the pseudonym until it is accepted by G-mail. When this part is almost done, Antonia accidentally deletes the information or doesn't save it).

Intern: What did I do? I just put—*Oh no! Vamos a hacerlo otra vez.* [Oh no! Let's do it again].

 (Transcript Day 1: March 4, 2010)

This routine became familiar to students and interns since in each new game, they had to go through the process of choosing names, passwords, and gender, and answering security questions. The students were instructed to use invented names during the games and never give their real names or dates of birth, and so the children came up with interesting names, such as El Hombre Araña (Spider Man) or in César's case Rey Misterio (Mystery King). As this excerpt shows, the interns mediated students' access to digital literacies, especially at the beginning, in very explicit and direct ways as they helped the children set up their email accounts or game accounts. The children eventually learned their self-selected names and their passwords and learned where to find Gmail on the website and how to search for games using Google.

Another important piece of information the interns and children soon learned was that some games offer the user a language choice. In the next excerpt César was using the Maya and Miguel website during the second day:

Intern: If you want, you can google it: Maya and Miguel.

César: *¿Cómo se escribe?* [How do you write it?]

 (Antonia spells Maya and Miguel for him).

César: Do I have to leave space?...

 (Finds the website)

Intern: *A ver, ¿lo quieres poner en español o en inglés?* [Let's see, do you want to have it Spanish or English?

César: *Español* [Spanish]

 (Transcript Day 2: March 10, 2010).

On this day, Antonia wrote in her field notes under computer skills: "I noticed that my student knew how use the space button, the use of the caps lock, and moving the cursor. I also learned that he is used to using Firefox." As we will show later, by the end of the program the interns would express amazement at the amount of learning their children had shown in comparison to their entry-level literacy performance.

Antonia also learned early on that César, like herself, was bilingual, but he preferred Spanish and read and wrote in Spanish although he used English often in their interactions. Although the interns were encouraged to use Spanish as much as possible, interns and children moved freely between Spanish and English and resisted any kind of language dichotomy. Through the use of borderland linguistic practices, interns and children had an opportunity to assert their bilingual and borderland identities (Martínez-Roldán & Sayer, 2006) while developing identities as tech savvy students. Spanglish, as described by Zentella (1997) and Bernal-Enríquez and Hernández Chávez (2003), was a crucial mediational tool in students' and undergraduates' interactions around computer games. Nevertheless, the interns used every opportunity they had to help students with their English and mediate the children's language learning. They spelled words for the children or translated for them, as the excerpt above shows. However, Antonia, like most of the interns, was a Latina English dominant, and there were instances in which they were the ones relying on the children as resources for their own Spanish language questions, as the following two short interactions illustrate. Right from the beginning, the relationship between expert and learner was not straightforward:

(They are getting to know each other before beginning the reading and play)

Intern:     *Mi perro se llama* Bullet. *¿Sabes que es* bullet? *En español es como "bala" como* bullet *porque como que le gusta correr bien de volada.* [My dog's name is Bullet. Do you know what does Bullet means? In Spanish is *bala* like bullet because he likes to run very fast.]
(They keep sharing. César talks about his dog...)

Intern:     *¿Cual es tu* subject *favorito?* [What is your favorite subject?]
César:      What's a subject? (Antonia provided examples of subjects).
(Transcript Day 1: March 4, 2010).

The next week:

Intern:     *¿A ti te gusta jugar* bowling? *¿Como se dice* bowling *en español?* [Do you like to play bowling? How do you say bowling in Spanish?]
César:      *Boliche.*
Intern:     *¿Sí?* [Yes?]
(Transcript Day 2: March 10, 2010)

The next day, while writing an email to El Maga, César asked Antonia: "How you do the eñe[2] [in the keyboard]? I forgot." Therefore, there were instances in which the children and the interns supported each other with language issues.

Although the program had some structure, it also had an informal character to it in addition to its focus on games. Within this context, power and authority presented themselves in a more distributed form (Salomon, 1993), as we illustrate later. In the next section, we offer additional examples of the children's learning from the interns' careful planning and assistance over time. We wanted to create the basis where students could begin to see themselves not just as consumers of games but as producers of digital media.

## Beyond the Consumption of Games to the Emergent Production of Digital Media

An analysis of the students and the interns' interactions during the last two weeks reveals how much progress the children made in the program. In Week Six all students prepared Glogs (http://edu.glogster.com/)—digital collages. The students had to produce a multimodal text. All children had been given digital cameras to take photos that they would be able to use in the creation of their Glogs. Some students used this experience as an opportunity to become producers of their own ideological materials (Black, 2009) at an introductory level, since they used videos from their popular culture, ideological signs from their environment (e.g., the use of the no-smoking sign to express their dislike for smoking), the creation of bilingual texts, and an integration of their families into their Glogs.

More than in previous weeks, the room buzzed with an active social interchange of ideas, sounds, and images. Spontaneously, the students began to share with others the videos and the background pages they were using. At the end of the session, two interns facilitated the sharing of the Glogs using a projector. There was a high level of excitement in the classroom as all students asked to show their Glogs, although the original intention was to show only a couple. Figure 2 shows César's Glog, with a video clip about soccer, photos from his family, and some text in Spanish. In case someone doubted his authorial role, he added: "created by César."

For the last week, Antonia decided to engage César further in digital media production and had him create short movies using the program Animoto. Animoto was definitely a more challenging site to use for the children, yet it appeared that the timing for using it was right for Antonia and César. Antonia had presented this website to the university class and so knew very well how Animoto worked. After having spent so many sessions with César, she also knew his abilities with games and felt confident about how to facilitate César's learning. César learned what to press to create a new video, how to add pictures, how to look for music, and how to add it to the video. He also knew how to open a new tab, how to make the computer window larger and smaller, how to save images to the desktop, or throw them away into the recycle bin, how to upload the pictures onto Animoto, and how to edit text into the video.

By exposing César for four days (two consecutive weeks) to the creation of multimodal texts (Glogs and movies), Antonia provided César with the prolonged engagement needed to gain as much as possible from the learning experience

FIGURE 2. César's Glogster page

(Gee, 2007a). Antonia commented. "I was really impressed by César's' performance during Animoto because I saw improvement, for the most part he knew what to do and wasn't depending on me." The production of his own Glog and three little movies could be considered the "buds" or "flowers" of development Vygotsky (1978) referred to rather than the "fruits" of development (p. 86) in terms of his digital literacy learning. The progression César showed from day one to the last day of the program is a clear example of the effective mediation provided by this bilingual program and Antonia to César's learning of some digital literacies that will support him in developing more complex 21st-century literacy learning. It illustrates how the child became more independent with appropriate guidance in an enjoyable and motivating learning activity, helping him navigate the zones of proximal development through which he acquired new levels of ability. His learning path thus did not follow the linear route suggested by the scaffolding metaphor and "containment" conceptions of the ZPD. Rather, his learning process under the mediation of the Amigos Clase Mágica—including his intern partner, the games, the trajectory suggested within the setting, and other factors—indicates instead that an interweaving of mediational tools and social processes contributed to César's learning.

## Spaces for Reciprocal Teaching and Learning

The zone of proximal development in this classroom was a permeable and reciprocal space for learning in which children learned from peers, and in which the Interns learned from the children. Both children and interns learned from the games, which offered particular affordances. Maya and Miguel offered very different learning experiences than did Neopets, Glogster, or Animoto. Being able to move across Spanish and English was also a major meditational tool. Likewise, the physical space had a role in mediating some interactions and limiting others, although students found ways to exercise some agency within the physical constraints of the seating arrangements. As in Wang and Carter Ching's (2003) study, the children found ways to reorganize the space and "enter" into their peers' games overcoming the limitations of the physical space (rows in which each student had his or her own computer) and overcoming pre-arranged interactions (one intern—one student) in very interesting ways creating new zones for themselves and their peers. The children sometimes just stood up around another peer playing a game (uninvited) and suggested strategies (sometimes almost at the end of the day), or just left their chairs to offer help even if that meant walking toward a different row to assist a student based on the sounds coming from their peers' computers. Gradually, the children developed ownership of the space and the activities by mediating their peers' navigation of the games, suggesting that they were learning through the mediation of others (Moll, 2001) including their bilingual peers.

Peer influence and mediation were evident in different ways, sometimes in subtle ways and at times in a more intentional way. The most common and indirect way the children influenced one another was when they learned what games the others were using as a way to inform their own decision-making about what to play or what strategies to use. César used this strategy when he was creating his Glog page. He noticed that his classmate next to him was looking at videos, and then he decided to see those videos and to eventually add a video to his own Glog. At other times, the children directly asked their peers for help or volunteered strategies to others by entering into the interactions the neighbors next to them were having with their interns, as the following two examples illustrate. In the next interaction, César was playing Panfu. In this game, the children had to create a Panda that represented them and had several options, tasks, and games to complete. At one point in the game, César's Panda was not doing well, and the following exchange took place:

César:      I already did this one. *¡Me estoy muriendo!* [I'm dying!] (His Panda)
Antonia:    Ah?
César:      *Me estoy muriendo.* [I'm dying.] (He said with a tired voice).
Kid 2:      *Agarra algo de comer.* [Pick something to eat.]
Antonia:    *¿Pescado a lo mejor?* [Maybe fish?]
            (Transcript Day 5: March 25, 2010).

In this game, as in others, Antonia suggested strategies to César to navigate the games, but he also received the advice of a peer. César was well into the game and had identified with his Panda to the point of saying that he was the one dying. Another child heard him and suggested a strategy to survive the challenge and keep playing: *"Agarra algo de comer"* [Pick something to eat]. This interaction is telling given that most of the time, between the children, there was an intern working with a student, obstructing possibilities for such interactions to begin. As Wang and Carter Ching (2003) found in their study of first-grade students interacting around computers, "children also reshape their goals and appropriate and transform the affordances of the cultural artifacts through their social practices" (p. 338).

Similarly, some students preferred to seek assistance from their peers rather than from adults (Chandler-Olcott & Mahar, 2003), destabilizing the traditional loci of authoritative knowledge. This preference was especially noticeable during the last day of the program in which the children were told they could choose which game to play. Some interns, as Antonia did, enticed their students into trying a specific game before choosing their own, but many of them allowed the student to choose which game to play during the whole session of that last day. The interns had to step back since many of the children chose games their mentors had not played before, creating the conditions where peer collaboration and mediation were more noticeable. For example, in the following interaction, after not getting initially a straight answer from the intern, a child preferred to go to his friends to solve a problem instead of following the intern's suggested strategy of using the "search option" to find information:

> Every now and then, he would ask me where he could find a game, but since I did not know the site, I could not tell him, so I told him he should search it using the search bar. He did this maybe twice, but he knew his friends knew where to find most of the games, so he would get up and ask them where to go. (Field Note, Luisa, April 22, 2010)

The decision of some interns to play *with* the children in games chosen by the child also contributed to decentering the loci of authoritative knowledge since the intern had to be guided by the children. Half of the undergraduates reflected upon this shift as the opening excerpt illustrated. We close this section with two additional examples representative of the dynamics that took place within the last week, in which many children acted as the experts and taught both their peers and the interns:

> During the time in the computer, they were interacting with each other and Axel guided Josué through the games. He would guide Josué by telling him how to play a game. (OC: I was happy to see that Axel would help Josué as needed. I was not familiar with this website and Axel guided us throughout the day.) (Field Note, Esterla, April 21, 2010)

> I really liked that she was able to show me, instead of me always showing her game. She showed me strategies about the game that we were both playing in order for me to advance to another level. (Field Notes, Myrta, April 22, 2010)

This distribution of power and knowledge was in great part enabled by the opportunities the students had to choose their own games that last week. Interestingly, the students chose games and websites that their classroom teacher had taught them. Thus, their teacher was also mediating the learning taking place in the Amigos Clase Mágica, even without being physically there, a possibility Vygotsky (1987c) noted: "When the school child solves a problem at home on the basis of a model he has been shown in class...it is a solution accomplished with the teacher's help. This help—this aspect of collaboration—is invisibly present" (p. 216). In this way, the collective zone of proximal development created by the after-school program was permeable enough as to incorporate elements of the students' learning history with their teacher in their regular classroom, along with their peers' expertise, the interns' assistance, and the repertoire of linguistic resources available to the children: those coming from their home-based discourse, the interns, and the language of the games. Within such collective zone, students' and interns' roles gradually began to shift resembling the kind of learning community Freire (1970) envisioned in which both (adults and children) are simultaneously teachers and students.

## Discussion

The collective zone of proximal development created by the Amigos Clase Mágica in which bilingualism, games, peers, and adults all mediated students' and interns' learning stands in sharp contrast to the pervasive efforts to standardize education for all children, which taken to an extreme, are exemplified in legislations that prevent schools from providing language minority children with the opportunity to use their linguistic resources to learn (Portes & Smagorinsky, 2010). Dramatic examples from Arizona, related by teachers to the first author, include stories in which they are forced to cover the Spanish part in bilingual children's books with sticky notes. In one first-grade class, a supervisor inspected the bilingual picture books on the shelves to see if the Spanish text in those books was indeed covered, leading the students to limit their contributions in class because they were afraid that they would speak Spanish and get their teacher in trouble. Another teacher reports that in classrooms with language minority students in Arizona, there can be no spoken or written Spanish, no work with cognates, and no bilingual buddies; her class must be conducted only in English. Moll (2010) describes such mandates as a regime of standardization that fails to mobilize the social, cultural, and linguistic processes of diverse communities as the most important resources for positive educational change. Within such subtractive contexts (Valenzuela, 1999), bilingual teachers' and students' borderland identities, far from being affirmed, must be jettisoned.

These trends to standardize education prevent teachers of minority students from incorporating in meaningful ways pedagogical practices that support students' learning of 21st-century digital literacies because the curricula most Latino/a children receive have to focus so heavily on providing just conventional basics literacy skills and these in English. When digital technologies are embraced, they are often incorporated in ways that keep conventional print-based literacy as the center of the curriculum (Reinking & Carter, 2007). By sharing the kinds of learning that took place in the Amigos Clase Mágica, we are not making an argument for incorporating games in and of themselves into the classroom. Rather, we are suggesting that classrooms serve as well-designed activity systems that include multiple means of mediation. Providing quality learning opportunities to language minority children that include access to digital literacy learning, not only for their consumption but for their production, is not a matter of making education fun for students, but it is an issue of social justice, since all students should be provided with the learning experiences needed to be successful in a society that demands much more than knowledge of the basics.

Restrictive language policies also limit the zones of proximal development available to children. By imposing a single developmental trajectory on young learners, schools, by implication, allow only for selective access to life experiences and the knowledge they afford. Students are thus deprived not only of a cultural identity and the sense of confidence and security it facilitates for them as learners, they are denied the opportunity to draw on the prior knowledge, including the cultural schemata they have learned through home and community socialization, that cognitive psychologists have long identified as the foundation for new learning (Bransford, 1979). Conceiving of classrooms as permeable zones of proximal development in which children's learning is interwoven with culturally appropriate mediational tools and multifaceted proleptic possibilities, we believe, affords the greatest learning potential not only for immigrant and multilingual children but for all involved in the settings of formal education.

## ACKNOWLEDGMENT

The first author would like to thank Angela Valenzuela from the University of Texas-Austin, who led an effort to establish LCM sites in Texas and who encouraged her to move forward with her own project the Amigos Clase Mágica. Special thanks also go to Olga Vásquez from the University of California-San Diego and Alba Ortiz from the University of Texas-Austin for their encouragement and support of this project.

## ENDNOTES

1   The Texas Center for Education Policy (TCEP) led by Angela Valenzuela served as an incubator for the creation of this project.

2   Indicated alphabetically as ñ

# · 1 0 ·

# An Integrated Approach to the Study of Transitions as Learning Activity

## Two Cases from Spanish Immersion Classrooms

*Patricia Baquedano-López, Ariana Mangual Figueroa, & Sera Jean Hernandez*

> [I]t was consistent with [Vygotsky's] general theoretical view
> that his work should be carried out in a society that sought
> the elimination of illiteracy and the founding of educational
> programs to maximize the potential of individual children
> (Cole & Scribner introduction to Vygotsky (1978), p. 9)

School-based transitions are generally understood as activities that take place between identifiable school periods such as circle time, language arts, or recess. Transitions are useful units of analysis for understanding the general structure of activity and for exemplifying the fluid boundaries of what we conceive of as "already completed" and "next activity." Drawing theoretically and methodologically from the fields of language socialization and ethnomethodology to examine school-based transitions, we offer an analysis of transitions as learning activities that illustrates how language organizes and mediates learning.

We hope to further the dialogue that Vygotsky started by focusing on the social aspects of learning and by situating language as the site *par excellence* for studying learning. We organize our chapter as follows: First we describe the motivation for our work. We then examine the structure of transitions as learning activities, and we draw from two preschool Spanish immersion sites in northern California to illustrate how classroom exchanges in transition activity socialize young children to the norms and expectations of their classroom communities. We conclude with a discussion of the importance and relevance of considering transitions as learning activities.

## Motivation for This Work

At a time when discriminatory policies disrupt decades of work that honors, teaches, and preserves linguistic and cultural diversity in the United States, educational researchers must channel their efforts to advocate for the educational rights of non-dominant communities. Clarifying our methods and theories strengthens our continued efforts to dispel myths about language use while asserting the social, political, and cultural legacies of multilingual children and families. We are concerned that recent mandates in Arizona that enforce linguistic purism by sorting out its multilingual teaching force on the misguided idea that "foreign accents" are detrimental to students' education, legally sanction the racial profiling of students and parents perceived to be "illegal" immigrants and erase ethnic studies curricula from high schools. These harmful policies are proposed in a state where, in the year 2000, Latino students were the largest minority group and comprised 33% of the students enrolled in the school system (United States Department of Education, 2002). Important work has been advanced to counter deficit thinking about the learning potential of Latinos in the United States (Valencia, 2002). Numerous researchers have demonstrated that the disproportionate lack of academic achievement among Latinos and other racial and linguistic minorities is the result of structural inequalities (e.g., poverty, underfunded schools, elimination of language programs) and not a linguistic or cultural deficit inherent to minority groups (Gutiérrez, Baquedano-López, & Asato, 1999; Gutiérrez, 2000; Moll, Amanti, Neff, & González, 1992; Orellana, 2009; Portes, 2005; Zentella, 2005).

This chapter, like the others in this volume, recognizes that Latino students participate in multiple learning experiences often mediated by more than one language across educational settings, social spaces, and national borders. A growing body of ethnographic, discourse analytic studies of preschool experiences has deepened our understanding of children's linguistic and social worlds (cf. Cook-Gumperz, Corsaro, & Streeck, 1986; Field, 1999; Kyratzis, 2001; Rosenkoetter, 2001; Sheldon, 1992), but to provide a comprehensive analysis of the critical transition and socialization of young children into schools, we need to utilize methods and theories that more fully express the link between language and learning in context. Learning, mediated by language and social interaction, is both a local and historically encoded act (Pavlenko & Lantolf, 2000) through which participants discursively construct and perform multiple cultural and linguistic identities. In our ethnographic studies of Spanish-immersion preschool programs, we observed how the use of Spanish or English articulated histories and ideologies about each language and their speakers. At one school, the Mexican teachers' shared frame of reference led them to include a song in Spanish infusing the preschool curriculum with knowledge from past experience in Mexico. It is relevant that the participants in these programs included Spanish-speaking teachers and that the instructional practices that we documented took place at a time when bilingual education was, as it continues to be, restricted by educational policy in the state of California (Parrish, Linquanti, & Merickel, 2002). We present insights from Spanish language immersion programs because we consider these settings to be excellent examples of the confluence of diverse experiences mediated by a language that may be familiar to some, but not all, students. The fact that students in these classrooms learn a linguistic code and an orientation to language, in this case a minority language, opens up analytical spaces for understanding language ideologies and politics and their effects on learning, that is, when to use a language and for what purpose, as well as who has the freedom to learn and be proficient in two languages in the United States (Moran, in press).

## Transitions in Educational Research

Educational transitions mark institutionally sanctioned changes that are temporal (e.g., recess at a specific time and duration), spatially organized (e.g., changes between classrooms within a school building), and developmental (e.g., early childhood, elementary or secondary education) (Hargreaves, Earl, & Ryan, 1996; Harter, Whitesell-Rumbaugh, & Kowalski, 1992; Kagan & Neuman, 1998; Solís, 2009). Educational research on transitions has primarily focused on shifts in time and space between home and school, within school, and from school to work. Within schools, transitions connect a number of instructional units and resources that often require a change in location or of material (Carta, Renauer, Schiefelbusch,

& Terry, 1998). Many preschool teachers and caregivers consider children's ability to make transitions between activities independently an essential skill and competency (Ostrosky, Jung, & Hemmeter, 2002). Transitions can be particularly significant given that they can take up to 25% of the school day in preschool and kindergarten classrooms (Carta et al., 1998). Transition activities for young students may involve moving from one area of the classroom to another or other routines such as cleaning up materials, washing up before taking a snack, or singing preparatory songs (songs that are usually about future activities).

A concern that surfaces in the review of the literature on transitions is that time spent orienting students to classroom procedures results in less instructional time. Transitions have even been conceived as periods of "wasted time" during the school day (see Davidson, 1982). While they provide us with a view of the instrumentality of transitions, these perspectives consider transitions to be predetermined or organized patterns of activity, and they do not account for the ways in which transitions are locally negotiated by participants. Recent studies address the temporal, spatial, and corporeal ordering of schooling practices, many of them transitions (Gordon, Holland, & Lahelma, 2000; Gordon & Lahelma, 1996; Lemke, 2000, 2002; McGregor, 2004; Orellana & Thorne, 1998; Solís, Kattan, & Baquedano-López, 2009a), yet there is still a need for studies to explain how transitions are ideologically configured, linguistically organized, and interactionally negotiated, and how they might contribute to the process of creating successful educational contexts.

## Language as the Tool of Tools: Methodological Approaches

Vygotskyan perspectives underscore the role that language plays as a semiotic tool in learning and problem solving. Vygotsky's (1978) discussion of Dewey's pragmatic rendering of "the tongue as the tool of tools" (p. 53) reminds us that the researcher's task is to uncover the real, not just figurative link, between behavior and auxiliary means (i.e., tools). To be sure, Dewey's conceptualization of tool underscored language as a mediational artifact and as social practice. In this respect, language was not just speech, but gesture, action and negotiated interaction (Dewey, 1925/1929, p. 184). As Garrison (1995) notes "tools have implications beyond themselves" (p. 97). In this sense, language is transcendent; it can facilitate, create, organize, and transform the social order.

To Cultural Historical Activity Theory (CHAT) researchers, Vygotsky's Zone of Proximal Development (ZPD) includes language use between novices and more expert others "as a tool for mediating misconceptions and consolidating misunderstandings" (Lee & Smagorinsky, 2000, p. 5). Language, in this sense, is a tool to reason and of reason. Wertsch (2000) elaborates indicating that language use underlies meaning making and learning in two ways: first, in the referential relationships between signs and objects (both linguistic and nonlinguistic) and second, as the process of developing meaning through increased generalization and abstraction (p. 20). The ways language functions as a tool for development during actual learning interactions, however, has not always been made methodologically and theoretically explicit. We will elucidate the mediational nature of language in learning through an analysis of teacher and student practices during transition activity. To do so, we employ principles from two theoretical and methodological approaches which complement CHAT's view on the primacy of language in collaborative learning activity: the language socialization paradigm and the ethnomethodological approach.

The language socialization paradigm focuses on the language of routine interactions in everyday activities, attending to processes of socialization *through* language and socialization *to* language (Garrett, & Baquedano-López, 2002; Schieffelin & Ochs, 1986). Socialization activities are thus mediated through language, yet at the same time they teach forms of language. The language socialization paradigm shares many of the fundamental principles found in sociocultural perspectives on learning, including an understanding of tool-mediated learning activity. A language code, material object, or the interaction with more expert others can all be considered tools utilized in the learning process.

The process of language socialization involves participation by novices and experts within culturally meaningful activities (Jacoby & Gonzales, 1991). This view complements the longstanding sociocultural view that learning takes place whenever there is a change in participation over time (Rogoff, 1991) or when learners move from peripheral to central participation in the mastery of new skills (Lave & Wenger, 1991). This perspective on learning expands theories of assisted learning and is part of the shift to a more dynamic, iterative notion of learning as activity (Engeström, 2001). A number of language socialization studies in educational settings have examined the ways that the negotiation and organization of classroom learning are reflective (and constitutive) of broader sociocultural structures. These negotiations include teaching and learning national or ethnic affiliations (Baquedano-López, 1997; Duff, 1995; He, 2003; Lo, 2009; Mangual Figueroa, 2010); acquiring ideologies of language (Fader, 2009; Schieffelin, 2002), and developing and enacting identities of "successful" or "less successful" learners (Nielsen, 2002; Rymes & Pash, 2001; Talmy, 2008; Willett, 1995). These studies illustrate how language is at the core of learning and how it is important to the development of individual and collective identities.

Our second approach to language analysis draws from ethnomethodology, which considers the organization of social interactions to be anticipated and managed by participants in everyday encounters (Garfinkel, 1967; Goffman, 1974, 1981; Goodwin, 1990; Sacks, Schegloff, & Jefferson, 1974). Interactional expectations and negotiations are realized at the turn-taking and the grammatical level (Schegloff, 1979), that is in micro-interaction, while also reflecting a view of the social order (Garfinkel, 2002; Goffman, 1974; Wetherell, 1998). The study of teaching and learning interactions offers opportunities to analyze power dynamics through examples of *breaches* (Garfinkel, 1967) or disruptions to normative classroom interaction. Such breaches to ongoing interaction illustrate the organization of learning and the adaptation of all participants, often invoking "a pull for coherence" even while holding conflicting positions stemming from diverse background knowledge (Ash, 2008; Baquedano-López, Solís, & Kattan, 2005). As "teachable moments," breaches offer novices and experts possibilities of realignment or change as they socialize one another to the norms of appropriate behavior (Jacobs-Huey, 2007). Through the use of spoken language and paralinguistic cues such as tone, prosody, and body language, interlocutors demonstrate that they have learned both discrete skills and the social norms for behavior in a particular activity setting. When breaches occur, the social and cultural norms that underlie language use and interaction are rendered visible and become negotiable. These processes provide opportunities for researchers to learn about and document the sociocultural conventions shared by members of a particular group. As we will show in the examples of data from preschool classrooms, teachers and children in transitional activities use both speech and gesture to negotiate meanings, as well as innovate and resolve breaches. These moments of socialization provide us with opportunities to learn how educators and young bilingual students negotiate academic and social expectations.

## The School Sites

Our analysis of transitions as learning activities draws on classroom data from two schools, Escuela Mundo and La Escuelita,1 located in northern California. These schools are linguistically, ethnically, and socioeconomically diverse, with subsidized, as well as unsubsidized, tuition fees. The school directors at both sites granted us access to record and analyze interactions during everyday instruction. Mangual Figueroa and Hernandez collected ethnographic data at the schools for the duration of two academic years as part of an initiative led by Baquedano-López to study bilingual language socialization during the first contact with school and the academic transition across the early grades. Our involvement at these sites, initiated by a common research interest between researchers and school leaders, included participation and mutual support at different academic levels. In addition to participant-observation in classrooms, we conducted professional development sessions at the sites and presented a workshop with one of the directors at a prominent statewide conference on child development. We wrote collaborative grants with school leaders and participated in curricular and board discussions at each site. We also want to acknowledge that our participation in the schools as researchers and as Spanish-speaking Latinas, who shared a similar ethnic and linguistic background with many teachers, parents, and students, also entailed negotiating institutional boundaries and expectations between university researchers and school and community members (Delgado-Gaitán, 1993; Villenas, 1996). These experiences remind us of the importance of acknowledging that our work was influenced by, and had an influence on, what we observed.

## Escuela Mundo

Located in an affluent area, Escuela Mundo is a private, alternative dual-immersion, pre-K to 8 school founded in 2006. According to the 2000 U.S. Census the racial/ethnic composition of this area was 35.4% White, 44.7% African American, 9.8% Latino, and 7.7% Asian. Residents rented their homes (72.6%), with only 27.4% owning the homes in which they lived. Among the residents, 19.6% spoke a language other than English within the home. During the period of data collection (fifteen months across two academic years, 2006–2007 and 2007–2008) the student population at Escuela Mundo was White, of mixed ethnicity, and Latino, and the school attracted students from over ten different cities, as some parents commuted 20-miles for their children to attend this school. Escuela Mundo's bilingual program adopted a Spanish immersion model in preschool, and lessons were conducted entirely in Spanish. While half of the student population came from a home with one Spanish-speaking parent, it was difficult for Escuela Mundo to recruit the Spanish-dominant students, largely because of the high cost of tuition, which ranged from $10,000 to $14,000 per year. While financial aid was available to some families, not enough funding was available to achieve the envisioned dual immersion model completely. Like many other small private schools, Escuela Mundo struggled with both financial sustainability and the integrity of its language program.

## La Escuelita

La Escuelita started as a non-profit program in 1975, and it is now one of the oldest preschool bilingual programs in the area. La Escuelita offered a preschool program that used a Spanish immersion model, a bilingual after-school program, and a Spanish-language family literacy program held on Saturdays. In 2000, according to the U.S. Census, the racial/ethnic composition of this area of the city was 37.4% White, 25.7% African American, and 23% Latino. Most residents rented their homes (66.7%), while fewer owned their homes (33.3%). A total of 41.7% of the residents reported speaking a language other than English at home. Data for this chapter came from observations recorded during a fifteen-month span across the academic years of 2005–2006 and 2006–2007. According to school records, 60% of enrolled students were Latino, and the remaining 40% percent were African American, Asian, Anglo, and biracial. La Escuelita thus served a culturally broad and economically diverse community of families where the majority was Latino.

Escuela Mundo and La Escuelita are rich sites to study language socialization interactions. Few language socialization studies have focused on bilingual programs. We note the emphasis on Spanish immersion in the preschool years at both schools, where bilingualism and biliteracy are the stated goals. While bilingual programs typically begin in kindergarten, Escuela Mundo and La Escuelita house several preschool classrooms for 3- and 4-year-old children. The opportunity to study the first socialization experiences of students at these sites was therefore unique. These settings are noteworthy because the study of language use in bilingual schools generally has focused on the education of poor linguistic minority students and their acquisition of English and/or the loss of the home language (Portes & Rumbaut, 2001; Suárez-Orozco, Suárez-Orozco, & Todorova, 2008). At Escuela Mundo, while many of the children were immigrants, the majority were from middle-class backgrounds who, in some cases, were acquiring a new language in addition to English. La Escuelita's commitment to community-building made it an ideal site to examine language socialization processes of a primarily Latino population in a community setting.

## Transitions as Activities

A cornerstone idea in sociocultural perspectives on learning is that the child learns with the assistance of others. The concept of the ZPD, or "the distance between the actual developmental level as determined by independent problem solving and the level of potential development as determined through problem solving under adult guidance or in collaboration with more capable peers" (Vygotsky, 1978, p. 86), has been taken up widely in the field of education. One of the challenges in defining and describing the ZPD is that the very process of learning from others and acquiring new ideas through interaction is difficult to observe and document empirically (Valsiner & van der Veer, 1999). The concept has been used to identify and design activities meant to support the cognitive development of learners, while overlooking Vygotsky's emphasis on the affective dimension of learning inherent in social interaction (Gonzalez Rey, 2009). Ratner (this volume) also suggests that the ZPD may not only be a site for learning but also for the social reproduction of group experiences of oppression and marginalization. These interpretations of the ZPD suggest that individual cognitive development is not the only link between learning activities and that affect and relationships are generated in the ZPD and are carried from one activity to the next (Mahn & John-Steiner, 2000).

Despite differing interpretations of the ZPD, scholars agree on two key points: To begin, learning is embedded in social interaction and second, development suggests a temporal frame that relates retrospective action (what is known) to potential action (what can be learned). We have traditionally identified learning as the advancement from one academic task to the next (e.g., moving from alphabet mastery to decoding and reading) where the space in between these learning activities, the ZPD, is considered a provisional site for actions that drive development. However, the actual moments of this zone of interaction are an important source for the analysis of learning activity. In this regard, the ZPD is an activity itself, that is, it is not simply a bridge to future action or a transitory space.

Following this understanding of the ZPD as activity, we consider transitions also to be learning activities in their own right. Transitions embody the tension between continuity and change that is inherent in any learning activity. While an examination of formal learning activities may predispose us to focus on continuity and cohesion across activities, transitions provide opportunities to foreground change and dissonance as central features of human social behavior and integral aspects of development. We consider transitions to have the following properties: first, they are goal-oriented; second, they are spatio-temporal and sequentially sensitive; third, they include expert and novice participants; fourth, they are structurally organized as a human activity system. We discuss each of these properties in turn.

## Goal Orientedness

During transition activities, participants orient toward a common goal and object often produced through requests, directives, or other discursive means. According to Engeström (1991), "[t]he central issues of activity theory remain the object—that is what connects my individual actions to the collective activity" (p. 31). In schools the object has traditionally been conceived as a formal academic task, for example, solving a mathematical problem or decoding a text. However, the object does not have to be limited to discreet academic tasks. The object of activity theory, situated collaboration among interlocutors, correlates with the language socialization perspective that everyday routine social events are rich sites for studying learning and development. Participation in a routine event demonstrates an individual's commitment to joint activity, a precondition for much of social interaction (Garfinkel, 2002).

## Expert and Novice Roles

Transition activities in schools provide the context for understanding the multiple roles that participants can take vis-à-vis the task at hand and each other. Vygotsky defined the ZPD as an interactional space of collaboration between individuals who lie on a continuum from more to less "capable," a collaboration which leads to learning. Like sociocultural theories of learning (Lave & Wenger, 1991; Rogoff, 1991), language socialization research supports the notion that learning is a bidirectional process in which adults and children can shape unfolding interaction and take up expert or novice roles (Schieffelin & Ochs, 1986; Whiting, 1980). This approach to the construction and potential shift in roles is based on the notion that participation in talk is action (Goodwin & Goodwin, 2004), and that the strategic coordination of talk and activity accomplishes tasks.

## Spatio-Temporal and Sequential Organization

Studies of classroom learning have examined alternative spatial constructs of interaction such as the official (teacher/institution sanctioned), the unofficial (student based) scripts (Gutiérrez, Rymes, & Larson, 1995), and hybrid practices and third spaces of classroom interaction (Gutiérrez, Baquedano-López, & Tejeda, 1999; Leander, 2002). Recent work has problematized the *chronos* of learning, and the ways learning activity occurs and creates a broad terrain of temporalities (Bloome et al., 2009; Solís, Kattan, & Baquedano-López, 2009a). These studies are based on an understanding of learning as an inherently complex process that is not predictable or unproblematic. Face-to-face interactions are important sites for examining how novices' and experts' discursive practices and strategies reconfigure spatial and temporal parameters of instruction and learning. By focusing on interactions during transitions, we gain a deeper understanding of how participants manage or shift the course of learning activities.

## Activity Theoretic Systems Structures

Transitions are comprised of the same structures as the human activity system. These structures include tools and signs, subjects, objects, rules, community, division of labor-mediating artifacts, sense, meaning, and outcomes. All transition activities contain accumulated knowledge of rules and tools of previous and next activity, yet they also project possibilities for novel understandings yet to be realized. As we noted earlier, transitions are goal oriented, sometimes in multiple and conflictive ways, responding to ongoing, as well as projected tasks.

Engeström's (2001) discussion of the three generations of activity theory is useful for explaining how the concept of transition activity fits within the scope of activity theory. Engeström notes that the first generation of activity theory research integrated cultural artifacts into learning through the concept of "mediation." In this formulation, learning was situated at the individual level and was portrayed through the triangle heuristic of subject—object—mediating artifact. The second generation shifted from a notion of individual learning to the collective and began to incorporate the idea of internal contradiction as central for change. In this approach there was still not much attention paid to cultural diversity despite other forms of inclusion accounting for learning sites ranging from young children and play to adults in the work place.

In the third generation, or the current stage of activity theory, Engeström highlights the continued need for attention to diversity of learners and settings, in his words, "The third generation of activity theory needs to develop conceptual tools to understand dialogue, multiple perspectives, and networks of interacting activity systems" (p. 135). This third generation of activity theory takes at a minimum "two interacting activity systems into account" (p. 136). Transition activity fits within this conceptual model as it necessarily engages more than one activity system given that it is structurally and pragmatically at the border of at least two activity systems, for example, between circle-time and play time or even a possible, emergent, other activity such as a discipline routine. Moreover, transitions may also include activity systems such as communicating in two languages, which may also create an alignment of code and activity, for example, alternating the use of a language during sets of activities. Such alignments are important to examine if we are to understand the diversity of learning experiences in schools.

# The Exemplars: Transition Activities as Opportunities to Learn

In this section we discuss examples of transition activities from Escuela Mundo and La Escuelita to illustrate how multiple goals, actions, and talk are managed. We focus on activities that involve spatial and temporal movement; in one case from indoors (circle-time) to outdoors (recess), in the other from story time to naptime. To examine how language mediates learning, we discuss two analytical points to help us understand transition as learning activity. The first concerns the notion of signification, that is, how an utterance encodes different levels of meaning. The second point centers around the analysis of the spatio-temporal sensitivity of transition activity. Earlier we discussed that structurally, transition activity involves at least two activity systems. We now explore how teachers and students use language to delimit the parameters of possible next-activity according to an evaluation of ongoing activity.

## Levels of Signification in Transition Activity

The first example we analyze comes from data collected at Escuela Mundo. It illustrates the ways a teacher, Susana, and her students negotiate the range of acceptable behaviors for next-activity as they move from circle-time to recess. Circle-time serves multiple purposes during classroom instruction, ranging from learning content matter, to storytelling activities, to building a sense of classroom community, and providing a setting to discipline and review rules of behavior and plans for the day (Michaels, 1981; Poveda, 2001; Solís, Kattan, & Baquedano-López, 2009b). Our analytical focus here is on the talk and ongoing actions that indicated to all participants in circle-time that they were engaged in a new activity, a transition activity, as well as how they were negotiating this new activity.

Borrowing a helpful heuristic from Hanks (1996), we outline different levels of meaning of a sample expression made by Susana while she was addressing her students at the conclusion of circle-time. We focus on three levels that include signification, the literal content, and the conveyed sense or the intended meaning of the phrase. These levels illustrate the multiple ways that one expression carries and amplifies meaning that socializes preschool students not just to the meaning of words but also to outcomes for appropriate behavior, that is, to forms of cultural competence. On this day, the classroom participants included 22 children, Susana, and two female teacher assistants. The majority of the students in this classroom were native speakers of English and second-language learners of Spanish. Susana and her teaching assistants were Latinas and native Spanish speakers. The interaction was carried out in Spanish and consisted of reviewing the rules for leaving the classroom and the appropriate behavior outdoors during recess. As the students sat around at the end of circle time, the teacher told the class the following phrase:

**"Acuérdense que afuera no jugamos a pelear"**
*Remember that outdoors we do not play fight/at fighting*

At the first level of meaning, signification, the teacher's directive to the students was to remember what they were not supposed to do outside. While they were supposed to play, they were not supposed to fight or play as if they were fighting. We note here the property of transitions of goal orientation, in this case achieving a goal that involved physical relocation from the inside of the classroom activity of circle-time to the outdoor activity of recess.

The second level of meaning, literal content, included information about where and how the subsequent activity was to take place, in this example, outside, and not inside, and it was not supposed to involve fighting. We note here the spatio-temporal and sequential organization of the activity, not only true for the unfolding activity itself, but also for the cumulative body of knowledge that was indexed, knowledge which had been acquired and brought to bear on the activity at hand. The teacher's directive to remember, as an act of collective remembrance, presupposed a shared history that was necessary for appropriate participation in their next activity. Finally, the third layer of meaning, the intended meaning or moral valence (an admonition in this case), exemplified how language in activity became the locus of shared culture and history. We outline these levels of analysis of the teacher's statement, from signification to the moralizing conveyed sense as follows:

Level 1:    [Acordar–comm-pres-2pl-refx que [afuera-LOC neg jugar-pres-1pl a pelear INF]][2]
            *Remember that outside no play to fight/at fighting*
Level 2:    Remember now what we do not do outside
Level 3:    Recall the morally acceptable terms of behavior within the physical spaces of the school setting

The students' uptake illustrates how they were able to interpret behavior according to the expectations of their teacher and school and confirms that learning is occurring during this transitional activity. Excerpt 1 below is a transcript3 of the video-recorded exchange following the teacher's statement just examined, "Acuérdense que afuera no jugamos a pelear." In the video still (Figure 1), we observe Peter, a male student, offering a negative behavior, "no guns," by pointing at the teacher as if he were holding a gun. As we can see in the transcript, the teacher's response verbally and gesturally overlapped with the student's turn, using her two hands to mimic guns pointing at each other:

Excerpt 1:
1 Tea:    **Acuérdense que afuer::a (.5) no jugamos a pelear**
          *Remember that outside we don't play fight*
2 Stu:    **No [a:rmas.**
          *No weapons*
3 Tea:    **[No jugamos con a:rmas.**
          *We don't play with weapons.*
          (Hands simulating guns)

As the excerpt illustrates, students can take up expert positions in learning activities. In this exchange, Peter displayed a competent, multilayered understanding of the teachers' utterance and provided an example of the inappropri-

FIGURE. 1 "No armas"

ate forms of play referenced by the teacher, in this case that the use of weapons, "armas," is a form of fighting. We note that the teacher framed next-activity in the negative—what they could not do outdoors. This framing highlighted, and invited, a listing of behaviors that were not acceptable. It also allowed for the possibility of recreating forbidden behavior as illustrated in the student's pointing of an imaginary gun towards the teacher. The enacted behavior, which would have constituted a breach to regular classroom behavior, was acceptable in this transition activity where rules were being negotiated. In this case, talk about and enactment of undesirable behaviors were not only possible, they were also defining features of this activity. We note, too, that the rest of the students physically oriented and visually attended to the exchange between the teacher and one of their peers. The language in this activity, through its multiple levels of significa-tion, reaffirmed the values held in this classroom community and expanded the students' knowledge of language and of the rules of behavior in prior, ongoing, and next activity.

## Spatio-Temporal Sensitivity in Transition Activities

As we have noted, while often discursively projecting other times and spaces, transition activity can take place between activity systems. In Excerpt 2 below we analyze an example of transition activity at La Escuelita, a transition at the margins of story and naptime, two recurrent and clearly defined activity systems at the school that serve expected developmental goals. Here, the activities took place in more than one code, Spanish and English, illustrating how participants in an activity utilize linguistic resources available to them. In Excerpt 2, about ten three-year-old students were seated on the floor in the school's library area waiting to be read a story before naptime. The teacher, Alma, who was about to read the story, was seated in a wicker chair at the front of the room. On this day, the children behaved in ways interpreted by the teachers to be restless, and their lack of sufficient attention to Alma while she was reading the story led to a reconfiguration of classroom goals. In this exchange, three teachers spoke and several children's names were mentioned. As in the previous example, the children's uptake and participation in transitional activity followed and supported the goals of the activity. Eventually, through displays of language and gestures they joined their teachers in song intoning the lyrics of a popular Spanish song in the 1960s4 as they began to march out of the library:

> Excerpt 2:
> 1 Alma: **¡Yo no sé porqué! Leemos una bien rápido solamente.**
> *I don't know why! We'll read one very quickly.*
> (Shakes head)
> 2 T1: **Uh, you now what Alma?**
> 3: **Manuel, Emilio, and George were not listening to you not one bit.**
> 4 T2: **Los niños que no están escuchando ya se pueden ir a las camas.**
> *The children who are not listening can go to bed now*
> 5: **porque las camas están listas.**
> because the beds are ready.
> 6 T1: **Ve a la cama Carlos. Adiós. Vámonos Jorge. Vámonos.**
> *Go to bed Carlos. Goodbye. Let's go Jorge. Let's go.*
> (Picks Carlos up and places him by the door)
> 7 T2: **Vamos chicos.**
> *Let's go kids.*
> 8 All: **Vamos a la cama, hay que descansar.**
> *Let us go to bed, we have to rest.*
> (Singing)
> 9 Lisa: (Orients to door and begins to march out)

This transitional activity has its own goal and structure, distinct from, and yet constituted by, the surrounding activities of story time and naptime. The teachers identified the children's inattentiveness as a breach in behavior that redefined the activity of story time into an activity of getting ready for naptime. The transition between story and naptime indicated by singing a song in line 8,

FIGURE. 2 "Vamos a la cama"

"vamos a la cama," cued children into physically moving from the library to their cots and shifting from being awake to projecting being asleep.

The language in this transitional activity emphasized the importance of listening and the consequences that failure to do so can have, in this case, an early shift to naptime. Movement towards a new goal, which now included socializing listening behavior and preparations to leave the room, was foregrounded in this interaction through Alma's explicit reference to not understanding the children's behavior "yo no sé porqué" (I don't know why) (line 1). This dynamic was further elaborated by the co-teachers noting that the students were not listening (lines 2 and 3), and by the collective of teachers framing "going to bed" as a consequence of not listening (lines 4 and 5). The disciplinary events that transpired during the transitional activity reframed the teachers' talk about naptime and their subsequent activity as a punishment, although naptime was not usually talked about in these terms. The construction of naptime as punishment was realized through the physical relocation of students when a teacher picked up Carlos and set him on the floor at the doorway between the library and classroom and through the issue of directives, including "go to bed" and "let's go" (line 6). When the teachers began to sing a song that accompanied transition activity to nap time (line 8), the children took up this cue, indicating that they understood the new goal of this transitional activity. This spatial quality of the transitional activity was also embodied through action.

This transition activity also opened up the possibility of reconfiguring participation frameworks and for expert and novice roles to be taken up. In this case, four major changes took place. First, the teachers, who usually worked together on a unified stance towards the activity, demonstrated shifts in alignment when they took up different roles ranging from storyteller to disciplinarian ("we can read a story quickly" and "go to bed, goodbye"). Second, students took up expert roles; for example, Lisa began marching out of the room, thus leading the way for the other students who were still seated on the rug in the library (Figure 2). Third, transitional activity included a shift in participation frameworks from teacher-led (story-time activities) to student-oriented (encouraging singing and body movement of all participants in the class). Finally, we note that a teacher switched from Spanish to English (lines 2 and 3) to address the lead teacher and to report student behaviors while conceivably the students were overhearing the exchange.

## Conclusion

Vygotsky is known for having articulated the relevance of the cultural and historical dimensions of learning and development. To elaborate on how history is made actual in learning, Leontiev (1981c) explained language as the object of activity of prior human generations, which is then appropriated by the child. Language is thus both preceded by the individual (that is, it is historical) and it is also appropriated by the individual in the present social learning context (that is, it is social and cultural). In this chapter we have supported a notion of language as the means through which children acquire competencies during transition activities. Children's intellectual work in schools is not bounded by typical notions of activity. Our analyses of transition activities at two Spanish immersion programs in California illustrated how Latino and non-Latino students, led in both settings by Latina teachers, participated, negotiated, and appropriated the norms, behaviors, and language of their classroom communities.

Throughout this chapter we have argued that transitions are not simply in-between states of activity systems and that instead, they are activities in their own right. In the examples we analyzed, we noted the collaborative construction of rules of behavior and participation in both transition activity and next-activity. We also observed that participants discussed the consequences for not displaying appropriate behavior. In one case, playing with weapons (a potential breach) would have constituted negatively sanctioned behavior. In another case, not listening to a story (an actual breach) meant a reconfiguration of ongoing activity and an early exit to nap time. We also noted how students took up expert positions illustrating shifts in participation during ongoing activity. In the first example, Peter displayed knowledge of forms of fighting, a negative expectation, that included the use of weapons. In the second example, we saw that teachers negotiated next courses of action in a temporary suspension of ongoing activity. The teachers' *keying*, in Goffman's sense (1974, p. 45), allowed them to display two different stances towards student inattention: in the midst of the activity of reading a story, the teachers disciplined the students *and* directed them to their cots using song to cue students transition to naptime.

Finally, we want to highlight the practice observed over time at La Escuelita concerning the use of English for disciplinary reasons. In the example of interaction we discussed, a teacher assistant's report to the lead teacher about misbehaving students was done in English. This suggests a form of domain-specificity where one language code is used for certain socialization exchanges (Garrett, 2005). A switch to English articulated a code of discipline in this preschool classroom. The teacher assistant's action also illustrates ideologies held about the power or status of languages (Woolard & Schieffelin, 1994; Schieffelin, Woolard, & Kroskrity, 1998). In this regard, the use of language within particular activities gives us insights into the ideologies and valences indexed by particular language codes within educational settings.

It has long been acknowledged that children's first contact with schooling is formative of their future success as students. With nearly two-thirds of all four-year-olds attending pre-school in the year before they enter kindergarten (U.S. Department of Education, 2002), it is imperative to compare and integrate findings on the effects of different forms of early childhood educational programs serving diverse student populations and to illuminate what social, linguistic, and cognitive opportunities are afforded to students. These efforts need to also support a view of language, no longer just as a resource, but as central to learning.

Transitions as central units of analysis have much to offer educational and language researchers who seek to understand socialization and development in the early academic years. Transitions are unique activities that by their very fluid and complex nature provide opportunities to enact a range of actions, from opportunities to test the parameters of permissible action to learning about the consequences of breaches to ongoing interaction. We hope the findings we have presented here move us toward an integrated understanding of the learning that is afforded in transition activity and of the language that helps realize it.

## ACKNOWLEDGMENTS

We would like to acknowledge the funding sources that made possible the research reported here. These include a Committee on Research grant from the University of California, Berkeley (Baquedano-López) and two Spencer Foundation Research Training Grants (Mangual Figueroa and Hernandez). We thank the members of the Laboratory for the Study of Interaction and Discourse in Educational Research L-SIDER at UC Berkeley for providing an intellectual space to share ideas and resources. We are grateful to teachers, parents, and students at Escuela Mundo and La Escuelita—their commitment to language learning and preschool education inspired this work.

## NOTES

1  We use pseudonyms for the names of the schools, teachers, and students.

2  Grammatical analysis abbreviations: COMM, command or directive; PRES, present tense; pl, plural; 1 or 2, first or second person; LOC, locative; INF, infinitive tense.

3  Transcription notations modified from Atkinson & Heritage (1984).

| | |
|---|---|
| **Bold** | Actual Speech |
| *Italics* | English gloss |
| . | Falling tone (not necessarily the end of a sentence) |
| , | Slight rising inflection |
| ? | Rising intonation (not necessarily a question) |
| ! | Animated tone |
| : | Sound elongations; the use of more colons indicate longer elongation of sound |
| [ ] | Overlapped speech |
| <u>Under</u> | Speaker emphasis |
| (1.5) | Length of pause in tenths of seconds |
| ((smile)) | Non-verbal behavior |
| Video still | Video stills (Figures) illustrate gestures relevant to the data excerpts. |

4  This was a popular theme song broadcast in the 1960s in Spain and Latin America that announced the end of the day's children's programming and the beginning of adult programming. It featured animated images of the six young children of La Familia Telerín who marched off to bed singing in single file (see Gasca, 1967; Guadarrama Rico, 1999).

## · 1 1 ·

# Faculty Views
# of Underrepresented Students
# in Community College Settings
## Cultural Models and Cultural Practices

*Leticia Tomas Bustillos, Robert Rueda, & Estela Mara Bensimon*

> *Research shows that instructor, instruction, and educational*
> *process in the classroom affect 25 percent of the student outcome.*
> *50 percent comes from who they are including genetics and the*
> *rest of the 25 percent depends on the socio-economic status of the*
> *students. This means that some students are doomed to failure*
> *when they come in. They have no motivation in them to succeed*
> *and they have no background in the first place. We affect such a*
> *small amount.—Professor, California Community College*

Many readers will find this community college faculty member's quote as disturbing as the authors do. It represents a view that we have often heard, in different versions and with different levels of intensity, in our work in community college settings. It is often heard in reference to students of color, who frequently enter community colleges less prepared and who often fall behind their White peers on a wide range of academic outcomes. It represents a perspective of resignation, of hopelessness, and lack of efficacy and of agency in being able to impact student outcomes because of factors beyond one's control. It raises a host of issues, including the question of who is responsible for student success at the college level.

What role can or should students play at this level of the education system? What role can or should faculty play at this level? It is clear that the educational system expects more from students once they leave high school, including basic academic skills as well as increased levels of independence, self-regulation, motivation, ability to set realistic goals, and so on. It is also the case that significant numbers of students enter community colleges without these skills and abilities, and they are commonly found in the remedial courses that are required of underprepared students in order to enter credit-bearing coursework. One possible response, as a faculty member, is to resign oneself to not being able to make a difference. However, another possible response is to assume a role with more agency and accept students as they come, moving forward from that point.

The role faculty members play in student educational outcomes is frequently overlooked in research in higher education, perhaps because more is expected of students when they approach adult age. Instead, a voluminous literature based on college student surveys correlates postsecondary education success with students' characteristics before they entered college and their self-reported experiences, behaviors, and accomplishments during the college years. Rarely are the institutional representatives themselves— faculty and administrators—given attention in terms of how they may or may not contribute to student success (Bensimon, 2007). At the same time, it is important to keep in mind, as Portes (2005) convincingly argues, there is a whole host of factors, including structural and financial factors that produce inequalities in educational outcomes and that merit attention. Moreover, the accountability issue, which has gained such prominence in the national education agenda, is not trivial, especially in light of the accountability problems that have plagued K-12 education (Nichols & Berliner, 2007; Orfield & Kornhaber, 2001) and the long-term impact they have on postsecondary outcomes. These problems include, among other issues, onerous testing requirements that rely on narrow measures, reshaping the curriculum to match those tests, negative views of teachers and school, and punitive approaches to bring about improvement.

We do not minimize the role of these factors, and we agree that they deserve attention. Even so, we certainly do not argue for importing any of K-12s problematic practices to higher education. Nor do we think faculty and administrators should be targeted or blamed for poor student outcomes. On the other hand, we do believe that faculty and administrators are an important part of the higher educational ecocultural system and can make a difference. As such, in our work we examine one piece of the equation that has received little attention, the role of faculty and administrators in closing the equity gap in higher education outcomes. In the interest of promoting more equitable outcomes in higher education, we have focused on how we can assist community college faculty to reframe their interpretations of the causes for racial inequities in educational outcomes so that instead of attributing student performance to factors such as the genetic makeup or social background of students, they will examine their own practices as well as those at the institutional level. Researchers at the Center for Urban Education believe that in order to address the problem of inequity, institutions of higher education need to recognize that their practices (e.g., curricular, pedagogical, relational, administrative, and so forth) are failing to produce successful outcomes for Latinos and Latinas (or other minority populations) and that in order to learn why their practices are failing to accomplish equitable outcomes they have to engage in a process of guided critical inquiry (Bensimon et al., 2004). To facilitate the process of learning and change among institutional actors the Center has created special tools and structures.

This chapter focuses on this approach specifically—promoting equitable outcomes in higher education by helping institutional actors examine the extent to which their views and actions can promote or impede student success. We focus on community college settings because they are the initial step in the pathway to higher education for the nearly 6% of Latino students (National Center for Education Statistics, 2008) in the United States who fare less well in terms of educational outcomes than other groups. The institutional change process that characterizes the work of the Center for Urban Education is informed by five theoretical strands: socio-cultural theories of learning, organizational learning, practice theory, participatory critical action research, and critical theories of race. In this chapter, we describe our application of sociohistorical perspectives on learning to foster change in community college settings related to how faculty view and address the problem of inequity. We both argue for broadening the range of factors seen as responsible for Latino/a student outcomes in these types of settings and illustrate how the sociohistorical principles and theory can be applied to bring about changes in faculty that have the potential to impact the educational outcomes of underrepresented students.

## Background of the Problem

While the demographic profile of the country is shifting, the patterns are most pronounced in some states such as California. In California's public K-12 schools, over 40% of students (2.6 million) come from households where a language other than English is spoken (Rumberger, 2007). Among Latino students, 25% complete the A-G course sequence, an indicator of college readiness (California Postsecondary Education Commission [CPEC], 2008). For many of these students, the pathway to higher education is characterized by community college attendance as a stepping-stone to four-year universities (Solórzano, Rivas, & Velez, 2005; Woodlief, Thomas, & Orozco, 2003). A significant factor for this trend is the high cost of higher education, which inordinately affects students from lower socioeconomic groups (Horn & Nevill, 2006; NCES, 2008).

Unfortunately, there is a long-standing pattern in higher education in which students of color from low socioeconomic backgrounds achieve at lower levels than their White peers. Not only do fewer students make it to higher education, but once there, they are more likely to be in remedial tracks and to transfer to four-year universities at lower rates (Attewell, Lavin, Domina, & Levey, 2006; Swail, Carbera, Lee, & Williams, 2005). In California, nearly 23% of Latino students transferred to the University of California (UC) or the California State University (CSU) systems, whereas 35% of white students did the same (CPEC, 2008). Of the entering Latino freshmen at the CSU's in the fall of 2009, 52% and 63% required remediation in math and English, respectively. This rate is nearly double that of Asian and White incoming freshmen requiring remediation in the same subjects (CSU, 2010). There are many indicators that suggest community college attendance and participation are stratified by students' racial-ethnic and socioeconomic backgrounds (Horn & Nevill, 2006).

These patterns point to the community college system as an important link in the higher education chain, especially for non-White and poor students; however, there are unequal outcomes for many of these students compared to their White counterparts. This combination of factors was the impetus for the work described in this chapter, specifically the creation of the *Math Project* housed at the Center for Urban Education (CUE) at the University of Southern California. A major goal of this project was the promotion of equity-mindedness and equity-focused practices within the community college setting with a particular focus on faculty. In this project, and in related action research (see Bensimon, Polkinghorne, Bauman, & Vallejo, 2004; Bustillos, 2007; Peña, 2007), "equity" was defined in terms of student outcomes (Dowd, 2005) rather than demographically representative enrollment.

There is a long-standing history in educational research in which student deficits are seen to be the primary factors related to inequitable outcomes. These explanations, often with little empirical foundation as the opening quote illustrates, have ranged from inadequate prior education, students' and family's lack of resources, deficits in prior knowledge, poverty, low motivation, low intelligence, language differences, and other factors (Valencia, 1998). Sadly, a common tendency is that an exclusive focus on these real or imagined deficits leads to lower expectations and to low-level or remedial instruction.

While it is clear that students arrive at college with differing opportunities-to learn-histories (i.e., varying amounts of exposure to factors which are related to school success such as economic resources, access to print materials, and so on), these are typically issues that cannot be easily addressed in the classroom. However, a major premise of our work is that it is also true that faculty and educational institutions *can* impact student outcomes through changes in their routine practices and by taking ownership of the problem. A major problem is that these types of changes are not easy to bring about, and there is often little existing scaffolding to foster them.

## Background and Goals of the Math Project

The Math Project emanated from the Center for Urban Education (CUE) at the University of Southern California. A major goal of the Center is to address inequitable outcomes in community college settings (Bensimon, 2004, 2005, 2007). The work we describe here is from one of the campuses that participated in a CUE-sponsored project focused on the area of mathematics. Previous work at this campus confirmed the patterns noted earlier, specifically low achievement for Latino students, their excessive representation in remedial courses, and a strong reluctance on the part of faculty and administrators to openly discuss or address issues of equity, race, and ethnicity. While previous work from CUE suggested that colleges regularly collect outcome indicators related to equity issues, they were rarely shared, were often not in a user-friendly form, and were not used in a proactive fashion to address equity issues. The issues we noted at the beginning of the Math Project could therefore be summarized as follows:

1. Inequitable outcomes were a problem (as recognized by the institution itself).
2. The problem of inequitable outcomes was especially pervasive within the math remedial course sequence.
3. Faculty often perceived these remedial courses as lower status courses and attributed student failure to within-student deficits (low motivation, low SES, lack of basic skills, or lack of ability).
4. While equity was an important issue, faculty most often felt that there was not much they could do to impact it.
5. While the school routinely collected data on student outcomes, this information was not used to address issues of equity, and was perceived to be primarily for administrative purposes.

6. There did not exist an "institutional culture" of focusing on equity, nor was there a physical or intellectual "space" in the institution for such a focus.

The project thus targeted these areas directly. A general overall goal was to foster a view of inequalities in outcomes, at least in part, as a problem of institutional accountability that calls for collective action. A specific goal of the project was for faculty to "take ownership" of the problem and look for ways that they could modify their professional practice to improve student outcomes. The project team, consisting of faculty members and administrators, had to therefore come to understand that taking ownership did not mean understanding inequitable outcomes in general, but recognizing inequitable outcomes at their own campus and in their own department. Thus, gaining expertise in accessing, understanding and asking questions of relevant data (what we called "sense-making") was an important element of the project. A collaborative action research approach (Bray, Lee, Smith, & Yorks, 2000) was adopted with the overall goal of creating a community of learners around the issue of student outcomes in math, fostering equity-minded[1] sense making of institutional data related to issues of equity, and considering ways to build on professional practice to foster these goals.

## Theoretical Framework

In thinking about how to engage faculty in the goals of the project, we found ourselves falling into the trap of attributing the same characteristics to them as they did to the students who failed math—low motivation, lack of relevant knowledge, and so forth. We therefore began to think systematically about how socio-historical principles could provide guidance. We quickly recognized that traditional approaches focused on lectures about equity and encouragement to engage in culturally responsive practices, characteristic of traditional "professional development" were doomed to failure (Brancato, 2003; Cranton & King, 2003). Thus, the Math Project intentionally built upon several sociohistorical traditions within an action inquiry framework.

A fundamental goal of our work with this institution was the collaborative construction of new knowledge and new practices for both individuals, as well as the institution related to fostering equitable outcomes for Latino students. The major premise was that learning and development are socially constructed and facilitated by engagement in a joint productive activity. We organized team meetings with the College we worked with (described below) as the primary vehicle of change. While the overall goal focused on fostering more nuanced understandings and cultural practices related to equity, the collaborative work that we used as a foundation for this work centered around participants' understanding and examination of their own institutional data related to equitable student outcomes. The meetings and artifacts around this work then became the vehicle for exploring existing knowledge and creating new knowledge around equity issues.

In this work we drew heavily from sociohistorical psychology related to teaching and learning, built on the early work of Vygotsky (Forman, Minick, & Stone, 1993; John-Steiner & Mann, 1996; Kozulin, Gindis, Ageyev, & Miller, 2003; Lave & Wenger, 1991; Moll, 1990; Rogoff, 1991; Rogoff, Turkanis, & Bartlett, 2001; Tharp & Gallimore, 1988; Wenger, 1998; Wertsch, 1998; Wertsch, Del Rio, & Alvarez, 1995). While there is variability in the family of perspectives, under the broad label of cultural-historical approaches, general features we drew on were the ideas that (a) learning is social, (b) learning is socially mediated by assisted performance that is responsive, (c) learning is mediated by cultural tools and artifacts, and (d) learning takes place in communities of practice and is indexed by changes in participation within these communities. We viewed the collaborative team meetings (to be described below) as teaching and learning situations, where a goal was to develop expertise as well as new ways of talking about and interacting with both institutional data as well as equity issues.

A particularly important extension of sociohistorial work for the current project was the idea of communities of practice, defined by Wenger (1998) as a social group developed over time through ongoing purposeful endeavor. These communities of practice can be formal or informal "groups of people who have some common and continuing organization, values, understanding, history, and practices" (Rogoff, 2003, p. 80). It is within these communities that learning takes place and individual identities, meaning, and social belonging are created. These communities of practice help shape what Gallimore and Goldenberg (2001) describe as cultural models, or shared mental schemata or normative understandings of how the world works, or ought to work, including what is valued and ideal, what settings should be enacted and avoided, who should participate, the rules of interaction, and the purpose of interactions. In this project, we intentionally tried to develop a community of practice around equitable practices in the instruction of mathematics.

We also drew on applications of sociohistorical theory to the areas of intercultural exchange in border and boundary crossing and to area literacy studies, in particular the notions of hybridity and re-mediation (Gutierrez, Morales, & Martinez, 2009). We were particularly interested in bridging the relatively sterile academic model of teaching and learning mathematics instantiated in many of the remedial math classrooms with the everyday lives of students who have few economic resources, poor academic preparation, and little of the social and cultural capital most valued in the academic world.

We also drew on related work in the Cultural Historical Activity Theory tradition (CHAT) (Cole, 1996; Engström, 1987), which allowed us to consider the nature of the activity settings that existed in the department as well as those that we attempted to create in the team meetings (described later in the chapter). The learning "unit" is not the individual, but the individual in a specific social context. Activity settings can be seen as the "who, what, when, where, why, and how" of the routines which constitute everyday life—in essence, a more elaborated version of what we commonly call a social context (Cole, 1996; Engeström, 1987; Engeström, Miettinen, & Punamäki, 1999; Tharp & Gallimore, 1988). The specific components of an activity setting include subjects (participants), objects (the goals participants are trying to achieve), tools (the forms of mediation available in the setting, which can be symbolic like language or concepts, or more tangible like physical artifacts), community, rules, and division of labor. The community refers to the specific community formed by those participating in the setting, but also the connections to the various extended communities with which they are associated. A major target of the Math Project was to create activity settings that did not currently exist, namely intellectual and physical spaces that focused on equity related issues and ownership of the problem of underachievement.

Finally, building on this CHAT tradition, we drew on the notion of "re-mediation" (Cole & The Distributed Literacy Consortium, 2006; Cole & Griffin, 1983; Gutierrez, Hunter, & Arzubiaga, 2009). Simply put, a re-mediation approach suggests that new learning is fostered when the means of mediation and cultural tools are changed, in stark contrast to traditional notions of remediation that seek to address learner deficits. This view suggests that learning and development are a complex result of one's interactions with others mediated by cultural tools and artifacts, both physical and symbolic, including language. When cultural tools are encountered in the environment, people do not interpret and act on them directly but rather through the mediation of how those tools are used by others. For example, a child learns the uses of a fork as a part of joint activity—by watching others use utensils during a family meal, by listening to their words (another kind of tool) in describing different utensils, and perhaps by becoming involved in the joint activity of dinner. Thus, as part of our project, we introduced new cultural tools and artifacts that were both material (among others, protocols around how to understand institutional data as well as tools to collect and use their own data) and symbolic (for example, new concepts and language).

In the following paragraphs, we elaborate on how we have drawn on these theoretical notions in the implementation of the project.

## The Math Project

The Math Project was a nearly two-year endeavour spanning from 2004 to 2006 that sought to refocus institutional concern from student deficits to one of institutional responsibility. Funded by the James Irvine Foundation, the Math Project provided six mathematics faculty members at California Community College (CCC) with a structured opportunity to study and discuss the myriad reasons for the persistent underachievement of Latino students enrolled in remedial mathematics courses. Specifically, the Project enabled faculty members to consider alternatives to their assumptions about underachievement by placing their own belief systems within the heart of inquiry.

California Community College was the site for this project, a large community college in the Southwest serving close to 17,000 students annually. The college offers 59 Associate of Arts/Science degree programs, 71 Career Certificate programs and the opportunity to complete up to two years in any of 58 baccalaureate programs for transfer to a four-year college or university. The college serves a diverse student population where Latino students made up 40% of students enrolled between 2004 and 2006, the years of the project. Students identifying themselves as Asian, Pacific Islander, and Filipino were 22%, White students 24%, and Black students represented 11% of the student population enrolled at CCC at the time of the project.

In December 2000, CCC was invited to participate as one of the partner institutions in the Diversity Scorecard Project because its student body demonstrated ethnic diversity. The Center for Urban Education purposefully invited colleges that were not struggling to diversify their student population so that the focus of the team would be on *student outcomes* rather than increasing diversity. Data from 2000 at this campus indicated that African American and Latino students had not attained a commensurate level of success compared to their Asian and White peers in critical pathway mathematics courses. However, institutional policies and structures were not in place at CCC that would enable institutional decision makers to undertake a systematic investigation into the persistent disparities between ethnic and racial groups in these courses.

Building on the previously described framework, the Math Project utilized a "practitioner-as-researcher" model in which practitioners took on the role of researchers, and researchers assumed the roles of facilitators and consultants. The practitioner-as-researcher model has elements of community (Smith, 1999), collaborative, and participatory action research (Bray et al., 2000; Stringer, 1996) in that the *purpose* of inquiry is to bring about individual and institutional change. The primary approach of the Project was to facilitate the regular and systematic interaction of researchers working as facilitators engaged with insider teams of practitioners in a process of collecting data and jointly *creating knowledge* about local problems related to equitable outcomes. The general purpose was to scaffold participants' construction of new knowledge about their own institutions that could then be used to bring about institutional change.

The practitioners involved in the work at the college setting were key players in the institution's formal learning systems and/or were viewed as key actors in informal institutional networks. Team members came from a specific department (Math) and were self-selected. The team was diverse, with White, African American, Latino, and Armenian faculty members present. In addition, other instrumental team members included the institutional researcher who provided data for discussion and analysis as well as the Learning Outcomes Coordinator.

The general process engaged team members in a series of meetings that initially revolved around "vital signs" (indicators of student degree progression and student outcomes that include academic pathways, retention, transfer readiness, and excellence). This work then quickly proceeded to the examination of "fine-grained measures" of the same types of indicators. An important difference between the vital signs and the fine-grained measures is the fact that the teams themselves selected the latter indicators and requested that they be provided for discussion to the team by the institutional research office. The process of defining the indicators and specifically requesting the data was designed to foster a sense of agency and to promote problem framing, ownership of the assessment results, and general data literacy around issues of equity.

There were specific cultural tools which were introduced within these specialized activity settings. For example, the Project provided access to special artifacts such as data sheets, "vital signs" protocols, interim reports templates, an equity index formula, and examples of graphic displays to help make data easy to decipher. The Project also introduced specialized vocabulary and concepts such as the differentiation between diversity and equity; deficit, diversity, and equity perspectives on institutional data; data vs. inquiry approaches to data; and the notion of global vs. local knowledge. Evidence teams met at least once a month for at least two hours. The team meetings served a "mediating" rather than a directive function in this respect. Rather than trying to change attitudes and practice directly, which emphasizes individual learning, the goal of the team meetings was to change the nature of the mediation and cultural practices that participants had at their disposal.

By creating communities of practice around equity, we attempted to help participants create new identities and new meaning or "sense-making" around issues of equity on their own campuses and in their own classrooms. In essence, we attempted to "re-mediate" thinking and practice around equity. In this context, then, re-mediation refers to changing the nature of mediation available to participants in the setting, rather than to the deficit-based connotation used to refer to compensatory programs and practices. Project researchers provided strategically assisted performance to the teams. Since learning was seen as social and mediated, we tried to reorganize key features of the social interaction and provide new cultural tools and artifacts and ways to use them (such as institutional data along with the strategies for becoming informed and critical consumers). Before the Project, there was no institutional "space" for this type of work, and thus it did not occur.

A Project researcher and at least one research assistant were present at each of the scheduled team meetings. Each of the team meetings over the 18-month period was transcribed for analysis. In addition, field notes from all contacts between project staff and team participants were kept. These contacts included records of formal meetings, informal meetings with individuals or subgroups of team members outside of the team meeting setting, phone calls, emails, and so on. In addition, all relevant documents that provided evidence of impact were kept for analysis. Finally, after the end of the formal project and the termination of formal team meetings, project staff continued to carefully document the participants' reports about their interactions with other people outside of the team meetings, their comments about institutional and organizational factors related to the project, and our own observations about institutional changes in activities or changes in practice or policy that took place and that could be directly attributed to the project, most often by the participants' or others' (e.g., administrators') reports.

## An Overview of Outcomes

It is useful to briefly summarize the major patterns that emerged related to participation in the team meetings. These can be briefly summarized as follows:

1.  Most team members believed data were essential, but few had the skills to examine it critically and ask relevant questions and use it as a tool for action. The process provided a context and setting for all evidence team members to engage in data-based inquiry and make sense of student outcome inequities revealed by examining disaggregated student outcomes data.

2.  Institutional researchers often saw their role as a technical activity rather than as helping others understand the data, ask questions of the data, or be proactive in looking at new data. The process assisted the institutional researcher to reconsider the formal role to which she was socialized and to view her role and that of the faculty as "teachers" and "facilitators" of data-based inquiry rather than as "gatekeepers" of information.

3. Leadership was not necessarily found in one individual, rather it was most often "distributed" among different members at different points in time. The most important leadership skill was being able to facilitate learning and equity mindedness by encouraging critical dialogue surrounding issues of race/ethnicity.

4. Many patterns of student outcome inequities may remain hidden without systematic "unpacking" of the data that already exist. The disaggregation of data helped to bring otherwise concealed inequities to the surface, thereby allowing evidence team members to better recognize these patterns.

5. The majority of the members of the Math Project were faculty members and were involved in frank discussions about subjects that were uncomfortably related to race, ethnicity, and equity. They were asked to reflect on the condition of equity on their campus and to share aloud what they believed to be the factors that contributed to the preponderance of Latino students in remedial mathematics courses and their lack of achievement. They were likewise asked to state their assumptions about students and to thoroughly articulate how they came to those conclusions with the intent to draw out deeply held beliefs and suppositions.

A major accomplishment of the Math Project was that it was able to create a previously non-existent activity setting with a specific focus on equitable student outcomes, and also the development of a new community of practice that did not previously exist.

In our analysis of the data, we found that team members displayed increased knowledge about their roles as instructors and more positive attitudes about indicators and equity. The following quote from a team member illustrates this point when she said, "So with this project, it's allowing me to get more of the student perspective opposed to our assumptions [be]cause there is a big difference." Another team member noted:

> I think the project provides some time and space for us to look [at the data] in addition to the information that we gather from the students. But in addition to that we, at least we spend some time looking at what it is that we're doing, what is going on also [in the classroom] because we never get to talk about that unless we do a retreat as we did a couple of years ago.

Qualitative analysis of meeting field notes and transcripts revealed that early in the Project, members of the inquiry team were alarmed by the institutional data that showed high rates of enrollment in remedial courses, significant gaps in transfer rates and degree attainment for Latino students. Prior to the Project, these "discoveries" were known about in an abstract way, informed more by anecdote rather than data, and as such, the extent of the inequities was not fully grasped by evidence team members. These findings were explored over the course of the project with the assistance of the data tools provided by the project. This new knowledge created within the team meetings became the impetus for team members to move their efforts beyond the confines of the team itself. Team members conducted both quantitative and qualitative inquiry activities to further understand the inequities persisting on their campus as made evident by the data. First, team members administered the LASSI, a diagnostic assessment of student strengths and weaknesses in 10 areas, so as to better gauge student attitudes, motivation and study skills to name a few. Second, using the results of the LASSI, team members devised an interview protocol they used with a select number of students enrolled in both remedial and advanced math courses to understand what happens inside and outside the classroom from the students' perspective. As a result of the combination of activities, team members were able to partially redefine their roles as faculty and administrators, including the ways that they interacted among themselves and in the larger campus around issues of equity.

At the conclusion of the Project, team members were able to move beyond this technical focus and significantly expanded the scope of their inquiry activities. Team members talked about how they planned to share the information they gathered with the rest of the Math Department. Moreover, there was the hope that additional math faculty would engage in similar inquiry activities to gain a better understanding of student experiences both inside and outside of the classroom. Having these qualitative data, team members believed, would challenge previously held assumptions about students and move them from a student deficit perspective. Reflecting on her interviews, a team member observed:

> And, you know, it's just hard for me to accept the fact that students, you know, they're just lazy, things of that nature, cause I really don't think that. That's not the main problem with students. I just think that every situation is different, everyone's work environment [and] home environment is [sic] different. So maybe they just need a different master plan 'til the system can be successful.

Above all, engaging in further inquiry activities meant that team members came to understand that no "magic bullet" exists to improve outcomes, but rather that change takes time, is deliberate, and often occurs in small, incremental steps.

## Conclusion

The overall design of the Math Project assumed that individual change is socially fostered and also leads to institutional change. Thus, fostering individual equity-minded thinking and practices is seen as a stepping-stone toward changing institutional practices and culture and ultimately improved student outcomes.

One problem with existing frameworks that address either one or both of these goals (changing individuals or changing institutions) is that they focus *exclusively* either on individual processes or else institutional factors. The socio-historical framework allows for a larger unit of analysis that includes both of these dimensions and thus helps to bridge and situate individual behavior and cultural practices to institutional ones. In essence, it situates individuals within specific communities of practice and incorporates not only individual goals and media-tional means but cultural norms and institutional goals as well.

An important change principle derived from this framework is that changes in any aspect of the activity setting can produce changes elsewhere in the sys-tem. Thus, by introducing new forms of cultural tools (for example, new ways of talking about and concepts for thinking about inequitable student outcomes, or data tools to track equity), it was possible to document changes in the larger sys-tem. The Math Project, in many ways, has served as an influencing agent for subsequent projects. Faculty at City College, for example, who were part of the Equity Scorecard Project (2007–2008), noted inequities among their African American student population enrolled in mathematics and shared this informa-tion with the Math Department. Consequently, the math faculty formed a Math Evidence Team that was modeled after the Math Project to explore the possible reasons for the underperformance of African American students in math through further data inquiry.

What began with the Math Project at one institution has yielded new com-munities of practice at other institutions with new goals focused around equitable outcomes. The division of labor related to making sure equitable outcomes are produced has shifted so that previously uninvolved actors and academic units are sharing the responsibility. The traditional roles that have separated coordi-nated efforts have begun to break down, particularly in the area of faculty and key staff (for example in the area of transfer and counseling), and are becoming less rigid. As these institutions begin to incorporate new cultural tools (equity-minded discourse, tools for unpacking and examining student outcome data, and so on), new activity settings are created such as a Transfer Academy at one of our partner institutions that serves to promote student success over time. In essence, new knowledge and understandings about the issue are being socially constructed and are serving as guides to future action.

While it is possible to think about producing changes in behavior by trying to change the behavior directly, through didactic or similar means, such an approach focuses only on individuals and also leaves several levels of learning unaccounted for. Consistent with the notion that learning is socially constructed, the Math Project incorporated a perspective that focused on a unit of analysis larger than the individual actors. Thus, rather than adopting a didactic instructional approach, the Project instead changed the nature of the mediation available to the team participants and also created a special activity setting (team meetings) that allowed the creation of new, situated knowledge leading to a critical and proactive stance toward institutional change. The active ingredients that appear to be critical thus include (1) creating special activity settings that help form new communities of practice, (2) situated learning, and (3) data-driven inquiry. The framework adopted here therefore is useful not only in how to change individual and institutional cultural norms and practices but where to look for that change as well.

## ACKNOWLEDGMENT

This chapter builds on data excerpted from the dissertation *Exploring Faculty Beliefs about Remedial Mathematics Students* by the first author. The authors are affiliated with the Center for Urban Education, Rossier School of Education, University of Southern California, Los Angeles. The Diversity Scorecard Project was funded by The James Irvine Foundation, and Estela Mara Bensimon served as the Principal Investigator.. The authors are grateful for the collaboration of colleagues at the community colleges involved in the projects, and to Professor Alicia C. Dowd, co-director of the Center for Urban Education for her intellectual contributions to this paper. Correspondence concerning this article should be addressed to Robert Rueda Rossier School of Education, University of Southern California, WPH 601B, 3470 Trousdale Parkway, Los Angeles, CA 90089 (Email: rueda@usc.edu).

## ENDNOTE

1   Throughout the chapter, the words *equity-minded, equity-mindful,* and *equity-mindedness* reflect the same meanings. These terms are used to describe individuals as well as institutional practices and structures.

## · 1 2 ·

# Praxis-in-Dis-coordination

*Margaret Gallego & Olga A. Vásquez*

Historically, the preponderance of educational research (including much of bilingual education research) has been concerned with identifying instructional interventions that positively influence individual student performance; in other words, it has primarily focused on "what works." Recently, researchers have used qualitative methods to investigate the conditions in which "best practices" are likely to be successful, including investigations regarding context, i.e., how it works. Absent in bilingual education research, however, is the question, "What's in it [bilingualism] for me or my community?" This question has particular resonance among monolingual individuals. Within research that addresses the dynamic relationship between individual and community (i.e., how participants and contexts work on each other), little research has expressly focused on the influence individuals have on the activity system in which they participate.

We continue the discussion of sociocultural theorists who examine the ways in which "relationships between human mental functioning, on the one hand, and the cultural, institutional, and historical situations in which this functioning occurs, on the other" (Wertsch, del Rio, & Alvarez, 1995, p. 3). Like Baquedano-López and colleagues (this volume), we look deeper into how learning is mediated by language and social interaction, in our case, in strategically engineered learning environments that make diversity the cornerstone of learning and development. We are particularly interested in the ways in which participants within an activity system draw on their own background experiences and the collective resources available in the context to reflect back on what those experiences offer the task at hand with new understandings. More specifically, we are interested in how the individual and the context work on each other in supportive ways.

## Linking Praxis to Dis-coordination

Points of interaction among cross-group participants within strategically designed learning environments that incorporate diverse resources are necessarily sites of negotiation, challenge, and resistance. While some may negatively perceive the confluence of a variety of cultural resources and traditions as problematic, we argue that problems—i.e., dis-coordinations—are moments that draw attention to difference and offer the context for adjustment, resolution and internalization. We agree with Engeström (1999), that the point of contact is the basis of dis-coordination and that contact has productive potential. Conflict, missteps, and mistakes are favorable conditions for learning when they are perceived as opportunities for understanding and reconstituting our views of self and culture; otherwise, they become lost opportunities.

We view praxis as theoretically grounded action, in this case, established practices that capitalize on difference normative of everyday life. By extension, praxis-in-dis-coordination is the practice of making the problems that arise from difference into opportunities for cultural awareness, resolution, and internalization. These individual gains reflect participant "agency" (Engeström, 2006). As Engeström suggests, "Human beings not only interpret, they also face contradictions between multiple motives embedded in and engendered by their historically evolving communities and objects" (p. 4) and act in ways that transform their own life activity. We are proposing that the new ways of seeing self, learning, and the "other" are reflective actions that individuals take. These actions are subsequently used by others, refined, and ultimately become established practice in the community. In essence, these are examples of the "self-regulatory process of personality at the moment of one's living a (a specifically engineered) concrete experience or series of experiences" as González Rey (this volume) makes clear. We refer to these experiences and the resultant transformation of the individual and their community, as praxis-in-dis-coordination.

In this chapter, we illustrate examples of praxis-in-dis-coordination in which difference, inherent in inter-group interactions, provides opportunity for cultural awareness, conflict resolution, and the subsequent influence on the context (both bilingual and monolingual participants). We draw examples from two strategically designed contexts that build on diversity as the founding principle. Fittingly, we begin with a general discussion of the context that influences our work. We provide a summary of the authors' experience within the organization and the development and implementation of two distinct versions of *La Clase Mágica*, an innovation of the Fifth Dimension model, an after-school educational activity founded on cultural-historical theories of learning and development (for details see Cole, 1996; Cole et al., 2006). Next, we discuss the theoretical grounding and conceptual tools we used in our analysis. We then distinguish the dual purpose of language and the role of context as cultural tools we apply to understand episodes of praxis-in-dis-coordination, situations in which individuals and context dialectically influence one another. Lastly, we propose several lines of research that we believe will be instrumental for making use of knowledge gained from "alternative" learning sites to inform and reform traditional educational settings.

## Two Projects, One Objective: Capitalizing on Diversity

*La Clase Mágica* and *La Clase Mágica*-Midwest are two efforts at integrating the participants' "complete linguistic, sociocultural, and academic repertoire" (Guttiérez et al., 2002). Variations of this after-school program, generically referred to as the Fifth Dimension, share several general features (for full description see Cole et al., 2006). First, the sites operate during after-school hours and purposefully combine the features of home and school into a productive "blend" that children find interesting enough to attend voluntarily and one that adults deemed educationally enriching enough to encourage their children's participation. Second, information and communication technologies are central to the activities, but, by and large, the level of technology is low, low-end microprocessors, and off the shelf software. Third, each site combines community institutions with university courses in support of intergenerational interaction and a culture of collaboration. College students enrolled in varied coursework related to learning and development participate alongside school-aged children. Each brings different expertise and talent to bear on the activity. Although, the content of each site may vary according to local preferences, software availability, resources, and the processes for participation are shared, resulting in sites with different "personalities" but shared characteristics (Gallego, Rueda, & Moll, 2003).

Below, we describe a bilingual and a multicultural variation of *La Clase Mágica* (Vásquez, 2003; Gallego, 2000). Both build on the intellectual resources of the participants and their communities by integrating the respective language and cultural practices into the system of artifacts (curricular materials) and the social interactions of adult-child participants. Both sites draw on the respective community funds of knowledge—i.e., the home language and culture of origin) and the norms and language of formal mainstream institutional contexts—to develop the material artifacts that guide participants' computer-based activity. *La Clase Mágica*, Solano Beach, California, has maintained sustainability and dissemination over the course of two decades and *La Clase Mágica*-Midwest operated for three years and closed due to other shut-downs within three years because of the lack of institutional support.

## La Clase Mágica

In 1989, Vásquez arrived at the Laboratory of Comparative Human Cognition (LCHC) as a postdoctoral fellow with the idea of exploring the cognitive aspect of oral-based literate activities she had found in a small Mexican immigrant community near Stanford University where she conducted her dissertation work. The Fifth Dimension project was in its third year of operation, and Vásquez was immediately drawn to the Fifth Dimension's protean nature to blend into its surrounding context and to its theoretically based organization in which participants routinely are active learners in the experience of play. On arrival at LCHC, Vásquez was charged with solving the puzzle of why the Fifth Dimension was unable to recruit or retain children from an adjacent Mexicano community. Using Cole's (1996) metaphor of culture as garden, she assessed that the culture of the Fifth Dimension did not offer the right conditions "to grow" immigrant youths from distinct language and culture backgrounds. In Engeström's (1987) terms, the Fifth Dimension instantiated dis-coordination, in which the apparent source of conflict was an unresolved culture clash. The challenge became how to organize the "right conditions" to support and enhance the learning and development of local bilingual, Mexican-origin youths. To reconcile the cultural worlds of youths living in a Mexican-origin community and those who resided in the high-income, English-dominant, area where the Fifth Dimension was located, required reorganizing the system of artifacts to include both the resources of both communities. A new site was opened at a nearby Catholic Mission ministering to the surrounding Mexicano community. Unable to bridge the language and culture of the two communities, the new version of the Fifth Dimension morphed into *La Clase Mágica* with its own cultural identity and new ambitions to make a difference in the schooling experiences of Latino English-language learners.

The attempt to incorporate the cultural and linguistic resources—i.e., Spanish and Mexicano culture—with those of the Fifth Dimension—English and mainstream culture, highlighted the first of many incidents in which the bringing together of multiple and varied resources resulted in the change of direction and practice of the context, the research and practice. The response to the individual needs of the target participants, i.e., making it relevant to their cultural and linguistic background and their academic needs, fundamentally changed the goals and objectives of the parent project into a new initiative, one that would address the under-achievement of Latino youths in P-12 education and their representation in higher education (Vásquez, 2003).

This initial adaptation led to 21 years of testing the flexibility of La Clase Mágica to capitalize on the intersecting worlds of minority youths whose language and culture differed greatly from that of the school. To support the multiple domains these children traverse as a matter of everyday life, the intellectual resources of the target populations and the requisite bilingual/bicultural competencies to succeed in both school and the world at large were integrated into the very essence of La Clase Mágica's raison d'être. Vásquez led the pursuant expansion of La Clase Mágica to four developmental activities, five local communities, and recently to two University of Texas campuses: UT San Antonio and UT Austin (Vásquez et al., 2010). Presently, she is pursuing the development of a second cycle of adaptation that extends the cultural and bilingual focus to a global relevance that prepares low-income bilingual learners to meet the social realities of an intensely interconnected world (Vásquez & Marcello, 2010).

## La Clase Mágica-Midwest

In the fall of 1991, LCM-Midwest was launched in a multiracial neighborhood flanked by the automobile factories of Lansing, Michigan, and by the academic community surrounding Michigan State University (MSU). Gallego sought to replicate the language and culture emphasis of LCM; however, the Latino population was one of several language minority groups residing in the neighborhood. A substantial number of Hmong, Chinese, and African American families also lived in the community. The multicultural/multilingual setting and an emphasis on teacher education research and instruction were two features that distinguished LCM-Midwest and La Clase Mágica situated in Southern California.

A modest two-story building, the Cristo Rey Community Center, became the site of LCM-Midwest. The community center was the focal point within the neighborhood where several educational programs already existed: adult English as a Second Language classes, GED preparations courses, and a tutoring program for children. Gallego sought to establish an environment in which the "educational experts" (researcher/Gallego, university graduate and undergraduate students) were positioned to "learn from" rather than "teach to" the neighborhood children. She also attempted to gain support for LCM-Midwest from teacher education colleagues by promoting it as an "alternative" professional development school.

LCM-Midwest physically existed for three years in relative obscurity save a few research articles (Gallego, 2000; Gallego & Cole, 2000; Gallego & Blanton 2002) and a few visits from Michael Cole and Vásquez. Regrettably, the type of efforts of LCM-Midwest, not more than eight miles from the Michigan State University campus, did not gain a foothold in the community or the university. The interest of the university at the time was in cultivating a very popular international program that sent College of Education professors abroad to teach at "American" schools. Funds as well as loyalties were divided between the local/domestic and the distant/international. In hindsight, LCM-Midwest was ahead of its time. In the interim decades, interest in after-school learning has mushroomed among educators seeking unique research sites (cf. Hull & Schultz, 2002; Garner, Zhao, & Gillingham, 2002) as well as novel opportunities to support and enhance students' school based knowledge in innovative ways (Schauble & Glaser, 1996). Furthermore, computer use at all levels of education has become ubiquitous.

## Praxis-in-Dis-coordination: A Theoretical Framework

The theoretical foundation of both versions of *La Clase Mágica* builds on Vygotsky's (1978) understandings of the social origins of human thinking, i.e., that higher intellectual functions occur in the social sphere before they become the property of the individual. Luria's (1978) assertion that behavior cannot be studied in isolation from the environmental conditions and general cultural context within which it develops brings to the fore the relationship of context and the individual. Contemporary sociocultural educational researchers argue that competence does not solely reside in the individual but rather in the interaction of the individual with others in culturally inspired activity systems and practices (McDermott, 1993). Individuals who engage in targeted activities in varied degrees of participation gain expertise as they move from legitimate peripheral participation toward central participation (Lave & Wegner, 1991). In other words, individuals are transformed through their participation in a community of practice (Rogoff, 1994). It is this transaction, this movement, that marks learning.

We use these ideas to frame our theoretical and methodological perspective to re-examine the relationship of individuals and communities in joint activity and to claim difference as an asset. Beyond the moment of participation, learning draws from "histories of participation" (Rogers, 2002) to constitute history and to shape future acts of participation. In other words, contexts exert influence on and are influenced by individuals' participation. However, the interaction between the individual and the context also "leaves a residue, it makes a mark on the participant" (Moje & Lewis, 2007, p. 16). We argue that individual learning leaves a residue within the context and that this learning also makes a mark on the community.

A full account of learning and development requires a methodology that acknowledges that the individual and the activity mutually work on each other (Engeström, 1998). Two constructs within the dialectic method: a) the dual function of language and b) the function of context are particularly useful to our work.

## The Role of Context on Learning

Studies of ecological psychology as well as sociocultural theories, as cited above, have documented extensively that the physical features of a setting and how people participate in such environments are related (Gump, 1978; Gump & Good, 1976). More specifically, the site or setting for learning influences what and how something is taught and/or learned (Johnson, 1985). Nonetheless, the consideration of context in the understanding of individual performance and learning is a major departure from the measure of individual accountability typical of traditional psychological and school achievement measures. More recent research conducted with a sociocultural perspective has confirmed that the social organization and underlying features of a given social context are central to understanding students' competence and participation (e.g., achievement). Individual measures provide an incomplete picture of achievement because they fail to record how individuals are influenced by their contexts/communities (Solano-Flores, 2008). Individual differences interact with the social organization of specific activity settings that mediate outcomes in significant ways.

## The Role of Language in Learning

When we examine learning from a Vygotskyan (1987) perspective, we acknowledge the important role that language, the most significant among "psychological tools" or signs and symbols, referring to language as the tool of tools (cf. Wertsch, 1985, 1991b), plays in supporting learning and development. Language serves as communication by enabling human beings to socially coordinate (or dis-coordinate) actions with others through shared meaning, and it also mediates intellectual activity through the internalization of this communication. Vygotsky assigned great importance to the development of self-regulation because one's inner speech helps bring actions under the control of thought (Shotter, 1993).

Language is tied to people's experiences of situated action in the material and social world (Gee, 1996), what cognitive psychologists refer to as situatedness (cf. Brown, Collins, & Dugid, 1989; Lave, 1996) or context. The point is that people interact with their worlds through cultural artifacts, principally through language in both its oral and written forms, and that resultant mediation of actions plays a crucial role in the formation and development of human intellectual capacities. These ideas are particularly interesting when it comes to the ways that multiple resources—both cultural and linguistic—play in the relationship between the individual and diverse contexts. In our case, we view bilingualism as a joint, concurrent, and interchangeable use of two languages in assorted combinations as well as a mixture of everyday and professional language registers or social languages (e.g., teacher-ese). Thus, the key to capitalizing on bilingualism for learning is to socially organize learning contexts where languages are tools for communication (overt and intended for others) as well as for thought and action (intended for self and others).

We use this perspective of context and language to analyze field notes, journal entries, and debriefing dialogue to examine how diversity/bilingualism positively influences interactions between individual participants and their community/context. In particular, we were interested in how languages are tools for communication and action and how this action transforms the context (Engeström, 2006). We analyze episodes in which bilingualism is the means for and the object of negotiation, i.e., dis-coordination. In each episode, the friction between participants' prior knowledge and expectations and the existing conditions within the site(s) provide a point of conflict in which language is used to mediate understanding and to influence community practices, i.e., praxis-in-dis-coordination.

## *La Clase Mágica* as Praxis-in-Dis-coordination

Located at the boundary between home and school, *La Clase Mágica* draws on the virtual and the material, English and Spanish, and mainstream and Mexican culture to create a strategic socio-ecological context that draws on these intersecting points of difference. These points of difference— practices, goals, and values—along with the mix of play and education become intellectual tools to accomplish the tasks set by a culture of optimal learning in which the right set of conditions are organized to support the development of the participants' optimal potential (Relaño Pastor & Vásquez, 2011). The opportunity to play and to imagine a future self presents a unique opportunity for children to see themselves above their social conditions and visualize other possibilities (Vygotsky, 1978). A young boy who is pressured to adopt gang affiliation is free to experiment with other productive and accepted identities, e.g., the image of "a school boy." At the same time, these intersecting points present abundant opportunities for praxis-in-dis-coordination, capitalizing and making use of difference to enhance everyday life (Martinez & Vásquez, 2007).

The site is further diversified by participants enrolled in an undergraduate practicum course linked to the after-school program. The university students attend the site as "Amigas/os" [friends], researchers, collaborators, and theorists. These young adults are different from the neighborhood children in several ways: level of income, education, and respective life experiences that offer a potential opening for praxis-in-dis-coordination. A large number come from a variety of Asian groups, and smaller numbers of White and Latino students are also enrolled in the program. In helping child participants to proceed through a series of tasks, they also cultivate new ways of understanding difference, one's self, one's language, and one's role in the world.

These reflections and subsequent understandings are uniquely illustrated in the reports of bi-directional relations exchanges among inter-group participants, the undergraduate students and the child-participants, who take place in face-to-face interactions in the context of the after-school site session. These experiences tend to produce deep reflections on learning and their own resources in both the child and the university students as expressed below by a university Amiga:

> As I come to spend more time with the them [children] I come to realize how much I've learned along my 15 or so years of being in a public school education system and how this process of learning or deep understanding did not happen overnight; instead, learning is indeed a process in which the interaction of people, artifacts, and tools on many dimensions is essential. [GS, 10/8/07]

Although the students often come endowed with cultural capital privileged in mainstream society, at times, they also experience a reversal of power relations in their interactions with Spanish-language speakers. Facing a context where English is not the primary means of communication and where children know more of how the system works than they do opens opportunities for praxis in dis-coordination. The discomfort they experience upon entering an unfamiliar context and the lessons they learn about the diversity in the society is often recounted in the reflection section of the field notes. For example, in a segment of her weekly field notes, JB related how she experienced "being scared and ashamed of speaking school-learned Spanish in a context where youngsters spoke it better than her" [JB, 2008]. It was an unsettling dis-coordination that led to a deep reflection that resulted in her conviction to "learn a second language in order to negotiate the diversity that awaits me upon graduation."

More often, however, undergraduate students also recognize the importance of a context that reflects the cultural and linguistic resources of the child participants and the benefits it has for both the children and themselves, as CJ recounts in a segment of her field note reflection below:

> I think the incorporation of language curriculum into *La Clase Mágica* is important for both the linguistic development of the children, as well as their social development. Not only do the children participating in LCM get to speak and read in both of their languages, they also are able to socialize using both languages. The way the program is set up allows the children to be comfortable in both languages, making it easier for them to build upon their knowledge of English and Spanish with the collaboration of older, more knowledgeable peers. In my work at site I have seen that this concept is two directional. Not only do I get to share my knowledge of my culture and language with the children, but they get to share their culture and knowledge with me as well. I have to do this more often. (CJ, 10/07/2009)

Children's participation, on the other hand, is often bound to a set of relationships that they establish with their undergraduate pals. These relationships are based on friendship and are theoretically informed. The stated goal for the undergraduates is to open a zone of possibilities (Moll, 1992) as they collaborate with the children on advancing them through a pre-arranged set of activities. It is a dynamic relationship in which each side offers its cultural and linguistic resources to reach the desired goal—in this case, understanding of the text. The example below illustrates the typical relationship-building that grows out of meaningful and instructive collaboration between the children and their undergraduate collaborators:

> I realized the book was in Spanish, and Mirko [German foreign exchange student] came back and wanted to see what Eziquel [8-year child] was reading, too. Eziquel looked at the first page for a bit in a thoughtful manner. Mirko said, "Just start reading it to him." Eziquel said, "Nooo, he won'...[understand]...and then started translating the story to me from Spanish to English. He did a good job, and Mirko helped him start translating. He did a good job until he got to the Spanish word for "snore." The dinosaur kept snoring and snoring during the story, which was hard for Eziquel to pronounce in English, and he kept forgetting the word. The structure of the story had the Dino snoring for five pages in a row, and the fifth time Eziquel could not say and translate snore properly, he let out a loud, "Ahhhhhh, ohhhhhh" and to put the book down and picked up the *Cat in the Hat*, which was bilingual. He started translating the Spanish into English for me again before he realized English was printed on the bottom of the page.

# Praxis-in-Dis-coordination: LCM-Midwest and Teacher Education

As a joint educational effort between the Julian Samora Research Institute (JSRI) MSU and the Cristo Rey Community Center in North Lansing, LCM-Midwest supplemented the conventional educational programming offered at the center with a more progressive approach while maintaining the academic benefits to children.

Typical of most community centers, the emphasis at Cristo Rey was oriented toward service to neighborhood residents. In contrast, with the LCM-Midwest program, the children provided the service in that they allowed teacher education students to learn from them. The students experienced both excitement and trepidation about their work with children who were different from themselves—since most of them were of Anglo American backgrounds, English monolinguals, and life-long residents of Michigan. All had read countless articles about diversity (as required of their teacher preparation courses). Nevertheless, few had any substantive interactions with "diversity" to critically assess the merit of the suggestions and cautions noted by authors of this chapter. Although only a few miles away from the MSU campus, LCM gave these students a legitimate reason to enter a neighborhood where they were the minority group. This opportunity to work with "those" children helped to ally residual trepidation and to reject negative assumptions regarding the children that are often mediated by popular culture and folk psychology.

Their concurrent participation in conventional and after-school field placements offered teacher education students rich contrastive experiences to examine the contexts of learning. The relatively rigid school structure and the demanding pace of the curriculum dramatically contrasted with the self-directed pace of the child participants at the LCM-Midwest site. At school, choice was limited and attendance mandatory, and the after-school site choice was a premium, and attendance was voluntary (intermittent). These contrastive characteristics proved advantageous according to the context: At school, limited choice provided consistency and structure—at LCM free choice served as a motivating tool as well as a distraction to progress.

Participation in LCM-Midwest also offered genuine communication opportunities. A friendly and encouraging audience allowed teacher education students to piece together sentences and questions using their school-learned Spanish without concern for pronunciation, tense, or grammar. Children who were reluctant to use their native or partial language fluency also benefited from the "any and all" language policy of the program. The university students coaxed hesitant participants by imitating adolescent mannerisms and at times verbally encouraged children in the tone of a well-intended older sibling. These situations gave the participants an opportunity to use language to mark multiple "identities" present at the site.

Each LCM visit served as a point of reference for collective reflection during the 20-minute debriefing sessions held immediately after each session, as well as the content core of individually written field notes. Using their authentic face-to-face experiences with children, the teacher education students re-assessed their conceptions of learning, the learning practices of minority youths, and the assumptions offered in the course readings. The students drew on their "histories of participation" (Rogers, 2002) to constitute a history, shape future participation, and to establish a more realistic vision of minority education.

Debriefing sessions were socially organized to provide and offer peer support and clearly illustrate the first function of language, i.e., to communicate with others (coordinated activity). For ease of following the topic thread, only the full comments made by the target speaker, Erin, are provided.

ERIN: When I was helping him with this game...we had tried to read the directions in Spanish...you know for extra credit like it says...well we get started then he decides he doesn't want to finish it...but to go back to the English version...this...

SARAH: [remembers a previous session having worked with the same child]

ERIN: I know the extra "credit" doesn't seem to mean anything to them...even if they get moved to another game...one that is more fun...I tried offering extra credit you know like "bonus" points at my student teaching classroom and it seemed to work there but here it was different....I think at school they you know want to please the teacher...here they want to please themselves...which is fine...but I think sometimes I don't think they know what is best for them, right?

KATE: [reminds ERIN that choice is part of the activity]

ERIN: When I was in middle school we had. extra credit and thought that actually motivated me...to learn more to do better...you know

KATE: [concurs but reminds them that maybe since they "liked" school and are going to be teachers...that they look at things differently]

BOB: [suggests that perhaps it was a language barrier, that he did want the extra credit but didn't want to do it in Spanish?]

ERIN: I guess maybe the instructions seem way harder in Spanish than they do in English...I read both of them...well sort of with my Spanish...I wonder if it was the Spanish thing...I guess I was just wanting to...you know move to the next level...when I have my own classroom I'll have the kids come up with the rules... like ownership of them...so maybe they will stick to them. (Group Debriefing, 4/10)

Although anchored by the immediate experience, these debriefing conversations often transported the students spatially and temporally away from the current experience. The experience with language at the site transports the undergraduates to other experiences at other times and in other contexts to form a "constellation" of experience(s). In the debriefing above, site-based experience was contrasted with a previous experience that occurred during the student teacher's classroom placement; her own academic past; and an imagined future classroom. This verbal play illustrates language as a key tool with which one gains understanding (Vygotsky, 1978; Wertsch, 1985, 1991b). These conversations served to help the individual and the community of peers understand the episode and gain general understanding useful to their future participation at the site, as well as their future professional lives.

There is another function of language at the site that connects the participants to their inner speech. Teacher education students' candid comments, assertions, wonderings, and over-generalizations recorded in field notes illustrate praxis-in-dis-coordination. For example, when Erin reflects upon the discord between the site norm of "choice" and her expectation for "rule compliance" illustrated in the field note below, she uses this public writing outlet to contemplate her own belief and understandings. Thus, publicly displayed field note writing functions as inner speech.

> Today went okay. I guess I'm a little frustrated with how the children seem one day to be totally into the games and the maze and everything and then other days they are not. I wonder if they are getting bored with the same games. I guess I would be bored too, but it's not like we are making them do anything...are we? I understand that choice, self-direction, and self-regulation are really important parts of the culture of LCM but sometimes I don't see it in the kids. I also need to be a bit more patient with them I guess I really want to be here like I really want to get to be with kids here and at my student teaching. I think I am getting more comfortable with letting them lead me but then at my school my teacher says to do that [let students lead] but then she makes all the decisions for them. I think it is important for kids to learn to choose and then to deal with the consequences of their actions or in some cases at LCM it is their non-action. I guess on paper like when you do lesson plans, you think you have thought about all that can happen and should happen and then you do it, you teach the lesson and it doesn't go according to plan at all. Here at LCM on paper, choice and all seem like that should be enough to motivate the kids...but I guess we are all entitled to a "bad" day. (Erin, Field Note, 4/13)

In the example above, personal assertions and beliefs regarding "following the rules" are in conflict with the social organizational site norms that guide curricular choice and voluntary participation. The language used in the field note above resembles "talking through" of a particular problem within one's inner speech. In this case, Erin weighs the merit of opposing views as well as others' opinions shared during the previous debriefing session as part of her professional development. In this way, direct interaction with children leaves a residue that is reconstituted during debriefing sessions with the assistance of peers. This collective reflection then influences, or "leaves a mark," on the individual student teachers (Moje & Lewis, 2007), and it is documented in individually written field notes.

## So, What Is in It for Me?

At the outset of this chapter, we introduced the question that monolinguals have about bilingualism: What is in it for me? What can we gain from learning or understanding another language? We hope that our theoretical framework and our examples drawn from a large quantity of data illustrate the benefits on the individual and the context. Bilingual participants served as conduits of information to reinterpret and translate aspects of the LCM site culture that are in discoordination with monolingual community members' expectations and experience, but whose participation is instrumental to the task completion. These "dis-coordinations" exposed warranted changes that have led to site innovation, in particular at *La Clase Mágica,* which is in a continuous process of refinement (Collins et al., 2004) as a result of some of these types of dis-coordinations. As new ways of mediating discord developed, other situations arose that triggered subsequent change at the site context. For instance, at LCM-Midwest, teacher education students came to understand that their "playing teacher" did not serve the norms of the context. Instead of a competition, monolingual/cultural members collaborated in an interdependent manner that was mutually productive to individuals and the community/context.

Arranging contexts of learning that are malleable to the various influences brought in by the multiple resources of the collective body of participants provides ample opportunities to capitalize on difference, e.g., the histories, interests, experiences, expertise, worldviews, as critical resources for supporting learning and development. In addition, , they prepare individuals for the social and intellectual realities of the 21st century. The use of language as a tool for communication (overt and intended for others) and an instrument of thought and reason (intended for self, though at times overtly stated) is critical to any kind of learning environment, in particular diverse environments in which praxis in dis-coordination can become a highly valuable instructional strategy. We argue that the physical location of the after-school sites described here is not their most important feature. Rather, the most important quality is the carefully (re-)engineering of context and language resources within the framework of praxis-in-dis-coordination.

Capitalizing upon bilingualism as a resource at the personal, social, and local community level is vital to strengthening our nation's political, economic, and social future. For a populace whose national identity is inextricably associated with rugged individualism and independence, acknowledging the ways bilingualism directly benefits individuals and their communities is the first step toward embracing an interdependence and a new sense of a collective self. We understand that it will not be easy to shift from a narrative of one individual people to a narrative of a collective of people. However, the tremendous diversity worldwide and the incessant advances in information and communication technologies compel us to move in this direction, especially as it relates to teaching and learning.

· 1 3 ·

# Development of Latino Family-School Engagement Programs in U.S. Contexts

## Enhancements to Cultural Historical Activity Theory Accounts

*Richard Durán*

This chapter is about the design and implementation of Latino family-school engagement programs, based on insights drawn from Latino Studies, the Latino social justice movement, critical pedagogy and ecological systems theory, and how they enhance Cultural Historical Activity Theory (CHAT) and related Vygotskyan approaches to strengthen the design, implementation, and investigation of programs by adding to the foregoing approaches. The chapter illustrates how scholars and implementers can adapt a CHAT perspective to improve Latino parents' organizational capacity for school involvement, coupled with civic engagement in a systematic and multi-level integrated manner. In so doing, the chapter also illustrates ways in which CHAT has been extended by scholars concerned with Latino education outcomes to encompass a broad, flexible conceptualization of "activity systems," so as to capture complex relationships among interconnected social and political institutions affecting parental school engagement systems design. The assertion of the voice and concerns of Latino parents and community members is an essential feature of this approach.

While there is no singular interpretation of CHAT, the basic tenets of the approach as adopted by contemporary theorists frame everyday human action in terms of learning and acquisition of adaptive social-cultural practices. These practices involve mental and physical tool artifacts or forms of mediation constructed and used purposefully by subjects (persons) in order to meet objectives (goals) in a manner that evolves over time and that can lead to human individual/social development of enduring capacity (see, e.g., Cole, 1996). The contemporary CHAT account characteristically acknowledges Vygotsky's notions of four types of interacting *genetic* development of humans: phylogenesis—species evolution; cultural historical genesis—development of social and cultural systems of representation and action over time; ontogenesis—individual human organism development; and microgenesis—a human organism's acquisition and development of particular skills and representational capacities.

Drawing on this foundation, CHAT theorists use the notion of "activity system" as a way of characterizing how human practices are organized as ongoing sociocultural resources to accomplish daily practice on the part of humans organized in "activity settings," allied with social affiliations and both informal and formal institutions. Family-school engagement programs can be treated as activity systems, though these activity systems may take many forms—an interesting and important issue when we consider that these forms themselves may interact with each other. For purposes of simplification, consider a Latino parent group that meets on weekday nights, say once every two weeks, to discuss the progress of children in school, their difficulties, and challenges and ways that teachers and the school may support children's school performance. Further, consider the possibility that the discussions among parents lead to follow-up actions involving communications with teachers, school staff and administrators, and a school board in order to implement changes in school practices.

Engeström (1999) has made a major contribution to activity theory perspectives by elaborating ways in which learning is expanded by characterizing interrelationships among interrelated activity systems. Furthermore, the ways that activity systems developed may show interdependence and the need to resolve contradictions in the aims and processes characterizing different activity systems. The parent program designed as described above could be characterized as interacting with activity systems representing the classroom, school, school district administration, school board, and any number and type of activity systems in the immediate and extended social surroundings—and everyday realization of mediational forms such as belief systems that are part of the cultural-social historical heritage of a community and its inhabitants.

In this chapter we consider how CHAT contributes to an understanding of Latino family-school engagement program structures as activity systems drawing on insights from the establishment of the Latino studies and social justice movement among scholars, critical pedagogy (Freire, 1970) and ecological systems theory (Bronfenbrenner, 1986).

As will be seen below, CHAT in its most classic and general sense does not provide an adequate foundation for studying the rationale and ends for Latino family-school engagement programs when such programs are viewed as tools for social justice. The work of investigators such as Engström on interacting and interdependent activity systems lights the way, but the unique circumstances that surround a Latino social justice treatment of Latino family-school engagement benefits from considering how the historical movement for social justice among Latinos creates insights into what CHAT can contribute to the understanding of human development, in its richer political and moral dimensions. It is not an accident that CHAT has appealed to Latino activist scholars. The ensuing discussion, preceding a discussion of CHAT and particular Latino school involvement programs from a CHAT perspective, illustrates the contributions of past family school involvement research, the history of the Latino studies movement, and critical pedagogy along with ecological systems theory to an enriched CHAT perspective. It will be clear that many of the basic tenets of CHAT are reflected and "brought to further life" when considered from these perspectives.

The final section of the chapter briefly explores three types of program structures: a) local school and classroom projects aimed at having Latino parents learn specific practices tied to literacy and schooling; b) regional and community programs of an ongoing nature such as that described above, aimed at increasing Latino parents' knowledge of school governance, policies, and parents' participation as school leaders influencing schooling practices; and c) diffusion programs at regional, state, and national levels whose aim it is to create new programs of type a) and b). Each type of structure is characterized by different (though potentially complementary) goals and activity systems. A further characteristic is that programs of the three types can interact and commingle, stimulating emergence of creative new types of activity systems that can influence educational policy and practice across educational tiers, schooling and policy institutions, thereby strategically positioning Latino communities as advocates for educational success.

## Latino Family School Involvement

The need for improvement of U.S. Latinos' involvement in their families' education is buttressed by extensive research and policy analyses showing that the education achievement and attainment gap faced by Latinos is induced by complex historical and structural inequities, leading to educational inequalities for U.S. Latinos and other underserved U.S. communities (Portes, 2005; Rodriguez-Brown, 2009; Epstein, 1995).

Existing reviews of research on Latino parent-school involvement show a mixed pattern of findings. Overall, it seems clear that Latino family households earn less income and have adult family members with less formal education and that there is a notable association between these characteristics and children's schooling achievement and educational attainment. This pattern exists regardless of parents' and children's nativity and is made more complex by intergenerational downward assimilation of some immigrant origin family members, who encounter barriers in society and schools because of failure to gain support for personal identities allied with motivation to succeed in school (Portes & Rumbaut, 2006). Some large scale survey research, e.g., indicates that Latino parents and their home environment are lacking in terms of activities such as parents reading to children in comparison to non-minority households, and that Latino children enter school with less familiarity with print concepts as compared to non-Latino children as a whole (Lopez et al., 2007). Other qualitative studies suggest that teachers inappropriately show a propensity to believe that Latino parents care less than other parents about their children's educational progress (Quiocho & Daoud, 2006).

As will be discussed here and more in depth in the next section on contributions of critical pedagogy to Latino parent program design, the research literature also provides evidence that Latino parents do care deeply about their children's education. Efforts to improve Latino parent-school involvements must build on bridging the cultural capital of families and the culture and belief systems of schooling in a way that honors this cultural capital (Trumbull et al., 2001). This dynamic goes beyond ameliorating cultural difference and inappropriate notions of eliminating cultural deficits. The research provides empirical evidence that culturally responsive parent school engagement programs and other efforts to connect Latino parents with classroom teachers, schooling activities, and schooling managers should be developed based on partnerships between Latino communities and their organizations—and the community at large and the power structures enacting schooling (see, e.g., Chrispeels & Rivero, 2001; Marschall, 2006; Cooper et al.,2005; Ferguson, 2008). Parent school engagement programs promoting the education of children and family members can take many forms. They differ from individual, isolated parent conversations and student status update meetings with teachers and individual parent participation in school organized briefing meetings for parents. Instead, they are formal organizations serving parents' systematic engagement with schools, school boards, and other institutional entities to address the learning and resource needs of children and family members in schools (Zarate, 2007). It is apparent that there are many organizational strategies and possible models for pursuing the design of school engagement programs.

It is a premise of this chapter that the design, development, and functioning of effective Latino parent school programs ought to be approached from a broad perspective that contextualizes the rationale for programs, and their theory of action, in light of the Latino social justice movement and its emergence as both an intellectual and practical force. As will be argued below, a coherent approach can build from critical pedagogy and ecological systems theories perspectives joined with a CHAT perspective. This combined approach brings out some of the unique ways that CHAT and Vygotskyan-based theories have been treated by U.S. Latino scholars and other scholars with similar perspectives, so as to contribute towards CHAT becoming a tool for social change, and not just an intellectual tool for understanding human development.

## Historical and Intellectual Roots of the Work

Cultural Historical Activity Theory (CHAT) and allied Vygotskyan accounts of learning and literacy development have provided valuable theoretical tools for contemporary scholar activists in the United States and Latin America concerned with understanding and promoting the educational advancement of communities of peoples in the Americas who have not had equitable access to institutional and economic resources in their host country. The appeal of CHAT for this purpose has historical, social, and intellectual roots that are important to understand in appreciating many of the unique characteristics of CHAT scholarship in the Americas as applied to Latino populations, and in particular, in the context of this chapter, how CHAT has been pursued by scholar activists such as those contributing to the present volume. The motivation of these scholar activists lies deep in the history of the Americas, the emergence of the Latino liberation and social justice movement, the emergence of Latino ethnic studies in colleges and universities, and the subsequent emergence of activist researchers devoting their careers to supporting the betterment of Latinos. These matters are of more significance than just providing a historical context. They are living concepts and ideas that guide the consciousness of many researchers, and their students and other advocates as they interpret CHAT and its importance for both change and scholarship. To be fair, it should also be noted that these same ideas are important to a broader range of scholars and advocates for social change in a number of fields that can be characterized as ethnic and cultural studies, critical race theory, or Marxist studies, to name a few.

Historically, more than 500 years have lapsed since the initial European settlements of the Americas. The majority of the current descendants of the indigenous peoples of the Americas, African slaves, and mixed-heritage persons descendant from intermarriage among these groups and with Europeans endure social, economic, and educational inequities in comparison to European-only origin American descendants. These descendants also show similar inequities compared to many groups from other parts of the world who immigrated later to the Americas. In the United States and the rest of America to the south, the indigenous peoples intermarried with the Hispanic settlers to create a predominantly mestizo population—termed "Latinos" in this chapter. Others falling under the rubric "Latino" in this chapter include descendants of mestizos who intermarried with persons of African origin. Ameliorating and eliminating inequities endured by Latinos and allowing Latinos to build their community identities and futures based on their cultural and linguistic assets are a root motivation for many, if not all, current Latino CHAT scholars (Sánchez Korrol, 1996).

While the roots of the U.S. Latino social justice movement emerged earlier, the movement became publicly prominent during the late 1960s and the early 1970s, with the emergence of ethnic studies programs in U.S. colleges and universities spurred by the activism of the first significant waves of U.S.-born Latinos and immigrant Latinos to attain admission to higher education in U.S. colleges (for a history see Lopez Pulido et al., 2009 and Rodriguez, 1996). A number of these Latino activist scholars entering higher education during this period went on to obtain advanced graduate degrees, ultimately becoming leading faculty members and professional researchers focused on ways that research might inform social transformation, and economic, political, and educational advancement. They were also prominent contributors to professional educator groups, such as the National Association of Bilingual Educators, and Latino civil rights groups such as the Mexican American Legal and Educational Defense Fund and PRLDEF, a sister organization serving the Puerto Rican Community. The fusion of the Latino ethnic studies movement coupled with the growth of Latino participation in professional organizations helped call public attention to the long-standing historical educational and social inequities faced by U.S. Latinos and to the importance of educational reform initiatives to improve educational and other outcomes for Latinos as a national priority.

The above assessment adds to a CHAT account of parent-school engagement programs the observation that the cultural historical context for the emergence and implementation of Latino family-school engagement programs is mediated by a deep concern for social justice among Latino community members stemming from the origins of Latinos in the Americas. This concern is a historical moral force and a set of beliefs that is alive in the consciousness of Latino community members, including social change activists and scholars.

## Contributions from Critical Pedagogy

Over the past 30 years, two leading scholar contributors to the Latino educational and social justice movement, in addition to some of the contributors to this volume, were Enrique (Henry) Trueba and Concha Delgado-Gaitán. They were among the earliest Latino scholar activists who called attention in the 1970s, and onward, to ways that the works of Vygotsky, Luria, Leontiev, and CHAT scholars could be united with Freirean critical pedagogy approaches (Freire, 1970; Freire, 1995). They discussed how this unification could be brought to bear on Latino education issues, and in particular, ways that this framing could assist Latino parents in advocating for their children's and family's education through action research projects (see Delgado-Gaitán & Trueba, 1991 and Trueba, 1999 for a discussion of the evolution of this direction). What follows below is a discussion of how a critical pedagogy perspective, such as that developed by Trueba and Delgado-Gaitán, informs an understanding of Latino parent programs that can be elaborated further and made useful for practical change by adopting a CHAT perspective. The ensuing discussion lays this foundation and goes on afterwards to review how ecological systems theory helps clarify further issues that can then also be informed by a CHAT perspective. The relevance of a CHAT perspective is then discussed explicitly following this context setting.

The Freirean critical pedagogy perspective is grounded in the notion of *conscientizacion*, the idea that underserved groups in society could develop the capacity to change the conditions of life around them by cultivating a critical awareness of the conditions of life, and how the power to alter these conditions was vested in and exercised by institutions and social groups controlling access to economic and other resources. The critical pedagogy perspective approach treats "literacy" as the key to conscientizacion and subsequently to action in the service of societal change. From a critical pedagogy perspective, "literacy" is a tool to "read," interrogate, and "re-write" the distribution of power. This power is rendered and controlled by institutions that make possible access to everyday resources for survival, well-being, and betterment of life for community members and social groups. In order for underserved groups to acquire critical awareness of societal conditions and strategies for change, groups must be able to "name" and characterize societal conditions as problems that need resolution, and how redistribution of power can serve this end. In so doing, group members must be able to communicate with one another via spoken and written language about social conditions and problems, and about strategies and actions to change social conditions and solve problems. Further, group members must be able to communicate these concerns to constituencies and institutions at large in surrounding communities in order to enact change through social and political processes, and other forms of action.

The notion of "action" from a critical pedagogy perspective is labeled "praxis." Praxis is much more than simple action undertaken to solve problems. It is reflective and reflexive in nature. Praxis is itself central to a Freirean notion of literacy—it entails that underserved groups continuously engage in a dialectic. This dialectic is reflective in that it requires group members to analyze whether the naming and characterization of problems, the strategies proposed to solve problems, and the outcomes of actions to solve problems are successful.

One further notion drawn from critical pedagogy that resonates with a CHAT perspective is that of "community cultural wealth" (Yosso, 2005). "Community cultural wealth" is another label for literacy from a critical pedagogy perspective. It refers to the broader cultural, linguistic, and social capital that is shared in common by underserved group members to read and write their worlds. Historically, this wealth is manifest in the belief systems, and knowledge of cultural practices and language resources that underlie the heritage of community members. This wealth is not just a heritage resource, and it is not just static knowledge. It also includes the living dynamic ways that group members adapt to their everyday circumstances. It is an evolving growing dynamic system that continuously creates new knowledge and practices, blending the old with the new and different, as group members navigate daily life and come into relationships with community institutions and different ways of life and practices occurring in communities. It is important to understand that community wealth itself represents power. It is the power to interpret the past, present, and future in the light of persons' identities, relationships with others, and ways of adapting to the contingencies of life.

A critical pedagogy perspective calls attention to the clash that unfolds when the community cultural wealth of underserved groups comes in contact with the incommensurate community cultural wealth of social groups and institutions that hold power. Nowhere is this confrontation more apparent than when Latino families encounter discrimination and lack of understanding of their own community wealth for furthering the educational and social progress of their children and families. Analysis of this clash is the focus of many intellectual contributions made by the Latino ethnic studies movement and social justice focus of Latino civil rights organizations. Fundamental to this analysis is that U.S. Latino communities must transform their relationships with other community members and surrounding institutions so as to accept the unique values, beliefs, cultural, and linguistic practices of Latinos as resources for overall community betterment, and not as "deficiencies" that represent barriers to educational and economic progress for Latinos and society at large (Rodriguez-Brown, 2009). Among other concerns, the "deficit" perspective arguing for improvement of the schooling outcomes of Latinos is founded on elimination of many Latino socialized cultural ways by new and contrasting cultural ways valued by dominant groups, in a community socialized to a great extent by European-origin cultural beliefs. These latter beliefs can be interpreted as "American" ways that have emerged historically as U.S. society and its economy have evolved nationally and globally. Primary examples of deficit model stereotypical beliefs include notions that

1.  the Spanish language is not to be valued and needs to be replaced by English;
2.  Latino parents do not care seriously about their children's educational outcomes;
3.  Parents fail to socialize their children to show motivation and discipline for schooling; and
4.  Parents fail to socialize children to be competitive as opposed to cooperative in attaining educational and other goals.

Research by investigators such as Delgado-Gaitán (1992), Zarate (2007), and Fernandez (2010) shows that these beliefs do not hold up empirically, and that parents do value bilingualism, concern for school involvement, and high educational aspirations for their children. Reese et al. (1995), in contrast, bring out how Latino parents' concern for *educación* of family members embodies a deeper notion of "education" socialized in their natal cultures that emphasizes a more holistic concept, showing concern for how betterment of family and community outcomes and well-being are the primary goals of a successful socialization of children and should support the formal educational schooling of children. Arguably, one of the most significant and important contributions of critical pedagogy is that it argues for "hope" and "democracy" from a humanist perspective (Freire, 1995). The very same *cariño por familia y pueblo* ("love of family and community" in English) that underlies *educación* is the same caring concern that extends from Latinos to the broader community and that flowers when Latinos are respected as community members and contributors toward societal well-being. When *educación* is allowed to flower, it becomes the basis for Latino families' civic engagement in a sustained manner tied to development of family members' identity and bonding to the larger community, coupled with increasing attainment of formal schooling, enabling enhanced community participation.

The importance of family members bonding and caring for each other and extended community members from the same or similar backgrounds is not just a brute idealization. These values and how they connect to family members' joint problem solving to meet survival and life-enhancement needs have been investigated empirically in ethnographic research studies by researchers such as Valdés (1996) and Orellana (2009), who studied these phenomena among recent Latino immigrants from perspectives resonating with a critical pedagogy orientation.

There are many parallels between concepts from critical pedagogy as described above in relation to Latino family issues and concern for education and parallel concepts developed in CHAT. For one, the concept of conscientizacion resonated very well with Vygotskyan notions of consciousness when treated as a mediational means to understand social being and sociocultural practices as ways toward societal ends, and human individual and collective development. The rich notion of literacy in critical pedagogy calls attention to the ways humans collectively learn how to interpret and construct their worlds for the purpose of interpreting experience, meeting goals, and building futures. This dynamic resonates very much with CHAT and Vygotskyan-based accounts of symbolic mediational systems and interwoven artifact systems that constitute the realization of culture, and the proleptic projection of possible futures as pathways facilitating individual and collective development. In addition, the critical pedagogy notion of "community wealth" very much resonates with CHAT theorists' notion of "funds of knowledge" and the extension of these into "zones of possibilities" for new learning and development akin to a broader notion of Vygotsky's notion of zone of proximal development (Moll & Greenberg, 1990). Parent participants in Latino family-school engagement programs are deeply immersed in thinking and planning their children's educational future. Qualitative studies of Latino parent-school engagement programs, e. g., the ones by Fernandez (2010) and by Rodriguez-Brown (2009), have carefully documented how Latino parents' self-consciousness raising about their children's current educational success and circumstances connects to possible educational and career aspirations for their children, the foregoing occurring under circumstances where a parent program is deliberately designed to activate these concerns (such as is the case of an implementation of a program based on the MALDEF Parent School Partnership Program, by Fernandez and the FLAME program by Rodriguez-Brown).

Like the movements to establish Latino ethnic studies programs and the Latino social justice movement, critical pedagogy perspectives on Latino families and Latino school engagement programs can greatly enrich a CHAT account regarding the functioning and evolution of Latino family-school engagement programs. The critical pedagogy perspective foregrounds the deep sense of social consciousness and drive to overcome inequality that motivates Latino parents to become engaged in such programs as an extension of their sense of *educación* and their commitment to community values.

## Contributions from Ecological Systems Theory

Ecological systems theory was developed by Bronfenbrenner (1979) as a means to understand and investigate human development and its connections to societal structures and dynamics surrounding, enabling, and constraining everyday activity and opportunities to develop. Bronfenbrenner and other proponents of ecological systems theory represent everyday contexts or *ecologies* in terms of a hierarchy of concentric levels of social organizational systems beginning with individuals and their ontogenetic experiences at the center and extending out into a range of increasingly distal social systems. Each system is composed of ecologies that correspond to institutions, societal structures, and their belief systems that can impact on everyday life through societal and political mechanisms. The description below, adapted and extended from an account by Weiss et al. (2010, p. xxvii), outlines the progression of ecologies in the form of concentric circles:

- *Child/person*: the individual and his/her ontogenetic experiences;
- *Microsystem*: e.g., nuclear family relations, immediate-peer relations, classroom experiences, community afterschool youth programs;
- *Mesosytem*: e.g., home, larger school context, neighborhood, residential community and institutions, peer groups;
- *Exosytems*: e.g., extended family, environments such as the workplace experienced by parents and other affiliated persons, broader community service agencies such as police, social service agencies, and school boards
- *Macrosystems*: e.g., attitudes and ideologies, cultural values, media communications, national and regional institutional agencies and resource providers, state and national policy entities.

The *Chronosystem* corresponds to yet another ecological system type. This system represents the idea that human development and its dependence on forces and influences arising from various ecological systems are a function of time and the life course of individuals and social groups.

An ecological systems approach is very helpful in understanding the design and implementation of family-school engagement programs (Weiss et al., 2010). This interpretation especially applies to Latino families because it highlights the importance of having parents and other family members develop capabilities to negotiate relationships, and accountabilities with a range of institutions and policy groups wielding power and resources affecting their children's education under circumstances where families have not been traditionally recognized for their rights in this regard because of their cultural and linguistic characteristics. Indeed, this may include climates of racism and discrimination against Latinos that have not been contested openly in communities.

Consistent with an activity theory orientation, every family-school engagement program can be characterized in terms of its participants, mission or objectives, and mediating actions intended to attain objectives. Ultimately, the specific objectives and actions of programs are intended to impact on children—e.g., improving children's access to learning opportunities in the classroom, though the means for impacting on children in this way may involve action by parents, teachers, and others in more distal ecologies, for instance, a school district providing teachers of children with staff development activities in learning new teaching techniques. This dynamic in turn could lead parents to speak at school board meetings and to civic community groups, or state legislators, for example, to raise support for such an initiative, thus exemplifying the extended nature of ecologies that family-school engagement programs might come to negotiate.

Accordingly, an ecological systems approach invites family-school engagement program designers, implementers, and evaluators/researchers of such programs to analyze explicitly the ecological social systems and their interrelationships that influence the schooling of children and how programs develop and exercise their capacity to reach goals. Importantly for Latino parents, the issue immediately arises about their acquisition of literacies in the critical pedagogy sense so as to understand the nature of social-political institutions affecting the well-being of families and school practices. Further consistent with a critical pedagogy perspective, parents need to acquire voice and agency in communicating with institutions in order to communicate their rights and expectations.

The important aspect to note about the contribution of an ecological systems perspective to an enhanced CHAT account of Latino family-school engagement programs is that it adds to CHAT the value of analyzing how Latino parents and family members must often navigate and interact with unfamiliar institutional systems that surround and influence educational practices and experiences faced by children and family members in concrete day-to-day experiences. Analyzing and investigating this empowerment process benefits from understanding the social justice perspective and struggle for rights and resources of Latino community members involved in implementing parent-school engagement programs. Attention is now turned to a brief description of three example program models that further illustrate how an enhanced CHAT perspective contributes to designing, implementing, and investigating programs.

## Three Program Models

Latino family-school engagement programs can take many forms. A basic characteristic is that they involve collective action and partnerships. They are not based on individual families and parents acting on their own in the interest of children's and family member's improved schooling; they involve groups of parents, family members, and others working through a formal organization with the universal goal of improving schooling for family members. Consider the following three examples of how such programs might be organized:

1. Local school and classroom projects aimed at having Latino parents learn specific practices tied to literacy and schooling;
2. Regional community and school-based programs of an ongoing nature aimed at increasing Latino parents' knowledge of school governance, policies, and parents' participation as school leaders influencing schooling practices; and,
3. Diffusion programs at regional, state, and national levels whose aim it is to create and disseminate new programs of type one and two.

An important characteristic of these three types of programs is that they can interact and commingle, stimulating emergence of creative new types of activity systems that can influence educational policy and practice across educational tiers, schooling, and policy institutions, thereby strategically positioning Latino communities as advocates for educational success.

What follows is a discussion of an example of each program type that has been implemented, with suggestions on how to understand possible interrelationships among programs. While the listing of programs above is ordered from the most micro-ecological system—projects tied to highly specific learning and practice goals in an activity setting, to the most macro-ecological system—a diffusion program operating over large geographical regions, the discussion of examples will alter this ordering slightly for purposes of highlighting possible forms of productive interaction among programs. The programs that are described are not fictitious. They are real programs that have been implemented.

# Parents, Children, and Computers Project:
# A Local School Project to Help Parents Do Internet Learning and Desktop Publishing

This project operated in school computer labs in the community of Goleta, California, for nearly 10 years before ending in 2009 due to lack of funding and loss of computer lab access and a meeting day and time that would attract sufficient numbers of parents (Durán et al., 2001). Project meetings were conducted in Spanish in an elementary school computer room. The participants were parents of children attending the school. University students and faculty coordinated the program and supported parents' acquisition of computer literacy skills and production of electronic publications.

While parents learned important computer and Internet literacy skills, this feature was not their sole focus, though there was statistical pre-post test evidence that they did improve dramatically in skill use and basic knowledge of computers and the Internet. Parents also pursued individualized projects, sometimes in collaboration with their children who also attended. These projects explored a diverse range of topics and "identity" work by parents such as their cultural and social values, and past and current family experiences expressed in a multimedia format combining written text with images and graphics (see Cummins, 2006 on multimedia "identity texts" and literacy empowerment). Parents, for example, wrote about their educational aspirations for their children and how these were connected to their reasons for immigrating to the United States in pursuit of a better life for their families. In one notable essay in this regard, a parent wrote at length about her tribulations in coping with the diagnosis that her nine-year-old son suffered from attention deficit disorder. The mother described her struggles in understanding English-language accounts of this diagnosis and its treatment given her limited English proficiency. She described how the situation faced by her son affected his identity at school and the prejudice he encountered from other students and school staff. She also described how her identity and her spouse's identity were affected, pointing out the desire that her family's experience become a learning opportunity for other immigrant Latino families encountering similar circumstances.

The contents of identity texts developed by parents and their children were not always about hardship and adversity. There was also a propensity to communicate an appreciation for cultural practices and values that were associated with adding meaning to life and the value of spirituality arising from cultural wisdom socialized as being Latino.

One poignant example followed a visit by the Chicana poet Norma Cantu, who presented to participants about how she authored her well-known autobiography *Canicula*, chronicling her significant experiences growing up in a south Texas community. She urged participants to think of the richness of their cultural background and how life's course was filled with important insights. Following this presentation, a father and adolescent daughter wrote pieces about their love of playing the guitar and singing traditional ballads and compositions they had written for children, expressing important social values and lessons of life. It was an awesome experience to have this father and daughter extend this love of music into the very conduct of parent computer literacy meetings, as they occasionally serenaded meeting participants or played in the background as participants worked on their desktop publications or practiced computer literacy skills.

From a CHAT perspective, the activity system represented by the Parents, Children, and Computers project is complex and nuanced. While participants' acquisition of particular computer literacy skills constitute forms of microgenetic development, the outcomes were deeper and broader, in ways that fit well with a critical pedagogy perspective and an ecological perspective that view outcomes as about creating voice and consciousness on a sociocultural plane derived from historical influences. The *ambiente* (cultural, affiliative climate) created by the participants expressed their worldviews in ways that cannot be understood well in the abstract and need to be understood for their force and power from the emic perspectives of the participants and analysts of data and accounts who can understand and interpret the sociocultural consciousness they express. This sense, whether labeled as *community wealth* or *funds of knowledge,* is not just a static entity; it is a source of power and motivation for Latino community members.

## The MALDEF Parent School Partnership (PSP) Program: A National Diffusion Program

The next program type discussed jumps up from a local school-based family-school engagement project with limited ends to a program diffusion activity system that is meant to start ongoing family-school engagement programs of broader scope and community impact than the former type of limited aims project. The reason for this skip in implementation levels is to highlight how the third program type to be discussed afterwards can emerge from a diffusion program, thereby contributing to an appreciation of how program types might interconnect into a broader notion of family-school engagement activity systems.

The Mexican American Legal and Education Defense PSP program (MALDEF, 2010a) is a trainer of a program implementers activity system operating at national and regional state levels. The PSP program primarily serves Latino community members and is most usually offered in Spanish, though materials and sessions can also be in English. The PSP program trains a cadre of local community program implementers in delivery of a 16-unit curriculum to parents with the goal of having them initiate a parents' school engagement organization. The PSP curriculum focuses on six core topics:

1. Parent Rights and Responsibilities;
2. Structure and Functions of Schools and School Districts;
3. Pathways to a University Education;
4. The Politics of Education;
5. Responsible Leadership Roles of Parents;
6. Access to and Use of Media to Promote Program Ends.

The curriculum is updated regularly as national and state education policies shift. Program implementers also are trained in helping parents identify priority problem areas in the schooling of children that can be attacked by specific action projects—the program also highlights ways that guest speakers who are school, higher education, community, and political leaders can be brought in to advise parents on their program agenda and projects.

The MALDEF PSP activity system has the benefit that it can accumulate and share resources and strategies gathered from around the United States and through systematic development of connections and relations with complex institutional entities such as state and national political and professional and civil rights organizations and foundations. Thus, in relation to parents and children at the local community level, the PSP operates at a *macrosystem* ecological level. The history of MALDEF as an organization, and its introduction and pursuit of the PSP, is very much aligned with the account of this chapter tracing how the emergence of the Latino social justice movement and allied scholarship in Latino studies and critical pedagogy contributes to CHAT accounts of family-school engagement programs serving Latinos (MALDEF, 2010b). For MALDEF the historical quest for Latino social justice is realized very directly in the consciousness it activates and stimulates in the implementers of programs. Further, in the narrative of this chapter, it also finds a home in the parents and family members who subsequently come to form and lead parent organizations. This claim is supported by the third program example discussed below.

## Padres Adelante: A Family-School Engagement Program in the Santa Barbara Community Founded by an Implementation of the MALDEF PSP

The Padres Adelante Program was implemented at César Estrada Chávez Dual Language Immersion beginning in 2005—a grade 1–6 charter school, established in 2001, and the only school offering bilingual education in the Santa Barbara region. The school was established as a charter school following abolition of bilingual education as a regular program offering by the school district, just prior to California's passage of Proposition 227 in 1998 that ended bilingual education in schools unless adopted by districts through a special parent petition process. From its beginning in 2001, the school developed as a base for Latino community members advocating for the language and cultural rights of their community, though it was not until 2005 that the Padres Adelante organization was founded.

Padres Adelante was initiated following a series of MALDEF PSP workshops in the community sponsored by what is now known as the UC Santa Barbara Office of Academic Preparation, a unit charged with outreach programs aimed at increasing access of students from underrepresented backgrounds to a college education. In the initial year of the program, the program coordinator was a staff member of the UCSB Office of Academic Preparation. Following an initial year of introducing the PSP program to Padres Adelante parents, parents elected their own officers and assumed full leadership of the organization with UCSB staff and students as assistants, including the role of participant observers from a research perspective (Fernandez, 2010). The organization convened at César Chávez School once every two to three weeks during the academic school year. The school principal was a frequent participant in meetings, especially during the initial two years. The program was both an autonomous self-governed group, while at the same time serving as the school district mandated English Language Advisory Committee for the school.

The agenda and proceedings of Padres Adelante connect very closely to the themes highlighted in this chapter (see Fernandez, 2010). From the beginning, parents showed deep concern for the *educación* of their children and families, education through formal schooling being one facet contributing to this more holistic sense of "becoming" a responsible community member. Parents also began to have organized contact with the local school board, attending its meetings and presenting at meetings. They also took the opportunity to develop a relationship with a local Latino county supervisor who, in one meeting, conducted a live phone conversation with the city mayor regarding parents' request that stop signs be placed in a busy intersection outside the school.

Parents expended considerable attention in meetings grappling with schooling issues surrounding the low test scores of children, the need for homework and supplemental education support for children, and the need to understand better what it meant to prepare children for completion of high school and pursuit of higher education. They also heard from speakers about the unique problems encountered by students who were undocumented as they proceeded through school and out into the workforce—though the program itself was careful not to create any records of the undocumented status of participating families.

In the 2009–2010 academic year, César Chávez School encountered a crisis. The district superintendent and school board withdrew their consent for a renewal of the school's charter status with the state department of education. This withdrawal of consent for a renewal was based on state test score data from the school that showed that the school performed at the very lowest level on the state index for academic performance and that the school had failed to show adequate growth in test scores in preceding years. A strong protest movement ensued involving not only parents at the school, but also local community members who viewed the school as an important resource for Latinos and the community at large, given the high proportion of Latino immigrants in the community and the high proportion of Latino students in the elementary schools (over 65%). In the end, following extended meetings, protests, involvement of dual immersion school proponents, and researchers, the school board approved a new dual immersion school charter proposal to the state that accommodated the concerns of the district for improving the quality of instruction, while at the same time maintaining bilingual education as the mode for instruction under a dual immersion model. This proposal was approved by the state; thus in 2010, Adelante Charter School was founded to replace the former school.

To be clear, the Padres Adelante family school program was not the only group advocating for establishment of the new charter school. At the same time, it is clear that the Padres Adelante program, its parents, and their children, represented a central vital force underlying establishment and pursuit of the school. Ending this chapter with this example also highlights the importance of extending CHAT approaches to the development and understanding of family-school engagement programs so that they encompass better the interplay of the complexities of historical dynamics and inter-ecological systems that underlie the development and evolution of programs, drawing on the cultural belief systems of families and the widespread concerns of Latino community members for social justice. Further, the narrative needs to be heard: Vygotskyan approaches to human and organizational development are of relevance to researchers and program implementers serving Latino community members beyond the abstract contribution to knowledge that is made by this perspective.

# References

Abuljanova, K. A. (1973). Subject psychicheskoi deyatelnosti [The subject of psychological activity]. Moscow: Nauka.

Abuljanova, K. A. (1980). Deyatelnost i psykjologiya lichnosti (Activity and Psychology of personality). Moscow: Nauka.

Abuljanova, K. A., & Bruchlinsky, A. V. (1989). Fiosofsko-psykjologicheskaya konsepsiya S. L. Rubinscheteina [Philosophical—psychological conception of S. L. Rubinstein] Moscow: Nauka.

Acanda, J. (2007). *Traducir a Gramsci*. La Habana, Cuba: Editorial de Ciencias Sociales.

Adler, A. (1927). *The practice and theory of individual psychology*, New York: Harcourt Brace.

Adler, A. (1982). *The pattern of life*. Chicago, IL: Alfred Adler Institute of Chicago. (Original work published 1930)

Adorno, T. (2006). *History and freedom*. London, UK: Polity Press. (Original work published 1964)

Akopov, G. V. (2009). The problem of consciousness in Russian psychology. *Journal of Russian and European Psychology, 47*(5), 3–25.

Alexander, L., & Tredoux, C. (2010). The spaces between us: A spatial analysis of informal segregation at a South African university. *Journal of Social Issues, 66*(2), 367–386.

Anojin, P. K. (1963). *La inhibición interna como problema de la fisiologia*. Buenos Aires, Argentina: Ediciones Nuestro Tiempo.

Ansbacher, H. L., & Ansbacher, R. (1964). *The individual psychology of Alfred Adler*. New York, NY: Harper & Row.

Anzaldúa, G. E. (1987). *Borderlands/La frontera: The new mestiza*. San Francisco, CA: Spinsters/Aunt Lute.

Anzaldúa, G. E. (1996). *Prietita and the ghost woman/Prietita y la llorana*. San Francisco, CA: Children's Book Press.

Argyris, C. (1977). Double loop learning in organizations. *Harvard Business Review, 55*(5), 115–125.

Argyris, C., & Schon, D. A. (1996). *Organizational learning II: Theory, method, and practice.* New Cork, NY: Addison-Wesley Publishing Co.

Arias, G. (1979). La Educación Especial en la República de Cuba. *Jornada Internacional de Estimulación Precoz.* España. (Material inédito).

Arias, G. (1986a). *La educación Especial en Cuba. Su desarrollo y perspectivas.* Conferencia Especiale. Congreso de PEDAGOGIA'86, Cuba. Materiales del Congreso.

Arias, G. (1986b, April to June). Algunas tendencias actuales sobre la educación especial. *Revista Educación,* pp. 75–81.

Arias, G. (1999a). Acerca del valor teórico y metodológico de la obra de L. S. Vygotski. *Revista Cubana de Psicología, 16*(3).

Arias, G. (1999b). *La orientación psicológica. Un intento de elaboración teórica.* En: Colectivo de autores: *La creación y evaluación de servicios de Orientación y Atención Psicológica.* Centro de Orientación y Atención Psicológica a la Población "Alfonso Bernal del Riesgo." Ciudad de La Habana, Cuba: Facultad de Psicología, Universidad de La Habana.

Arias, G. (2001). *Evaluación y Diagnóstico en la Educación y el Desarrollo.* Sao Paulo, Brazil: Editor Independiente.

Arias, G. (2002a). *Por una mejor vida y aplicación del enfoque histórico cultural.* CD Convención HOMINIS´02. Palacio de las Convenciones, Ciudad de la Habana, Cuba.

Arias, G. (2002b). *El proceso de construcción del Enfoque Histórico Cultural en sus Inicios.* CD Convención HOMINIS´02. Palacio de las Convenciones, Ciudad de la Habana, Cuba.

Arias, G. (2002c). *Las unidades funcionales en la psicología. Una tarea inconclusa y no continuada.* CD Convención HOMINIS´02. Palacio de las Convenciones, Ciudad de la Habana, Cuba.

Arias, G. (2004). *Los aportes de L. S. Vygotski a la Psicología de todos los tiempos.* Ponencia en la Conferencia Internacional L. S. Vygotski. Instituto Vygotski, Moscú, Rusia.

Arias, G. (2005a). *Un intento de sistematización teórica acerca de la relación de ayuda psicológica.* Ponencia presentada en la III Convención Intercontinental de Psicología y Ciencias Humanas, HOMINIS´05 "Crecimiento Humano y Diversidad" CD.

Arias, G. (2005b). *La persona en el enfoque histórico cultural.* Sao Paulo, Brasil: Editorial Linear B.

Arias, G., & Llorens, V. (1982). *La educación especial.* Ciudad de La Habana, Cuba: Editorial Pueblo y Educación.

Ash, D. (2008). Thematic continuities: Talking and thinking about adaptation in a socially complex classroom. *Journal of Research in Science Technology, 45*(1), 1–30.

Ashley, M. (2004). Evaluation of traumatic brain injury following rehabilitation. In M. Ashley (Ed.), *Traumatic brain injury* (pp. 613–640). Boca Raton, FL: CRC.

Asmolov, A. G. (1984). *Lichnost kak predmet psikjologicheskoi isledovanii* (Personality as subject of psychological research). Moscow: Moscow University Publishers.

Atkinson, J. M., & Heritage, J. (1984). Structures of social action: Studies in conversational analysis. New York, NY: Cambridge University Press.

Attewell, P., Lavin, D., Domina, T., & Levey, T. (2006). New evidence on college remediation. *Journal of Higher Education, 77*(5), 887–924.

August-Rothman, P., & Zinn, B. (1986). *Application of instrumental enrichment principles to a mathematics course for young Ethiopian adults.* Jerusalem, Israel: Hebrew University.

Avinor, E. (1995). Academic difficulties and early literacy deprivation: The case of Ethiopians in Israel. *Language, Culture and Curriculum, 8,* 201–210.

Bacon, F. (1961). *Novum organum.* Buenos Aires, Argentina: Editorial Losada S. A.

Bakhtin, M. M. (1981). *The dialogic imagination: Four essays by M. M. Bakhtin.* M. Holquist (Ed.), (C. Emerson & M. Holquist, Trans.). Austin, TX: University of Texas Press. (Original work published in the 1930s)

Bakhtin, M. M. (1984). *Problems of Dostoyevsky's poetics.* C. Emerson (Ed. and Trans). Minneapolis, MN: University of Minnesota Press.

Bakhtin, M. M. (1986). *Speech genres and other late essays* (V. W. McGee, Trans.) C. Emerson & M. Holquist (Eds.),). Austin, TX: University of Texas Press.

Bandura, A. (1991). Social cognitive theory of self-regulation. *Organizational Behavior and Human Performance, 50,* 248–287.

Baquedano-López, P. (1997). Creating social identities through *doctrina* narratives. *Issues in Applied Linguistics, 8*(1), 27–45.

Baquedano-López, P., Solís, J., & Kattan, S. (2005). Adaptation: The language of classroom learning. *Linguistics and Education, 6,* 1–26.

Bargh, J. A., & Ferguson, M. J. (2000). Beyond behaviorism: On the automaticity of higher mental processes. *Psychological Bulletin, 126*(6), 925–945.

Bauman, G. L. (2002). *Developing a culture of evidence: Using institutional data to identify inequitable educational outcomes* (Doctoral dissertation, University of Southern California, Los Angeles).

Bauman, G. L., & Bensimon, E. M. (2002). *The promotion of organizational learning through the use of routine data.* Paper presented at the Association for the Study of Higher Education conference, November, Sacramento, CA.

Bazerman, C., & Russell, D. R. (Eds.). (2003). *Writing selves/writing societies: Research for activity perspective.* Fort Collins, CO: The WAC Clearing House Perspective on Writing.

Bensimon, E. M. (2004, January/February). The diversity scorecard: A learning approach to institutional change. *Change,* 45–52.

Bensimon, E. M. (2005). Closing the achievement gap in higher education: An organizational learning perspective. In A. Kezar (Ed.), *Higher education as a learning organization: Promising concepts and approaches: Vol. 131.* San Francisco, CA: Jossey-Bass.

Bensimon, E. M. (2007). The underestimated significance of practitioner knowledge in the scholarship of student success. *The Review of Higher Education, 30*(4), 441–469.

Bensimon, E. M., Polkinghorne, D. E., Bauman, G. L., & Vallejo, E. (2004). Doing research that makes a difference. *Journal of Higher Education, 75*(1), 104–126.

Bensimon, E., Rueda, R., Dowd, A. C., & Harris, F. (2007). Accountability, equity, and practitioner learning and change. *Metropolitan Universities, 18*(3), 28–45.

Berhanu, G. (2001). *Learning-in-context: An ethnographic investigation of mediated learning experience among Ethiopian Jews in Israel.* Goteborg, Sweden: Goteborg University Press.

Bernal-Enríquez, Y., & Hernández Chávez, E. (2003). La enseñanza del Español en Nuevo México: ¿Revitalización o erradicación de la variedad Chicana?. In A. Roca & M. Colombi (Eds.), *Mi lengua: Spanish as a heritage language in the United States* (pp. 96–122). Washington, DC: Georgetown University Press.

Betancourt, J. (2002). *Papel de las Vivencias en los escolares con trastornos del comportamiento y emocionales* (Tesis de Doctorado. Instituto Central de Ciencias Pedagógicas, MINED, Ciudad de la Habana).

Black, R. W. (2009). English-language learners, fan communities, and 21st century skills. *Journal of Adolescent & Adult Literacy, 52*, 688–697.

Blackman, L. (2008). Affect, relationality and the problem of personality. *Theory, Culture, and Society, 25*(1), 1–22.

Blanck, G. (2001). *Prólogo a psicología pedagógica. Un curso breve.* Aique grupo. Buenos Aires, Argentina: Editor S. A.

Bloome, D., Beierle, M., Grigorenko, M., & Goldman, S. (2009). Learning over time: Uses of intercontextuality, collective memories, and classroom chronotopes in the construction of learning opportunities in a 9th grade language arts classroom. *Language and Education, 23*(4), 313–334.

Blunden, A. (2009). Soviet cultural psychology. In *Archives of Soviet Psychology.* Retrieved from http//www.marxistarchive.com.

Bozhovich, L. I. (1976). *La personalidad y su formación en la edad Infantil.* La Habana, Cuba: Editorial Pueblo y Educación.

Bozhovich, L. I. (1978). K razvitiyu affektivno-potrebnosti sfery cheloveka. (On development of the affective based on needs sphere). In V. V. Davydov (Ed.), *Problemy obschei, vozrastnoi and pedagogicheskoi psykjologii* [Problems of general, aged and pedagogical psychology] (pp. 168–179). Moscow: Pedagogika.

Brancato, V. C. (2003). Professional development in higher education. *New Directions for Adult and Continuing Education, 98*, 59–66.

Bransford, J. D. (1979). *Human cognition: Learning, understanding, and remembering.* Belmont, CA: Wadsworth.

Bray, J. N., Lee, J., Smith, L. L., & Yorks, L. (2000). *Collaborative inquiry in practice: Action, reflection, and making meaning.* Thousand Oaks, CA: Sage.

Bronfenbrenner, U. (1979). *The ecology of human development: Experiments by nature and design.* Cambridge, MA: Harvard University Press.

Bronfenbrenner, U. (1986). Ecology of the family as a context for human development: Research perspectives. *Developmental Psychology. 22*(6), 723–742.

*Brookdale memo on integration of Ethiopian immigrants in education and workforce.* (2004). [In Hebrew] Jerusalem: Brookdale Institute.

Brown, J. S., Collins, A., & Dugid, P. (1989). Situated cognition and the culture of learning. *Educational Researcher, 18*(1), 32–42.

Bruner, J. S. (1990). *Acts of meaning.* Cambridge, MA: Harvard University Press.

Bruner, J. S. (1995). Reflecting on Russian consciousness. In L. Martin, K. Nelson, & E. Tobach (Eds.), *Sociocultural psychology: Theory and practice of doing and knowing.* New York, NY: Cambridge University Press.

Bruschlinsky, A. V. (1977). K predistorii problemy "Soznanie i Deyatelnosti." [About the pre-history of the problem of "Consciousness and Activity"], (pp. 7–12). V Tesisi i dokladov on v Ciezdy Ochestva Psykjologov Sovestkoi Soyuza. In *Problema deyatelnosti v sovietskoi psykjologii.* [The problem of activity in Soviet psychology. Thesis and materials of the 5th Congress of the Society of Psychologists of the Soviet Union], Moscow.

Bruschlinsky, A. V. (1996). Suject: mischlenie, ushenie, voobrachenie [Subject: Thinking, learning and imagination]. M.-Boronochets. Institut Prakticheskoi Psykjologii. ( Institute of practical psychology). Voronesh.

Bruschlinsky, A. V. (2002). Psykjologiya subjekta i teoriya razvivayochee obrazobanie: Dialog c V. V. Davydovym. [Psychology of the subject and education in development: Dialog with V. V. Davydov] (pp. 128–135). Institut Psykjologii Ruskoi Akademii Pedagogicheskoi nauk (Institute of psycholgy of the Russian Academy of Pedagogical Sciences). Moscow: APK I PRO.

Budilova, E. A. (1983). Sotcialtno- psikjologicheskie problemy v ruskoi nayke [Socio-psychological problems in Russian science]. Moscow: Nauka.

Bustillos, L.T. (2007). *Exploring faculty beliefs about remedial mathematics students: A collaborative inquiry approach.* (Doctoral Dissertation). Retrieved from Proquest Dissertations and Theses. 3261848.

Caballero, A. (1999). *Obras. biblioteca de clásicos cubanos.* La Habana, Cuba: Editorial Imagen Contemporánea..

Cahan, E. D., & White, S. H. (1992). Proposals for a second psychology. *American Psychologist, 47*(2), 224–235.

California Postsecondary Education Commission. (2008). *Ethnicity snapshots.* Retrieved from http://www.cpec.ca.gov/StudentData/EthSnapshotMenu.asp

California State University. (2010). *California State University Fall 2009 regularly admitted first-time freshmen remediation campus and systemwide.* Retrieved from http://www.asd.calstate.edu/remediation/09/index.shtml

Callahan, R. (2005). Tracking and high school English learners: Limiting opportunities to learn. *American Educational Research Journal, 42*(2), 305–328.

Cammarota, J. (2007). A social justice approach to achievement: Guiding Latina/o students toward educational attainment with a challenging, socially relevant curriculum. *Equity & Excellence in Education, 40*(1), 87–96.

Cammarota, J. (2008). The cultural organizing of youth ethnographers: Formalizing a praxis-based pedagogy. *Anthropology & Education Quarterly, 39*(1), 45–58.

Cannella, C. (2009). *Opening windows, opening doors: Marginalized students engaging in praxis to become sociohistorical analysts and actors* (Doctoral dissertation, University of Arizona, Tucson).

Carnevale, A. P., & Fry, R. A. (2000). *Crossing the great divide: Can we achieve equity when generation Y goes to college?* Princeton, NJ: Educational Testing Service. (ERIC Document Reproduction Service No. ED 443907).

Carta, J. Renauer, M. Schiefelbusch, J., & Terry, B. (1998). *Effective instructional strategies to facilitate: Classroom transitions, group instruction, independent performance and self-assessment.* Kansas City, KS: Project Slide.

Chabrán, R. (2007). Francisco Hernández. In W. F. Bynum & H. Bynum (Eds.), *Dictionary of Medical Biography* (Vol. 3: pp. 632–637). Westport, CT: Greenwood Press.

Chaiklin, S., (2003). The zone of proximal development in Vygotsky's analysis of learning and instruction. In, A. Kozulin, B. Gindis, V. S. Ageyev, & S. M. Miller (Eds.), *Vygotsky's educational theory in cultural context*. Cambridge, UK: Cambridge University Press.

Chaiklin, S., & Lave, J. (Eds.). (1993). *Understanding practice: Perspectives on activity and context.* Cambridge: Cambridge University Press.

Champion, R. (2002) Taking Measure: Choose the right data for the job. *Journal of Staff Development, 23*(3).

Chandler-Olcott, K., & Mahar, D. (2003). Tech-savviness meets multiliteracies: Exploring adolescent girls' technology-mediated literacy practices. *Reading Research Quarterly, 38*, 356–385.

Cheyne, J. A., & Tarulli, D. (1999). Dialogue, difference, and the "third voice" in the zone of proximal development. *Theory and Psychology, 9*, 5–28.

Chomsky, N. (1959). A review of Skinner's verbal behavior. *Language, 35*(1), 26–58.

Chrispeels, J. H., & Rivero, E. (2001). Engaging Latino families for student success: How parent education can reshape parents' sense of place in the education of their children. *Peabody Journal of Education. 76*, 119–169.

Christensen, A. L. (1975). *Luria's neuropsychological investigation.* New York, NY: Spectrum.

Chudnovsky, V. E. (1988). Problema subjektivnosti v svete sovremennyx zadach psikjologii vospitaniya [The problem of subjectivity in the light of the current tasks of educational psychology]. *Voprocy psikjologii* [Questions of psychology], *4*, 15–24.

Chudnovsky, V. E. (2009). L. I. Bozhovich as a person, a personality, and a scholar. *Journal of Russian and Eastern European Psychology, 47*(4), 3–27.

Clark, R. E., & Estes, F. (2002). *Turning research into results: A guide to selecting the right performance solutions.* Atlanta, GA: CEP Press.

Cohen, A. M., & Brawer, F. B. (2003). *The American community college.* San Francisco, CA: Jossey-Bass.

Cohen, J. (1988). *Statistical power analysis for the behavioral sciences* (2nd ed.). Hillsdale, NJ: Lawrence Erlbaum.

Cole, M. (1978). *The selected writings of A. R. Luria.* White Plains, NY: M. E. Sharpe.

Cole, M. (1990). Cognitive development and formal schooling. In L. Moll (Ed.), *Vygotsky and education* (pp. 89–110). New York, NY: Cambridge University Press.

Cole, M. (1996). *Cultural psychology: A once and future discipline.* Cambridge, MA: Belknap Press of Harvard University Press.

Cole, M. (1999). Culture-free versus culture-based measures of cognition. In R. J. Sternberg (Ed.), *The nature of cognition* (pp. 645–664). Cambridge, MA: The MIT Press.

Cole, M., & Engeström, Y. (1993). A cultural–historical approach to distributed cognition. In G. Salomon (Ed.), *Distributed cognitions: psychological and educational considerations* (pp. 1–46). New York, NY: Cambridge University Press.

Cole, M., & Griffin, P. (1983). A socio-historical approach to re-mediation. *Quarterly Newsletter of the Laboratory of Comparative Human Cognition, 5*(4), 69–74.

Cole, M., & Scribner, S. (1974). *Culture and thought*. New York, NY: Wiley.

Cole, M., & The Distributed Literacy Consortium. (2006). *The Fifth Dimension: An after-school program built on diversity*. New York, NY: Russell Sage Foundation.

Collins, A., Joseph, D., & Bielaczyc, K. (2004). Design research: Theoretical and methodological issues. *The Journal of the Learning Sciences, 13*(1), 15–42.

Cook-Gumperz, J., Corsaro W., & Streeck J. (Eds.). (1986) *Children's worlds and children's language*. Berlin, Germany: Mouton de Gruyter.

Cooper, C., Chavira, G., & Mina, D. (2005). From pipelines to partnerships: A synthesis of research on how diverse families, schools, and communities support children's pathways through school. *Journal of Education for Students Placed at Risk. 10*(4), 407–430.

Corral Ruso, R. (1999). Las lecturas de la Zona de Desarrollo Próximo. *Revista Cubana de Psicología, 16* (3).

Costa, A. (1999). *Developing minds: A resource book for teaching thinking*. Alexandria, VA: Association for Supervision and Curriculum Development.

Cranton, P., & King, K. P. (2003). Transformative learning as a professional development goal. *New Directions for Adult and Continuing Education, 98*, 31–37.

Cummins, J. (2006). Identity texts: The imaginative construction of self through multiliteracies pedagogy. In O. Garcia, T. Skutnabb-Kangas, & M. Torres-Guzman (Eds.). *Imagining multilingual schools: Language in education and globalization* (pp. 51–68). Clevendon, UK: Multilingual Matters.

Daniels, H. (2002). *Uma introdução a Vygotski*. São Paulo, Brasil: Edições Loyola.

Davidson, J. (1982). Wasted time: The ignored dilemma. In Brown, J. F. (Ed.) *Curriculum planning for young children* (pp. 196–204). Washington, DC: NAEYC.

Davydov, V. V. (1988). Problems of developmental teaching. Parts 1–3. *Soviet Education, 30*, 8–10.

Davydov, V. V. (1999). A new approach to the interpretation of activity: structure and content. In S. Chaiklin, M. Hedegaard & J. Jensen (Eds.), *Activity Theory and Social Practice*. Aarhus: Aarhus University Press.

Davydov, V. V. (2002). Novii padjod k ponimaniyu struktury i soderchaniya deyatelnosti [New approach to comprehension of structure and content of activity]. In *Razvivayochee obrazobanie: Dialog with V. V. Davydov*]) (pp 24–34). Moscow: AKP & PRO.

Davydov, V. V., & Radzikhovskii, L. (1980). Teoriya L. S. Vygotsky i deyatelnostnii padxod v psykhologii [L. S. Vygotsky's theory and based activity approach in psychology]. *Voprocy Psykjologii* [Questions of Psychology], 6, 48–59.

Del Río, P., & Álvarez, A. (2007). Inside and outside the zone of proximal development: An eco-functional reading of Vygotsky. In H. Daniels, M. Cole & J. V. Wertsch (Eds.), *The Cambridge companion to Vygotsky*. New York, NY: Cambridge University Press.

Delgado-Gaitan, C., & Trueba, H. (1991). *Crossing cultural borders: Education for immigrant families in America*. London: Falmer.

Delgado-Gaitán, C. (1992). School matters in the Mexican-American home: Socializing children to education. *American Educational Research Journal, 29*(3), 495–513.

Delgado-Gaitán, C. (1993). Researching change and changing the researcher. *Harvard Educational Review, 63*(1), 389–411.

Dergan, J. (1987). La batería neuropsicológica Luria-Nebrazca. *Avanzes de Psicología Clínica Latinoamericana.* Bogota, Colombia, 5, 27–36.

Dergan, J. (1997). *Protocol for pain management.* Unpublished manuscript.

Dergan, J. (2007a). El rol de la neuropsicología en pacientes con lesiones cerebrá les.*Revista Peruana de Psicología. 1,* 5–12.

Dergan, J. (2007b). *Neuropsicología de la esquizofrenia.* Bogota, Colombia: ECOE.

Dewey, J. (1925/1929). *Experience and nature.* New York, NY: Open Court Publishing.

Dewey, J. (1938/1963). *Experience and education.* New York, NY: Macmillan.

Dixon, J., Tredoux, C., & Clack, B. (2005). On the micro-ecology of racial division: A neglected dimension of segregation. *South African Journal of Psychology, 35,* 395–411.

Donaldson, M. (1978). *Children's minds.* London, UK: Fontana/Croom Helm.

Dowd, A. C. (2005). *Data don't drive: Building a practitioner-driven culture of inquiry to assess community college performance* (Research Report). Indianapolis, IN: Lumina Foundation for Education.

Dowd, A. C., & Tong, V. P. (2007). Accountability, assessment, and the scholarship of "best practice." In J. C. Smart (Ed.), *Handbook of higher education: Vol. 22* (pp. 57–119). New York, NY: Springer.

Dreier, O. (1997). *Subject and social practice.* Center of Health, Humanity, and Culture, Department of Philosophy, University of Aarhus, Denmark.

Duff, P. A. (1995). An ethnography of communication in immersion classrooms in Hungary. *TESOL Quarterly, 29*(3), 505–537.

Durán, R. P., Durán, J., Perry-Romero, D., & Sanchez, E. (2001). Latino immigrant parents and children learning and publishing together in an after-school setting. *Journal of Education for Students Placed At-Risk, 6*(1&2), 95–113.

Durkheim, E. (2005). The dualism of human nature and its social conditions. *Durkheimian Studies, 11,* 35–45. (Original work published 1914)

Dyson, A. H. (1990). Weaving possibilities: Rethinking metaphors for early literacy development. *The Reading Teacher, 44*(3), 202–213.

Dyson, A. H. (2001). Where are the childhoods in childhood literacy? An exploration in outer (school) space. *Journal of Early Childhood Literacy, 1*(1), 9–39.

Echemendía Tocabens, B. (2006). *Los niveles de ayuda en la relación psicoterapéutica. Un análisis desde el enfoque histórico cultural.* Cadernos ECOS: *Educação, Cultura e Desenvolvimento Humano,* Vol. 1 (pp. 145–154). São Paulo, Brazil: Editorial Terceira Margem.

Elliott, A. (1992). *Social theory and psychoanalysis in transition.* Oxford, UK: Blackwell.

Engeström, Y. (1987). *Learning by expanding.* Helsinki, Finland: Orinta-Konsultit Oy.

Engeström, Y. (1991). Activity theory and individual and social transformation. In Y. Engeström, R. Miettinen, & R. Punamaki (Eds.), *Perspectives on activity theory* (pp. 19–38). New York, NY: Cambridge University Press.

Engeström, Y. (1999). Activity theory and individual and social transformation. In Y. Engstrom, R. Miettinen, & R. Punamäki (Eds.), *Perspectives on activity theory.* New York, NY: Cambridge University Press.

Engeström, Y. (2001). Expansive learning at work: Toward an activity theoretical reconceptualization. *Journal of Education and Work, 14*(1), 133–156.

Engeström, Y. (2006). Development, movement and agency: Breaking away into mycorrhizae activities. In K. Yamazumi (Ed.), *Building activity theory in practice: Toward the next generation.* (CHAT Technical Reports #1). Osaka, Japan: Center for Human Activity Theory, Kansai University.

Engeström, Y., & Cole, M. (1997). Situated cognition in search of an agenda. In D. Kirshner & J. Whitson (Eds.), *Situated cognition: Social, semiotic, and psychological perspective* (pp. 301–309). Mahwah, NJ: Lawrence Erlbaum.

Engeström, Y., Miettinen, R., & Punamäki, R. (1999). *Perspectives on activity theory.* New York, NY: Cambridge University Press.

Epstein, J. L. (1987). Toward a theory of family-school connections: Teacher practices & parent involvement. In K. Hurrelmann, F. Kaufmann, & F. Losel (Eds.), *Social intervention: Potential and constraints* (pp. 91–121). New York, NY: DeGruyter.

Epstein, J. L. (1995). School/family/community partnerships: Caring for the children we share. *Phi Delta Kappan, 76* (9), p. 705-707.

Erasmus, Z. (2010). Contact theory: Too timid for "race" and racism. *Journal of Social Issues, 66,* 387–400.

Erikson, E. H. (1968). *Identity, youth, & crisis.* New York, NY: Norton.

Espenshade. T., & Radford, A. (2009). *No longer separate, not yet equal: Race and class in elite college admission and campus life.* Princeton, NJ: Princeton University Press.

Eysenck, H. J. (1973). *Eysenck on extroversion.* London, UK: Crosby Lockwood Staples.

Fader, A. (2009). *Mitzvah girls: Bringing up the new generation of Hasidic Jews in Brooklyn.* Princeton, NJ: Princeton University Press.

Fariñas, G. (1999). Acerca del concepto de vivencia en el Enfoque histórico cultural. *Revista Cubana de Psicología, 16*(3), 222.

Fariñas, G. (2005). *Psicología, educación y sociedad (un estudio sobre el desarrollo humano).* La Habana, Cuba: Editorial Félix Varela.

Fariñas G., & Arias, G. (2002). *L. S. Vygotski, por una psicología general: A favor y en contra. Problemas teóricos y metodológicos.* CD de la Convención HOMINIS´02. Palacio de las Convenciones, Ciudad de la Habana, Cuba.

Febles, M. (2001). La concepción histórico del desarrollo: Principios y leyes. In *Psicología del desarrollo.* La Habana, Cuba: Editorial Félix Varela.

Ferguson, C. (2008). *The school-family connection: Looking at the larger picture. A review of current literature.* Austin, TX: SEDL National Center for Family and Community Connections with Schools.

Fernandez, G. (2010). *Abriendo caminos para la educación:* A case study of a parent outreach initiative building on the knowledge, skills, and resources of the Latina/o community (Doctoral dissertation, University of California, Santa Barbara).

Feuerstein, R., Falik, L., & Feuerstein, Ra., (1998). Feuerstein's LPAD. In R. Samuda (Ed.), *Advances in cultural assessment.* Thousand Oaks, CA: Sage.

Feuerstein, R., & Feuerstein, S. (1991). Mediated learning experience: A theoretical review. In R. Feuerstein, P. Klein, & A. Tannenbaum, (Eds.), *Mediated learning experience: Theoretical, psychosocial, and learning implications.* Tel Aviv, Israel, and London, UK: Freund.

Feuerstein, R., Rand, Y., & Hoffman, M. (1979). *The dynamic assessment of the retarded performer.* Baltimore, MD: University Park Press.

Feuerstein, R., Rand, Y., Hoffman, M., & Miller, R. (1980). *Instrumental enrichment: An intervention program for cognitive modifiability.* Baltimore, MD: University Park Press.

Feuerstein, R., & Kozulin, A. (1995). The bell curve: Getting the facts straight. *Educational Leadership, 52*(7), 71–74.

Feuerstein, R., Rand, Y., Falik, L., & Feuerstein, Ra. (2002). *Dynamic assessment of cognitive modifiability.* Jerusalem: ICELP Press.

Field, T. (1999). Preschoolers in America are touched less and are more aggressive than preschoolers in France. *Early Child Development and Care, 151*(1), 11–17.

Figueredo, H. (1999). *La atención a los escolares con insuficiencias leves en el lenguaje*(Tesis de Doctorado. Instituto Central de Ciencias Pedagógicas. MINED, Cuba).

Flavell, J. (1962). Historical and biographical note. In W. Kessen & C. Kuhlman (Eds.), *Thought in the young child: Report on a conference on intellective development with particular attention to the work of Jean Piaget.* Monographs of the Society for Child Development. Serial number 83. Antioch, OH: The Antioch Press.

Fodor, J. A. (1972). Some reflections on L. S. Vygotsky's thoughts and language. *Cognition, 1,* 83–95.

Forman, E. A., Minick, N., & Stone, C. A. (Eds.). (1993). *Contexts of learning: Sociocultural dynamics of children's development.* New York: Oxford University Press.

Frank, T. (2005). *What's the matter with Kansas? How conservatives won the heart of America.* New York, NY: Holt.

Freire, P. (1970). *Pedagogy of the oppressed.* New York, NY: Continuum.

Freire, P. (1973). *Education for critical consciousness.* New York, NY: Seabury Press.

Freire, P. (1998). *Pedagogy of freedom: Ethics, democracy, and civic courage.* Lanham, MD: Rowman & Littlefield.

Freire, P. (1995) *Pedagogy of Hope: Reliving Pedagogy of the Oppressed,* New York: Continuum.

Freud, S. (1922). *Beyond the pleasure principle* (C. J. M. Hubback, Trans.). London: The International Psycho-Analytical Press.

Freud, S., Strachey, J. & Freud, A. (1966). *The psychopathology of everyday life.* London: Benn.

Fuster, J. M. (2002). *Cortex and mind: Unifying cognition.* New York, NY: Oxford University Press.

Gaitan, C., & Trueba, H. (1990). *Crossing cultural borders: Education for immigrant families in America.* Bristol, PA: Falmer Press, Taylor & Francis Inc.

Gallego, M. A. (2000). Is experience the best teacher? *Journal of Teacher Education, 52*(4), 312–325.

Gallego, M. A., & Blanton, W. (2002). Cultural practices in Fifth Dimension sites around the world. In E. R. Garner, Y. Zhao, & M. Gillingham (Eds.), *Hanging out: Community based after-school programs for children* (pp. 137–147). Westport, CT: Bergin & Garvey.

Gallego, M. A., & Cole, M. (2000). Success is not enough: Challenges to sustaining new forms of educational activity. *Computers in Human Behavior, 16,* 271–286.

Gallego, M. A., Rueda, R., & Moll, L. C. (2003). Mediating language and literacy: Lessons from an after-school setting. In G. G. Garcia (Ed.), *English learners: Reaching the highest level of English literacy* (pp. 387–407). Newark, DE: International Reading Association.

Gallego, M. A., Rueda, R., & Moll, L. C. (2005). Multilevel approaches to documenting change: Challenges in community-based educational research. *Teachers College Record, 107*(10), 2299–2325.

Gallimore, R., & Goldenberg, C. (2001). Analyzing cultural models and settings to connect minority achievement and school improvement research. *Educational Psychologist, 36*(1), 45–56.

Gándara, P., Rumberger, R., Maxwell-Jolly, J., & Callahan, R. (2003). English learners in California schools: Unequal resources, unequal outcomes. *Education Policy Analysis Archives, 11*(36). Retrieved from http://epaa.asu.edu/epaa/v2011n2036/

Garb, E., & Kozulin, A. (2004). Cognition and metacognition: Tools for change. In R. Wilkinson (Ed.), *Integrating content and language: Meeting the challenge of a multilingual higher education.* Maastricht, Netherlands: University of Maastricht Press.

García, O., Bartlett, L., & Kliefgen, J. (2007). From biliteracy to pluriliteracies. In P. Auer & L. Wei (Eds.), *Handbook of applied linguistics. Vol. 5: Multilingualism* (pp. 207–228). Berlin, Germany: Mouton/de Gruyter.

García Tejeda, C. (2007). *El papel de la familia en la potenciación del desarrollo infantil. Una propuesta para su fortalecimiento.* Trabajo de Diploma. Facultad de Psicología. Universidad de La Habana.

Garfinkel, H. (1967). *Studies in ethnomethodology.* Englewood Cliffs, NJ: Prentice-Hall.

Garfinkel, H. (2002). *Ethnomethodology's program: Working out Durkheim's aphorism.* Lanham, MD: Rowman & Littlefield.

Garner, R., Zhao, Y., & Gillingham, M. (Eds.). (2002). *Hanging out: Community based after-school programs for children.* Westport, CT: Bergin & Garvey.

Garrett, P. (2005). What a language is good for: Language socialization, language shift, and the persistence of code-specific genres in St. Lucia. *Language in Society, 34,* 327–361.

Garrett, P., & Baquedano-López, P. (2002). Language socialization: Reproduction and continuity, transformation and change. *Annual Review of Anthropology 31,* 339–361. Palo Alto, CA: Annual Reviews.

Garrison, J. (1995). Dewey's philosophy and the experience of working: Labor, tools, and language. *Synthese, 105*(1), 87–114.

Garza, X. (2005). *Lucha libre: The man in the silver mask: A bilingual cuento.* El Paso, TX: Cinco Puntos Press.

Gasca, L. (1967). Influencia del "comic" en la publicidad. *Revista Española de la Opinión Pública, 8,* 125–142.

Gauggel, S. (1997). Hirnverletztenlazarette und der Anfang der Neurorehabilititation. In S. Gauggel, & G. Kerkhoff (Eds.). *Fallbuch der klinischen Neuropsychologie* (pp. 15–24). Göttingen, Germany: Hogrefe.

Gauvain, M., & Munroe, R. L. (2009). Contributions of societal modernity to cognitive development. *Child Development, 80,* 1628–1642.

Gee, J. P. (1996). *Social linguistics and literacies: Ideology in discourses.* London, UK: Taylor & Francis.

Gee, J. P. (2007a). *Good video games + good learning: Collected essays on video games, learning and literacy.* New York, NY: Peter Lang.

Gee, J. P. (2007b). *What video games have to teach us about learning and literacy* (rev. ed.). New York, NY: Palgrave Macmillan.

Gibson. N. (2005). The limits of Black political empowerment. *Theoria: A Journal of Social and Political Theory, 55,* pp. 89-118.

Gibson, N. (2011, forthcoming). What happened to "the promised land?" A Fanonian perspective on post-apartheid South Africa." *Antipode.*

Glick, J., (1983). Piaget, Vygotsky and Werner. In S. Wapner & B. Kaplan (Eds.), *Toward a holistic developmental psychology.* Hillsdale, NJ: Lawrence Erlbaum.

Glick, J. (1995). Intellectual and manual labor: Implications for developmental theory. In L. Martin, K. Nelson, & E. Tobach (Eds.), *Sociocultural psychology: Theory and practice of doing and knowing.* New York, NY: Cambridge University Press.

Goffman, E. (1961). *Asylums: Essays on the social situation of mental patients and other inmates.* New York, NY: Doubleday.

Goffman, E. (1974). *Frame analysis: An essay on the organization of experience.* New York, NY: Harper and Row.

Goffman, E. (1981). *Forms of talk.* Philadelphia, PA: University of Pennsylvania Press.

Goldberg, E., & Bougakov. D. (2009). Neuropsychology and A. R. Luria's concept of higher cortical functions in the beginning of the 3rd millennium. In A. L. Christensen, E. Goldberg, & D. Bougakov (Eds.), *Luria's legacy in the 21st century* (pp. 15–22). New York, NY: Oxford University Press.

Golden, C., & Moses, J. (1984). *Clinical neuropsychology: Interface with neurological and psychiatric disorders.* New York, NY: Rune & Stratton.

González, N. (2005). Children in the eye of the storm: Language ideologies in a dual language school. In A. C. Zentella (Ed.), *Building on strength: Language and literacy in Latino families and communities* (pp. 162–174). New York, NY: Teachers College Press.

González, N., & Moll, L. C., & Amanti, C. (Eds.). (2005). *Funds of knowledge: Theorizing practices in households, communities, and classrooms.* Mahwah, NJ: Lawrence Erlbaum.

Gonzales Bertrand, D. (2003). *The empanadas that Abuela made/Las empanadas que hacía la abuela.* Houston, TX: Arte Público Press.

González Rey, F. L. (1983). Obschenie y evo znachenie v razrabotke problemy lichnosti [The community and its significance for the reelaboration of personality theory]. *Psikjologichiskii Journal* [Psychological Journal], *4,* 40–47.

González Rey, F. L. (1991). *Problemas epistemológicos de la psicología.* Colegio de Ciencias Sociales y Humanidade. Universidad Nacional Autónoma de México.

González Rey, F. L. (1995). *Comunicación personalidad y desarrollo.* Habana, Cuba: Editorial Pueblo y Educación.

González Rey, F. L. (1999). Personality subject and human development. In S. Chaiklin, M. Hedegaard, & U. Jensen (Eds.), *Activity theory and social practice* (pp. 253–274). Aarhus, Denmark: Aarhus University Press.

González Rey, F. L. (2001) La categoría sentido y su significación en la construcción del pensamiento psicológico. *Contrapontos, 1*(2), 13–28.

González Rey, F. L. (2002). *Sujeto e subjetividade: Una aproximación histórico-cultural.* São Paulo, Brazil: Thomson,.

González Rey, F. L. (2007). Social and individual subjectivity from an historical cultural standpoint. *Critical Social Studies. Outlines, 9*(2), 3–14.

González Rey, F. L. (2008). *Different periods in Vygotsky's work: Their implications for arguments regarding his legacy.* Paper presented at the Annual Meeting of the International Society for Cultural and Activity Research, San Diego, California.

González Rey, F. L. (2009). Historical relevance of Vygotsky's work: Its significance for a new approach to the problem of subjectivity in psychology. *Outlines. Critical Practice Studies, 1,* 59–73.

González Rey, F. L. (2010). A *Psicologia soviética: Vygotski, Rubinstein e as tendências que a caracterizaram até o fim dos anos 1980.* In A. M. Jacó-Vilela, A. A. Leal Ferreira, & F. Texeira (Eds.), *Historia da psicologia. Rumos e percursos.* (2nd ed.) (pp. 349–366). Portugal: Editora NAU.

González Serra, D. (2003). Martí, Vygotski y el carácter sociohistórico del ser humano. *Revista Cubana de Psicología, 20*(3), 256–259.

Goodwin, M. H. (1990). *He-said-she-said: Talk as social organization among Black children.* Bloomington, IN: Indiana University Press.

Goodwin, C., & Goodwin, M. H. (2004). Participation. In A. Duranti (Ed.), *Companion to linguistic anthropology.* Malden, MA: Blackwell.

Gordon, T., & Lahelma, E. (1996). "School is like an ants' nest"—Spatiality and embodiment in schools. *Gender and Education, 8*(3), 301–310.

Gordon, T., Holland, J., & Lahelma, E. (2000). *Making spaces: Citizenship and difference in schools.* London, UK: Macmillan.

Gouzman, R., & Kozulin, A. (2011). Helping minority students to succeed in technological college. *International Journal of Inclusive Education, 15* (2), 1-12.

Gredler, M. E., & Shields, C. C. (2008). *Vygotsky's legacy: A foundation for research and practice.* New York, NY: Guilford Press.

Green, M., Kern, R., Blaff, D., & Mintz, J. (2000). Neurocognitive deficits and functional outcome in schizophrenia: Are we measuring the "right stuff"? *Schizophrenia Bulletin, 26,* 119–136.

Greenfield, P., Maynard, A., & Childs, C. (2003). Historical change, cultural learning, and cognitive representation in Zinacantec Maya children. *Cognitive Development, 18,* 455–487.

Greeno, J. G. (1998). The situativity of knowing, learning, and research, *American Psychologist,* 53, 5–17.

Griffin, P., & Cole, M. (1984). Current activity for the future: The zo-ped. In B. Rogoff & Wertsch, J. V. (Eds.), *Children's learning in the "zone of proximal development"* (pp. 45–64). San Francisco, CA: Jossey-Bass.

Gruber, H., & Vonêche, J.J. (1977). *The essential Piaget: An interpretive reference and guide*. New York, NY: Basic Books.

Guadarrama Rico, L. (1999). Géneros televisivos en México: Un paseo por la geografía de cuatro décadas. *Convergencia, 6*(19), 179–125.

Guattari, F. (1992). Caosmose—Um novo paradigma estético. Rio de Janeiro, Brazil: Editora 34.

Guevara Valdés, J. (1984). *Apuntes para una historia de la psicología en Cuba*. Unpublished manuscript.

Gump, V. (1978). School environments. In I. Altman & J. F. Wohlwill (Eds.), *Human behavior and environment: Advances in theory and research: Vol. 3* (pp. 131–169). New York, NY: Plenum Press.

Gump, P. V., & Good, L. R. (1976). Environments operating in open space and traditionally designed school. *Journal of Architectural Research, 5*, 20–27.

Gutiérrez, K. D. (1999). Rethinking diversity: Hybridity and hybrid language practices in the third space. *Mind, Culture, and Activity, 6*, 286–303.

Gutiérrez, K. D. (2000). Teaching and learning in the 21st century. *English Education, 32*(4), 290–298.

Gutiérrez, K. D. (2008). Developing a sociocritical literacy in the third space. *Reading Research Quarterly, 43*(2), 148–164.

Gutiérrez, K., Asato, J., Santos, M., & Gotanda, N. (2002). Backlash pedagogy: Language and culture and the politics of reform. *The Review of Education, Pedagogy & Cultural Studies, 24*(4), 335–351.

Gutiérrez, K., Baquedano-López, P., & Asato, J. (2001). English for the children: The new literacy of the old world order. *Bilingual Review Journal, 24*(1 & 2), 87–112.

Gutiérrez, K., Baquedano-Lopez, P., & Tejeda, C. (1999). Rethinking diversity: Hybridity and hybrid language practices in the third space. *Mind, Culture, & Activity: An International Journal, 6*(4), 286–303.

Gutiérrez, K., Hunter, J. D., & Arzubiaga, A. (2009). Re-mediating the university: Learning through sociocritical literacies. *Pedagogies: An International Journal, 4*(1), 1–23.

Gutiérrez, K., Morales, P. D., & Martinez, D. C. (2007). Re-mediating literacy: Culture, difference, and learning for students from nondominant communities. *Review of Research in Education, 33*, 212–235.

Gutiérrez, K., & Rogoff, B. (2003). Cultural ways of learning: Individual traits or repertoires of practice. *Educational Researcher, 32*(5), 19–25.

Gutiérrez, K., Rymes, B., & Larson, J. (1995). Script, counterscript, and underlife in the classroom: James Brown versus *Brown v. Board of Education*. *Harvard Educational Review, 65*(3), 445–471.

Habib, J., & Associates. (2001). *Integration of Ethiopian immigrants into Israeli society*. Jerusalem, Israel: JDC Brookdale Institute.

Hanks, W. F. (1996). *Language and communicative practices*. Boulder, CO: Westview.

Hargreaves, A., Earl, L., & Ryan, J. (1996). *Schooling for change: Reinventing education for early adolescents*. Philadelphia, PA: Falmer Press.

Harter, S., Whitesell-Rumbaugh, N., & Kowalski, P. (1992). Individual differences in the effect of educational transitions on young adolescents' perceptions of competence and motivational orientation. *American Educational Research Journal, 29*(4), 777–807.

He, A. (2003) Novices and their speech roles in Chinese heritage language classes. In R. Bailey & S. Schecter, (Eds.). *Language socialization in bilingual and multilingual societies* (pp. 128–146). Clevendon: Multilingual Matters.

Heath, S. B. (1983). *Ways with words.* New York, NY: Cambridge University Press.

Hegel, G. W. F. (1969). *The science of logic* (A. V. Miller, Trans.). New York, NY: Humanity Books.

Herbert, B. (2010, July 31). A sin and a shame. *The New York Times.* Retrieved from http://www.nytimes.com/2010/07/31/opinion/31herbert.html

Herrnstein, R., & Murray, C. (1994). *The bell curve.* New York, NY: The Free Press.

Horn, L., & Nevill, S. (2006). Profile of undergraduates in U.S. postsecondary education institutions: 2003–04: With a special analysis of community college students (NCES 2006-184). U.S. Department of Education. Washington, DC: National Center for Education Statistics.

Hull, G., & Schultz, K. (2002). *School's out!: Bridging out of school literacy with classroom practice.* New York, NY: Teachers College Press.

Jackson, J. H. (1874/1932). On the nature of the duality of the brain. In *Selected writings of John Hughlings Jackson: Vol. 2.* London: Hodder & Stoughton.

Jacobs-Huey, L. (2007). Learning through the breach: Language socialization among African American cosmetologists. *Ethnography, 8*(2), 171–203.

Jacoby, S., & Gonzales, P. (1991). The constitution of expert-novice in scientific discourse. *Issues in Applied Linguistics, 2*(2), 149–181.

Jantzen, W. (2004). Methodologische Grundfragen der kulturhistorischen Neuropsychologie. In W. Jantzen (Ed.), *Gehirn,Geschichte und Gesellschaft: Die Neuropsychologie Alexandr R. Lurijas (1902–1977)* (pp. 115–136). Berlin, Germany: Lehmanns Media.

John-Steiner, V. (1987). *Notebooks of the mind: Explorations in thinking.* New York, NY: Harper & Row.

John-Steiner, V. (1995). Cognitive pluralism: A sociocultural approach. *Mind, Culture, and Activity, 2*(1), 2–10.

John-Steiner, V., Souberman, E., Cole, M., & Scribner, S., (1962) Editor's preface to Vygotsky, L.S. (1978) In M. Cole, V. John-Steiner, S. Scribner, & E. Souberman (Eds.), *Mind in Society: The development of higher psychological processes.* Cambridge, MA: Harvard University Press.

John-Steiner V., & Holbrook, M. (1996). Sociocultural approaches to learning and development: A Vygotskian framework. *Educational Psychologist, 31*(3/4), 191–206.

John-Steiner, V., & Mann, H. (1996). Sociocultural approaches to learning and development: A Vygotskian framework. *Educational Psychologist, 31,* 191–206.

Johnson, N. B. (1985). *West Haven: Classroom cultures and society in a rural elementary school.* Chapel Hill, NC: The University of North Carolina Press.

Kagan, S. L., & Neuman, M. J. (1998). Lessons from three decades of transition research. *Elementary School Journal, 98*(4), 365–379.

Kaniel, S., Tzuriel, D., Feuerstein, R., Ben-Schachar, N., & Eitan, T. (1991). Dynamic assessment: Learning and transfer abilities of Ethiopian immigrants to Israel. In R. Feuerstein, P. Klein,

& A. Tannenbaum (Eds.), *Mediated learning experience: Theoretical, psychosocial, and learning implications* (pp. 179–209). Tel Aviv, Israel, and London, UK: Freund.

Kaplan, R. S., & Norton, D. P. (1998). The balanced scorecard: Measures that drive performance. In *H. B. Review* (Ed.), *On measuring corporate performance* (pp. 123–145). Boston, MA: Harvard Business School Press.

Karpov, Y., & Haywood, H. C. (1998). Two ways to elaborate Vygotsky's concept of mediation: Implications for instruction. *American Psychologist, 53*(1), 27–36.

Katz, N., & Hadas, N. (1995). Cognitive rehabilitation: Occupational therapy models for intervention in psychiatry. *Psychiatric Rehabilitation Journal, 19*(2), 29–36.

Kenner, C., & Kress, G. (2003). The multisemiotic resources of biliterate children. *Journal of Early Childhood Literacy, 3*(2), 179–202.

Kessen, W., & Kuhlman, C. (Eds.). (1962). *Thought in the young child: Report on a conference on intellective development with particular attention to the work of Jean Piaget.* Monographs of the Society for Child Development, *27* (Serial no. 83). Antioch, OH: The Antioch Press.

Kezar, A. (2005). What campuses need to know about organizational learning and the learning organization. In A. Kezar (Ed.), *Organizational learning in higher education* (pp. 7–22). San Francisco, CA: Jossey-Bass.

Kinard, J., & Kozulin, A. (2008). *Rigorous mathematical thinking: Conceptual formation in the mathematics classroom.* New York, NY: Cambridge University Press.

Kirkpatrick, D. L. (1994). *Evaluating training programs: The four levels.* San Francisco, CA: Berrett-Koehler.

Knight, N. (2007). *Rethinking Mao: Explorations in Mao Zedung's thought.* Lanham, MD: Lexington Books.

Knobel, M., & Lankshear, C. (2008). Remix: The art and craft of endless hybridization. *Journal of Adolescent & Adult Literacy, 52*, 22–33.

Kozulin, A. (1990a). *La psicología de Vygotski.* Madrid, Spain: Alianza Editorial..

Kozulin, A. (1990b). The concept of regression and Vygotsky's developmental theory. *Developmental Review, 10*, 218–238.

Kozulin, A. (1995). The learning process: Vygotsky's theory in the mirror of its interpretations. *School Psychology International, 16*(2), 117–129.

Kozulin, A. (1998). *Psychological tools: A sociocultural approach to education.* Cambridge, MA: Harvard University Press.

Kozulin, A. (2005a). Immigrant parents' aspirations for their children and the required family support system: A lack of confluence. *Journal of Cognitive Education and Psychology, 4*(3), 352–361.

Kozulin, A. (2005b). Cognitive enrichment of adult new immigrant students from Ethiopia [in Hebrew]. *Hed Ulpan HaHadash on Web, 89.*

Kozulin, A. (2006). *Learning potential assessment as a tool for professional advancement of cultural minority young adults.* Paper presented at the Northumbria EARLI Assessment Conference, University of Northumbria, UK.

Kozulin, A. (2008). Evidence of culture-dependency and modifiability of spatial memory of young adults. *Journal of Cognitive Education and Psychology, 7*(1), 70–80.

Kozulin, A., Gindis, B., Ageyev, V., & Miller, S. (2003). *Vygotsky's educational theory in cultural context*. Cambridge: Cambridge University Press.

Kress. G., & van Leeuwen, T. (2006). *Reading images: The grammar of visual design* (2nd ed.). New York, NY: Routledge.

Kretschmer, E. (1936). *Physique and character: An investigation of the nature of constitution and of the theory of temperament*. Harcourt Brace.

Kyratzis, A. (2001). Emotion talk in preschool same-sex friendship groups: Fluidity over time and context. In N. Budwig (Ed.), Language socialization and children's entry into schooling. *Early Education and Development, 12*, 359–391.

Labarrere Sarduy, A. (1996a). *Interacción en zona de desarrollo próximo. Qué puede para bien y qué para mal*. La Habana, Cuba: ICCP-ARGOS.

Labarrere Sarduy, A. (1996b). *Pensamiento, análisis y autorregulación de la actividad cognitiva de los alumnos*. La Habana, Cuba: Editorial Pueblo y Educación.

Lave, J. (1996). Teaching, as learning, in practice. *Mind, Culture, and Activity: An International Journal, 3*, 149–164.

Lave, J. (1993). Situating learning in communities of practice. In L. B. Resnick, J. M. Levine, & S. D. Teasley (Eds.), *Perspectives on socially shared cognition* (pp. 17–36). Washington, DC: American Psychological Association.

Lave, J. (1988). *Cognition in practice: Mind, mathematics, and culture in everyday life*. New York, NY: Cambridge University Press.

Lave, J., & Wenger, E. (1991). *Situated learning: Legitimate peripheral participation*. Cambridge, UK: Cambridge University Press.

Leander, K. (2002). Polycontextual construction zones: Mapping the expansion of schooling, space, and identity. *Mind, Culture, and Activity, 9*, 211–237.

Lee, C. D., & Smagorinsky, P. (Eds.). (2000). *Vygotskian perspectives on literacy research: Constructing meaning through collaborative inquiry*. New York, NY: Cambridge University Press.

Lee, V. E., & Burkam, D. T. (2002). *Inequality at the Starting Gate*. Washington, DC: The Economic Policy Institute.

Leiman, M. (1992). The concept of sign in the work of Vygotsky, Winnicott and Bakhtin: Further integration of object relations theory and activity theory. *British Journal of Medical Psychology, 65*, 209–221.

Lektorsky, V. (1999). Historical change of the notion of activity: Philosophical presuppositions. In S. Chaiklin, M. Hedegaard, & U. Jensen (Eds.), *Activity theory and social practice* (pp. 100–113). Aarhus, Denmark: Aarhus University Press.

Lemke, J. (2000). Across the scales of time: Multi-level organization in activity networks and ecosocial systems. *Mind, Culture, and Activity, 7*(4), 273–290.

Lemke, J. (2002). Language development and identity: Multiple timescales in the social ecology of learning. In C. Kramsch (Ed.), *Language acquisition and language socialization: Ecological perspectives*. London, UK: Continuum Press.

Leontiev, A. A. (1992). Ecco homo: Methodological problem of the activity theoretical approach. *Newsletter for Activity Theory, 11*(12), 41–44.

Leontiev, A. A. (2001). *Deyatelnii Um: (Deyatelnost, snak, lichnost)/The active mind (Activity, sign, personality)*. Moscow: Moscow. Smisl.

Leontiev, A. N. (1965). Predislovie (Prólogo) Psikjologiya Iskusstva (L. S. Vygotsky) (Psicologia del Arte) Izdatelstva "Iskusstva" ( Editorial "Arte") Moscow.

Leontiev, A. N. (1966/1974). *El concepto de reflejo. Su importancia para la Psicología Científica.* Discurso inaugural del XVIII Congreso Internacional de Psicología Científica, Moscú. Publicado en el *Boletín de Psychologie, 254,* XX, No. 5, diciembre de 1966 y traducido y publicado en *Publicaciones Ligeras* de la Universidad de La Habana por el Dr. Ernesto González Puig el 20 de agosto de 1974.

Leontiev, A. N. (1978). *Activity, consciousness and personality.* Englewood, NJ: Prentice Hall.

Leontiev, A. N. (1981a). *Actividad conciencia y personalidad.* Ciudad de la Habana, Cuba: Editorial Pueblo y Educación.

Leontiev, A. N. (1981b). The problem of activity in psychology. In J. V. Wertsch, (Ed.), *The concept of activity in Soviet psychology* (pp. 33–71). Armonk, NY: Sharpe.

Leontiev, A. N. (1981c). Problems of the development of the mind. Moscow: Progress Publishers.

Leontiev, A. N. (1986). Problema deyatelnosti v istorii sovestskoi psikhologii. (The problem of activity in the history of Soviet psychology) *Voprocy Psykhology, 4,* 109–120.

Leontiev, A. N. (1991). *Prólogo al tomo I de las obras escogidas.* Madrid, Spain: Editorial Visor.

Leontiev, A. N., Luria A. R., & Teplov, B. M. (1987). *Prólogo de los redactores de la edición soviética, a Historia del desarrollo de las funciones psíquicas superiores.* Ciudad de La Habana, Cuba: Editorial Científico Técnica.

Leontiev, D. (1994). The concept of personal sense through the ages. *Multidisciplinary newsletter for Activity Theory, 15/ 16,* 13–16.

Leontiev, D. (2007). *Psykjologiya smysla.* [Psychology of sense]. Moscow: Smysl.

Levin, T., & Shohamy, E. (2008). Achievement of immigrant students in mathematics and academic Hebrew in Israeli school: A large scale evaluation study. *Studies in Educational Evaluation, 34,* 1–14.

Lewis, J. (1989). Mother's love: The construction of an emotion in nineteenth-century America. In A. Barnes & P. Stearns (Eds.), *Social history and issues in human consciousness* (pp. 209–229). New York, NY: New York University Press.

Lifshitz, C., Noam, G., & Habib, J. (1998). *The absorption of Ethiopian immigrant youth.* Jerusalem: JDC-Brookdale Institute.

Lo, A. (2009). Evidentiality and morality in a Korean heritage language school. In A. Reyes & A. Lo (Eds.). *Beyond yellow English: Toward a linguistic anthropology of Asian Pacific America* (pp. 63–83). New York: Oxford University Press.

Lomov, B. F. (1978). Kategorii obtyscheniya i deyatelnosti v psykjologii [The categories of communication and activity in psychology]. *Voprocy Filosofii* [Questions of philosophy], 8, 34–47.

Lomov, B. F. (1984). Metodologicheskie i teoreticheskie problemy psykjologii [Methodological and theoretical problems of psychology]. Moscow: Nauka.

Lomov, B. F. (1989). *La categoría de Comunicación y de actividad en la psicología.* En: *Temas sobre la actividad y la comunicación,* Colectivo de autores. La Habana, Cuba: Editorial de Ciencias Sociales.

Lopez, M., Barrueco, S., Feinauer, E., & Miles, J. (2007, June). *Young Latino infants and families: Parental involvement implications from a recent national study.* Harvard Family Research Project. Retrieved from www.hfrp.org.

López Hurtado, J., & Siverio A. M. (1986). Dominio del arte de construir y usar modelos materiales evidentes en la infancia preescolar. In *Particularidades del desarrollo de las capacidades cognoscitivas en la edad preescolar* (pp. 15–25). Moscow: URSSCUBA: Vneshtorgizdat.

López Hurtado, J., & Siverio A. M. (1996). *El diagnóstico: un instrumento de trabajo pedagógico de preescolar a escolar.* La Habana. Editorial Pueblo y Educación.

López Hurtado, J., León, S., & Siverio A. M. (1991). Formación y desarrollo de las capacidades intelectuales. *Simientes, 3,* 28–33.

López Hurtado, J., León, S., & Siverio A. M. (1992). La modelación como mediatización en la solución de tareas. In *Estudio sobre las particularidades del desarrollo del niño preescolar cubano.* La Habana, Cuba: Editorial Pueblo y Educación.

Lopez Pulido, A., Driscoll de Alaorado, B., & Samora, C. (Eds.). (2009). *Moving beyond borders: Julian Samora and the establishment of Latino Studies.* Champaign, IL: University of Illinois Press.

Luke, A. (2008). Race and language as capital in schools: A sociological template for language education reform. In R. Kubota & A. Lin (Eds.), *Race, culture and identities in second language education* (pp. 286–308). London, UK: Routledge.

Lukes, S. (2005). *Power: A radical view* (2nd ed.). Basingstoke: Palgrave Macmillan.

Luria, A. R. (1925/1978). Psychoanalysis as a system of monistic psychology. In M. Cole (Ed.), *The selected writings of A. R. Luria* (pp. 3–44). New York, NY: Sharpe.

Luria, A. R. (1929/1978). The development of thought. In M. Cole (Ed.), *The selected writings of A. R. Luria* (pp. 97–144). New York, NY: Sharpe.

Luria, A. R. (1973). *The working brain: An introduction to neuropsychology.* New York, NY: Basic Books.

Luria, A. R. (1976). *Cognitive development: Its cultural and social foundation.* In M. Cole, (Ed.). Cambridge, MA: Harvard University Press.

Luria, A. R. (1978). *The nature of human conflicts.* New York, NY: Liveright. (Original work published 1932)

Luria, A. R. (1979a). *Mirando hacia atrás.* Madrid, Spain: Ediciones Norma.

Luria, A. R. (1979b). *The making of mind: A personal account of Soviet psychology.* Cambridge, MA: Harvard University Press.

Luria, A. R. (1980). *Higher cortical functions in man* (2nd ed.). New York, NY: Basic Books.

Luz y Caballero, J. (2001). *Obras y Elencos de discursos académicos. Biblioteca de clásicos cubanos.* Vol. 3. La Habana, Cuba: Editorial Imagen Contemporánea.

Mahn, H., & John-Steiner, V. (2002). The gift of confidence: A Vygotskian view of emotions. In G. Wells & G. Claxton (Eds.), *Learning for the 21st century.* Oxford, UK: Blackwell.

MALDEF (2010a). Parent School Partnership (PSP) Program. Retrieved from http://maldef.org/leadership/programs/psp/

MALDEF (2010b). MALDEF's 40th Anniversary. Retrieved from http://www.maldef.org/about/40th_anniversary/

Mangual Figueroa, A. (2010). *Language socialization experiences of mixed-status families in the New Latino diaspora* (Doctoral dissertation, Graduate School of Education, University of California, Berkeley).

Mannheim, K. (1952). *Essays on the sociology of knowledge.* London, UK.

Marschall, M. (September 2006). Parent involvement and educational outcomes for Latino students. *The Review of Policy Research, 23*(5), 1053–1076.

Martí, J. (1975). *José Martí. Obras Completas.* Editorial de Ciencias Sociales. La Habana.

Martinez, M., & Vásquez, A. O. (2007, April). *Sustainability: La Clase Mágica beyond its boundaries.* Paper presented at the Annual Meeting of the American Educational Research Association, Chicago, Illinois.

Martínez-Roldán, C. M., & Sayer, P. (2006). Reading through linguistic borderlands: Latino students' transactions with narrative texts. *Journal of Early Childhood Literacy, 6*(3), 297–326.

Marx, C., & Engels, F. (1986). *Obras escogidas: Vol. 1.* Moscú: Editorial Progreso.

Marx, K. (1952). *A history of economic theories: From the physiocrats to Adam Smith.* New York, NY: The Langland Press.

Massey, D. (2007). *Categorically unequal: The American stratification system.* New York, NY: Russell Sage Foundation.

McDermott, R. (1993). The acquisition of a child by a learning disability. In S. Chaiklin & J. Lave (Eds.), *Understanding practice: Perspectives on activity and context* (pp. 269–305). New York, NY: Cambridge University Press.

McGregor, J. (2004). Spatiality and the place of the material in schools. *Pedagogy, Culture and Society, 12*(3), 347–72.

McIntyre, R. P. (2008). *Are worker rights human rights?* Ann Arbor, MI: University of Michigan Press.

Mehl, M. (1991). Mediated learning experience at university level. In R. Feuerstein, P. Klein, & A. Tannenbaum (Eds.), *Mediated learning experience* (pp.157–178). Tel Aviv, Israel, & London, UK: Freund.

Melamed, J. (2006). The spirit of neoliberalism: From racial liberalism to neoliberal multiculturalism. *Social Text, 24,* 1–24.

Meshcheryakov, B. G., & Zinchenko, V. P. (2000, March/April). L. S. Vygotski y sovremennaya kulturno-istoricheskaya psijologiya. *[Kriticheskii analyz knigi M. Koula]. Voprosy psijologii.* Editorial Rosiiskaya Akademiya Obrazovaniya, , *15* (pp. 102–116). Moscú: Idioma: Ruso.

Michaels, S. (1981). Sharing time: Children's narrative style and differential access to literacy. *Language in Society 10,* 423–442.

Michaels, W. (2006). *The trouble with diversity: How we learned to love identity and ignore inequality.* New York, NY: Holt.

Mignolo, W. (2000). *Local histories/global designs: Coloniality, subaltern knowledges, and border thinking.* Princeton, NJ: Princeton University Press.

Miltenburg, R., & Singer, E., (1999). Culturally mediated learning and the development of self-regulation by survivors of child-abuse: A Vygotskian approach to the support of survivors of child abuse. *Human Development, 42,* 1–17.

Miltenburg, R., & Singer, E. (2000). A concept becomes a passion. Moral commitments and the affective development of the survivors of child abuse. *Theory & Psychology, 10,* 503–526.

Moje, E., & Lewis, C. (2007). Examining opportunities to learn literacy: The role of critical socio-cultural literacy research. In C. Lewis, P. Enciso, & E. Moje (Eds.), *Reframing sociocultural research on literacy*. Mahwah, NJ: Lawrence Erlbaum.

Moll, L. C. (1990). *Vygotsky and education: Instructional implications and applications of sociohistorical psychology*. New York, NY: Cambridge University Press.

Moll, L. C. (1992). Bilingual classroom studies and community analysis: Some recent trends. *Educational Researcher, 21*(2), 20–24.

Moll, L. C. (2001). Through the mediation of others: Vygotskian research on teaching. In V. Richardson (Ed.), *Handbook of research on teaching* (4th ed.) (pp. 111–129). Washington, DC: American Educational Research Association.

Moll, L. C. (2010). Mobilizing culture, language, and educational practices: Fulfilling the promises of *Mendez* and *Brown*. *Educational Researcher, 39*, 451–460.

Moll, L. C., Amanti, C., Neff, D., & González, N. (1992). Funds of knowledge for teaching: Using a qualitative approach to connect homes and classrooms. *Theory into Practice, 31*(2), 132–141.

Moll, L. C., & Cammarota, J. (2010). Cultivating new funds of knowledge through research and practice. In K. Dunsmore & D. Fisher (Eds.). *Bringing literacy home* (pp. 290–306). Newark, DE: International Reading Association.

Moll, L. C., & González, N. (2004). Engaging life: A funds of knowledge approach to multicultural education. In J. Banks & C. McGee Banks (Eds.), *Handbook of research on multicultural education* (2nd ed.) (pp. 699–715). New York, NY: Jossey-Bass.

Moll, L. C., & Greenberg, J. (1990). Creating zones of possibilities: Combining social contexts for instruction. In L. C. Moll (Ed.), *Vygotsky and education: Instructional implications and applications of sociohistorical psychology* (pp. 319–348). New York, NY: Cambridge University Press.

Moll, L. C., Sáez, R., & Dworin, J. (2001). Exploring biliteracy. *Elementary School Journal, 101*(4), 435–449.

Moll, L. C., & Whitmore, K. (1993). Vygotsky in the classroom practice: Moving from the individual transmission to social transaction. In E. A. Forman, N. Minnick, & A. C. Stone (Eds.), *Context for learning: Sociocultural dynamics in children's development* (pp. 19–42). New York, NY: Oxford University Press.

Montgomery, S. (2002). *Science in translation: Movements of knowledge through cultures and time*. Chicago, IL: University of Chicago Press.

Moran, R. (in press). New twist on "The One Best System": Structured immersion initiatives, equal opportunity, and freedom to learn. In G. P. McField (Ed.), *Structured immersion in comparative contexts: History, politics, and practice*. Bristol, UK: Multilingual Matters.

Moscovici, S. (2000). The history and actuality of social representations. In G. Duveen (Ed.), *Social Representations: Explorations in social psychology* (pp. 120–155). London, UK: Polity Press

Nash, R. (2003). Inequality/difference in New Zealand education: Social reproduction and the cognitive habitus. *International Study in Sociology of Education, 13*, 171–191.

National Center for Education Statistics. (2003). *Postsecondary attainment attendance, curriculum, and performance: Selected results from the NELS: 88/2000.* Washington, DC: U.S. Department of Education.

National Center for Education Statistics. (2005). *First-generation students in postsecondary education: A look at their college transcripts.* NCES 2005–171, by X. Chen. Project Officer. C. Dennis Carroll. Washington, DC: U.S. Department of Education.

National Center for Education Statistics. (2008). *Digest of education statistics: 2008.* Retrieved from http://nces.ed.gov/programs/digest/d08/index.asp

Neliubin, N. I. (2009). On the functional correspondence of meaning and sense in the structure of consciousness. *Journal of Russian and Eastern European Psychology, 47*(5), 26–43.

Nepomnichaya, N. I. (1977). Deyatelnost, soznanie lichnost i predmet psykjologii [Activity, consciousness, personality and the object of psychology]. In *The problem of activity in Soviet psychology.* Thesis and materials of the 5th Congress of the Society of Psychologists of the Soviet Union, Moscow.

The New London Group. (1996). A pedagogy of multiliteracies: Designing social futures. *Harvard Educational Review, 66,* 60–92.

Newman, R., & Holzman, L. (1993). *Lev Vygotsky: Revolutionary scientist.* London, UK: Routledge.

Nichols, S. L., & Berliner, D. C. (2007). *Collateral damage: How high-stakes testing corrupts America's schools.* Boston, MA: Harvard Education Publishing Group.

Nielsen, S. E. (2002). *Josh's worlds: Developing literacy skills at home and at school* (Doctoral dissertation, School of Education, University of California, Davis).

Novoselova, S. (1981). *El desarrollo de pensamiento en la edad temprana.* La Habana, Cuba: Editorial Pueblo y Educación.

Oakes, J., Joseph, R., & Muir, K. (2004). Access and achievement in mathematics and science: Inequalities that endure and change. In J. A. Banks & C. A. Banks, (Eds.), *Handbook of research on multicultural education* (2nd ed.) (pp. 69–90). San Francisco, CA: Jossey-Bass.

Oberst, U. E., & Stewart, A. E. (2003). *Adlerian psychotherapy: An advanced approach to individual psychology.* New York, NY: Routledge.

Orellana, M. F. (2009). *Translating childhoods: Immigrant youth, language and culture.* New Brunswick, NJ: Rutgers University Press.

Orellana, M. F., & Thorne B. (1998). Year-round schools and the politics of time. *Anthropology and Education Quarterly, 29*(4), 1–27.

Orfield, G., & Kornhaber, M. L. (Eds.). (2001). *Raising standards or raising barriers? Inequality and high-stakes testing in public education.* New York, NY: The Century Foundation Press.

Ortner, S. (2006). *Anthropology and social theory: Culture, power and the acting subject.* Durham, NC: Duke University Press.

Ostrosky, M. M., Jung, E. Y., & Hemmeter, M. L. (2002). *Helping children make transitions between activities: What works brief.* Champaign, IL: Center on the Social and Emotional Foundations for Early Learning.

Panofsky, C. (2003). The relations of learning and student social class: Toward re-'socializing' sociocultural learning theory. In A. Kozulin & B. Gindis, V. S. Ageyev, & S. M. Miller (Eds.), *Vygotsky's educational theory in cultural context* (pp. 411–431). New York, NY: Cambridge University Press.

Parker, I. (1999). Deconstruction and psychotherapy. In I. Parker (Ed.), *Deconstructing psychotherapy* (pp. 1–18). London, UK: Sage Publications.

Parrish, T. B., Linquanti, R., & Merickel, A. (2002). *Proposition 227 and instruction of English learners in California: Evaluation update.* American Institutes for Research and WestEd.

Pavlenko, A., & Lantolf, J. (2000). Second language learning as participation and the (re) construction of selves. In James Lantolf (Ed.). *Sociocultural theory and second language learning* (pp. 155–177). New York: Oxford University Press.

Pavlov, I. P. (1957). *Essays in psychology and psychiatry.* New York, NY: The Citadel Press.

Pedrol, R., & Casanova, A. R. (2005). *La unidad y la diversidad en los métodos de estudios de la Biología.* Publicación electrónica en la editorial DESOFT S. A.

Peña, E.V. (2007). *The responsive academic practitioner: Using inquiry methods for self-change.* (Doctoral Dissertation). Retrieved from Proquest Dissertations and Theses. 3262771

Piaget, J. (1923). *Le langage et la pensée chez l'enfant.* Neuchâtel-Paris: Delachaux et Nestlé.

Piaget, J. (1924). *Le jugement et le raissonement chez l'enfant.* Neuchâtel: Delachaux et Nestlé.

Piaget, J. (1964). Development and learning. In R. E. Ripple & V. N. Rockcastle (Eds.), *Piaget revisited.* Ithaca, NY: Cornell University Press.

Politzer, G. (1965). *Psicología concreta, prologo y apéndice de José Bleger.* Buenos Aires: Editor Jorge Álvarez.

Polkinghorne, D. E. (2004). *Practice and the human sciences: The case for a judgment-based practice of care.* Albany, NY: State University of New York Press.

Pontecorvo, C. (1993). Forms of discourse and shared thinking. *Cognition and Instruction, 11* (3 & 4), 189–196.

Portes, A. (1971). On the emergence of behavior therapy in modern society. *Journal of Consulting and Clinical Psychology, 36*(3), 303–313.

Portes, P. R. (1990). Political upheaval, cultural assimilation and the origins of counseling needs. *International Journal for the Advancement of Counseling, 13,* 11–18.

Portes, P. R. (1993, April). *The Vygotsky thread: Semiotics in education and counseling.* Paper presented at the American Educational Research Association, Atlanta, Georgia.

Portes, P. R. (1996). Ethnicity in educational psychology. In R. Calfee & D. Berliner (Eds.), *Handbook of educational psychology.* New York, NY: Macmillan.

Portes, P. R. (1999). Social and psychological factors in the academic achievement of children of immigrants: A cultural historical puzzle. *American Educational Research Journal, 36*(3), 489–507.

Portes, A., & Rumbaut, R. (2001). *Legacies: The story of the immigrant second generation.* Berkeley, CA: University of California Press & Russell Sage Foundation.

Portes, P. R. (2005). *Dismantling educational inequality: A cultural-historical approach to closing the achievement gap.* New York, NY: Peter Lang Publishing.

Portes, A., & Rumbaut, R. (2006). *A portrait of immigrant America* (3rd ed.). Berkeley, CA: University of California Press.

Portes, A., Fernandez-Kelly, P., & Haller, W. (2008). *The adaptation of the immigrant second generation in America: Theoretical overview and recent evidence.* Center for Migration and Development Working Paper #08-02. Retrieved from http://cmd.princeton.edu/papers.shtml

Portes, P. R., Nixon, C. B., & Sandhu, D. S. (2008). *Development of a cultural adaptation and adjustment scale-revised: The persisting issue of cultural validity.* Paper presented at the Society for Crosscultural Research, Annual Meeting, New Orleans.

Portes, P. R., & Salas, S. (2010). In the shadow of Stone Mountain: Identity development, structured inequality, and the education of Spanish-speaking children. *The Journal of the National Association for Bilingual Education, 33*(2), 241–248.

Portes, P. R., & Smagorinsky, P. (2010). Static structures, changing demographics: Educating teachers for shifting populations in stable schools. *National Council of Teachers of English, 42*(3), 236–247.

Portes, P. R., Smith, T. L., Zady, M. F., & Del Castillo, K. (1997). Extending the double stimulation method in cultural-historical research: Parent-child interaction and cognitive change. *Mind, Culture, and Activity, 4*(2), 108–123.

Portes, P. R., & Vadeboncoeur, J. (2003). Mediation in cognitive socialization: The influence of socioeconomic status. In A. Kozulin, B. Gindis, V. S. Ageyev, & S. M. Miller (Eds.). *Vygotsky's educational theory in cultural context* (pp. 371–392) New York, NY: Cambridge University Press.

Postone, M. (2006). *Tiempo, trabajo y dominación social. Una reinterpretación de la teoría crítica de Marx.* Madrid, Spain: Marcial Pons Ediciones Jurídicas y Sociales, S. A. Politopias.

Poveda, D. (2001). La Ronda in a Spanish kindergarten classroom with a crosscultural comparison to sharing time in the U.S.A. *Anthropology and Education Quarterly, 32*(3), 301–325.

Pred, A. (1984). Place as historically contingent process: Structuration and the time—geography of becoming places. *Annals of the Association of American Geographers, 74*(2), 279–297.

Prensky, M. (2001). Digital natives, digital immigrants. *On the Horizon, 9*(5).

Prigatano, G. (2009). Neuropsychological foundations of human personality and Luria's legacy. In A. L. Christensen, E. Goldberg, & D. Bougakov (Eds.), *Luria's legacy in the 21st century.* New York, NY: Oxford University Press.

Public Policy Institute of California. (2007). Immigrants in California. Just the facts. Retrieved from http://www.ppic.org/main/publication.asp?i=221

Pushkin, V. N. (1997). Deyatelnost kak otbiekt psykjologii [The activity as object of psychology]. In *Problema deyatelnosti v sovietskoi psykjologii. Tezici y dokladov 5th Vcecoyusnomy siesdy Obchestva Psikxologov.* [The Problem of activity in Soviet psykjologii] (pp 52–58). Theses and materials of 5th Congress of the Society of Psychologists of the Soviet Union. Moscow.

Puziréi, A., & Guippenréiter, Y. (1989). *El proceso de formación de la psicología marxista: L. Vygotski, A. Leontiev, A. Luria.* Moscú: Editorial Progreso.

Puzyrei, A. (2007). Contemporary psychology and Vygotsky´s cultural-historical theory. *Journal of Russian and Eastern European Psychology, 45*(1), 8–93.

Quiocho, A., & Daoud, A. (2006). Dispelling myths about Latino parent participation in schools. *The Education Forum, 70*(3), 255–267.

Radzijovsky, L. A. (1982). G. I. Chelpanov—organizator Psykjologicheskovo Instituta. *Voprocy Psykjologii* [Questions of Psychology], *5*, 47–60.

Raphael, D. (2009). *Social determinants of health: Canadian perspectives.* Ontario: Canadian Scholars' Press Inc.

Ratner, C. (1991). *Vygotsky's sociohistorical psychology and its contemporary applications*. New York, NY: Plenum.

Ratner, C. (2002). *Cultural psychology: Theory and method*. New York, NY: Kluver Academic/ Plenum.

Ratner, C. (2006). *Cultural psychology: A perspective on psychological functioning and social reform*. Mahwah, NJ: Lawrence Erlbaum.

Ratner, C. (2009a). The cultural psychology of oppression and liberation. *Journal of Social Distress and the Homeless, 18*(3 & 4), 231–268. Retrieved from http://www.sonic.net/~cr2/psych liberation.pdf

Ratner, C. (2009b). Cooperativism: A social, economic, and political alternative to capitalism. *Capitalism, Nature, Socialism, 20*, 2, 44–73.

Ratner, C. (2011a). Macro cultural psychology. In Jaan Valsiner (Ed.), *Oxford handbook of culture and psychology*. New York, NY: Oxford University Press.

Ratner, C. (2011b). *Macro cultural psychology: A political philosophy of mind*. New York, NY: Oxford University Press.

Reason, P. (1994). Three approaches to participative inquiry. In N. K. Denzin & Y. Lincoln (Eds.), *Handbook of qualitative research*. Thousand Oaks, CA: Sage.

Reason, P., & Bradbury, H. (2001). Introduction: Inquiry and participation in search of a world worthy of human aspiration. In P. Reason & H. Bradbury (Eds.), *Handbook of action research: Participative inquiry and practice* (pp. 1–14). Thousand Oaks, CA: Sage.

Redlich, D., Hadas-Lidor, N., Weiss, P., & Amirav, I. (2010). Mediated learning experience intervention increases hope of family members coping with a relative with severe mental illness. *Community Mental Health Journal, 46*(4), 409– 415.

Reese, L., Balzano, S., Gallimore, R., & Goldenberg, C. (1995). The concept of educación: Latino family values and American schooling. *International Journal of Educational Research, 23*(1), 57.

Reinking, D., & Carter, A. (2007). Accommodating digital literacies within conceptions of literacy instruction for a new century. In B. J. Guzzetti (Ed.), *Literacy for the new millennium: Vol. 2* (pp. 139–155). Westport, CT: Praeger.

Relaño Pastor, A. M., & Vásquez, O. A. (2011, July). Accountability of the informal: Challenges and new directions. *Pedagogies: An International Journal*.

Resnick (1991). Literacy in and out of school. In S. R. Graubard (Ed.), *Literacy: An overview of fourteen experts* (pp. 169–185). New York, NY: Noonday Press.

Resnick (1994). Developing understanding of the idea of communities of learners. *Mind, Culture and Activity, 1*(4), 209–229.

Reyes, M. L. (in press). (Ed.). *Biliterate against the odds*. New York, NY: Teachers College Press.

Rico Montero, P. (1996). *Reflexión y aprendizaje en el aula*. La Habana, Cuba: Editorial Pueblo y Educación.

Rieber, R. W., & Carton, A. S. (1993). *The collected works of L. S. Vygotsky: Vol. 2: The fundamentals of defectology*. New York, NY: Plenum Press.

Ríos-Aguilar, C. (2007). *An examination of the effect of Latino households' funds of knowledge on Latina/o students' reading achievement and literacy outcomes* (Doctoral dissertation, University of Rochester, NY)

Rivero, M. (2001). *Influencia de la modelación en el desarrollo intelectual de retrasados mentales leves* (Tesis de Doctorado, ICCP, La Habana).

Roche, O. (2000). *Una aproximación a la Psicoterapia Científica desde una perspectiva histórica y dialéctica* (Tesis de Maestría en Psicología Clínica, Facultad de Psicología, Universidad de La Habana).

Rodriguez, R. (1996). The origins and history of the Chicano movement. Occasional Paper No. 07. Julian Somara Research Institute. Retrieved from http://www.jsri.msu.edu/RandS/research/ops/oc07.html#anchor731432

Rodriguez-Brown, F. (2009). *Home-school connection. Lessons learned in a culturally and linguistically diverse community.* New York, NY: Routledge, Taylor and Francis.

Rodríguez Ibáñez, B., & García Báez, R. (1996). *El derrumbe del modelo eurosoviético: visión desde Cuba* (3rd ed.). Ciudad de la Habana, Cuba: Editorial Félix Varela.

Rogers, R. (2002). Between contexts: A critical analysis of family literacy, discursive practices, and literate subjectivities. *Reading Research Quarterly, 37*, 248–277.

Rogoff, B. (1991). *Apprenticeship in thinking: Cognitive development in social context.* New York, NY: Oxford University Press.

Rogoff, B. (1995). Observing sociocultural activity on three planes: Participatory appropriation, guided participation, and apprenticeship. In J. V. Wertsch, P. Del Rio, & A. Alvarez (Eds.), *Sociocultural studies of mind* (pp. 139–164). Cambridge, UK: Cambridge University Press.

Rogoff, B. (1994). Developing understanding of the idea of communities of learners. *Mind, Culture and Activity, 1(4)*, 209-29.

Rogoff, B. (2003). *The cultural nature of human development.* New York, NY: Oxford University Press.

Rogoff, B., Baker-Sennett, J., Lacasa, P., & Goldsmith, D. (1995). Development through participation in sociocultural activity. In J. Goodnow, P. Miller, & F. Kessel (Eds.), *Cultural practices as contexts for development* (pp. 45–65). San Francisco, CA: Jossey-Bass.

Rogoff, B., Matusov, E, & White, C. (1996). Models of teaching and learning: Participation in a community of learners. In D. R. Olson & N. Torrance (Eds.), *The handbook of education and human development* (pp. 388–414). Oxford, UK: Blackwell.

Rogoff, B., Turkanis, C. G., & Bartlett, L. (2001). *Children and adults in a school community.* New York, NY: Oxford University Press.

Roloff, G., et al. (1987). *Investigaciones psicopedagógicas acerca del escolar cubano.* Ciudad de la Habana, Cuba: Editorial Pueblo y Educación.

Rosenkoetter, S. E. (2001). Lessons for preschool language socialization from the vantage point of the first day of kindergarten. *Early Education and Development, 12(3)*, 325–342.

Rotter, J. B. (1954). *Social learning and clinical psychology.* Englewood Cliffs, NJ: Prentice-Hall.

Rubinstein, S. L. (1957). *Bitiye u Coznaniye. (Social Being and Consciousness).* Moscow: Academy of Sciences.

Rueda, R., Gallego, M. A., & Moll, L. C. (2000). The least restrictive environment: A place or context? *Remedial and Special Education, 21*, 70–78.

Rueda, R., & Mehan, H. (1986). Metacognition and passing: Strategic interactions in the lives of students with learning disabilities. *Anthropology and Education Quarterly, 17(3)*, 145–165.

Rumberger, R. W. (2007). California's linguistic minority public school students, 2005. *EL Facts, 9*.

Ryle, A. (1991). Object relations theory and activity theory: A proposed link by way of the procedural sequence model. *British Journal of Medical Psychology, 64*, 307–316.

Rymes, B. R., & Pash, D. (2001). Questioning identity: The case of one second language learner. *Anthropology & Education Quarterly, 32*(3), 276–300.

Sacks, H., Schegloff, E. A., & Jefferson, G. (1974). A simplest systematics for the organization of turn-taking for conversation. *Language, 50*, 696–735.

Saenz, V. (2002). *Hispanic students and community colleges: A critical point for intervention* [Electronic Version]. ERIC Clearinghouse for Community Colleges, ED477908. Retrieved from http://www.gseis.ucla.edu/ccs/digests/dig0208.htm.

Salomon, G. (Ed.). (1993). *Distributed cognitions: Psychological and educational considerations*. New York, NY: Cambridge University Press.

Sánchez Korrol, V. (1996). The origins and evolution of Latino history. *Organization of American Historians Magazine of History, 10*.

Santamaría Santigosa, A. (2005). La noción de interiorización desde una visión cultural del desarrollo. In M. Cubero & J. D. Ramírez Garrido (Eds.), *Vygotski en la psicología contemporánea* (pp. 81–111). Madrid, Spain: Editorial Miño y Dávila.

Schauble, L., & Glaser, R. (1996). *Innovations in learning: New environments for education*. Mahwah, NJ: Lawrence Erlbaum.

Schegloff, E. A. (1979). The relevance of repair to syntax-for-conversation. In T. Givon (Ed.) *Syntax and semantics 12: Discourse and syntax* (pp. 261–288). New York, NY: Academic Press.

Schieffelin, B. B. (2002). Marking time: The dichotomizing discourses of multiple temporalities. *Current Anthropology, 43*, 5–17.

Schieffelin, B. B., & Ochs E. (Eds.). (1986). *Language socialization across cultures*. Cambridge University Press.

Schieffelin, B. B., Woolard, K., & Kroskrity, P. V. (1998). *Language ideologies: Practice and theory*. Oxford, UK: Oxford University Press.

Schunk, D. H. (1984). Self-efficacy perspective on achievement behavior. *Educational Psychologist, 19*, 48–58.

Scribner, S., & Cole, M. (1981). *The psychology of literacy*. Cambridge, MA: Harvard University Press.

Serpell, R. (1993). *The significance of schooling: Life-journey in an African society*. New York, NY: Cambridge University Press.

Shaffer, D. W. (2006). *How computer games help children learn*. New York, NY: Palgrave Macmillan.

Sheldon, A. (1992). Preschool girls' discourse competence: Managing conflict and negotiating power. In K. Hall, M. Bucholtz, & B. Moonwoman (Eds.). *Locating power* (pp. 528–539). Berkeley, CA: Berkeley Women and Language Group, University of California.

Sherif, M., Harvey, O., White, J., Hood, W., & Sherif, C. (1988). *The robber's cave experiment: Intergroup conflict and cooperation*. Middletown, CT: Wesleyan University Press. (Original work published 1954)

Shotter, J. (1993). Becoming someone: Identity and belonging. In N. Coupland & J. F. Nussbaum (Eds.), *Discourse and lifespan identity: Language and language behaviors*. Thousand Oaks, CA: Sage.

Shuare, M. (1990). *La psicología soviética tal y como yo la veo*. Moscú: Editorial Progreso.

Siverio Gómez, A. M. (1988). *Investigaciones psicológicas y pedagógicas acerca del niño preescolar*. La Habana, Cuba: Editorial Pueblo y Educación.

Siverio Gómez, A. M. (1995). *Estudio de las particularidades del desarrollo del preescolar cubano*. Editorial Pueblo y Educación. La Habana.

Skandrani, S., Baubet, T., Taïeb, Ol, Rezzoug, D., & Moro, M. R. (2010). The rule of virginity among young women of Maghrebine origin in France. *Transcultural Psychiatry, 47*, 301–313.

Smagorinsky, P. (1995a). Constructing meaning in the disciplines: Reconceptualizing writing across the curriculum as composing across the curriculum. *American Journal of Education, 103*, 160–184.

Smagorinsky, P. (1995b). The social construction of data. Methodological problems of investigating learning in the zone of proximal development. *Review of Educational Research, 65*, 191–212.

Smagorinsky, P. (2001). If meaning is constructed, what is it made from? Toward a cultural theory of reading. *Review of Educational Research, 71*, 133–169.

Smagorinsky, P. (2010). The culture of learning to teach: The self-perpetuating cycle of conservative schooling. *Teacher Education Quarterly, 37*(2), 19–32.

Smirnov, C. D. (1993). Ovshepsikjologisheskaya teoria deyatelnosti: Perspektivy i ogranicheniya [K 90-leitiu so dinya roshdeniya A. N. Leonteva] The general psychological activity theory: Perspectives and constrains [On 90th anniversary of the birth of A.N. Leontiev). *Voprocy psykjology* [Questions of psychology], *4*, 94–101.

Smith, L. T. (1999). *Decolonizing methodologies: Research and indigenous peoples*. New York, NY, and London, UK: Zed Books Ltd. and Dunedin: Otago Press.

Smolka, A. L., B., M. C., R. De Goes, A. Pino (Eds.). (1995). The constitution of the subject: A persistent question. In J. V. Wertsch, P. Del Río, & A. Alvarez (Eds.), *Sociocultural studies of mind*. New York, NY: Cambridge University Press.

Sohlberg, M., & Mateer, K. A. (1989). *Introduction to cognitive rehabilitation*. New York, NY: Guilford.

Solano-Flores, G. (2008). Who is given test in what language by whom, when and where? The need for probabilistic views of language in the testing of English language learners. *Educational Researcher, 37*, 189.

Solórzano, D. G., Rivas, M. A., & Velez, V. (2005). *Community College as a Pathway to Chicana/o Doctorate Production*. Latino Policy and Issues Brief No. 11. Los Angeles: UCLA Chicano Research Studies Center Press.

Solís, J. (2001), Immigration status and identity: Undocumented Mexicans in New York. In Augusto Laó-Montes & Arlene Dávila (Eds.), *Mambo montage*. New York, NY: Columbia University Press.

Solís, J. (2004). Narrating and counternarrating illegality as an identity. In C. Daiute & S. Lightfoot (Eds.), *Narrative analysis: Studying the development of individuals in society*. Thousand Oaks, CA: Sage Publications.

Solís, J. (2009). Theorizing educational transitions: English Language Learners (ELLs) across academic settings (Doctoral dissertation, Graduate School of Education, University of California, Berkeley).

Solís, J., Kattan, S., & Baquedano-López, P. (2009a). Locating time in science learning activity: Adaptation as a theory of learning and change. In K. Richardson Bruna & K. Gomez (Eds.), *Talking science, writing science: The work of language in multicultural classrooms* (pp. 139–166). New York, NY, and London, UK: Routledge.

Solís, J., Kattan, S., & Baquedano-López, P. (2009b). Socializing respect and knowledge in a racially integrated science classroom. *Linguistics and Education, 20*(3), 273–290.

Steiner, S. (1970). *La Raza: The Mexican Americans*. New York, NY: Harper and Row.

Stephens, S. (Ed.). (1995). *Children and the politics of culture*. Princeton, NJ: Princeton University Press.

Sternberg, R. (2000). Group and individual differences in intelligence: What can and should be done about them. In A. Kozulin & Y. Rand. (Eds.), *Experience of mediated learning*. Oxford, UK: Pergamon.

Street, B. (2003). What's "new" in New Literacy Studies? Critical approaches to literacy in theory and practice. *Current Issues in Comparative Education, 5*(2), 77–91.

Stringer, E. T. (1996). *Action research: A handbook for practitioners*. Thousand Oaks, CA: Sage.

Suárez-Orozco, C., Suárez-Orozco, M. M., & Todorova, I. (2008). *Learning a new land: Immigrant students in American society*. Cambridge, MA: Harvard University Press.

Sutton-Smith, B. (1997). *The ambiguity of play*. Cambridge, MA: Harvard University Press.

Swail, S., Carbera, A., Lee, C., & Williams, A. (2005). *Latino students and the education pipeline: Part III of a three-part series*. Stafford, VA: The Educational Policy Institute.

Talmy, S. (2008). The cultural production of the ESL student at Tradewinds High: Contingency, multidirectionality, and identity in L2 socialization. *Applied Linguistics, 17*(1), 1–22.

Terrell, K. (2009). Review of *Why students in Cuba do better in school,* by M. Carnoy, A. Gove, & J. Marshall. *Journal of Educational Change, 10*, 401–404.

Tharp, R. G. (1993). Institutional and social context of educational practice and reform. In E. A. Forman, N. Minick, & C. A. Stone (Eds.), *Contexts for learning: Sociocultural dynamics in children's development*. New York, NY: Oxford University Press.

Tharp, R. G., & Gallimore, R. (1988). *Rousing minds to life: Teaching, learning, and school in social context*. New York, NY: Cambridge University Press.

Tharp, R. G., Rivera, H., Youpa, D., Dalton, S, Guardino, G. M., & Lasky, S. (1998). ASOS: *Activity setting observation system (Coding Rule Book)*. Santa Cruz, CA: Center for Research on Education, Diversity, and Excellence.

Thomas, M. (2005). I think it's just natural: The spatiality of racial segregation at a US high school. *Environment and Planning A, 37*, 1233–1248.

Thomas, M. (2008). The paradoxes of personhood: Banal multiculturalism and racial-ethnic identification among Latina and Armenian girls at a Los Angeles high school. *Environment and Planning A, 40*, 2864–2878.

Toiviainen, H., & Engeström, Y. (2009). Expansive learning in and for work. In H. Daniels, H. Lauder, & J. Porter (Eds.), *Knowledge, values and education policy: A critical perspective* (pp. 95–109). New York, NY: Routledge.

Torres, C. A. (Ed.). (1995). *Education and social change in Latin America*. Albert Park, Australia: James Nicholas Publishers.

Torres, L. (1995). *El Sancocho del sábado*. New York, NY: Farrar, Straus and Giroux.

Torres Dávila, M. (2006). *¿Qué tipos de Factores de Riesgo se pueden detectar en una población de Niños con Problemas de Aprendizaje?* (Trabajo de Diploma. Facultad de Psicología. Universidad de La Habana).

Troitsky, M. (1882). Obschaya svistba i zakony chelavecheskaya duja. [The general quality and laws of the human soul]) T. I. Moscow: A. Gatnulka Publisher.

Trueba, H. (1999). *Latinos unidos: From cultural diversity to the politics of solidarity*. Lanham, MD: Rowman & Littlefield.

Trumbull, E., Rothstein-Fisch, C. Greenfield, P., & Quiroz, B. (Eds.). (2001). *Bridging cultures between home and school: A guide for teachers*. Mahwah, NJ: Lawrence Erlbaum.

Tulviste, P. (1991). *Cultural-historical development of verbal thinking*. New York, NY: Nova Science Publishers.

United States Census Bureau. *American Fact Finder* [Data file]. Retrieved from http://www.census.gov/

U. S. Department of Education, Planning and Evaluation Service (2002). *State education indicators with a focus on Title I, 1999–2000*. Washington, DC. Retrieved from http://www2.ed.gov/rschstat/eval/disadv/2002indicators/arizona/edlite-arizona.html

Valdés, G. (1996). *Con respeto. Bridging the distances between culturally diverse families and schools: An ethnographic portrait*. New York, NY: Teachers College Press.

Valencia, R. R. (1998). *The evolution of deficit thinking: Educational through and practice*. Bristol, PA: Falmer Press, Taylor & Francis, Inc.

Valencia, R. R. (2002). *Chicano school failure and success: Past, present, and future*. (2nd ed.). London, UK: Routledge.

Valenzuela, A. (1999). *Subtractive schooling: U.S.-Mexican youth and the politics of caring*. Albany, NY: State University of New York Press.

Valsiner, J. (1987). *Culture and development of children's action: A cultural historical theory of developmental psychology*. New York, NY: Wiley.

Valsiner, J., & Van der Veer, R. (1992). The encoding of distance: The concept of the "zone of proximal development" and its interpretations. In R. R. Cocking & K. A. Renninger (Eds.), *The development and meaning of psychological distance* (pp. 35–62). Hillsdale, NJ: Erlbaum.

Valsiner, J., & Van der Veer, R. (1999). The encoding of distance: the concept of the zone of proximal development and its interpretations. In P. Lloyd and C. Fernyhough (Eds.) *Lev Vygotsky: Critical assessments: Vol. 3* (pp. 3–31). London, UK: Routledge.

Van der Veer, R. (2007). *Lev Vygotsky*. London, UK, & New York, NY: Continuum.

Van der Veer, R.., & Valsiner, J. (1993). *Understanding Vygotsky: A quest for synthesis*. Oxford, UK: Blackwell.

Van der Veer, R., & Valsiner, J. (1994). *The Vygotsky reader*. Oxford, UK: Blackwell.

Van der Veer, R., & Valsiner, J. (1996). *Vygotski uma sintese*. São Paulo, Brazil: Editora Unimarco, Edições Loyola.

Varela, F. (1999). *Ética y anticipación del pensamiento de la emancipación cubana*. Memorias del Coloquio Internacional de la Habana, diciembre 1997. La Habana, Cuba: Editorial Imagen Contemporánea.

Varenne, H., & McDermott, R. (1998). *Successful failure: The school America builds*. Boulder, CO: Westview.

Varey, S., & Chabrán, R. (1995). Mexican medicine comes to England. *Viator: Medieval and Renaissance Studies, 26*, 333–353.

Vásquez, O. A. (1993). A look at language as a resource: Lessons from La Clase Mágica. In M. B. Arias & U. Casanova (Eds.), *Bilingual education: Politics, practice, and research* (pp. 199–224). Chicago, IL: The University of Chicago Press.

Vásquez, O. A. (2003). *La clase mágica: Imagining optimal possibilities in a bilingual learning community of learners*. Mahwah, NJ: Erlbaum.

Vásquez, O. A., Underwood, C., Razfar, A., Bustos Flores, B., Rojas Clark, E., & Claeys, L. (2010). *Laboratories for learning: Collaborative research-based after-school programs: A research policy brief*. Paper presented at the National Latino Children's Institute Annual Conference, Washington, DC.

Vásquez, O. A., & Marcello, A. (2010). A situated view at "Scaling up" in culturally and linguistically diverse communities: The need for mutual adaptation. Paper submitted for publication to the Revista de Educación of the Universidad Nacional Abierta y Distancia (UNAD) of Colombia.

Veléz-Ibáñez, C. G. (1988). Networks of exchange among Mexicans in the U.S. and Mexico: Local level mediating responses to national and international transformations. *Urban Anthropology 17*, 25–51.

Venguer, L. A. (1976). *Temas de psicología preescolar*. La Habana, Cuba: Editora Científico-Técnica.

Veresov, N. (1999). *Undiscovered Vygotsky*. Berlin, Germany: Peter Lang.

Villenas, S. (1996). The colonizer/colonized Chicana ethnographer: Identity, marginalization and co-optation in the field. *Harvard Educational Review, 66*(4), 711–732.

Vives, J. L. (1997). *Las disciplinas*. Valencia, Spain: Artes Gráficas Soler, Ayuntamiento de Valencia,

Voyat, G. (1984). The Work of Henri Wallon. In G. Voyat (Ed.), *The world of Henri Wallon*. New York, NY: Aronson.

Vygotsky, L. S. (1962). *Thought and language*, E. Hanfmann & G. Vakar (Eds. & Trans.). Cambridge, MA: MIT University Press.

Vygotsky, L. S. (1964). *Pensamiento y lenguaje: Teoria del desarrollo cultural de las funciones psiquicas* (M. Rotger, Trans.). La Habana, Cuba: Edicion Revolucionaria.

Vygotsky, L. S. (1933/1966). *Play and its role in the mental development of the child* (C. Mulholland, Trans.). *Voprosy psikhologii, 6*. Retrieved from http://www.all-about-psychology.com/support-files/play-and-its-role-in-the-mental-development-of-the-child.pdf

Vygotsky, L. S. (1978). *Mind in society: The development of higher psychological processes.* (M. Cole, V. John-Steiner, S. Scribner, & E. Souberman, Eds. & Trans.). Cambridge, MA: Harvard University Press.

Vygotsky, L. S. (1979). Consciousness as a problem in the psychology of behaviour. *Soviet Psychology,* 17 (4), 3–35.

Vygotsky, L. S. (1984). *A formãcao social da mente.* São Paulo, Brazil: Martins Fontes.

Vygotsky, L. S. (1986). *Thought and language* (A. Kozulin, Trans.). Cambridge, MA: MIT University Press.

Vygotsky, L. S. (1987a). *Pensamento e linguagem.* São Paulo, Brazil: Martins Fontes.

Vygotsky, L. S. (1987b). *Historia del desarrollo de las funciones psíquicas superiores.* Ciudad de La Habana, Cuba: Editorial Científico Técnica.

Vygotsky, L. S. (1987c). *L. S. Vygotsky, collected works: Vol 1.* In R. Rieber & A. Carton (Eds.), (N. Minick, Trans.). New Cork, NY: Plenum. (Original work published 1934)

Vygotsky, L. S. (1989). *Obras completas.* [Asnovi defektologuii]. Vol. 5. La Habana, Cuba: Editorial Pueblo y Educación.

Vygotsky, L. S. (1991). *Obras escogidas: Vol. 1.* Madrid, España: Editorial Visor.

Vygotsky, L. S. (1993a). Compensatory processes in the development of the retarded child. In R. W. Rieber & A. S. Carton (Eds.), *The collected works of L. S. Vygotsky, Vol. 2: The fundamentals of defectology* (pp. 122–138). New York, NY: Plenum Press.

Vygotsky, L. S. (1993b). Defects and compensation. In R. W. Rieber, & A. S. Carton, (Eds.), *The collected works of L. S. Vygotsky, Vol. 2: The fundamentals of defectology* (pp. 52–64). New York, NY: Plenum Press.

Vygotsky, L. S. (1993c). *Obras escogidas: Vol. 2.* Madrid, Spain: Editorial Aprendizaje/Visor.

Vygotsky, L. S. (1993d). The diagnosis of development and the pedological clinic for difficult children. In R. W. Rieber & A. S. Carton (Eds.), *The collected works of L. S. Vygotsky, Vol. 2. The fundamentals of defectology* (pp. 122–138). New York, NY: Plenum Press.

Vygotsky, L. S. (1994). The socialist alteration of man. In R. Van der Veer & J. Valsiner (Eds.), *The Vygotsky reader* (pp. 175–184). Oxford, UK: Blackwell.

Vygotsky, L. S. (1995). *Obras escogidas: Vol. 3.* Madrid, Spain: Editorial Aprendizaje/Visor.

Vygotsky, L. S. (1996). *Obras escogidas: Vol 4.* Madrid, Spain: Editorial Aprendizaje/Visor.

Vygotsky, L. S. (1997a).Consciousness as a problem for the psychology of behavior. In R. W. Rieber & A. S. Carton (Eds.), *The collected works of L. S. Vygotsky: Vol. 3* (pp. 63–79). New York, NY: Plenum.

Vygotsky, L. S. (1997b). *Educational psychology.* Boca Raton, FL: St. Lucie Press. (Original work published 1926)

Vygotsky, L. S. (1998). *The collected works of L. S. Vygotsky: Vol. 5.* New York, NY: Plenum.

Vygotsky, L. S. (1999). *Imaginación y creación en la edad infantil* (2nd ed.). Ciudad de la Habana, Cuba: Editorial Pueblo y Educación.

Vygotsky, L. S. (2004). *Teoría de las emociones: Estudio histórico-psicológico.* Madrid, Spain: Ediciones Akal, S. A.

Vygotsky, L., & Luria, A. (1993). *Essays on the history of behavior.* Mahweh, NJ: Lawrence Erlbaum. (Original work published 1930)

Wacquant, L. (2010). Crafting the neo-liberal state: Workfare, prisonfare, and social insecurity. *Sociological Forum, 25,* 197–220.

Wallon, H. (1937). Psychologie und Technik. In H. Wallon (Ed.), *Die Wissenschaft im Lichte des Marxismus* (pp. 130–153). Zurich, Switzerland: Jean-Christophe-Verlag.

Wallon, H. (1984). The role of the other in the consciousness of the ego. In G. Voyat (Ed.), *The world of Henri Wallon* (pp. 91–103). New York, NY: Aronson.

Wang, X. C., & Carter Ching, C. (2003). Social construction of computer experience in a first-grade classroom: Social processes and mediating artifacts. *Early Education & Development, 14,* 336–361.

Weber, M. (1964). *The sociology of religion* (E. Fischoff, Trans.) Boston, MA: Beacon Press.

Weiss, H., Kreider, H., Lopez, M. E., & Chatman-Nelson, C. (2010). *Preparing educators to engage families: Case studies using an ecological systems framework* (2nd ed.). Los Angeles, CA: Sage.

Wells, G. (1990). Talk about text: Where literacy is learned and taught. *Curriculum Inquiry, 20,* 369–405.

Wenger, E. (1998). *Communities of practice: Learning, meaning, and identity.* New York, NY: Cambridge University Press.

Wertsch, J. V. (1985). *Vygotsky and the social formation of mind.* Cambridge, MA: Harvard University Press.

Wertsch, J. V. (1990). A meeting of paradigms: Vygotsky and psychoanalysis. *Contemporary Psychoanalysis, 26,* 53–73.

Wertsch, J. V. (1991a). *Voices of the mind: A sociocultural approach to mediated action.* Cambridge, MA: Harvard University Press.

Wertsch, J. V. (1991b). Vygotsky and the social formation of mind. Cambridge, MA: Harvard University Press.

Wertsch, J. V. (1998). *Mind as action.* New York, NY: Oxford University Press.

Wertsch, J. V. (2000). Vygotsky's two minds on the nature of meaning. In C. D. Lee & P. Smagorinsky (Eds.), *Vygotskian perspectives on literacy research: Constructing meaning through collaborative inquiry* (pp. 19–30). New York, NY: Cambridge University Press.

Wertsch, J. V. (2007). Mediation. In H. Daniels, M. Cole, & J. V. Wertsch (Eds.), *The Cambridge companion to Vygotsky* (pp. 178–192). Cambridge, UK: Cambridge University Press.

Wertsch, J. V. (2008). From social interaction to higher psychological processes. *Human Development, 51,* 66–79.

Wertsch, J., del Rio, P., & Alvarez, A. (1995). 'Sociocultural studies: history, action, and mediation'. In J. Wertsch, J., P. del Rio & A. Alvarez (Eds.) *Sociocultural studies of mind.* Cambridge, MA: Harvard University Press.

Wertsch, J. V., Hagstrom, F., & Kikas, E. (1995). Voices of thinking and speaking. In L. Martin, K. Nelson, & and E. Tobach (Eds.), *Sociocultural psychology: Theory and practice of doing and knowing.* New York, NY: Cambridge University Press.

Wetherell, M. (1998). Positioning and interpretive repertoires: Conversation analysis and post-structuralism in dialogue. *Discourse & Society, 9*(3), 387–417.

Wheatley, T., & Wegner, D. M. (2001). Automaticity of action, Psychology. In N. J. Smelser & P. B. Baltes (Eds.), *International encyclopedia of the social and behavioral sciences* (pp. 991–993). Oxford, UK: Elsevier Science Limited.

Whiting, B. W. (1980). Culture and social behavior: A model for the development of social behavior. *Ethos, 8*(2), 95–116.

Wikan, U. (2008). *In honor of Fadime: Murder and shame.* Chicago, IL: University of Chicago Press.

Wilhelm, J., Baker, T., & Dube, J. (2001). *Strategic reading: Guiding students to lifelong literacy.* Portsmouth, NH: Heinemann.

Willett, J. (1995). Becoming first graders in an L2: An ethnographic study of L2 socialization. *TESOL Quarterly, 29*(3), 473–503.

Williams, R. (1973). Base and superstructure in Marxist cultural theory. *New Left Review, 82,* 3–16.

Wilson, A., & Weinstein, L. (1990). An investigation into some implications of a Vygotskian perspective on the origins of mind: Psychoanalysis and the Vygotskian psychology, Part 1. *Journal of the American Psychoanalytic Association, 40,* 349–370.

Wisman, J., & Capehart, K. (2010). Creative destruction, economic insecurity, stress, and epidemic obesity. *American Journal of Economics & Sociology, 69,* 939–982.

Woodlief, B., Thomas, C., & Orozco, G. (2003). *California's gold: Claiming the promise of diversity in our community colleges.* Oakland, CA.

Woolard, K. A., & Schieffelin, B. B. (1994). Language ideology. *Annual Review of Anthropology, 23,* 55–82.

Wundt, W. (1921). *Elements of folk psychology.* London, UK: Allen and Unwin.

Wurtzburger, R. (2003). *Community of immigrants from Ethiopia* [in Hebrew]. Jerusalem: Knesset Israel— Center for Research and Information.

Yakimanskaya, I. C. (1989). Princip aktivnosti v pedagogisheschoi psykjologii. *Voprocy psykjology* [Questions of psychology], 6, 5–13.

Yaroshevsky, M. (1989). *Lev Vygotsky.* Moscow: Progress.

Yaroshevsky, M. (1993). *L. S. Vygotsky: In the search for the new psychology.* Moscow: LGI.

Yarochevsky, M. (2007). *L. S. Vygotsky: In the search of a new psychology.* Moscow: LGI.

Yosso, T. J. (2005). Whose culture has capital? A critical race theory discussion of community cultural wealth. *Race Ethnicity and Education, 8*(1), 69–92.

Zaporochets, A. V. (1986). *Izbranye psikjologicheskie trudy ( Selected psychological works).* Moscow: Pedagógica.

Zarate, M. E. (2007). *Understanding Latino parental involvement in education: Perceptions, expectations, and recommendations.* University of Southern California, School of Policy, Planning, and Development: Tomas Rivera Policy Institute.

Zentella, A. (1997). *Growing up bilingual: Puerto Rican children in New York.* Malden, MA: Blackwell.

Zentella, A. (Ed.). (2005). *Building on strength: Language and literacy in Latino families and communities* (pp. 162–174). New York, NY: Teachers College Press.

Zinchenko, V. P. (1997). La psicología sociocultural y la teoría psicológica de la actividad: revisión y proyección hacia el futur. In J. V. Wertsch, P. Del Rio & A. Alvarez (Eds.), *La mente socio-cultural. Aproximaciones teóricas y aplicadas* (pp. 35-47). Madrid: Fundación Infancia y Aprendizaje.

Zinchenko, V. P. (2001). External and internal: Another comment on the issue. In S. Chaiklin (Ed.), *The theory and practice of cultural-historical psychology* (pp. 135–147).

Zinchenko, V. P. (2002). Problematika mischleniya v pazvivayochevo obucheniya [The problematic of thinking in an education in development] In *Education in development*. Dialog c V. V. Davidovym. T. I. (pp. 46–102). Moscow: APK & PRO.

Zinchenko, V. P. (2007) Thought and word: The approaches of L.S. Vygotsky and G. Shpet. In H. Daniels, M. Cole, & J. Wertsch (Eds.), *The Cambridge companion to Vygotsky*. New York, NY: Cambridge University Press.

Zinchenko, V. (2009). Consciousness as the subject matter and task of psychology. *Journal of Russian and East European Psychology, 47*(5), 44-75.